D0294878

Dogs closest to point of origin followed Pleistocene move toward Giantism.

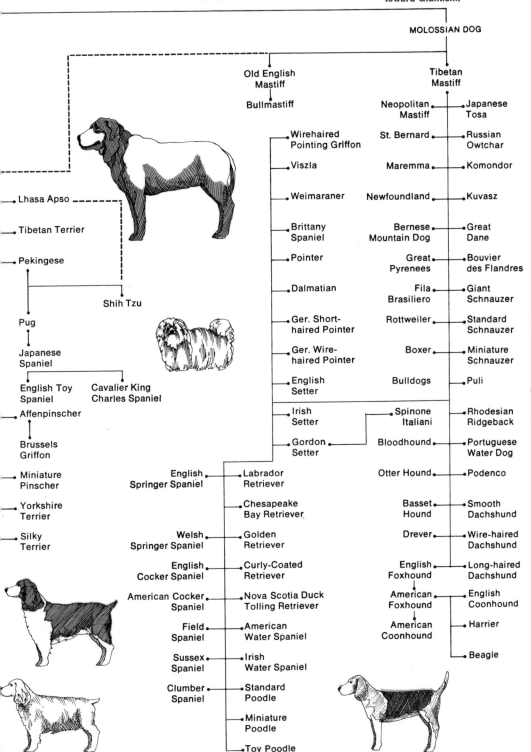

MOLOSSIAN DOG

Old English Mastiff

Bullmastiff

Tibetan Mastiff

Neopolitan Mastiff — Japanese Tosa

Wirehaired Pointing Griffon

St. Bernard — Russian Owtchar

Viszla

Maremma — Komondor

Weimaraner

Newfoundland — Kuvasz

Lhasa Apso

Tibetan Terrier

Brittany Spaniel

Bernese Mountain Dog — Great Dane

Pekingese

Pointer

Great Pyrenees — Bouvier des Flandres

Shih Tzu

Dalmatian

Fila Brasiliero — Giant Schnauzer

Pug

Ger. Short-haired Pointer

Rottweiler — Standard Schnauzer

Japanese Spaniel

Ger. Wire-haired Pointer

Boxer — Miniature Schnauzer

English Toy Spaniel   Cavalier King Charles Spaniel

English Setter

Bulldogs — Puli

Affenpinscher

Irish Setter

Spinone Italiani — Rhodesian Ridgeback

Brussels Griffon

Gordon Setter

Bloodhound — Portuguese Water Dog

Miniature Pinscher

English Springer Spaniel — Labrador Retriever

Otter Hound — Podenco

Yorkshire Terrier

Chesapeake Bay Retriever

Basset Hound — Smooth Dachshund

Silky Terrier

Welsh Springer Spaniel — Golden Retriever

Drever — Wire-haired Dachshund

English Cocker Spaniel — Curly-Coated Retriever

English Foxhound — Long-haired Dachshund

American Cocker Spaniel — Nova Scotia Duck Tolling Retriever

American Foxhound — English Coonhound

Field Spaniel — American Water Spaniel

American Coonhound — Harrier

Sussex Spaniel — Irish Water Spaniel

Clumber Spaniel — Standard Poodle

Beagle

Miniature Poodle

Toy Poodle

YOUR
FAMILY
DOG

YOUR FAMILY DOG

The Complete Guide to Choosing, Caring for, Training, and Showing

Maxwell Riddle

DOUBLEDAY & COMPANY, INC.
Garden City, New York

A portion of the material in this book is adapted, with permission, from two books by Maxwell Riddle, *Your Show Dog,* copyright © 1968 by Maxwell Riddle, and *A Quick Guide to Standards for Show Dogs,* copyright © 1972 by Maxwell Riddle. Both books are published by Doubleday & Company, Inc., Garden City, New York.

The information in this book on breed standards is based on the official standards of the American Kennel Club.

Library of Congress Cataloging in Publication Data

Riddle, Maxwell.
    Your family dog.

    Includes index.
    I. Dogs.   I. Title.
SF426.R55   636.7

Introduction

The man-dog relationship began at least fifteen thousand to seventeen thousand years ago, according to discoveries in which the bones of men and dogs were found near each other. The bond between man and dog has continued ever since and is probably stronger today than ever before.

The number of dog owners today has increased substantially. Thirty years ago a marketing survey indicated that one out of every ten families owned a dog. Today at least one out of every five families has one dog and sometimes more than one.

It used to be that people owned dogs for the assistance they provided in hunting, herding, drawing carts, and guarding property. Today there are many other reasons that account for the increased ownership of dogs, including dog shows, obedience competition, and field trials. But to most people it is the simple pleasure of enjoying a dog as a household pet that has enabled the dog to retain the title "man's best friend."

Other people have become seriously interested in the breeding of purebred dogs. Breeding such dogs is an art; some would say it is a science. But it is also a sport in itself. Breeders spend hours studying pedigrees, dogs and their records, as well as diets and dog foods. It should be noted that the support and demand of people interested in purebred dogs have contributed immensely to improved modern dog foods and better veterinary care for animals.

The number of owners of purebred dogs has greatly increased over the years as more and more people realize the advantages of owning a purebred. Thirty years ago the ratio of mongrels to purebreds owned was nine to one; today two out of every five dogs owned is a purebred, about a 30 per cent increase.

But whether it is purebred or not, a dog can be a joy to own as a family pet. He (or she) is the welcome bark that greets you when you return from work. Your dog is the faithful companion who is always (or usually) there when you are lonesome and need a friend. Children and dogs have a built-in rapport, romping and playing together to the delight of both. It is as though both children and dogs feel themselves to be pygmies in a world of giants and so join forces to create their own small world of pleasure. And do not forget that dogs are a boon to millions of senior citizens, who find great pleasure in their quiet companionship.

The purpose of this book is twofold: to explore the many aspects of dog ownership, such as training and caring for your dog, and to explain all the various activities, such as dog shows, obedience training, and field trials, that you as a dog owner can enjoy and in which you can participate.

MAXWELL RIDDLE

Contents

part one

DOGS: BACKGROUND AND OWNERSHIP

chapter one
The Origin of the Dog

The dog belongs to the family Canidae, to which the wolf, coyote, jackal, fox, Dingo, and African hunting dog also belong. There are a number of theories of the dog's origin. None of them can be proven, and all of them present difficulties in explanation.

One theory is that the dog is only a tamed, or domesticated, wolf. Ivan Sanderson, author of *Living Mammals of the World,* is an excellent advocate of this view. Another theory, suggested by the English zoologist Richard Fiennes in *The Order of Wolves* and other works, is that dogs descend from four species of now extinct wolves. Anthropologist Dr. William Haag, at the University of Kentucky (currently at Louisiana State University), has suggested yet another theory for the origin of the dog; he postulates that the dog descends from some still unknown canid of Asia, probably neither dog nor wolf, that may have existed twenty thousand to a million years ago. Let us consider these theories and see how they relate to discoveries in recent years of fossil ancestors of the dog.

Sanderson has written that "if you skin a wolf, a coyote, and a dog, you would be hard put to identify any one of them even if you were an anatomist." This is certainly not true. If it were, the bones of prehistoric dogs could never have been identified, and yet they have been.

Sanderson questions Dr. Haag's theory regarding some earlier form of animal from which the dog descends and asks: Then where are the fossil remains of such an ancestor? This is perhaps no answer at all. New discoveries are constantly pushing back our horizons. For example, most authorities believe that men populated the Americas by crossing the Bering Strait and that they brought their dogs with them. They used to think this occurred four thousand or five thousand years ago. However, in recent years radioactive carbon dating of ancient campsites has placed man in both North and South America twenty-five thousand years ago and perhaps even earlier. (As though to prove the speciousness of Sanderson's question, no fossil human remains have been found to tell us who occupied those campsites.)

Until recently it was thought that the dog was domesticated between 9,500 and 10,500 years ago. (This was the period in which pigs, cattle, sheep, and most of our food plants were domesticated.) Dr. Barbara Lawrence, of the Museum of Comparative Zoology at Harvard University, discovered the partial remains of a dog estimated to be about 10,500 years old in Jaguar Cave in Idaho. We now know, however, that the dog existed as a dog at least 14,000 years ago, for the fossil jaw and teeth of a dog were discovered at a site in Iraq known as Palegrawra, near Kirkuk.

If we are to assume that the dog is only a tamed wolf, as reported by the New York *Times* in October 1975 in an article on the Iraq fossil, then we must ask: How many centuries or millennia did it take for this tamed wolf to become osteologically distinct from the wolf? And distinct it must have been — as was Dr. Lawrence's fossil — or it could not have been identified as a dog.

The discovery of the Iraq fossil also raises other questions for which, at the present time, there are no answers. If the fossil ancestors of the Canidae developed in North America, why was the dog developed in Asia? Why did it have to be brought to North America over the land bridge at the Bering Strait? Was it brought over by its human masters, or did it migrate by itself? Did it precede human migrants?

We say quite glibly that man domesticated the dog, but what men? When? And where? Theories have been proposed, but they are only that. Other researchers in the fields of anthropology, zoology, and history have said that within the history of modern man no animal has been domesticated. Two possible exceptions are the partially domesticated turkey and budgerigar, or parakeet.

Here let us discuss a point that the zoologists and anatomists do not. There is a vast psychological gulf between *tame* and *domestic,* and that same chasm exists between the *wild* and the *domestic.*

Lions and tigers have been tamed for the circus, but they remain wild animals. A trainer once told me that the lions he thought were the tamest and most reliable were actually the most likely to attack. I have been told by elephant trainers in Ceylon that elephants born in captivity are very dangerous because they have lost their fear of man. Therefore, wild elephants are always caught for work because they do fear men.

There is no authenticated case in North America of a wild wolf attacking a human being, but a tamed wolf that was taken to schools did attack a child. Also, wolves being trained for a motion picture have attacked a person.

Consider the meaning of the word *domestic*. In regard to animals one definition might be an animal that has cast its lot with that of man. The rat is such an animal. We trap, poison, and shoot rats, but they are determined to live with us, and when allowed to be, they are gentle and surprisingly intelligent pets. This is in direct contrast with the wolf, which has not become domesticated.

In his famous fable Aesop has a fat dog suggest to a starving wolf that it join its master. The wolf agrees, but after learning that the bare ring around the dog's neck was caused by a collar, it declines, saying, "Better to starve free than to die a fat slave." And so it has always been for the wolf. Wolves have been trapped or killed for thousands of years and have been driven from their homes into the Arctic, where they are only partially safe, but even though they face extinction, none has ever decided to be the fat dog of Aesop's fable.

Fiennes's theory that dogs developed at different times and places from four now extinct species of wolves is not easy to believe for two important reasons.

First, wolves have relatively perfect sight; whereas all dogs suffer from severe eye defects. The dog cannot focus sharply; it is myopic (short-sighted). The wolf is not. The dog suffers from astigmatism (inability to get a sharp focus at the edge of the picture). The wolf has no such problem. As many people get older, the lenses of their eyes harden, and they cannot see things at close range, such as the numbers in a telephone directory, clearly, a condition known as presbyopia. The dog is born with presbyopia. It is believed that the wolf's eyes are far superior in this respect.

Second, zoologists and anatomists can, by dissection, identify several dozen species of wolves, all of which are very similar. However, hundreds of dog breeds have been developed over the centuries, varying from a two-pound Chihuahua to a two-hundred-pound St. Bernard.

Moreover, ever since the earliest days of Arctic exploration many observers have noted the deadly hatred of the wolf for the dog. Wolves have killed dogs whenever they have had the chance; they have not even spared a bitch nursing her puppies.

Considering the refusal of so many animals to become domesticated, and remembering the unbridgeable chasm that separates the wild from the domestic, I agree with Dr. Haag's theory that the dog descends from some as yet unknown ancestor. It might have been a cousin to a wolf, and I believe it branched off and by genetic mutation, began to travel the long road toward partnership with man.

The process was not instantaneous. The Iraqi dog of 14,500 years ago may have been a descendant of thousands of generations of psychologically different wolflike animals. During those centuries or millennia it underwent the physical changes that, along with psychological ones, made it a true dog.

Dr. Haag has theorized that the dog originated in central Asia and developed into its modern forms while spreading almost worldwide. As populations both human and canine grew, the weaker peoples moved or were pushed farther from this area, and their dogs would have moved with them. Eventually the most primitive peoples settled at the ends of the earth, where they were least disturbed. The most primitive of the true dogs are: the Dingo of Australia, the Sinhala Hound of Sri Lanka (Ceylon), the Basenji and its relatives in Africa, the dogs of the Ainu of northern Japan, and the Pariah Dogs of the Middle Eastern deserts.

My theory is that those dogs that moved away from their area of origin and into the high mountains of Tibet developed the giantism common to many animal forms during the Pleistocene period, the time of the Great Ice Age. These dogs developed the skull formation, the deep stop, and the large sinuses characteristic of the St. Bernard. The large sinuses were necessary to warm air before it entered the dog's lungs. As it left the lungs, the warmed air helped to warm the frontal areas of the skull, including the eye sockets.

Those dogs that entered desert areas had no need for such a skull formation. They became sight hunters or coursing hounds and developed the heads and bodies typical of the Greyhound family of racing hunters.

Other dogs entered the northern forest regions. As an adaptation to the climate, they developed moderate stops and sinuses, a double coat, and a heavily furred tail, all characteristic of sled dogs, the Norwegian Elkhound, the Chow Chow, and other northern breeds. Their distribution became worldwide, extending to the subarctic forests and even to warmer northern areas.

The remains of Dingos have been found together with the remains of a marsupial lion near at least two sites in Australia. Radiocarbon dating of some remains has indicated these animals' existence about nineteen thousand years ago. It is assumed that man took the Dingo with him when he first migrated to Australia (about five thousand years ago). Therefore, scientists tend to doubt the evidence of these two finds because this would mean that a previously unknown race of people arrived before the aborigines.

The Dingo.

The Dingo has always been considered a feral dog (i.e., a domestic dog returned to the wild), and it mated enthusiastically with the dogs brought in by the white colonists. The importation of German Shepherds to Australia was banned in 1935 because of a fear that German Shepherd–Dingo crosses would go wild and decimate flocks of sheep. (That ban has since been lifted.)

Today the Save the Dingo Society is trying to prove that the Dingo is really a wolf, and an American authority on wolves, Stanley J. Olsen, wishes to exclude it from the line of dogs. Yet these facts remain: Psychologically, the Dingo is a dog. Moreover, Dingo–sheep dog crosses were used to produce the world's finest cattle dog, the Australian Cattle Dog.

A dog can be a joy to own if it is given special care, training, and love. Here, an energetic Cocker Spaniel is shown jumping a fence hedge.
Ralston Purina Company

chapter two
The Right Dog for You

Dog World magazine allows column space for all the popular breeds of dogs. When the late Will Judy was the magazine's owner and editor, he had a standard feature that used to run once a year for each breed. A newcomer to a certain breed of dog would be asked to write a short article on "Why I Like the . . ." The newcomer would be flattered, and the article would be forthcoming. Someone who read the magazine from cover to cover (as I did) soon realized the articles were always the same for all breeds: The writers invariably claimed that their breeds were the best family dogs, the best with children, the most easily housebroken, the best home guardians, the most intelligent, and the most easily trained. For the most part they ignored the problem of grooming unless they could actually claim their breeds were easily groomed, as would be the case with a Whippet.

The owners of mongrels would usually write in equally extravagant praise of their dogs. Invariably they said that their mongrels were healthier and more intelligent than purebreds (or as most of them incorrectly said, thoroughbreds).

Many or even most dogs live up to all the proud claims of their owners at least partially. Dogs have a remarkable ability to adjust to almost any environment, which, in this case, includes owners.

Do not choose a dog on a whim. There are many different factors to consider in order to pick just the right dog for you and your family. In this chapter I discuss some of the major considerations you must take into account in making this choice.

Pet Shops?

Should you buy from a pet shop? Absolutely not! Insofar as you, the prospective buyer, are concerned, pet shops depend on two things: the impulse to buy a cute puppy and your pity for a poor puppy in a cage.

Pet shops rely on what are known as *puppy mills* for their puppies. Puppy mills are only one of the ways in which the modern world has put living beings into a heartless production line. For example, chickens, either for the market or for egg production, are placed in small crates from which they are never released during their productive lives. Pigs are kept in cribs that prevent them from turning around and are fed hormones so that they can produce three litters a year instead of two. Calves are raised in cribs and forced to the veal stage.

In the case of puppy mills a dozen bitches — purebred but usually of poor stock — are kept in barns, often in unsanitary conditions. They are mated to equally poor males. At five to six weeks of age the puppies are crated by the litter and shipped hundreds, even thousands of miles to pet shops.

The pups may be afflicted with all sorts of parasites, both internal and external. They may have mange (which is transmitted by mites). They may be inadequately protected against the killing diseases of distemper, leptospirosis, and hepatitis.

A puppy's registration papers may be falsified, or you may be told that they will come later — which, of course, they never do. Pet shops have to buy entire litters, often paying $10 to $25 for each puppy. They may then sell a puppy for $100 to $200. Some puppies will die before they can be sold; others may have to be held for weeks. It is obvious that you could buy a puppy of better quality and better health from a reputable source for the same amount of money and often for less.

Some pet shops guarantee to replace a puppy if it dies from any cause within a given time, sometimes up to a year. Even so, the pet shop will still make a nice profit. Remember, your $150 puppy cost them $25; if that puppy is replaced, it will be by another $25 pup. Sometimes the pet shop may be gone or under new ownership when you arrive to claim the guarantee. As for the puppy that gets sick — because you love it, you won't want to take it back to ask for another pup.

Never buy a puppy on impulse, and stay away from pet shops.

Mongrel or Purebred?

A mongrel is any dog whose parents were not purebred or, if they were purebred, were of different breeds. For the most part mongrels have mongrel parents. Mongrel puppies seldom cost more than $10, and they may cost nothing at all. In contrast, a purebred puppy may cost anywhere from $75 to $500 and up.

Should a family get a mongrel puppy? The answer is, as a rule, no. The major reason is that mongrel puppies are almost always the offspring of a bitch (female dog) who was not guarded when she was in heat. Instead she was allowed to roam and mated with a neighborhood dog. Furthermore, the sire of mongrels is not always the strongest of the bitch's suitors. Sometimes the strongest males fight, and meanwhile she selects a weaker male.

Neither parent may have been in good health at the time of the mating, and prenatal care may not have been good. So the pups get a poor start both at conception and in utero. The dam (mother) may have a tapeworm or hookworm infestation. Or she may be afflicted with the parasite Coccidia, with no effort having been made to rid her of these parasites before whelping. Adequate whelping arrangements may not have been made, either because of the irresponsibility or because of the ignorance of the dam's owner.

When the puppies are born, they may become infested with other parasites, such as roundworms. While nursing, the pups might ingest fleas, which are carriers of roundworms during one stage in their life cycle. Also, sometimes the mother's milk will be inferior in quality if she did not enjoy optimum health at the time of mating or of whelping.

The sole advantage these puppies may have is that because their mothers were wanderers, they will have been constantly exposed to distemper virus. Therefore they will have a high resistance to this disease and will pass on a "passive resistance" to distemper to their puppies through their milk; this will protect the puppies for the first five or six weeks of their lives.

It has been estimated that 80 per cent of mongrel puppies die before they are eight weeks old. Indeed, their mortality rate is about 60 per cent during the first three weeks. And those that do survive may be relatively unhealthy most of their lives.

It is very important that the owner of a dog keep it in good health; see that it has annual distemper, hepatitis, and leptospirosis shots; and is free from internal parasites.

When the time comes to mate a bitch, a male of equal quality and good health should be selected. Before the mating the bitch should be given a careful health check that ensures, among other things, that she is not carrying internal parasites, such as hookworms, tapeworms, or Coccidia.

As whelping time approaches, adequate whelping facilities should be prepared for her. A veterinarian should check to determine that the bitch is strong and is properly structured anatomically for normal delivery.

If the litter is large and the mother's milk supply appears inadequate, or if all breasts are not functioning, the puppies will be given an adequate supply of simulated bitch's milk. The veterinarian will give the puppies protective shots even before they are weaned when there are indications that the mother's milk does not contain passive resistance factors to distemper. The puppies' stool should be checked by a veterinarian for the presence of roundworm eggs, whipworms, hookworms, and Coccidia. If parasites are found, the puppies should be treated for them.

The result of all this will be that at weaning time (about six weeks of age), the puppies will be in optimum health and perfectly ready to go into new homes.

Of course, all this careful preparation costs money. It has been estimated that the costs can easily run to $50 a puppy, and that does not include the stud (mating) fee, the cost of travel with the bitch to the stud dog, or the cost in time lavished on the bitch during her pregnancy and postnatal days.

The proud owner of the purebred puppy, having paid a considerable sum for it, will be a responsible owner who will want to safeguard his or her puppy, rear it carefully, and pay whatever expenses that may entail.

In the case of a purebred puppy you should be able to see or obtain information about its mother and sire. With that knowledge you will better understand what your puppy will be like when it grows up. But if you buy a mongrel pup, you will probably be unable to get such information, and whether the dog you choose will grow up to be intelligent, have personality problems, be average in size or oversized or undersized, be healthy or not, will all be left to chance.

Puppy or Grown Dog?

Should you buy a puppy or a grown dog? In most cases it is advisable to buy a puppy. Generally people who want to buy a grown dog are those who do not want the responsibility of raising a puppy. But these same people are also not likely to accept the responsibility of giving a grown dog adequate care. Hundreds of people — usually parents who feel that although they don't want a dog, the children should have one — have been quite frank in telling me that they don't want the nuisance of housebreaking a puppy or correcting its chewing. These families should not have a dog because in the end the parents usually have to do most of the work of caring for it.

If you get a puppy, you can discipline it at the start, before its initially cute and mischievous pranks become bad habits. But if you buy a grown dog, you might not be able to correct habits that you dislike. Also, if the dog has been in a kennel until you get it, it may have trouble adjusting to your home. If it has been in another home, its loyalties may forever remain with that first home and it might not be a fully satisfactory friend for you. Finally you will miss the delight of watching a puppy play and grow.

Of course there will always be exceptions. I have taken in several dozen older dogs. Some have had incurable bad habits, and some have been neurotic. Others have been remarkably good pets, have adjusted readily, and have been a joy to own.

Male or Female?

There have been times when I have had all males and other times when I have had all females. There are many arguments for and against each sex, but most of them are not valid. More depends on you than on the sex of the dog.

Female dogs are in heat twice a year, and male dogs may be drawn to your home during those times. If you do not intend to breed your bitch, then she should be spayed, if she's in good health, three months or so after her first heat. Male dogs are said to be in heat all year round. Although it is said that males are likely to become roamers and thus neighborhood nuisances, the truth is that dogs of either sex can become incurable vagabonds. Many owners feel that a male pup should be castrated before it reaches maturity. This is less expensive than spaying but is still fairly costly and not necessarily a solution.

As far as a puppy's intelligence and trainability are concerned, I do not believe that there is any difference between the sexes.

The Runt of the Litter?

Should you buy a runt, a puppy stunted in growth at birth? Many people claim that runts are the smartest of the pups in a litter. This is true only in the sense that the struggle to survive has forced them to become more aggressive and to use their inborn talents earlier than their litter brothers and sisters. In the long run, however, a runt may not be smarter and may be less so. Actually there are some sound reasons for not selecting the runt of the litter.

The struggle for survival does not begin at the moment of birth; it begins at conception and continues during the puppies' entire uterine life. The runt has survived, but the very fact that it is a runt illustrates that it has not been as successful as the other puppies.

During the first six weeks after birth the puppy must fight its littermates just to get to a nipple. It may fail to get to one that yields a plentiful supply of milk. Consequently its battle is not entirely successful, even though it continues to survive.

This battle for survival may have two results. First, the puppy's character may have been affected; it may be an aggressive, ill-natured animal all its life. Second, it may be less healthy than others in the litter. This means that although the purchase price for a runt may be lower, veterinary expenses may be far higher.

The Lhasa Apso is a practical pet for people with small living quarters or with limited time to walk a dog. Its coat needs regular grooming to keep it neat and clean. Photo of Ch. Quang-Te van de Blauwe Mammouth, owned by Rev. & Mrs. D. Allan Easton.

Temperament

Another important consideration in choosing a dog is to select a breed whose temperament will match your own personality or the preferences of your family. For example, some people love to walk — whether on city streets or in the country, where they can stroll through fields or on little-used country roads — and they enjoy having their dog accompany them. I know an aged man who has an aged Collie. They walk slowly, the dog matching the pace of its owner, for long distances in the morning and early evening.

Toy breeds do not require much exercise, so they make excellent pets for people who live in apartments or small houses or people unable to take or uninterested in taking lengthy walks (yet I must add that one does see many owners walking Toy dogs).

Some people are highly disciplined, are meticulous in their work, and require well-ordered homes. This kind of person may wish to choose a dog like a Doberman Pinscher or German Shepherd, which can take stern discipline without having its personality injured.

If you like noise and excitement, then choose a dog that fits that description. If you like a dog that challenges other dogs to a fight, you will no doubt enjoy the personality of most Terriers. (Of course you should never let a Terrier, no matter how feisty, get into a battle!) People who get Terriers and take them for walks will get all the excitement they want. (There is a rule in judging Scottish Terriers that any Scottie that does not show proper Terrier spirit should not be given championship points. Terrier judges often apply the rule to all Terriers. They ask the handlers to turn their dogs toward each other, whereupon the dogs set up a terrific racket, growling, snarling, hurling themselves at the end of the leash, trying to reach each other. If one puts its tail between its legs and turns away, the judge is likely to withhold either a first prize or a winners' ribbon or both.)

Many of the Toy dogs are also noisemakers and can be quite effective burglar alarms. These dogs seem to compensate for the fact that they are dogdom's dwarfs by raising a racket — in the car, at the door, at passersby. Many owners get real pleasure just from the absurdity of such a little dog making such a racket and challenging dogs that could kill it with one bite. However, if you are partial to getting a puppy from one of the Toy breeds and the dog is yappy, some training will be necessary to prevent excessive barking.

There are noisy dogs in every breed and there are quiet ones. One breed, the Basenji, is barkless. However, the dog is not mute; under certain circumstances it may scream.

If you are selecting a dog for your children, Terriers, that love to romp and play, are wonderful to own. (However, children will adjust to a puppy of any breed and vice versa.) But suppose you want to come home at night to a dog that will greet you enthusiastically but then calm down, sit quietly by your side as you read, or be satisfied just to have your hand on it as you sit in your yard watching the evening flight of birds. There are many breeds that will fit your needs: Collies, Shetland Sheepdogs, Golden Retrievers, and a dozen more.

For many people a less energetic, more protective, or quieter dog is the most suitable as a companion, especially in the case of the senior citizen. Consider the following examples: An unfortunate choice of a dog was made by an elderly friend who was badly crippled. He wanted a canine companion and remembered a dog of his youth, a Smooth Fox Terrier. He would not agree to get any other breed, and consequently a Terrier was obtained for him. This man was delighted with it, but the dog was too lively, too brimming with energy for him. One night he hobbled into the yard on his crutches to exercise the dog, which was on lead. It was raining slightly. Hours later, he was found on the ground, tangled in the crutches and leash and unable to get up.

Another senior citizen wanted a Doberman Pinscher, which is a strong and very active dog. Against all advice he bought one. The man had severe arthritis in his hands and found that trying to restrain the Doberman while it was on leash was more painful than he could bear. These examples suggest that elderly people should own quieter, less energetic dogs. Bulldogs and French Bulldogs may snort and snuffle when sleeping, but that gentle snoring often has a calming effect on the people who own them. Moreover, these dogs do not have a superabundance of energy that must be relieved by rough play, a lot of yard running, or long walks. Pugs, Cavalier King Charles Spaniels, English Toy Spaniel varieties, and the Japanese Chin (formerly known as the Japanese Spaniel) have similar characteristics. Both of the Welsh Corgis, Pembroke and Cardigan, are small, reasonably quiet house dogs. So are the show-type Beagles. Beagles bred solely for hunting and field trials are too high-strung to be good companions to elderly people. Among the larger dogs the Golden Retriever is an excellent choice.

As you can see, there are breeds of dogs to fit a wide variety of human needs. It should be pointed out, however, that within a breed it is entirely possible that individual temperaments will differ, just as they do in human beings. There are headstrong, super-active Golden Retrievers, and there are very docile Dobermans. So don't expect a particular dog inevitably to fit a pattern or stereotype. It is hard to tell precisely what a very young puppy's temperament will be when he is grown up, although your treatment and training will have much to do with the results. Still, you will get the most satisfaction if at least you choose the sort of breed that best complements your own personality and living arrangements.

Children and dogs have a built-in rapport and enjoy each other's company. This three-month-old Bouvier puppy is owned by Col. & Mrs. Charles McLean and is shown with their daughter Chari Raye McLean.

Canine Longevity

When choosing a dog, many people request a breed that is long-lived. Some say that it is too hard to get over the loss of a dog; they don't want to repeat that sorrowful experience too soon. Of course, no one can predict how long a given dog will live, even without disease or accident.

However, there are some breeds that are known to be short-lived. In general this applies to all the giant breeds: Great Danes, St. Bernards, Mastiffs, Great Pyrenees, and Irish Wolfhounds. Borzois and Scottish Deerhounds may also have slightly shorter life-spans than, for example, English Springer Spaniels.

Modern nutrition and health care are responsible for a longer life-span for most dogs. But this has also meant that dogs are now subject to diseases previously unknown to them. Although some dogs in all breeds develop heart problems, bloat, and so on, these ailments are more often seen in the larger breeds, such as German Shepherds, Doberman Pinschers, Bloodhounds, Mastiffs, and Bullmastiffs. Bone cancer in the legs seems to occur more often in Great Danes than in most other breeds. However, cancers of all kinds are appearing in all breeds whose lives have been extended through better health care and nutrition.

Dogs as Home Guardians

There are some people who want dogs solely to protect their homes, to guard both residents and property. Many people feel that the bigger the dog, the better, so they choose a Great Dane, a Newfoundland, or another large breed, despite considerations such as the increased cost of food.

Size alone does not make a guard dog. The dog must have strongly developed guard instincts. Doberman Pinschers, German Shepherds, Rottweilers, Belgian Sheepdogs, Belgian Tervurens, Bouviers des Flandres, Boxers, Belgian Malinois, and Briards are superb for this.

Many others, though not especially bred for guard work, may have guardian instincts. These include such breeds as Dalmatians, Bernese Mountain Dogs, Giant Schnauzers, Komondors, Kuvaszok, and Rhodesian Ridgebacks.

Contrary to popular opinion, a dog does not really have to be large in order to protect a home from burglars. Burglars are not going to enter any home in which there is a noisy barker. So actually all the Terriers and most of the Toy Breeds fit into this "guard dog" group, as do Poodles, Lhasa Apsos, Shih Tzus, Keeshonden, Norwegian Elkhounds, and Cocker Spaniels. Most of the Sporting Breeds make poor watchdogs, although there are exceptions in all breeds. And, of course, no dog is likely to prevail over a determined intruder with a gun or a knife.

Aid to the Handicapped

Deaf people can almost always benefit from a noisemaker. Such dogs attract the attention of their owners when strangers are at the door. They can even be taught to alert a deaf person when the phone rings.

Dogs have proven to be remarkably good aids to retarded people, particularly children. They learn how to train dogs for obedience competition, and in taking on this responsibility, show great improvement in their own development.

On the whole, breeds noted for fairly placid and gentle dispositions should be selected. These include some of the Sporting Breeds, such as English Setters, Gordon Setters, Golden Retrievers, English and Welsh Springer Spaniels, American Cocker Spaniels, English Cocker Spaniels, and Brittany Spaniels. Show-type Beagles and Bassets, the two Welsh Corgis (Pembroke and Cardigan), some of the larger Toy Breeds (such as the Pug and Toy Poodle), Bulldogs, Keeshonden, Miniature and Standard Poodles, Collies, and Shetland Sheepdogs are also suitable.

The feats of the Guide Dogs, especially trained to help the blind, are well known. German Shepherds are most commonly used, but other breeds, including Boxers and Labrador Retrievers, have also been employed successfully.

Of course, these are generalizations. You should always try to see the parents of the puppies that appeal to you; this will give you some idea of what the puppy's adult disposition will be like. If you can't see both, at least study the mother. Do not select a shy or fearful puppy.

The German Shepherd Dog is the breed most often trained as a guide for the blind. *Ralston Purina Company*

Grooming

Different breeds need varying degrees of attention to maintain proper grooming. You should be prepared to give your dog the necessary grooming to keep it clean, neat, and in conformance with the style of its breed.

Smooth-coated, short-haired dogs need the least grooming; just a simple brushing and then wiping a dampened cloth over their bodies are usually all that is necessary. Among these breeds are Smooth Dachshunds, Basenjis, Whippets, Italian Greyhounds, Miniature Pinschers, American Staffordshire Terriers, Staffordshire Bull Terriers, Bull Terriers, Beagles, Smooth Fox Terriers, Boston Terriers, Bulldogs, Vizslas, Rhodesian Ridgebacks, and Dalmatians.

On the other hand some Spaniels, English and American Cockers, and the English Springers need constant combing, trimming, and even the use of clippers. Otherwise they soon look like animated mops. In particular, hair on the dog's feet must be trimmed out to keep the dog from tracking dirt or mud into your home. Collies, Shetland Sheepdogs, and similar long-coated dogs need constant combing, but foot hair is not a problem. For further grooming information for the various breeds, see Chapters 16 to 19.

When Not to Get a Dog

A family should never have a dog if the responsibility of caring for it is to be a hotly debated issue or if the dog will be unappreciated and not properly attended to. Sometimes children promise that they will take care of a dog, but after the first few weeks, they no longer do, and a parent who may dislike the responsibility has to take over.

Allow me to elaborate on this. For the past forty years I have been hearing constant complaints from parents who do not want a "dirty, unsanitary" dog in the house. Their children wanted a dog and were so insistent that the parents felt they must give in and buy one. In such homes the children and the dogs are martyred for the sake of cleanliness. The dog is purchased. For a while all goes well, but gradually the parent begins to complain: "That dirty dog is spreading germs." "The children aren't taking care of the dog like they promised." Finally the parent issues an ultimatum, and the dog has to leave. Often it is taken to an animal shelter, where it will probably be destroyed. It may pick up a disease at the shelter that could cause its death. Its second home, if it gets one, may be less satisfactory than the first. Its next trip to the animal shelter will probably be its last, for most such abandoned animals are destroyed.

Another person who should not have a dog is someone who requests a grown, fully housebroken dog that does not smell, bite, or need expensive shots. When breeders hear such demands, they should simply say, "Go away. You don't deserve a dog." Such a person will never be willing to give a dog the care it will need. Such an owner will almost invariably send the dog to an animal shelter, give it away, or just allow it to exist under miserable conditions. Many reputable breeders recognize such people and refuse to sell them a puppy.

Finally no home should have a dog if all the family members are gone during the day. Dogs that are left alone all day usually develop personality problems. Some become very shy. Others try to amuse themselves by chewing on rugs or chair legs or by tearing down curtains. Still others show their resentment by relieving themselves on beds, near the front door, and so on. Such dogs may end up at an animal shelter because their owners do not wish to put up with their misbehavior. And certainly no one should own a dog if it is going to be kept tied all the time. This is a cruel practice that more often than not leads to injuries, excessive barking, escapes, and, eventually, produces a vicious animal.

Breed Characteristics in Brief

It is always difficult to be specific on such a subject because there will always be dogs that prove you wrong. There are always master-dog relationships that should not work out but somehow do, even if only satisfactorily at best. Keep these points in mind as you consider these general comments about the six major dog types.

Sporting Breeds. In general, all Sporting breeds make good house dogs and pets. (There are exceptions, however; see Chapter 35.) A prime consideration may be the shedding and grooming of long-haired dogs. (Dogs that may present a shedding and grooming problem are the English and American Cocker Spaniels, particularly the latter; Irish and American Water Spaniels; Clumber Spaniels; and Curly-Coated Retrievers.) Some of the bigger dogs, such as Labrador Retrievers, Pointers, and Irish Setters, may be too strong and boisterous for elderly people. Chesapeake Bay Retrievers make good guard dogs but are sometimes unfriendly with strangers and may like to fight. Avoid all dogs that have been specifically bred for field trials. Most will be too high-strung to make good house pets, and they may also be headstrong.

Hound Breeds. Most Hounds make excellent house pets. People who want Bassets, Bloodhounds, and Black and Tan Coonhounds should like wearing tweeds, and should not mind avoiding solid-color clothes, because these dogs are droolers. The breeds that require the least amount of grooming care are Smooth Dachshunds, Basenjis, and Whippets. Special training may be necessary to keep the big coursing dogs, such as Greyhounds and Afghans (which also require a lot of grooming), from

Labrador Retrievers can be obedient home companions and are also among the most popular of field trial dogs. *Bettmann Archive*

Bloodhounds have an affectionate, gentle nature. Ch. The Rectory's Rebel Yell and Ch. The Rectory's Reward are owned by The Rev. & Mrs. George E. Sinkinson, Jr.

racing over the entire neighborhood. Norwegian Elkhounds make excellent watchdogs, but require constant grooming and sometimes fight with other dogs, although they are gentle with people. Avoid Beagles bred specifically for field trials unless you want one for this sport; most, in contrast to the gentle show-bred ones, are too high-strung to be good house pets.

Working Breeds.   Most dogs in this category are excellent watchdogs. Some — German Shepherds, Doberman Pinschers, and Rottweilers, for instance — are great guard dogs, but avoid them unless you are prepared to be a strict disciplinarian. They are exceptionally alert and intelligent and will try to take advantage of you. In the wrong hands they can be dangerous.

St. Bernards, Newfoundlands, Old English Sheepdogs, Komondorok, Mastiffs, Bullmastiffs, and a few others are droolers, and they require special grooming attention. Collies, Border Collies, Bearded Collies, Shetland Sheepdogs, and others of the herding group are usually excellent

The Collie is a beautiful, highly intelligent dog, and it requires special grooming attention. *Bettmann Archive*

and quiet house dogs, but they, too, require special grooming attention. The Cardigan and Pembroke Welsh Corgis are easily kept and compact enough to fit into even the smallest house or apartment.

Terrier Breeds. Most Terriers are noisy. If you like a bundle of energy, are always ready for excitement, and like to play, a Terrier is for you. Because they bark a lot, they are excellent burglar alarms and are sometimes more feared by housebreakers than more recognized guard dogs. Terriers make great playmates for children.

You will have to learn special grooming techniques to keep hard-coated Terriers looking the way they are meant to look. Ragged-coated Terriers, such as Cairns and Australians, on the other hand, need little grooming. There are also short, bristle-coated dogs, such as the Border, Norwich, American Staffordshire, and Smooth Fox Terriers. There are even some Terriers that have short, slick coats, such as the Standard Manchester and Staffordshire Bull Terriers.

Toy Breeds. An advantage of the Toy breeds is that they are all small enough never to need to leave the home. Most are housebroken to use paper, unlike larger dogs, which should always be taken out. Smaller dogs also cost less to feed. Grooming is sometimes a problem, however. The excessively long-coated dogs — Maltese, Yorkshires, and Shih Tzus — need particular care in order to keep their hair from breaking. Their size makes all Toy breeds susceptible to broken bones if they are allowed to jump from high furniture, such as beds. The Miniature Pinscher is a slick-coated dog but a bundle of nervous energy; ear and tail cropping add to the expense of owning this breed. The Pug is usually quiet. The Toy Manchester is another short, slick-haired dog requiring little grooming care, as is the Italian Greyhound.

Non-Sporting Breeds. Poodles, including Toy Poodles, may cost their owners more than $150 a year for proper grooming. Lhasa Apsos also need careful grooming. Bulldogs, Boston Terriers, and French Bulldogs may require Cesarean section to give birth. Dalmatians make excellent watchdogs and guard dogs, particularly on farms or around racetracks because they have an affinity for horses and stables. Keeshonden are good watchdogs, but they need steady grooming. Schipperkes are excellent barkers and require little coat care. But Tibetan Terriers and Bichon Frises require regular grooming.

A Final Note. These comments about the various breeds are not intended to be definitive. The intent has been to give you a set of values to use in selecting a breed of dog for you. More complete descriptions of all the breeds are given in Part Seven, "Breed Standards."

chapter three
Buying a Puppy

Visiting a Kennel or Breeder

I assume that you want to buy a good, healthy puppy, one that has a good temperament, is purebred, and is either registered or comes from a registered litter. You should follow these steps.

First, stay away from pet shops or at any rate from those that sell puppies. Some shops refuse to sell puppies. A few of these may keep lists of reputable kennels and will refer you to them.

Second, visit a dog breeder. Look around to ascertain whether the pups are kept in sanitary conditions. If they are, the breeder has passed the first test. Next, notice whether the pups appear to be healthy and strong. A dog's eyes should be clear, and its coat should have a gloss. If a puppy appears to have a severely bloated belly, diarrhea, matter in its eyes or coming from its nose, then the breeder has failed the second test.

Third, ask to see the pups' mother. And if the breeder owns the sire, ask to see him as well. If either parent appears to be very shy or very aggressive, wend your way home and wait to look at another litter.

Fourth, find out if the litter is registered. If it is not, you should not buy. Thousands of times each year people buy pups from breeders who say that their registration application for the litter has been sent to the American Kennel Club but that it has not come back yet. In most of those cases application was never made, and you will be stuck with a puppy that cannot be registered, shown, or used in breeding. If a litter application has been sent in on the day that puppies are born, the application will be registered and the certificate sent back to the breeder by the time the pups are six weeks old.

Do not choose a puppy on a whim. Make sure that it is the right dog for you and your family. *Bettmann Archive*

Often the owner of the dam has not bothered to register the dog, or the owner of the sire has not done so. Both parents may have pedigree certificates, but these are worthless. You would not believe that a man has a five-hundred-dollar savings account just because he shows you a handwritten statement to that effect. You would want to see an official bank statement. The same principle applies to registration papers: Only official certificates are proof. In thousands of cases a dog owner may have lost the papers for one of his dogs, a sire or dam. Being unfamiliar with registration procedures, he or she figures that it is a simple procedure to get new ones. It is not; it is almost impossible.

The papers that the breeder must show you are a certificate of litter registration and an application to register a pup from a registered litter. Again, do not be misled by a three- or five-generation pedigree. Even if it is accurate, it is worthless without the certificate of litter registration and the signed application to register the individual puppy.

Fifth, you should observe the puppies in their kennel run. Do they scrabble on the fence, barking and trying to get out or to get your attention? If they do, fine. But maybe one sits alone. The kids may love that lonely, forlorn little fellow, but that is one you must forget.

Ask to see the puppies out in the yard, away from the world of their pen. Do they scrabble on your legs, get between your feet, try to jump up to your face? If so, great. If one sneaks quietly back into the kennel or pen, discard it as a possibility.

The puppies I have told you not to choose are shy. They were born that way and will remain that way all their lives. They will be unsatisfactory in dozens of home situations, as well as when they are away from home. They may become fear biters; they may be storm-shy, noise-shy, or gun-shy.

You should watch the pups while you are talking to the breeder. After crawling all over you, jumping at your face, and yelping for attention, several puppies may wander off and begin to explore the world. Now you are seeing the bravest and most intelligent of the litter. Those are the ones that will be the most satisfactory for your home.

Sixth, you should ask the final questions: Have the puppies been wormed? If so, when? Has the dam had distemper? If so, then she will have passed antibodies to her puppies in the colostrum, the first milk she gives them. They will then be protected for a week or two after weaning. If the dam has not had distemper, was she immunized recently? Were the puppies given the weakened measles virus for protection?

Negative answers to these final questions should not necessarily prevent you from buying a puppy. However, they do indicate your future course in caring for your dog, and that is important.

By watching puppies outside in the kennel's yard, you will be able to see what kind of temperament they have. *Gaines Dog Research Center*

These are energetic, playful St. Bernard pups. *Ralston Purina Company*

Other Sources for Buying a Dog

Is it all right to get a puppy or dog from an animal shelter? Yes, but remember, animal shelters are potentially places where disease can spread. The shelter is constantly bringing in many wandering, lost, or sick dogs. They may take in dozens of litters of unwanted puppies whose background in regard to disease exposure is not known.

Some shelters will give puppies shots and examine them for worms. However, they cannot afford to do this for puppies that are going to be destroyed within a couple of weeks. So the puppy you choose will probably get its shots just before you take it home. In some cases the puppy may have been exposed several days before to a disease, and incubation may be too far along for the shots to be effective.

You are taking a risk. Although you are getting a puppy at very little cost, you may have to pay later in high veterinary bills, at a time when you or your family will have already developed a strong affection for the dog. And yet I have known many gentle, affectionate, and healthy pups that have come from animal shelters.

If you are unsure where to locate a breeder who has puppies for sale, consult the "Pets for Sale" listings in the classified advertising section of your local newspaper. Also, most major cities and many smaller ones have active kennel clubs that sponsor many kinds of events for owners and their dogs. Watch for announcements of their meetings. Plan to attend so that you can ask for a directory of breeders. (The American Kennel Club does not have a referral service.)

Most dog magazines orient their articles and information toward dog shows. However, *Dog World,* the world's largest dog magazine, carries more advertisements for puppies than any other magazine. It is available on newsstands in many cities across the country. *Dog World* separates its advertisements into both breeds and states, which makes it easy for you to locate breeders near you.

Finally, ask your friends. One of the largest and oldest kennel clubs in America was founded because a salesman met a company officer who had a litter of puppies. The salesman's friends bought the entire litter, founded a club for that breed, and eventually branched out to become an all-breeds club.

The Formative Weeks

A puppy will make the best adjustment to its environment, to a new home, and to a new family during the first six to fourteen weeks of its life. The rudiments of all a dog needs to know are learned during this period, and animal psychologists consider it the most critical time in a dog's entire life.

For example, many guide dog schools give basic obedience training to puppies when they are six to eight weeks old. The training is very light — walk at heel, come when called, walk on a leash. Afterward the puppy is placed in a private home, and it adjusts to life there. The early training it has been given at school will remain fixed in its memory and reactions. When it is later returned for formal training, it will progress swiftly and more easily.

If you want your puppy to be a happy, well-adjusted, and intelligent family pet, you should plan to get it when it is between six and fourteen weeks old. The closer to the age of six weeks, the better. After the puppy is about fourteen weeks old, it becomes harder for the owner to train.

Dog Breeders

Dedicated breeders trying to produce champions are sometimes unwilling to sell very young puppies. They do not want to sell the best puppy in the litter as a pet by mistake, so they keep the entire litter until the pups are seven or eight months old, sometimes longer. This gives the breeder a chance to determine which puppies will become good show dogs. Owners who want to develop field trial champions may require an even longer period to decide; meanwhile, they give the dogs tests in the field and hunting exercises.

The breeder of show dogs faces two problems: How can he or she adequately socialize a gang of puppies during the critical period of their lives? How can the puppies be prevented from deciding that the kennel runs are their entire world? The breeder can do this with one or two puppies, but with half a dozen or more, it is nearly impossible.

Some highly experienced breeders can perceive a puppy's championship potential when it is still very young. Toy or Miniature Poodle breeders can often tell at six weeks which puppies are likely to grow over the size limits of 10 and 15 inches, respectively. Other breeders may be able to make similar educated guesses.

The problem of when a breeder should sell a puppy can also be solved in another way. The buyer who wants to acquire a puppy during its critical growth period may be asked by the seller to sign a special agreement which states that if the puppy appears to have show potential, the buyer agrees to put it into show competition when it is old enough. Similarly, dedicated breeders of rarely seen dogs may want every pup

Puppies will make the best adjustment to a new home during their first 6 to 14 weeks of life. *Ralston Purina Company*

they sell to be shown so that the breed gets as much public exposure as possible.

Of course, runts will be excluded, as well as puppies with serious or disqualifying faults. This point may seem negligible; however, several examples will show that it is not. Blue Weimaraners and white German Shepherds are barred from the show ring because both colors are disqualifying faults according to the breed standards. Parti-color Poodles are also excluded from show competition. Of course, such puppies are born, and people buy them and like them. Owners may spend years agitating to have these colors recognized. As a result we have a Blu-Mar Club and a White German Shepherd Club. One man I know spent years breeding parti-color Poodles and trying to get them recognized in shows.

Most reputable breeders will, to the best of their judgment, select which of a litter are "show quality" and which are "pet quality." The latter will cost less and have only minor faults that would handicap them in showing but in no way lessen their potentials as good pets. Of course, even the wisest breeders make mistakes sometimes! Just be sure that the "pet quality" pup does not have any really serious fault that would be a hazard to its health or activity, an aesthetic disappointment, or a disqualification for showing if you should change your mind.

Registering Your Dog

Now let's discuss the procedure you must follow to obtain your dog's papers. Every step in registering a dog must be taken in order. If one step is left out, your puppy cannot be registered.

1. The sire and dam must be registered, and their registration papers must be certified in the name of the owners at the time of mating.

2. The litter must be registered.

3. One application to register a puppy from a registered litter is issued for each puppy in the litter. The owner of the litter must personally endorse the dog over to you. That is, he or she cannot just sign the form and give it to you. Your name must be filled in at the time of sale. If the puppy has been sold and returned, or if you bought it from the first purchaser but before it was registered, that seller must endorse the papers over to you on a supplemental form issued for this purpose by the American Kennel Club. (Registration procedures for the *Field Dog Stud Book* and United Kennel Club may differ slightly.)

The day you bring home your puppy, you should sign the registration application, enclose the registration fee, and mail it to the American Kennel Club. Literally thousands of people fail to do this. Then they mislay the papers or just forget about them. The result: You have a purebred dog, but you will never be able to get it registered.

chapter four
Bringing Your Puppy Home

You should make adequate preparations for your puppy's arrival before you bring it home. Remember that you are dealing with a highly sensitive and rather fragile bit of life. Here are my suggestions for getting ready for your puppy.

Necessary Purchases

First, find out from the breeder whether there is a **book on the breed** you have chosen. Such a book will help you to understand your puppy and will increase your pride in ownership. When such books are available, smart breeders give a copy to puppy purchasers. They knòw that by doing so, they are increasing the puppy's chances of being in a really superior home.

Find out from the breeder the type of **dog food** that is being used. You may want to change to a different brand, but it is advisable to continue the puppy on the food it is used to until it has adjusted to life in your home.

Your next concern is for your dog's **sleeping place.** One alternative is to purchase a wire travelling crate such as those seen at dog shows for your dog to sleep in. A wood or metal crate is preferable because it will simulate the den in which the ancestors of the dog lived. Den dwellers inherit an instinct to keep their dens clean, and this is important in housebreaking your puppy. No one who has ever watched a litter of coyote puppies tumble into their den at the first sight or sound of danger can fail to realize that the den represents a place of security to them, a place where they will be safe.

Your dog will grow accustomed to a crate that becomes its private sleeping place, and will associate it with safety and security. *H. Armstrong Roberts*

Your dog will learn to consider the crate its private sleeping place unless you corrupt it into thinking it has become "people." Once you have decided to discard the crate and let the dog sleep where it chooses, you are asking for trouble. The dog may resent being left alone in the house while you go shopping or out for the evening. You have taken away its security, and now its only security is you. You have gone off and left it defenseless.

At least a hundred times a year desperate people have complained to me about this. They come home to find a big stool on the rug just in front of the front door. Others find stools in the middle of their beds. Some dogs become positively destructive and tear down curtains, destroy pillows, or chew up table legs or sofas.

Your dog should use the crate you get it for its entire life. It will know that it is a secure den and that when you put it inside, it is to stay there and be quiet.

If your dog is to sleep in a wire crate, the crate should be covered on all sides, including the back and top, except the door. This will also give the puppy the feeling of being in a den. A high-sided old cardboard box with no top will not do. The puppy will simply spend unhappy hours trying to escape. Pups can escape from surprisingly high-sided boxes.

Sometimes people put up barriers in order to make a small section of their kitchen or another room the pup's bed. This does not always work satisfactorily. The puppy may feel that it has been exiled, and this may cause personality problems. It may also be difficult to make the space small enough so that the puppy won't sleep in one part of the area and relieve itself in another.

Some people buy a puppy and chain it outside, with just enough room so that it can get into a doghouse or have just a small area to move around in. To me, as I've said earlier, this is cruelty to animals. The dog will want to be with you, and being with you means being in your home. A pup left outside will show its resentment and loneliness by howling or barking at every passing person or thing, and that may prompt neighbors to call the police.

One solution is to set up a doghouse in your backyard. Surround it with portable fencing, allowing a large area for your dog to run around in, plus a gate for you to enter. Then you can put your dog outside for exercise, and it won't be run over by a car or chase children on bikes, and it can go into the doghouse to lie down or to get out of the sun or rain. Bring your dog inside if barking becomes a nuisance, and keep it in the house at night. In cold weather your dog should be left outside for only a few minutes.

Other important purchases for your dog are a **leather collar** and **light leather leash,** and a **chain collar** and **light chain leash.** The leather collar will

Keep your dog on leash when you take him for a walk, so that he cannot run away. Photo of Telomian, courtesy of Audrey M. Palumbo.

Give your puppy some small toys — the indestructible type — that he can call his own. Photo of Maltese, owned by Neil N. Joseph.

be for regular wear; the chain collar and leash are for housebreaking your pup. When it is time for your dog to relieve itself, put the chain collar and leash on your dog, and take it outside. The dog will quickly learn to associate this collar and leash with going to the relief area.

You can expect a new puppy to make some puddles, and you should be prepared for this with some **cleanup equipment.** To remove the stains those inevitable puddles will cause, use club soda or a stain remover to clean the area and deodorize it. In addition, you might buy one of the "housebreaking odor" aids that are now on the market. These are used to give the puppy the idea that it has used this spot to relieve itself before and should do so again. (For more details on housebreaking and cleaning up after your pet, see Chapter 5, "Housebreaking Your Dog.")

You should also buy your dog its own **food dish** and **water bowl.** These should be durable and safe (not made of a substance poisonous to dogs) and should remain stationary while your dog is eating.

In Chapter 16, there is a detailed discussion of the kinds of **grooming equipment** that you can use to care for your pet. Keep your dog neat and clean, and as it grows older, see that it is groomed according to the style of its particular breed.

Finally, buy some small **toys** — and be sure they are the indestructible type — with which your puppy can play. These will be useful in teaching it not to chew on your shoes or the bedspread. If the toys have metal bells inside them, remove the bells before giving the puppy the plaything.

Early Adjustment

Now you are ready to bring your puppy home. Do this in the morning, never at night. The puppy will then have a full day to forget its littermates and to begin its adjustment to your home.

When you arrive home, give the puppy a chance to meet the family. It is important for it to recognize the smell of each person, particularly the person who will be considered its special master.

After a period of play and family introduction the pup should be placed in its crate. Never pick up a puppy by its front legs. Instead, place one hand under its abdomen and the other hand under its throat. With puppies of small breeds, use one hand to lift it by the scruff, or nape, of the neck and place the other hand under its abdomen.

A puppy needs a lot of sleep, and it will be tired from being in a new environment and from all the excitement. After it is placed in its crate, the puppy may cry at first and may even try to get out. It's probably feeling lonely. Tolerate this; the puppy will soon tire and fall asleep. It should have at least four rest periods during that first day. By night it will have grown partially used to the crate and will begin to think of it as its home and fortress.

Here is an additional thing to do: Place some small article of clothing worn by the dog's special master in its bed. It will recognize the odor, and this will add to its sense of security. If it cries longer than you can stand, slap the side of the crate, and in a moderately stern voice, order it to lie down and be quiet.

If your puppy was not immunized before you brought it home, it will need to have shots for distemper, leptospirosis, and hepatitis. But give your dog about a week to settle down and learn the routine in your home before bringing it to the veterinarian. The doctor will choose the right time to give your dog these shots, depending on circumstances such as the pup's age and what shots it might already have had.

For registration purposes, or if you eventually want to enter your dog in shows, you may want to give it a fancy name, such as Prince of Jones Street, Queen of Arlendale, Sir Roger of Cranston. For a call name, choose a simple one- or two-syllable word that will quickly get your dog's attention.

License

Most states require dogs to be licensed, and the license tag should be worn on the dog's collar. The practice of licensing dogs began as an excise tax imposed on the dog owner to cover losses sustained by farmers whose sheep, chickens, goats, or other animals had been killed by marauding dogs. It is not a personal property tax.

Dogs should be licensed when they are three to six months old, depending on the law in your area. If you purchase an older dog, apply for its license at that time. Licenses should be renewed annually. Your dog's license tag serves as its identification if it wanders away from you and becomes lost. Personal property tax will permit you to recover the value of your dog if it is maliciously killed, that is, destroyed without valid reason as set forth in state law or local ordinance. Check in your community to find out what agency will issue your dog a license.

A license tag serves as a dog's identification and should be worn on its collar. *Ralston Purina Company*

part two
BASIC CARE

chapter five
Housebreaking Your Dog

Because the *way* you feed your puppy and *what* you feed it will have an effect on housebreaking, let me offer a few general suggestions.

The best time of day for feeding is generally in the morning because then the dog will relieve itself before the work of the day begins. (Hunting and heavily exercised dogs are exceptions; see Chapter 6.)

Do not feed your puppy milk. A puppy's stomach produces an enzyme known as *rennin,* which is used to coagulate milk in the stomach and slow its passage into the intestine. However, the puppy's stomach ceases to produce rennin at the time of weaning; consequently milk passes into the intestine in an undigested form. There it will putrify, causing foul odors and loose bowels.

Do not give the puppy water after 6 or 7 P.M., depending on your own bedtime hour. Then if you take the puppy to its spot before you retire for the evening, it will relieve itself and be able to go the entire night without urinating.

Outdoor Housebreaking

Your first step is to select a spot at the back end of your yard or outside your house or apartment building that will be the puppy's toilet area. If the puppy urinates in the house, wipe the puddle up with a rag, and then anchor that rag to the spot you have selected. The next time your puppy has to go, take it to that spot outside. It will smell the urine and use that spot. The housebreaking odor aids that are now on the market will also help to remind the puppy to use that toilet area again.

A puppy should relieve itself when it wakes up from a nap, after meals, the first thing in the morning, and the last thing before being put to bed for the night. Excitement may cause a bladder-emptying reaction. To prevent this, the puppy should be taken to its spot before any play period. If the excitement of moving from a kennel to its new home is too great, a puppy may have to relieve itself in its crate-den. It will probably not do so again because its instinct is to keep its bed clean.

If the puppy howls to get out at 4 or 5 A.M., ignore it, or slap the side of the crate and tell it to be quiet. If you let it out at that early hour, all you will be doing is training it — or should one say the puppy is training you? — to relieve itself at that hour every morning.

Do not let rain, snow, or bitter cold prevent you from taking your dog out to its toilet area. Puppies are born with an unusually thick insulating coat. They will not get chilled in the short time that they are out. And they will be just as anxious to get it over with as you are. If you use weather conditions as an excuse, you are excusing yourself, not the pup. In addition, you will be breaking the very habits you are trying to instill in your dog.

There is one rule that you absolutely must not break. For at least the first six weeks, never put your puppy out; *take* it out. If you put it out, it may not know why and may become interested in everything else but relieving itself. It may forget to go to its spot. Then, when you let it in, you will not know whether it emptied itself and whether it may make a puddle inside shortly after you have let it in.

In Chapter 4, I suggested purchasing two types of collars and leashes for your dog, a leather collar and leash and a chain collar and leash. Use the chain collar and leash when you take the puppy to its spot. Almost immediately it will identify them with going to the relief area.

If you begin this as soon as you bring your puppy home, you will be grateful the rest of the dog's life. For example, there will be times when you will be on a trip and want your dog to relieve itself at a stopover. Then all you will have to do is put the chain collar and leash on your dog, and it will relieve itself on the spot.

Remember to compliment the puppy as soon as it urinates or defecates. Within a week or so you should be able to housebreak your dog.

Also remember that if dogs are to be walked on city streets, they must be on leash and kept under control. If you walk your dog without a leash through the fields out in the country, it is more likely to stay close to you if you do not take a second dog along. Two dogs may run off if they are allowed to roam freely and not kept on leashes.

Unless you expect to allow the puppy to relieve itself on paper all its life, never start it on papers. If you do, you will be corrupting its instincts to keep its home clean. Hundreds of thousands of dog owners make this mistake and afterward can never teach the dog to go outside. Such owners write to me or call me, and their complaint is always the same: "No matter how long I have him out or walk him, he won't do a thing. Then the minute

I get him back to the house, he does it. He seems to be smart enough, but we just can't make him understand.''

In such cases the dog often cannot be retrained. When it can, the retraining may take months. The dog must be put into its crate or cage and kept there except for those times when it is with you and on its chain leash. You must deodorize every spot in the house that the dog has used. The notions sections in department stores may have odor destroyers (rather than odor maskers) that you can purchase. When you take your dog to its toilet area, and it refuses to relieve itself, insert a suppository into its rectum. An ordinary paper book match will do. (Never use a household, strike-anywhere match.) And remember that you will need to be very patient when trying to retrain your dog.

Many dog owners housebreak their pets by using a chain collar and leash exclusively for that purpose. *H. Armstrong Roberts*

Housebreaking on Paper

If you own a dog from the Toy breeds, you may decide to teach it to relieve itself on paper, so that taking the dog outdoors to relieve it will be unnecessary. In that case select the spot it should use, cover the floor with paper, and set up a small portable exercise pen. Place your puppy in this pen, and keep it there until it has relieved itself. Reward your dog with petting and compliments. If you want your puppy to exercise but not relieve itself, move the portable pen to another area, and do not use paper in the exercise area. It is important that the dog always associate a given area — and *only* that area — and paper with relief.

Cleaning up

For the first week or two the puppy should not be allowed in rooms where there are shag or oriental rugs. Actually it is best if puppies are allowed only in rooms where there are no rugs, so that, if necessary, you will be able to clean up puddles in the easiest possible manner. Shag rugs are the most difficult to remove stains from; oriental rugs are too valuable.

Wipe up the puddle quickly, and then pour a little club soda over the area. This will help to remove any residue that might otherwise have sunk into the warp. It will also help to deodorize the area, as will soapy water. Do not use vinegar, ammonia, or an acid to clean up the puddle. Dry the spot as well as you can. One carpet manufacturer suggests that you cover the area with a Turkish towel and put your clothes iron on it, set to "hot." This is the best possible way to remove any remaining moisture.

A dog can easily detect the smells of blood, sweat, urine, and other acids. In fact it can smell one part of urine in ten thousand parts of water. Therefore, it is very important for you to remove all residue of odor so that the puppy won't be tempted to use that spot again. An indoor repellent can be used on the spot, but test it first to be sure that it will not stain the rug.

Whenever a puppy makes a puddle, show it the spot where it made the mistake, and scold it. Then take it to the paper, encouraging the puppy to relieve itself there. Under no circumstances should you rub the dog's nose in the mess. After the first several days of using this discipline, if your puppy still makes a puddle where it shouldn't, the fault is probably yours, not the dog's.

Many pet supplies stores sell stain removers; so do notions departments in large department stores. These usually come in two types: one for use on dry stains, the other for use on fresh wet ones. Keep these handy, and use them. Do not try to remove stains by other means first; chances are that you will set the stain and make it impossible to remove later.

If your dog makes a puddle in your home, he should be reprimanded; do not rub the dog's nose in the mess.   *H. Armstrong Roberts*

A Dog Owner's Responsibility

Antidog feeling and antidog legislation are growing as the American population increases, particularly in urban areas. This could be greatly reduced if dog owners would recognize their responsibility toward their pets and be more considerate of their needs and of the concerns of the community. For instance, I believe it is the dog owner's responsibility not to allow his or her dog to run at large, ruin the neighbors' shrubbery or leave stools in their yards.

People love to take their dogs for walks. But they must realize that during a walk, the dog may relieve itself on the strip of lawn between the sidewalk and the curb. Normally cities claim ownership of this lawn, but homeowners are responsible for keeping it mowed and clean. In many city areas there is no such lawn strip, and so dogs are taken to the curb to relieve themselves. As we shall see, this is not a valid solution to the problem.

If you take your dog for walks, you should purchase a stool scooper at your local pet shop. Do not pick up the stool with the scooper and then drop the stool over the curb. More and more cities have laws against this for ecological reasons as well as for general cleanliness. It is argued that storm drainage and sewer water flow into rivers and lakes, and therefore dog feces simply add to the pollution.

Earlier I explained how to train your dog to relieve itself in a special spot outside. However, if your dog has not learned to do this, you should remove the stools you scoop up to a spot in your yard or outside your home. Many people dispose of dog feces in their garbage despite the fact that some refuse collectors will not pick up garbage cans if they know that dog stools are in them. Discuss this with your garbage collector, and perhaps he will not object if the stools are placed in plastic bags that are tied shut.

Another way to dispose of unwanted stools is to buy an enzyme digester that will reduce them to little more than fiber and will prevent odors. If your pet store does not carry one, it should be able to order one for you or tell you where you can order one.

You might also consider using the stools for fertilizer; dog manure is about as good as horse or cow manure for gardening and can be used around trees and shrubs. Let the stools dry out and crumble; then mix them with the topsoil. You will also be saving on the high price of buying another kind of manure.

If you live in an apartment house or condominium that permits dogs, you might suggest that a dog exercise area be built. I once designed such an area for an apartment building in Cleveland: it consisted of a concrete slab that sloped to a gutter to drain off urine and a six-foot storm fence to surround the area. People were grateful for the dog run, and later a roof was placed over the higher part of the area to protect the dogs from inclement weather. The dogs learned to keep this part clean and to relieve themselves on the lower end of the slab. And the owners were able to leave their dogs in the area for an hour or more.

I would also like to suggest that when you take your dog for a walk, you should keep it away from shrubs. Repeated wettings with urine will kill plants. Moreover, the shrubs may contain ticks, which will jump onto a passing dog. Trees and fireplugs serve as newspapers for dogs. A dog will smell around a tree, ascertain that other dogs have been there — male, female, sick, healthy, in heat — and then leave its own "watermark." Let the dog sniff these, instead of shrubs.

chapter six
Feeding Your Dog

The Cleveland Press once ran a survey in its dog column asking people to tell what they fed their dogs. Did they use a fine, meal-type food; a biscuit-type food; or a canned food? Did they mix two of these types? Did they add fresh or cooked meat?

Many people wrote long letters giving the intricate details of the feeding systems they used for their dogs. There were some surprising answers in these letters that showed a tragic lack of knowledge about what you should feed a dog.

One person wrote that because his dog liked to eat grass, he had started to cultivate the species of grass he felt his dog enjoyed the most. Another person, who lived near a horse farm, wrote that his dog would sometimes eat horse manure. He figured that "the dog knows best," and so he began adding horse manure to the dog's diet because "it keeps the dog from getting distemper."

Some people said that they fed their dogs eggs, either raw or cooked; others mixed horsemeat with a meal-type food. Several owners said they would feed their dogs only chicken or beef. One person cooked chicken and beef hearts and mixed portions of each with ground biscuits soaked in beef consomme for his dog. Another mixed ground beef with Shredded Wheat.

Other people who wrote in asked questions that revealed their misconceptions about feeding a dog. One man wrote that his Scottie was now a year old and had been given only soup and milk, no solid food. Could he now switch his dog to solid food? Was the dog old enough to stand the change? In fact it should have been weaned on solid food starting at four to five weeks of age.

Another person had been feeding her puppy eight times a day, including a midnight supper and a 5:30 A.M. breakfast. Could it now be cut down to five or six meals per day? Several dozen people wanted to know if it was true that feeding a dog meat or raw milk could give it worms. (It does not.)

This chapter will provide you with basic information on what, when, and how to feed your dog so that it will get proper nourishment.

Kinds of Dog Food

Canned dog food used to have the largest sales volume of all canned foods except evaporated milk, and even a fair amount of the canned milk sold went to dogs. Today the greater acceptance rate of dry and soft-moist dog foods has put these products ahead of canned dog foods.

Before proceeding any further, let me give some definitions.

Canned meat is designed to be fed as a supplement to some other kind of food. Vitamins and minerals are added to the meat of livestock or meat by-products. Canned meat will contain 75 to 80 per cent water.

Canned dog food is designed to be fed just as it comes from the can. It will contain meat, meat by-products, cereals, soybeans, vitamins, minerals, and about 75 to 80 per cent water. Probably 50 per cent of canned dog food's protein comes from meat by-products (i.e., udders, stomachs, spleens). The ingredients are blended, cooked, and sealed in cans. Government inspection monitors the ingredients and the packing equipment of many companies.

Dry foods can be classified separately in a number of ways. There are the *hard-baked biscuits,* which are marketed whole or ground into small chunks, generally called *kibbles* or *kibbled biscuits.* Another classification is *homogenized dog food.* The ingredients are carefully mixed and balanced, then made into pellets or various-sized particles or are expanded into nugget sizes. Still another form is *meal,* which is a blend of ingredients in granular size.

The **soft-moist dog foods,** which look like hamburger or meat cutlets, are the latest to come onto the market, and are made to appeal to people as well as to dogs. So are other impulse or gourmet dog foods called *hash, stew,* and so forth, which are as nutritious as the other forms of dog food.

The two most important definitions that every dog owner should know are those of balanced and complete. A **balanced dog food** is one that contains all the nutrients, in proper balance, which are required by the dog. For example, if you are buying a puppy food, that food should be balanced according to the needs of growing puppies. If it is a food for older dogs, it should be balanced according to their requirements. Consult your veterinarian regarding the nutritional needs of your dog.

A **complete dog food** is one that if fed as the dog's sole diet, is sufficient for growth, pregnancy, rearing of puppies, and work, such as hunting. Sometimes the label of a food will say "a complete and balanced diet," which means that it should supply the dog with adequate nourishment under almost any circumstance.

Dog foods that are sold in interstate commerce come under the regulations of the Federal Trade Commission. Insofar as "a complete and balanced diet" is concerned, the FTC requires manufacturers to prove the claims on their labels. This is of vital importance. If the food is not as complete as claimed, your dog's health may be impaired. Foods made and sold solely within the state of origin fall under that state's laws, and these may not be stringent enough to guarantee the product's worth. As a prospective buyer, there are several ways you can check.

Read the label. If the food is made locally, do not buy it until you have learned what your own state laws require of a manufacturer. Most law offices and county agricultural offices will be able to supply such information.

If the label says anything like two I have seen recently, do not buy the food. One label said: "Our finest product"; and the other said: "Good for the dog."

A grown dog should be fed one well-balanced meal a day. It is wise to discuss your dog's nutritional needs and diet with a veterinarian. *Ralston Purina Company*

Dog foods that are misrepresented to the public can impair a dog's health. For example, a kennel owner became friendly with the sales manager of a local dog food company and as a result switched to that company's food. In less than a month his dogs developed a deficiency disease that actually ruined his breeding stock.

In another case complaints came in that dogs eating a certain manufacturer's food were suffering from diarrhea. The company ordered a recall of the remaining dog food and apologized for the mistake, saying that a foreign ingredient had somehow gotten into the food. However, when the food was returned to the manufacturer, the labels were changed, and the same food was sent back for distribution.

Major dog-food companies study the effectiveness of their products by monitoring the health and growth of dogs that are fed special rations. *Ralston Purina Company*

An officer in another company said to me, "We sell our food at a lower price than the big companies do. The market is highly competitive, so at times we may have to leave out certain ingredients and substitute other substances. A given shipment might not be nutritious except in the sense of keeping the animal alive. But over the long haul our food is okay."

"Over the long haul" the diet of one unfortunate dog might consist of nothing but substandard food. Consequently, here are my words of warning: The dog food market is competitive, but you are dealing with your dog's life. Do not buy a product just because it is cheaper.

There are economical ways to feed your dog. The canned foods look nice and meaty and may be balanced and complete, but they contain from 75 to 80 per cent water. Why buy water when you can take it from the tap?

Dry dog foods, whether biscuit, meal, or the homogenized foods that have been blended, cooked, and then pelleted or puffed (expanded), contain about 10 per cent water. The meal types are usually the most economical to buy because they require the least processing; however, these granular foods have one disadvantage. When the food is shipped, the balanced blending of the ingredients may be disturbed and separated into pockets. Then, at a given meal, the dog might not be getting a balanced ration.

The soft-moist foods contain about 25 per cent water. They keep well after the package has been opened, and they do not need refrigeration. They may be the most expensive, but they have a high level of palatability, and spoiled pets will often eat them when they reject other foods. At a nutrition conference one authority told me, "They have a high biological level. Their one fault may be that they do not have enough roughage [volume] for the ordinary dog."

Should You Prepare Your Own Dog Food?

I do not suggest that you try to prepare your own dog food. Modern commercial dog food is a highly complex mixture based on years of research involving dogs and other animals. The major dog food manufacturers maintain large kennels in which they study the performance of their own products and that of their competitors by using dogs as test subjects. At least five of these companies maintain kennels of 400 or more dogs, with breeds ranging from Chihuahas to St. Bernards. One company has maintained in good health — and, more important in good reproductive health — seven generations of Labrador Retrievers. Another has raised five generations of English Setters, with three bitches producing as many as 100 puppies each before being retired.

At least two of these kennels also test their foods on dogs that are under stress to perform, such as hunting dogs. All of them finance studies at veterinary colleges on the needs of lactating bitches, aged dogs, and the requirements of males being used regularly at stud.

Read the label on the next package, sack, or can of dog food that you buy. Could you hope to locate all the nutrients listed? If so, could you mix them in exact proportions? Where could you get the trace elements, such as cobalt carbonate and copper oxide, and the vitamins listed? Could you blend them properly and protect the vitamins from spoilage? Obviously you could not.

Supplements and Snacks

The dog food you buy should be a complete and balanced ration. Therefore, any supplement that you use will unbalance that carefully balanced product. In most homes there are table meat scraps, dishes to lick, and doggie bags brought home from restaurants. Most authorities agree that adding these will not seriously unbalance the ration, provided it is not overdone by adding meat or fat to the ration daily. A hard dog biscuit is a good choice for a snack for your dog. This exercises its jaws and helps to clean its teeth.

In regard to other food in your kitchen that you might be tempted to feed your dog, heed this advice: Do not give your dog eggs unless they have been cooked hard. Many dogs cannot digest milk, so avoid it. As a rule do not feed a dog any vegetables, cookies, or candy that it cannot easily digest. Small amounts of bacon and sausage fat are all right, and most dogs will enjoy a snack of toast or cheese crackers. But the total of all these snacks should not equal more than 10 per cent of the day's total diet.

Vitamins and mineral supplements are a different story. We have been called a "vitamin-crazy people." If what some nutritionists tell us about the junk foods we buy and consume is true, perhaps many of us are well advised to be so. Remember, however, that the major brands of commercial dog foods are balanced by nutritionists who have spent their lives studying the needs of dogs. Moreover, they have overadded certain vitamins when they have felt that these might deteriorate during the product's shelf life.

Oversupplementation of vitamins and minerals in a dog's food can lead to serious consequences, including skeletal defects and abnormalities. As children many of us were given cod-liver oil as protection against rickets, and we gave it to our dogs, too. It is nearly a quarter of a century since a noted English kennel of Irish Setters began to have whole litters of puppies with rickets. The Royal College of Veterinary Surgeons made an investigation. Its researchers concluded that over-

Snacks should not exceed 10 per cent of a dog's daily diet. Dog biscuits are not only a welcome snack but also help to keep the dog's teeth clean. Photo of Samoyed, courtesy of W. Earl Salmon.

dosing with cod-liver oil was causing the problem it was supposed to prevent.

In the late 1960s, a major American dog food company divided a litter of twelve puppies in half. Six were left with their mother, who was on a self-feeding program on the company's standard dog food. (*Self-feeding* means the dog's dish is kept constantly full of food.) These six puppies were weaned by the mother on this food. The other six puppies were given the same food; however, it was heavily supplemented with a vitamin-mineral product. These six puppies developed hip dysplasia; the six puppies left with their mother had perfect hips.

A noted Swedish researcher repeated this experiment at the College of Veterinary Medicine, Cornell University, using Great Danes. Those on the supplement developed hip dysplasia; those given only the dog food did not. That scientist's warning: Don't supplement.

In many cases the fault may rest with the owner, rather than with the supplement. For example, imagine that your dog is sick and that the veterinarian has suggested a vitamin-mineral supplement. The vet has explained that a certain brand is more expensive than another but twice as strong. You buy it. The directions say to give a quarter teaspoonful twice a day to the kind of dog you own. But how many people will give their dog just a quarter teaspoonful? A lot of people will give a half teaspoonful or more. Overdosing your dog should definitely be discouraged.

How Much to Feed Your Dog

Here are two useful rules for feeding an adult dog.

First, feed only the amount your dog will eat at one time, without leaving the dish. If the dog leaves some food in the dish, take the food away, and feed it that much less at the next meal.

Second, give one-half ounce of food per pound of your dog's weight each day. For instance, if a dog weighs thirty pounds, give it fifteen ounces of food. This is about the contents of a single can of dog food. Remember that canned dog food will average 75 per cent water. So if you give a dry ration, you must add water to the food before weighing it.

All major dog food companies print on their labels the weights of several dogs and the corresponding amounts to feed such dogs. These instructions are meant to be a general guide, rather than specific. Dogs differ individually in their caloric requirements. How much food they need will also depend on such factors as the amount of exercise they get, whether they are kept indoors or out, and whether they are recovering from an illness.

We do know that small dogs have far greater energy requirements than large dogs. Moreover, growing puppies require twice as many kilocalories (the amount of heat necessary to raise water from 15 to 16°C.) as an adult dog the same weight would require simply for maintenance.

For example, the National Research Council, National Academy of Sciences, estimates that an adult dog weighing 3.3 pounds will require 122 kilocalories per kilogram of body weight daily for maintenance. A puppy of the same weight would require 244 kilocalories. An adult dog weighing 44.1 pounds would need only 62 kilocalories per kilogram of body weight, whereas a puppy of that weight would need 124. A 110-pound Great Dane would need about 50 kilocalories per kilogram of body weight; a puppy would need twice as many kilocalories per kilogram of its weight.

It used to be possible to work out the maximum number of calories or kilocalories in a pound of dog food by studying the label. The labels of most commercial foods give the maximum per cent of protein, fat, and carbohydrates in the food. (If fully utilized, 1 gram of protein or 1 gram of carbohydrate would yield 4 calories; 1 gram of fat would yield 9 calories.) However, the government has allowed manufacturers to delete

A comical look at feeding your dog. He will learn to adjust to whatever time is convenient for you. *H. Armstrong Roberts*

the carbohydrate listing, which makes it impossible for consumers to calculate calories. Also, the figures on a label can be misleading because the actual digestibility of the food is not taken into account. Chicken feathers and horses' hooves are particularly rich in protein, but they are indigestible. For this reason the label should list them as "crude protein."

At least one major company lists the number of calories in each pound of its dry foods: "Calculated calories, 1518 per pound; 95 per ounce; 292 per cup.'' No more honest or valuable statement can be given.

Foods formulated for puppies are usually higher in protein than standard varieties of dog food. Foods for aged dogs are usually sold through veterinarians. Your vet should examine your dog, make tests, and then decide whether it should be fed such foods.

How to Feed Your Dog

Canned foods can be given to the dog directly out of the can; soft-moist ones, out of the package. There are several ways to feed a dog dry foods.

Most labels on dry dog foods suggest that you serve the contents just as it comes from the sack or mix it with a certain amount of water. With the first method you allow a dog to drink the amount of water it wants; with the second method you add the amount you think the dog needs. The second method permits you to add small amounts of gravy or leftover fats, although at the risk of slightly unbalancing the food.

It might be advisable to add bacon grease or lard to a dog's food when the dog is being strenuously exercised—for example, during the training period prior to hunting or during the hunting season. The fat supplies quick energy when the dog needs it. A reasonable estimate is a tablespoon of lard once a day.

Another method of feeding dry dog food is called the *self-feeding system*. The dog's food pan is kept constantly filled with food. Because a dog tends to eat only when it actually requires, it will maintain a normal weight. Gluttons (greedy dogs) soon learn there is no point in stuffing themselves; after all, food is always available.

The self-feeding method is the best one for reducing a fat dog. Because the food is always available, the dog tends to take a few bites off and on all day; and with food in its stomach, it is never very hungry. Soon the dog loses its excessive appetite, and then it reduces slowly and safely over a long period of time. This will not work, of course, if you add fats and meats to the dog's diet which increase the dog's total calorie intake.

If you feed your dog the expanded or homogenized dry dog foods, use the self-feeding program. This kind of food makes a larger bulk in the dog's stomach than other kinds of foods do and quickly satisfies its appetite. Be sure your dog's water bowl is always kept full.

Feeding a sick dog is the province of a veterinarian. He or she may suggest added meat protein because this is easily digested. The doctor may decide that the dog should be given extra vitamins and minerals (sometimes called stress vitamins). Or perhaps the dog should be fed very small quantities of food four or five times a day. Do whatever your veterinarian suggests.

When to Feed Your Dog

Many studies indicate that a puppy does best on two meals a day (three meals if it is one of the giant breeds) during its growing period and that adult dogs require only one meal. An adult dog will waste as much as 20 per cent of its food intake when fed twice a day; that is, it will eat one-fifth more than it needs. Consequently it may get fat, and you will have to dispose of more and bigger stools.

The best time of day for feeding is the morning, primarily because the dog will then relieve itself before the work of the day begins. This method is generally used by kennels; it allows them to clean the kennel runs before visitors come later in the day.

An exception to this rule should be made for the hunting dog or for any dog that will be heavily exercised just after eating. It is believed that bloat, a dreaded and usually fatal ailment, starts at such times. If you have a hunting dog, it is best to condition it to evening feeding. However, some friends of mine who use night-hunting dogs (Coonhounds and Foxhounds) feed them at noon. A number of breeders and owners of large dogs, which seem particularly susceptible to bloat, especially if not given much exercise, now believe it is safer to feed smaller quantities twice a day rather than to give one large meal.

In a recent case neighbors brought nuisance complaints against a woman who had eight dogs. Their complaint: She fed them early each morning, and their barking for food prevented the neighbors for a block around from sleeping. The dogs were quiet after they were fed. The problem was settled when the dog owner agreed to feed them at 10 A.M. A conclusion you can reach from this episode is that when it comes to feeding, dogs will adjust to whatever time is best for you. (But keep in mind the previous suggestions given in this section.)

chapter seven

Worms, Parasites, and Vaccinations

Dogs may be afflicted with both internal parasites, such as roundworms, tapeworms, and hookworms, and external parasites, such as fleas, ticks, and lice. As a responsible dog owner, you should have a basic understanding of how to keep your dog healthy, including the prevention, symptoms, and treatment of worms and parasites and the basic immunizations that every dog should have.

Internal Parasites

Let's begin with the assumption that most puppies have **roundworms** (ascarids). Mature dogs often become infested with the eggs of an ascarid known as *Toxocara canis*. For some unknown reason the developing larvae do not complete their life cycle in the normal way; instead they become encysted in body tissues. They remain there for an indeterminate length of time and cannot be killed by any known chemical that would not also kill the dog.

If a bitch with such encysted larvae becomes pregnant, the hormonal changes in her body activate the larvae, and they cross the placental wall, infecting the unborn puppies. Heavy infestations can kill the puppies even before they are weaned.

Give your new puppy a few days to settle into the routine and feeding arrangements in your home; then take a stool sample to your veterinarian. The doctor will examine it microscopically not only for

ascarid eggs but also for other parasites. If the puppy is severely infected, adult worms (which are four to five inches long) will be present in
the puppy's stools and will usually be in constant motion.

Any drugstore or pet store can supply you with salts of piperazine, a
safe drug with which you can treat your puppy at home. However, it is
best to get the drug and instructions from your veterinarian. During this
period you must be absolutely fastidious about sanitation. Pick up and
destroy all stools, and use a disinfectant on any toilet area inside the
home.

For disinfecting an outside toilet area, mix 1 pound of lye with 10
quarts of cold water in a pail large enough to hold the mixture. Wear
gloves while doing this, and remember that when lye is mixed with warm
water, it tends to effervesce — so use cold water. Do not allow the
mixture to splash on your face or clothes. Keep the mixture in a watering
can, and sprinkle the area after each stool is picked up. After an hour,
pour fresh water over the area so that it will no longer be toxic.

It is safe to treat your dog for roundworms at home, but for all
other internal parasitic infections, such as hookworms and whipworms,
you should take your dog to a veterinarian. (The doctor may make an
exception in the case of tapeworms.) If you treat your puppy at home,
get the worming drug from the doctor. Generally drugs available without
prescription are not fully effective.

An adult **tapeworm** will shed segments of its body, which will appear in the dog's stools. The worms are flat and rectangular, sometimes
swell and contract, and are pearly white. They may darken slightly after
prolonged exposure to the air. Because fleas play a major part in the life
cycle of the tapeworm, keep fleas off your dog in order to prevent
reinfestation.

Hookworms are dangerous to the life of a puppy. These worms are
so small that they can be overlooked by all except the very careful,
experienced observer. They attach themselves to the wall of the small
intestine and suck blood. Because there are usually swarms of them, they
cause anemia and diarrhea, generally debilitating the puppy to such an
extent that it is an easy mark for other diseases.

Hookworm larvae can penetrate the skin and may enter through the
feet. Treat the puppy's toilet area to kill the hookworms and their eggs,
using the lye mixture outside and a nonstaining disinfectant inside.
Remember to pour water over the outside area one hour after applying
the lye mixture so that the area will be safe for the puppy.

Again, it is important to take the dog's stools to the veterinarian for
a microscopic check. Under no circumstances should you treat the puppy
yourself. The most effective drugs are also the most dangerous when
used by inexperienced people.

Fleas are very annoying to a dog and can contribute to allergic reactions or skin irritations.   *H. Armstrong Roberts*

Whipworms live in a dog's cecum, which corresponds to the human appendix. They may be present in the puppy or the adult dog and can cause diarrhea, an upset stomach, and anemia. Because the worms live in a sac between the large and small intestines, drugs may not exterminate them, and a microscopic stool examination will be necessary to determine their presence. Medication or an injection by a veterinarian are effective in destroying the worms.

The **heartworm,** which was once limited to the southern United States, the Caribbean, South America, and Japan, has spread as far north as Canada. However, the infection occurs most frequently where there are heavy mosquito populations. A mosquito bite transfers this parasite which can be fatal, to your dog. The embryos (microfilariae) of the heartworm swarm through the dog's bloodstream, where they may live and be active for nearly a year. Very careful veterinary treatment is required. Semiannual blood checks should be given to your dog whenever your doctor suggests. (Although human beings get bitten by mosquitos, we don't develop heartworm infections because our bodies are an unnatural and unsuitable host for this parasite.)

Coccidiosis is a disease caused by a protozoan parasite. This parasite is not commonly found in well-run kennels; it appears most frequently in pet shop puppies that have been bought from "puppy mills," usually farm kennels where sanitation is lacking and where farm animals in the area can transmit disease.

The affected animal becomes weak and has chronic or acute diarrhea and blood in its stools. Unless it is given appropriate treatment, the puppy will be susceptible to other ailments because of its weakened condition.

Microscopic stool checks made at a veterinary hospital are the only means of detecting the infestation, and only a veterinarian can treat the problem. Careful sanitation in the home and around the puppy's toilet area is essential.

There are many other worms that can affect dogs, but they are rare. If your dog is given an annual checkup by the veterinarian, their presence will be detected.

External Parasites

Fleas, are slender-bodied creatures designed to run between the hairs of a dog and have astonishing jumping powers. They go through several larval stages and may be inactive for weeks at a time before latching onto their prey. Fleas are unusually sensitive to vibrations and at the first sign of an approaching dog or person they prepare to hop onto their victim. They often climb walls or chair legs where they wait to jump onto a passing dog or person. (However they seldom climb higher than two feet.) If fleas discover a sick dog, they will migrate from other animals to join the feast. A weak, ill puppy may be covered with hundreds of fleas.

Persistent scratching is not necessarily a sign of fleas. The dog may have a skin irritation caused by allergies. If you suspect fleas, part your dog's hair so that you can see its skin. Carefully examine the dog all over. If it has fleas, you'll see them scurrying off into the hair with remarkable speed. Sometimes larger orange-colored fleas are seen. Their bites may contribute to allergic reactions or skin irritations in a dog.

The simplest way to control fleas on your puppy is to dust it every three or four days with a flea powder. Because fleas migrate to the head, one way to get rid of most of them is to dust between the dog's shoulder blades, along the top of its neck, and between its ears. Flea sprays, soap, dips, and collars are available. In my experience collars are the most expensive and the least effective. Some veterinarians consider them dangerous, and even manufacturers warn against using them on certain breeds of dogs. Flea collars and flea tags are actually insecticide generators, and the insecticide can be inhaled by a dog. Warnings are usually given not to use them on Whippets and Greyhounds. Some veterinarians will refuse to perform surgery on some dogs until a week or so after the collar or tag has been removed because they believe the collar or tag can cause a serious allergic reaction.

If you suspect the presence of fleas in your home, take special care to vacuum along the edges of rugs and baseboards. Fleas mate on a dog, but they lay their eggs elsewhere, so it is wise to take special precautions in cleaning. Also, spray chair legs and walls up to a height of two feet.

If you prefer, get a fogger from a pet store. After covering all food and putting away all dishes, start the fogger, and leave the house for three or four hours. However, because this is the least-safe method to use, it should only be used as a last resort.

Ticks spread everywhere; I've even heard complaints from people with dogs living near the top of high-rise apartments in major cities as far north as Ottawa, Ontario.

The female tick is about ten times the size of the male. He attaches himself beneath her, and she hops on a dog. After a blood meal the ticks mate and leave the animal. The female lays her eggs, after which both male and female die. The eggs then go through a series of trans-formations. Later, both seed ticks (the larvae, which are miniscule) and adult ticks climb upward, seeking branches, tall grass, or weeds along paths that dogs travel. They may remain there up to six months, in winter as well as summer. Ticks are extraordinarily heat-sensitive; when a dog comes along, its body heat alerts the ticks, and they jump onto it.

In a house, seed ticks and mature ticks crawl up a wall or sometimes on chair legs. As a rule the female lays her eggs along the edges of rugs, enabling the seed ticks as well as adult ticks to crawl up the walls from there. They do this by instinct. Then they can drop onto a dog.

At the time of this writing our Curly-Coated Retriever has a severe tick problem. After swimming in a nearby pond, the dog usually dries himself by rubbing against the surrounding bushes or comes back to our yard and rubs against the fence and the climbing vines of morning glories. I could spray the entire area with an insecticide, but hum-mingbirds frequent the morning glories, and other birds and bees gather in the bushes and flowers around the pond. To use an insecticide would mean killing some of these birds and bees, and so I was reluctant to use it unless all else failed.

We examine the dog daily, particularly after swimming; however, seed ticks are hard to find in his curly coat. Some seed ticks, as well as some adult ticks, naturally elude our scrutiny. We spray and use powder, but the dog's swimming, which gives him so much pleasure, cannot be denied, and the swimming negates the powder and spray. Tick collars do not seem to work, and can cause severe skin irritations in some dogs. We now use a special spray for ticks.

Our dog is confined to two rooms in the house, and we watch for ticks crawling up the walls. (By the way, the ticks do not go behind pictures, presumably because they sense that they cannot jump onto a passing dog from such a hiding place.) We spray along the edges of rugs, and those we find crawling up the walls we trap in a shot glass and kill.

Dog experts have warned for years not to try to pull ticks off a dog. Their heads and mouths are buried in the dog's skin, and the mouths of the ticks refuse to let go. Consequently the heads of the ticks, but not the mouths, are pulled off, and small infections arise. Sprays and powders do not work while the tick is feeding, but they do kill the attached males.

Sometimes ticks get on the eyelids, very close to the eye, or along the rectum of a dog. If they do, you must try to pull them off with tweezers. Take hold as close to the head of the tick as you can, and pull gently but steadily until the weakened tick lets go.

The folklore methods of removing ticks, such as touching the tick with a burning cigarette or heating a needle with a lighted match and piercing the tick, are dangerous and do not really work.

If you are careful, you can try a couple of other methods. Touch the tick with a drop of nail polish or 90 per cent rubbing alcohol. These substances are helpful in making the tick release its hold. Be careful not to touch the dog's skin, which will already be irritated by the tick's bite and a substance in the tick's saliva.

The **spinose ear tick** can come to live deep in a dog's ear in its earwax. If your dog holds its head at a strange angle, rubs its ear on the floor, or tries to put its foot in its ear, it may have an ear tick. Sometimes the dog will flop its ears very hard and, in doing so, discharge foul-smelling matter. Because the inner ear is very tender, a veterinarian should be called immediately to treat this condition. Otherwise a serious irritation may result that could cause severe trouble of some other kind. In my experience, ear ticks are more likely to be found on country dogs, and they also pose a problem to cattle and horses.

Lice are small, wingless, parasitic insects that suck blood and inhabit the hair of a host animal. They will lay their eggs in a dog's hair, to which they adhere. Many people fail to notice the eggs and think that the dog has only picked up some dirt. Moreover, the eggs are difficult to remove. Acids such as lemon juice will loosen them, and soap and water will finish the job.

I remember seeing a litter of English Springer Spaniel puppies, only two weeks old, each of which had hundreds of lice. We took the entire litter and their mother to a veterinarian, where they were given a special anti-lice bath. Their home quarters were thoroughly treated, and all the dogs returned to good health.

Dogs can become infested with a variety of **mites,** including chiggers (*Trombicula*) and ear mites (*Otodectes cynosis*), which are the most serious. These mites live in the ear canal and cause headshaking, which could also be a symptom of other ear problems. Mites can also cause dark brown or black wax to form in the ear. If your dog tries to put its foot in its ear, it is time to visit a veterinarian because only a doctor should treat such cases.

The most common and worst mite parasites are those that cause mange. Sarcoptic mange (*Sarcoptic scabiei*) is produced by mites' burrowing beneath the dog's skin, which causes intense itching.

A dog with mange should be taken to a veterinarian, who will make skin scrapings to identify the trouble and then prescribe treatment, which may include a cortisone preparation to ease the itching.

Demodectic mange is caused by the mite *Demodex canis* (as distinguished from *Demodex folliculorum,* which infects people). *Demodex canis* is transferred to puppies by their mothers when they begin to nurse. In demodectic mange, there is loss of hair and there are red bumps on the skin — a condition commonly referred to as red mange. Not all puppies in the litter may be infested, and the mother may show no signs of it. Some dogs have an immunity factor that prevents mange from developing. Healing of demodectic mange may be spontaneous, and treatment sometimes fails — both for as yet unknown reasons.

Puppies usually get a form of mange in which hair loss occurs on the foreface and forelegs and sometimes around the eyes. These areas are obvious exposure sites for nursing puppies. In older dogs, mange may spread over the entire body; and when treatment fails, death ultimately results. In such cases, poor health will be a contributing factor.

Another common infection is **ringworm,** which is caused by. a fungus. It affects puppies more often than it does mature dogs, and any rapidly expanding circular area should be suspect. Children can spread this infection to puppies, and sometimes the reverse occurs, although it is less common. Medical and veterinary attention are needed for both children and dogs.

Vaccinations

Distemper, hepatitis, leptospirosis, and canine parvovirus are three potentially fatal diseases for which dogs should receive immunization. Multiple immunization shots for these diseases are available and should be renewed annually. Keep a careful record of the dates on which your dog is immunized, as well as other relevant information, so that you will have your dog's complete health record.

On the basis of your dog's history the vet may suggest a method other than the multiple immunization shot—for example, a temporary type of vaccine that is used until a puppy has reached a certain age. Sometimes the hepatitis and leptospirosis vaccines may be eliminated when a puppy reaches maturity, but bear in mind that your veterinarian will know which diseases are prevalent in your area. He or she will be in the best position to tell you what type of shots your dog should receive.

Distemper is a highly contagious disease of dogs caused by a virus that appears to be almost identical with the human measles virus. Six to nine days after exposure, a dog will experience a sudden high rise in its temperature. This may last about three days, during which time the dog will appear otherwise normal. A second phase of the illness begins when the dog's temperature drops to normal and then quickly rises again. This phase lasts about a week, during which time the dog loses its appetite and appears dull and sick.

Meanwhile the leucocyte count in its blood will drop below normal and will fluctuate along with its temperature. In addition to lack of appetite, the dog develops an ugly discharge from its eyes and nose. There will be diarrhea, and often mucus and blood will be in the watery stools. Pneumonia and nervous disorders, such as chorea, may then develop.

Dogs may be exposed to both distemper and hepatitis at the same time. The mortality rate is then much higher than for the individual diseases. However, if the dog survives, it will be immune to both.

Dogs should be immunized against distemper once a year. Most dogs today are restricted, and because they are not continually exposed to the virus, the immunity level in their blood is low.

Hepatitis is also a viral disease. It kills about 10 per cent of the dogs that are infected with it. Six to nine days after exposure, a dog's temperature rises to above 104 degrees. Temperature fluctuations are great, often rising and falling on a day-to-day basis. Infected dogs are apathetic, may refuse food, and show an intense thirst. There may be a discharge from the nose and eyes and intestinal soreness. A dog that is injured while suffering from the disease may bleed to death.

Leptospirosis is caused by a spiral-shaped bacterium that is able to live in water. There are several large families of these spirochetes, and in one is the causative agent of human syphilis.

Leptospira canicola is a common type of this infection in dogs, and it is spread by infected urine. Dogs who sniff rat urine or urine from other infected dogs inhale bacteria that invade their bodies.

The disease begins to appear after an incubation period of five to fifteen days. The dog appears weak, vomits, refuses to eat, and runs a temperature of 103 to 105 degrees. Since these are the symptoms of many other illnesses, it may be impossible to make a correct diagnosis until the disease is further advanced. Sometimes this is not possible until after the dog has died.

Aside from being vaccinated, dogs should be kept on leash and away from possible urine deposits, particularly near water puddles. They should also be given enough drinking water at home so that they will not be tempted to lap from puddles.

A strange new, and potentially fatal, intestinal disease called **canine parvovirus** has recently swept America and Europe. Puppies are particularly susceptible to a fatal form. A vaccine has just been developed. Consult your veterinarian.

Some states require a **rabies** vaccination. If your state does not, do not have your dog treated. You should base your judgment on the presence of rabies in your community and on the care you give your dog. Rabies is very rare in dogs today. If there is no known rabies in your area, or if you keep your pet under close watch, then it should not have to get the shots.

Some virologists are warning today that a virus from a live virus vaccine may live in the body for many years, then undergo a mutation and become active as some other disease. With distemper, hepatitis, and leptospirosis, it is worth taking the chance and having your pet inoculated. However, if you do take adequate care of your dog, then it is not worth the risk of administering a rabies vaccine, unless you wish to travel with your dog to Canada, abroad, or into states that do require inoculation against rabies.

Visiting the Veterinarian

Here are some guidelines for you to follow when you take your dog for treatment or observation by a veterinarian.

First, select one veterinarian and stick with him or her during the life of your dog. The doctor will keep a complete medical record for your dog, which will always be a great help whenever it needs special care. Remember that your dog cannot talk, but its record can give indications about causes of problems.

It is possible that the breeder you got your dog from had a veterinarian give immunization shots to your dog before it was weaned. If not, take your puppy to the doctor for its first shots as soon as it has adjusted to your home.

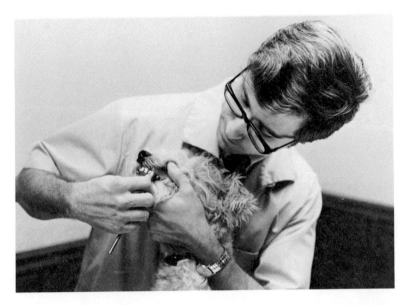

A veterinarian will check your dog's teeth and remove any tartar from them as part of a general examination. *Ralston Purina Company*

If your dog is generally healthy, you will only have to take it to the vet once a year to keep up its immunization. At this time the vet can also give it a general examination, checking the dog's teeth, nails, stool (in case you are concerned about worms), and emptying its anal glands if necessary.

Do not bring your puppy in and dump it on the examination table. The cold table, the strange odors, and the doctor will all combine to frighten it. Hold your dog in your arms, let the doctor talk to it and reassure it while a shot is being given.

If you do this when your dog is young, you may prevent its having a lifetime fear of a table, in addition to a lifetime fear of the doctor and veterinary hospitals. It may be vitally important — in case of serious illness — for your dog to know and like the doctor and to have confidence in the care and treatment it will get at the hospital.

chapter eight
Accidents and Emergency Treatment

A veterinarian wants to assure your dog the best medical care possible. Emergency treatment, in particular, should be left to the doctor's professional judgment. But sometimes a veterinarian cannot be reached immediately or not until the next day. Therefore the owner should know some basic first aid to treat a dog without further injuring it in case of burns, poisoning, severe cuts, or other accidents. Your dog's life could be at stake.

However, keep in mind that your emergency treatment could actually kill a dog. Let me give an example. An Irish Setter that disappeared from a yard out in the country was found in a quicksand bog. Boards were laid across the bog, and the dog was finally pulled out, caked with mud. The only veterinarian in town was away, so the owners began washing the mud off the dog with a garden hose. Because the dog was too weak to stand, a stimulant, a very strong mixture of instant coffee made with warm water, was poured down the dog's throat. A few minutes later the dog struggled to its feet, stood for a minute or two, and then died.

The stimulant caffeine probably caused the dog's body to release energy that it could not spare; thus the coffee probably contributed to the dog's death. Also, the dog should not have been washed, just kept warm. As a quick-energy food, it might have been given sugar water or even whiskey and water.

Shock

Common forms of shock are caused by heat stroke, burns, or being struck by an automobile.

Heat stroke often occurs when people leave dogs in parked cars for a long time. Usually a car is left in the shade, but the sun moves and then shines in. All the car's windows should be left open as far as possible without permitting the dog to escape. The dog should also be checked up on occasionally.

In case of heat stroke or burns, ice packs should be applied and the dog should be taken immediately to a veterinary hospital. *H. Armstrong Roberts*

In heat stroke a dog's temperature is elevated to the danger point. Therefore its body must be cooled as quickly as possible. Ice packs should be placed on the dog, or the dog should be immersed in cool water. Cool water enemas will also help. Keep the dog as quiet as possible; then rush it to a veterinary hospital, where supportive treatment, such as injections or oxygen, may have to be given.

Burns should be treated with cool water. Or an ice pack can be placed on the area; these should not be left on longer than fifteen to twenty minutes. For very deep burns ice cubes could be used instead of an ice pack, which might irritate. Supportive treatment by the veterinarian will depend on the depth and size of the burned area and will undoubtedly include a pain-killer such as Demerol.

Physical trauma may occur if a dog is hit by a car. Because this involves serious injury, the dog must be treated as soon as possible by a veterinarian. Your job will be to get the dog out of the street without injuring it further. The dog may be in great agony and may try to bite you when you lift it. Therefore your first step should be to bandage its mouth shut. A necktie can be used. Then slip a coat, large towel, or blanket under the dog so that it can be lifted to a safe place.

Poisoning

In any case of poisoning it is absolutely essential that you phone the doctor to report the type of poisoning you suspect, and then rush the dog to the hospital.

There are nearly two hundred thousand potentially toxic substances on the market, and dozens of them can be found in the average household. These range from cleaning fluids and insecticides to aspirin, shampoo, and even certain ornamental plants and shrubs. Other toxic preparations found in or around the home include furniture polishes and waxes, paint solvents and removers, metal cleansers and polishes, shoe polishes, cosmetic preparations, dish or laundry detergents, hair preparations, nail polish and remover, and rat poisons (such as red squill, Antu, thallium, phosphorus, and warfarin).

Practically any household or garden product that carries the warning "Keep out of the reach of children" should also be kept out of the reach of a dog. Prevention is better than emergency treatment and antidotes.

"Strike anywhere" matches are dangerous because they contain phosphorus, as does the striking strip on paper book matches. However, paper matches themselves are not toxic and are sometimes used as suppositories (see Chapter 5).

In their *Handbook of Veterinary Procedures and Emergency Treatment,* Kirk and Bistner list fifty-eight potentially dangerous ornamental plants. These include narcissus, mistletoe, hyacinth, daffodil, iris, and poinsettia. The sap of the poinsettia is only mildly irritating but might be dangerous if a dog happened to be suffering from some serious stomach problem. Lily of the valley can be fatal if eaten by a dog, particularly a dog suffering from a heart ailment.

I do not advocate banning all such plants and flowers from the house. What you should do is place them with care. Mistletoe might best be kept out of your home, however, because the poisonous berries may fall to the floor where a dog could eat them.

One hears quite regularly of children who have been poisoned by overdoses of aspirin. Usually such aspirin has been sugarcoated for use by children, who consequently think of the tablets as candy. If a dog eats these tablets, about the only emergency treatment you can give is an *emetic* (a substance that will cause vomiting) to empty its stomach. Fresh hydrogen peroxide can be given, about a tenth of an ounce poured down the dog's throat. However, a teaspoonful of salt placed in the dog's mouth would be more practical. Any other treatment must be given by the veterinarian.

Insecticides are always dangerous, although malathion and methoxychlor are relatively less so than others. When dieldrin first came on the market, the label said "Not harmful to children or animals if used as directed." Do not be fooled by such labels. Too many times the directions are incomplete or will not be followed exactly. Even momentary carelessness can result in tragedy. For example, a farm worker who washed out a pail that had contained dieldrin dumped the water on the ground. Subsequently the family's Great Dane licked the spot and died of poisoning.

There are few (if any) true antidotes for insecticides, but there are measures that the veterinarian can take. Tell the doctor what substance the dog has ingested. He or she will prepare emergency treatment and tell you what you can do on the way to the hospital.

Lead poisoning usually occurs slowly over a long period of time. You should be concerned if you find your dog licking up dried paint chips, chewing on painted sticks and swallowing the slivers, or swallowing putty. Veterinary treatment should be solicited because lead poisoning will probably result. Of course you should take preventive measures to try to assure that the dog does not get at such substances.

In most cases in which a poison has been swallowed, an emetic should be given to induce vomiting. A common method is to put a teaspoonful of salt into the dog's throat. Or you can make a heavy salt solution with water (add 2 tablespoons salt to 1 cup water), make a pouch of the dog's lips, and pour in the solution so that the dog has to swallow it. But you should remember that for some poisons, emetics must *not* be given. Your veterinarian will advise you.

If you do induce vomiting, save the vomit; it may help the veterinarian make a diagnosis. While you are on the way to the hospital, the doctor will be preparing the antidotes and whatever supportive treatment is necessary.

Here is a list of the antidotes or treatment for various toxic substances.

ACIDS (acetic, carbolic, hydrochloric, and so on)
> *Do not induce vomiting.* Neutralize the acid by giving the dog the whites of several eggs. Or give magnesium hydroxide (an ingredient in some antacid preparations for human use). If in powder or tablet form, crush, and mix with water.

CAUSTIC SODA (lye)
> *Do not give an emetic.* Give milk of magnesia, crushed chalk in water, or milk and egg whites.

ARSENIC (rat and weed poisons)
> Give 1 teaspoon of Epsom salts in 2 ounces of water to induce vomiting. Then bicarbonate of soda. Rush the dog to a doctor.

PHOSPHORUS (rat poisons, "strike anywhere" matches)
> Give equal parts of hydrogen peroxide and water (about 1 ounce for each 10 pounds of body weight) as an emetic.

CLEANING AGENTS (alkalies)
> Give 2 tablespoons of vinegar or lemon juice.

SODIUM BISULFATE (toilet bowl cleaners)
> Give milk of magnesia, chalk in water, or milk and egg whites.

PAINT AND VARNISH REMOVERS
> Use salt to induce vomiting. Make a heavy saltwater solution and use to cause repeated vomiting.

CLEANING FLUIDS, GASOLINE, KEROSENE, CARBON TETRA-CHLORIDE
> Treatment must be by a doctor as quickly as possible.

DEODORANTS
> Induce vomiting.

BLEACHES
> Induce vomiting. Follow with olive or other bland oil or egg whites.

FURNITURE POLISH
> Home treatments of little help. Rush dog to doctor.

WARFARIN (rat poison)
   Consult label. Rush dog to doctor.

HOUSEHOLD PLANTS
   Tell the doctor the suspected source of the poison. Give emetic, and rush the dog to the hospital.

GARDEN SPRAYS (lindane, chlordane)
   Give emetic.

STRYCHNINE (animal poison)
   Give sedative. Consult vet, giving the weight of the dog.

FOOD POISONING
   Give hydrogen peroxide, then enema.

Cuts

Most cuts are not severe. If the dog can reach a cut with its tongue, allow it to do so. It will clean the wound, and enzymes in its saliva will kill bacteria and promote healing. If the dog cannot reach the wound, clean it yourself with fresh hydrogen peroxide. You will have to do this with long-haired dogs or where the wound is on the neck or shoulder.

Deep puncture wounds should be treated by a veterinarian, who will check for foreign matter in the wound and may recommend antitetanus treatment. However, if there will be a delay in reaching the veterinary hospital, apply hydrogen peroxide to the wound.

Cuts on the legs may cause severe bleeding. If you feel about on the inside of the dog's leg, you may find a pressure point (i.e., one that when pressed will slow or stop the bleeding), or you may have to apply a bandage above the wound with sufficient pressure to stop the bleeding. This tourniquet must be loosened and then reapplied every ten minutes. Similarly, ease up on the pressure point every ten minutes. While you are applying pressure to the wound, someone should be driving you to the veterinary hospital.

If you have watched a football game, you may have observed first aid being given to a player who has sprained an ankle or knee. The injured joint is immediately packed in ice to prevent swelling. You can give your dog the same treatment for any injury that is likely to swell and become congested. Many pharmacies and all surgical supply houses have gel packs that can be kept in your freezer at home. Some of these can be used either hot or cold. However, hot compresses can promote congestion, so do not use them unless instructed to do so by your veterinarian.

Choking

If your dog seems to be choking, it may have something caught in its throat. Open its mouth wide. If you cannot see anything, push your finger into the dog's throat as deeply as possible and rub the surface gently. This may dislodge a small article stuck there. If you cannot determine the cause of the choking, take the dog to a veterinary hospital.

On rare occasions a dog will get a bone lodged across the back of its mouth between its teeth. I once noticed one of my own dogs licking and trying to put a foot into its mouth. Sure enough, there was a bone lodged between the right and left rear molars in its upper jaw. To dislodge the object, remove it with your fingers while you or someone else holds its mouth open. If you are unsuccessful in reaching the object, take the dog to a vet immediately.

Drowning

Dogs can, and sometimes do, drown. A dog may splash with its front legs and let its rear end drop into what for a person would be a tread-water position. However, a dog cannot maintain this position.

I was once present when such a dog was rescued from the water. It was unconscious. I held the dog up by its hind legs; this got the water out of its lungs. I then applied gentle artificial respiration using light, rhythmic pressure on the lungs. Soon the dog began to breathe on its own and it eventually recovered fully.

Your Dog's Medicine Chest

This should include a small vial (the standard size holds 2 teaspoons of liquid) for administering liquid medicines to your dog. Your veterinarian may give you one when prescribing liquid medicine for the dog.

To administer liquid medicine, pull out the dog's cheek to form a pouch, and pour in the liquid. The dog will have to swallow as the liquid runs into the back of its throat.

To administer pills, place your hand over the dog's muzzle, and press against the lips until the dog opens its mouth. With your other hand and fingers, push the pills deep into the dog's throat; then hold its mouth shut until it swallows. Stroking the dog's throat may help.

Your dog's medicine chest should contain a rectal thermometer, which is heavier than the normal mouth thermometer. The normal temperature for a dog averages 101.2 degrees, although this may vary from 101 to 102.

A veterinarian will keep a complete medical record of your dog, which will be a great help whenever the dog needs special care. *Gaines Dog Research Center*

In addition you should have 91 per cent isopropyl alcohol for sterilizing instruments and the thermometer. Hydrogen peroxide, an emetic, should be kept in your medicine cabinet; it can also be used to cleanse deep wounds or wounds with dirt in them. Keep a fresh, unopened bottle on hand at all times, and have your veterinarian recommend an antiseptic solution that will be as nonirritating as possible. Other common emetics to keep handy are salt and Epsom salts, bicarbonate of soda, vinegar, and lemon juice.

Other items that may come in handy are bandages (one-half-inch, one-inch, and two-inch widths), compress pads, adhesive tape of various widths, blunt-ended scissors, and a medicine dropper.

chapter nine
Breeding

Over the years I have frequently been approached by people asking my opinion on the subject of breeding one's own dog. I always give the same answer: It is an extremely poor idea; it is much more practical to find a reputable professional dog breeder. A professional dog breeder will be knowledgeable about the genetics of mating certain dogs to each other and about the lineage of the stud dogs he or she recommends. Keep in mind that a person with one or two bitches who breeds them with care may have greater success than a person with a hundred-dog kennel. Important requirements are a knowledge of the breed involved and the objectivity to see the dogs' major faults and good points.

People usually want to breed their own dog for one of two reasons: to produce another dog with characteristics similar to their present dog or to permit their children to view the actual birth of puppies. I do not consider either of these reasons valid. It is very rare that your dog will produce a mirror image of itself or its father. Your dog is unique, and so is a new puppy. It is unfair to try to turn that puppy into a carbon copy of its parent.

Another problem is that dogs with temperamental problems, such as extreme shyness or aggressiveness, inevitably pass these particular traits on to their offspring. For example, there are dogs who are apt to bite when suddenly frightened. There is every possibility that one or more of their puppies will be born with the same tendency to bite, often to a greater degree.

Teaching your children about birth is one of the poorest excuses for breeding your dog. We all know parents who feel there is a great lesson to learn from witnessing the birth of puppies and later from observing

Breeding puppies requires an understanding of the health and temperament of the female dog and the lineage of the stud dog.   *H. Armstrong Roberts*

the mother care for them, but very few people stop to think about the size of the litter and what will eventually happen to the puppies.

It is true that there is seldom a problem in finding homes for cuddly, cute puppies. As long as the novelty is there, no problem exists. However, five or six weeks later, parents who no longer want to cope with their youngster's puppy may take the dog to an animal shelter. In a survey on homeless animals the Humane Society found that approximately seven and a half million unwanted animals are put to death annually. I have been involved in humane work for forty years, and I can truthfully say that out of a litter of ten casually bred puppies, only one will find a good home; the others must bear the risk of being put to death.

There is no reason why your children cannot be present at the birth of puppies without your having to breed your own dog. There are many recognized breeders who will allow children to watch dogs being mated. Later they will advise you when the bitch is going into labor, and children can be present for the whelping. They can also see the puppies being cleaned after birth and watch the pups' instinctive motions toward their mother's nipples for food.

When to Breed a Dog

Bitches come into heat twice a year. Most breeders feel that a bitch should not be mated until her third or fourth heat period. However, nature designed a bitch to conceive at the time of her first period. Studies have shown that the earlier the breeding, the less the chance of whelping problems and the greater the supply of milk. Nevertheless, careful breeders prefer to wait before breeding a bitch in order to determine whether she will qualify as a show or field trial dog. They may not want the dog to become a mother until her show or field career is finished.

I do not suggest breeding a bitch that is four years of age or over because there could be serious whelping problems, particularly if the bitch is one of the large-headed breeds, such as the Boston Terrier or Bulldog. Many dogs belonging to these breeds have problems whelping at any age, and a Cesarean section is necessary in approximately 75 per cent of the births.

Once you have established that your bitch is in heat, it is possible to determine when the puppies will be born and when they will be ready for sale. The full heat period lasts about twenty-one days, but the bitch can conceive during only a portion of that time, which is when she has ovulated, that is, when the eggs are ready for the male sperm. The bitch is usually ready for mating between the seventh and twelfth days after she goes into heat, but some bitches will ovulate later, even to the eighteenth or twentieth day! Only experience can tell you what your bitch's cycle will be, though sometimes a veterinarian can analyze the stage she's in from a smear taken through the vagina.

The puppies will be born sometime between the sixtieth and sixty-third day after mating. Generally breeders figure on the sixty-third day. Another six weeks should be added, which is the usual time between birth and weaning. You will then have established the date when the puppies will be ready for sale. Later in this chapter I will discuss the optimum times for you to sell or place the pups from a litter.

The first sign that a bitch is coming into season is called *spotting*. You will notice tiny spots of blood on the floor and an enlargement of the sex organs in preparation for penetration by the male. Begin to count the days after the first sign of spotting. When the spots become lighter, almost straw-colored, this indicates that the mating time is drawing near.

Another sign that a bitch is coming into heat is that she may become restless and seem to have a wanderlust. Instinctively the bitch is looking for a mate; this instinct may be so strong that a bitch may seek every opportunity to run away. If she does find a means of escape, she will not return until she has actually mated.

Male dogs are strongly attracted to the sex odors of a female in heat and will come to your house from the surrounding area. They may urinate at your front door or nearby; this is part of a male's courtship. You may suddenly find groups of dogs in your backyard, many of them fighting among themselves. You will undoubtedly become exasperated, and so will your neighbors.

It is best to keep your bitch in the house while she is in heat and before she is mated. There are special menstrual napkins for dogs, which they can wear in the house or yard. This precaution can help to save your rugs and furniture from stains. When your dog goes outside, make sure she is on a leash. If there is a problem of male dogs being in the area, you may have to take her in the car to a place where she can relieve herself without being subjected to the attentions of other dogs.

Dogs should be checked for internal parasites before being bred. If for some reason this is not done, the test should be made within the first week after mating. It is also wise to have your dog tested for heartworm infestation before mating.

Breeding Terms

A stud fee is paid by the owner of the bitch to the owner of the male. The cost will vary according to the quality and fame of the male dog and the rarity of the breed.

In a case where the stud fee is extremely high, you might request a free return breeding in the event that the mating is not successful. This should be a written agreement signed by you and the owner of the male dog.

A breeder may ask for pick of the litter or even two puppies, as well as a stud fee. This can cause a great deal of bitterness or unhappiness if the bitch produces only one or two puppies. The owner of the stud dog might decide to take both pups, leaving you with none. Under other circumstances you might be left with a malformed puppy. Regardless of how you handle the arrangements, be certain that any agreement is in writing.

If you plan to register your puppies, make certain the owner of the stud dog signs the litter registration form on the correct line. The day the litter is born, you can fill in the necessary information and send the registration application to the American Kennel Club, *Field Dog Stud Book,* United Kennel Club, or other appropriate organization. The papers for the individual dogs should be ready by the time the puppies are six weeks old and ready to be sold. In case of error you will have had time to make the necessary corrections.

Mating

The sex drive is instinctual, but mating is not. Wild dogs, for instance, learn to mate in the pack. Because your bitch will not have had this kind of experience with other dogs, she might fight off the attempts of a male to mount her. Therefore, the sensible approach is to introduce the bitch and her prospective mate to each other well in advance of the mating time so that they can become accustomed to each other. In that way there will be a much greater chance that the mating will be successful. Allow them to play together, and when she does come into season, allow her to visit the male while both are kept on leash.

In regard to a place for mating, I would not recommend your house. Because the male urinates frequently during this period, you would risk having your rugs stained and a strong odor permeate the house.

A garage is often a good place for mating your dog. You must be careful about closing the doors tightly so that neither of the dogs can wander away. It could be disastrous if the bitch escaped and was mated to the wrong dog.

The dogs will enter into a considerable amount of sex play before mating. They push and nip at each other. This courtship is important in the production of sperm and in the maturing of the eggs.

The bitch will determine the time when she is ready to accept the male. She will turn her rear toward him and move her tail to one side. The male will then insert his penis which suddenly begins to swell. As the bitch's sphincter muscle tightens around the penis a "knot" or "tie" forms, holding the penis in the vagina. The two may turn rump to rump, or an experienced dog owner may turn them. It is not unusual for the dogs to remain in a tie for twenty minutes or more. Although the tie is supposed to ensure adequate fertilization of the eggs, fertile matings do occur when there has been no tie.

After the dogs have separated, many breeders hold the bitch up by the hind legs to give the uterus a chance to close, thus preventing semen from escaping. However, this is obviously not a necessary procedure; dogs manage to mate successfully even when no humans are in attendance.

The acceptance period is usually three days, so you must watch your bitch carefully at this time and not allow her to run off and find another mate. There are owners who arrange a second mating a day or so after the first in order to ensure fertilization. However, this precaution is rarely necessary.

In regard to breeding, there is a little story I would like to tell that also serves as a warning to avoid an embarrassing situation. A woman from Cleveland came to my home near Ravenna; she wanted to breed her bitch with my dog. Unfortunately the first attempt was unsuccessful, so it was decided that both dogs would return to Cleveland and that a second mating would be arranged two or three days later. The woman was staying at a very fancy hotel in downtown Cleveland. When she arrived back at the hotel with the dogs, the woman stopped at the lobby elevator to chat for a minute. Suddenly there was a great deal of commotion in the background, punctuated by loud gasps. She turned around, and there she found the dogs tied together in the middle of the lobby.

Pregnancy

You will notice changes in your bitch in approximately the fifth week of her pregnancy. Her appetite will increase considerably, necessitating a larger intake of food. Her shape will also change. It is wise to have a veterinarian examine your bitch and give you special instructions for her feeding and care.

This is the time when you should decide where the puppies will be born. The dog's bed or box should be moved to that area or one should be provided.

It is important that the bitch have comfortable, warm surroundings during this waiting period. She will have almost four more weeks to grow accustomed to the place you have chosen for her. Chances are that when she is ready to deliver the puppies, she will automatically go to her bed or box. If you do not provide her with a place well in advance, she might decide to have the puppies on your bed or in some other inappropriate place.

The basement is often an ideal place for whelping, provided it is warm enough. Ordinary boards can be used to close off a section of the basement for your dog. The boards should be approximately one inch thick, six to eight inches wide, and six feet long. It is important that the whelping area is not too small. (If it is, you will risk the chance of your bitch turning over and rolling on the puppies. This is not an infrequent occurrence, and puppies are often harmed or even killed in that manner.) A six-foot-square area should be large enough for the average dog, but extremely large dogs might need a somewhat larger space (eight feet is better).

Newspaper should be placed on the floor, and I would suggest a large blanket later for the puppies. The blanket does present sanitary problems, but it gives the puppies something to hold onto as they try to move toward the nipples. A rubber mat will also provide traction, and is easier to keep clean. Kennels often use straw. Although straw is not quite as effective, it does soak up moisture.

Your bitch should receive plenty of exercise during her pregnancy. This exercise need not be strenuous, but it should include walking up hills or other inclines. It is important for your dog to strengthen the muscles of her legs and abdomen so that they are in good condition when it comes time to deliver the puppies. I recommend that you have your dog on a leash whenever she is exercised.

The gestation period lasts between eight and nine weeks. The last day or two before whelping, the puppies will drop down to the bitch's lower abdomen. This is a sign that the whelping time is approaching. The bitch may become quite excited just before giving birth and may ignore the whelping box. If this happens and she gives birth elsewhere, the first puppy should be put in the whelping area; chances are that the other puppies will be born there.

Whelping

Some dogs resent the presence of a person during whelping; others welcome your company. It is different with each dog. It is wise to be close by or to have a veterinarian in attendance in case there is a problem in the delivery. Labor is not always easy, and if it is protracted, particularly between the arrival of puppies, it is important that a veterinarian be present. There is always the possibility that a puppy can become stuck in the birth canal, which requires immediate attention.

A puppy is connected by an umbilical cord to a placenta. It is both natural and instinctive for the mother to devour these placentas, or af-

The whelping area should be warm and large enough for the pups to move around. Photo of Vizsla puppies, courtesy of Burnt Hills Boarding Kennels.

Puppies will seek the comfort and nourishment of their mother while learning to adjust to the outside world.   *H. Armstrong Roberts*

terbirth. Some breeders do not allow this, but I do not think there should be any interference; there is some evidence that this is beneficial to the mother.

Early Care of Puppies

The mother will give quite a bit of attention to her puppies to keep them clean. You will notice, however, that even the puppies have an instinct to keep their beds clean. As soon as they are able to crawl, even before their eyes are open, they will crawl away from the nesting area to relieve themselves and then return to their mother.

A puppy is usually weaned on dry food by the time it is six weeks old. Photo courtesy of W. Earl Salmon.

The first sense to develop in a puppy is that of smell, which is functional at the time of birth. Hold the puppies in your arms a few days after birth so that they will recognize the smell of a human being. This is enormously helpful in having pups learn to adjust to people.

Consult your veterinarian or a breeder if the puppies are of a breed that requires cropping of the ears or docking of the tail for showing. A puppy's tail is cut by means of a simple operation when it is only two or three days old. This is before its pain reflexes are fully developed and before anesthesia is necessary. A puppy might give one cry as its tail is cut off, but it will turn back to its mother's nipple almost immediately. This is also the time when dewclaws are removed. You should, of course, be well versed in your breed's standard regarding ears, tail, and dewclaws. The ears are done later, when their size and shape are more apparent. If your veterinarian is not an expert in this phase — and not all are when it comes to the fine art, say, of cropping the ears of Dobermans — you should consult experienced breeders to find such an expert who can advise the vet.

The puppies will usually scramble for the nipples supplying the most milk, and the weaker or smaller puppies may well be shortchanged. You must watch those puppies that are not as aggressive as the others, for they are often forced off the nipples before they are full.

The mother will begin to wean her puppies after about four weeks. You can help the process by giving the puppies simulated bitch's milk. It will take a little practice, but if you stick the puppies' noses in the milk, the lapping instinct will take over in time.

Several research kennels and some breeders feed adult dogs a dry food that is kept in hoppers so that the dogs can eat as much as they want whenever they want. Often a kennel also allows its mothers to wean their puppies on this food. The puppies waddle over to the feeders and nibble on the food. By the time they are six weeks old, they are weaned. This has proved to be a very satisfactory method. In fact, when the puppies are sold, the kennel or breeder should give the new owner enough of this food for a few days to help the puppy through the adjustment period. There are also a number of dry puppy foods that can be substituted for whatever food the puppy originally received.

Selling Puppies from the Litter

You must take into consideration the time of year when the puppies will be born. For example, if the litter is born in October or November, the prospective buyer might ask you to hold several puppies for him or her until after Christmas, when things are less hectic and proper attention can be given to the pups. This means that you will have to keep the puppies at your own expense and at a time in their development when they should be adjusting to their permanent homes. Mid-December is another poor time because the demand for Christmas puppies will be over before they are weaned. Then you may have trouble selling the puppies or even giving them away.

One advantage of having puppies born in the winter is the fact that they do not suffer as many problems with worms or fleas. Also, contrary to what people believe, the winter is not a bad time to housebreak a puppy; it will not want to be outdoors very long before it relieves itself.

In my experience the least successful months to sell puppies are January, August, and late November. August is a poor month because many families are on vacation and do not want to cope with a brand-new puppy. The best times of the year for selling puppies are Christmas and Easter, late June when schools close, and September when schools start.

Be absolutely certain that your dog is properly registered. There are many purebreds that do not have the correct registration papers. Read your dog's credentials carefully, and do not mistake a pedigree paper or a registration application for actual registration papers. You must have a registration certificate for your own dog as well as one for your dog's mate. Remember, it is difficult enough to sell puppies that are registered, but it may be impossible to sell those that are not registered.

chapter ten
Traveling and Your Dog

Riding in Cars

The first difficulty to overcome in training your dog to ride in a car is car sickness. Small puppies usually get car sick on their first trip, but they soon get over it. Take along paper towels, sponges, water. To help your puppy adjust to riding in a car, take it for very short rides, then longer ones.

Some dogs do not adjust and continue to get sick. Experiments with people and dogs have shown that a cause of car sickness is the buildup of static electricity as the car moves along. Tests have proven that this can be avoided when a chain is attached to the rear axle of a car and allowed to bump along the pavement, as is done on some fuel trucks. Sometimes exhibitors have explained their dogs' pallidness in the show ring by saying, "I got here late, and the dog was car sick all the way." Many later reported that the use of the dangling chain worked.

My experience has been that travel sickness drugs do not work well with dogs. Hundreds of people have told me the same thing. If one is determined that they should work, it is often necessary to begin using them the day before the trip.

If your car will hold an ordinary wire traveling crate (such as I recommended in Chapter 4 for your dog to sleep in), teach your dog to ride in it. The advantages of such a crate are numerous: The dog cannot climb into the front seat to disturb you while you are driving, and it cannot bolt out of the car when you open the door. In case of accident the crate could save your dog's life; the dog will probably not be seriously hurt unless the crate itself is smashed. A frightened dog that escapes from a car after an accident might get lost or possibly get hit by a passing car. Also, in case of injury to the passengers of the car, a

A dog should never be allowed to have its head outside a window when the car is in motion.   *H. Armstrong Roberts*

crated dog will be taken care of by the police or someone recommended by the police until a family member can pick it up.

If you are not going to use a crate, you should teach your dog to ride on the floor of a car, which is the next-safest way for it to travel. Fashion a seat belt for your dog by having your garage mechanic set a special anchor in the car floor or by attaching a chain to the anchor of your seat belt on the right side. When driving, put a harness over the dog's regular collar. Attach the dog's harness with a short lead to the anchor, or fasten the chain to his harness. He should have enough leeway to sit up and lie down, but not to get under your feet.

Dogs should not be allowed to ride on the back seat of a car. In case of an abrupt stop or collision, the dog could be thrown forward, injuring both itself and you.

Dog supply companies have fence sections designed to keep dogs from climbing into the back or front seats of station wagons. For safety's sake, fasten the dog's leash to the fence.

Never allow your dog to ride with its head out the window. The wind will dry out its eye sockets, and dust particles may be blown into its eyes and/or ears, causing serious irritation and pain.

If your dog is not trained, or if you cannot follow these instructions, then leash the dog and fasten one end of the leash to some sturdy object to prevent the dog from bolting from the car — and possibly into the path of passing cars — as soon as the door opens.

Identification Plate

Attach a plate to the dog's collar, giving your name, address, and phone number, but not the dog's name. If your dog gets lost and is taken in by a larcenous individual, that person will not be able to call the dog by its true name and will have to give it another name. Later, in a court case, for example, you may be required to prove the dog's identity by asking it to respond to its real name. This could win the case and get your dog back.

Many owners of Coonhounds, Foxhounds, and other hunting dogs buy an inexpensive, simple-to-use tattoo set. This causes the dog only momentary pain, and even that pain can be avoided if your veterinarian uses a pain-killer on the area (usually the inside of the ear flap or a bare spot on the inner thigh). Or get in touch with your local kennel club regarding tattoo clinics which are now held all over the country. Your Social Security number is tattooed by an expert on the inside of a hind thigh, and you can have the dog registered with the National Dog Registry, which keeps a central file and has been instrumental in getting many lost or stolen dogs returned to their owners. Experimental laboratories have agreed not to use tattooed dogs, so dognappers are very likely to turn such dogs loose.

Feeding on Trips

The advent of dry and soft-moist dog foods has made feeding during a trip quite simple. The expanded foods can be fed right from the bag, and the soft-moist (hamburger or meat cutlet) types can be served directly from the package (see Chapter 6). Take along the kind of food you normally feed the dog; if you do, the dog is less likely to get diarrhea. If you bring canned dog food, don't forget to take along a can opener. If your dog does not eat all the can's contents, destroy the rest. An additional item to take along is a water pan.

Rest Stops

Taking your dog for a walk on a leash is the best way to give it both exercise and relief while traveling. An alternative is to take along a stake that can be shoved into the ground with a swivel on top that rotates. You can attach a fairly long chain to it and fasten the chain to your dog's collar so he can move about easily.

If your dog is fed once a day, it will normally have a bowel movement immediately after eating. If it does not, insert a suppository into its rectum. This will bring an immediate stool ejection.

No Dogs Allowed

Many motels and hotels have signs saying No Dogs Allowed or No Pets Permitted. To be better prepared for your trip, consult publications or directories such as "Touring with Towser" (Gaines Dog Research Center, White Plains, N.Y. 10625) to find listings of motels and hotels nationwide that welcome guests with pets, as well as the conditions under which they will do so. This way you'll be able to make advance reservations for your entire trip.

Even if there is a No Dogs sign, you might ask the hotel or motel manager whether a dog is permitted if you keep it in a crate. You might also suggest that the dog be charged as an extra guest in your room. In some cases a motel manager will allow you to leave a deposit, refundable after a room inspection shows that no damage has been done.

The barking dog is a prime cause of No Dogs restrictions. However, if you have trained your dog to live in a crate and be quiet, it should cause no noise problem when it is away from home because the crate is the dog's private, secure castle, and it will be content there.

Air Travel

All the major airlines make provisions for shipping dogs. Most will sell or rent approved, lightweight shipping crates for dogs to travel in. These vary with the size of the dog. If you are traveling with your dog, this crate is usually supplied when you check your own luggage. The dog will ride in the forward hold, which is pressurized and heated.

If your trip involves several stops along the way, it will probably be impossible to check on your dog. If there is a change of planes but not airlines, you may be able to do so. Bear in mind that the airline is responsible for the dog, and once you have checked it in, the airline has complete control.

Generally airlines will not transfer dogs to other airlines if the second one is going to a foreign country. Even if they could, you would be well advised to hire a brokerage firm to handle the transfer. However, if the dog is accompanying you, the situation is somewhat different.

Take the case of a Standard Poodle being shipped from Los Angeles to Bermuda, with intermediary stops in Cleveland and Newark. The owner was accompanying her dog. She was unable to see the dog during the stopover at Cleveland, but she was able to retrieve the dog on arrival at

Newark, exercise it, and complete arrangements for its shipment to Bermuda. In this case there was no change of airline, and there was adequate time. If another airline would have taken the dog from Newark to Bermuda, it would have been even more imperative for the owner to be there to co-ordinate flight schedules and see that the dog was transferred to the proper airline.

If you do not plan to accompany your dog on a flight, then you will probably have to make reservations for its handling at least several days in advance. The dog may also need to be at the airline's freight office several hours before the plane's scheduled departure.

Make arrangements to stay with your dog until it is actually loaded onto the plane. This is important because a variety of mishaps might occur. For instance, because of an unexpected delay or cancellation of a flight, a dog may have to stay over in an airport for hours or even days or might have to be transferred to another airline. It is wise for you to be present. In an extreme case a dog can die in transit because of the carelessness of freight handlers. They may leave the crated dog out on the runway for an hour or more in one hundred-degree weather or in below-freezing weather. I have known of dogs that have died under such circumstances.

New York City's Kennedy International Airport has an Animalport. There the owner can arrange for his or her dog to be picked up, exercised, fed, watered, housed, and put on the correct flight to its destination. Find out if the airport your dog will arrive at has similar facilities.

Be sure that your dog has had water and a bowel movement before you crate it. If the trip is to be a long one, you may have to supply or rent a crate that contains a water pan. Because there may be unforeseen travel delays, it is wise to fasten a sack of food, with feeding instructions, to the outside of the crate.

Travel to Another Country

Traveling with your dog to foreign countries is a more complicated procedure. Those countries that permit you to bring dogs in usually require a health certificate signed by a veterinarian and sometimes by a U. S. Public Health Service officer, as well as a rabies vaccination certificate.

Dogs brought into Canada or Mexico need to have had a rabies vaccination. Without proof of this, a veterinarian in those countries will have to vaccinate your dog. The cost may be four to five times higher than what you would pay in the United States.

Dogs cannot be taken to Iceland under any circumstances. England requires a six-month quarantine, as do most of the Caribbean Islands. Puerto Rico follows U.S. procedure and does not require quarantine. Hawaii requires a four-month quarantine. An American dog being shipped to Australia must first be sent to England via boat for a six-month quarantine and may still face months of quarantine in Australia. South Africa requires a six-month quarantine.

Countries that require a quarantine usually have kennels for this purpose at certain ports of entry. Dogs are quarantined at your expense. A country's consulate can give you full information about when health certificates are issued, how long before departure a dog should have a rabies vaccination, the port of entry your dog will be shipped to, and any costs you must assume. Dogs are given regular veterinary inspection and care at quarantine stations, and you are allowed visiting privileges.

Many people think they can arrange an exception to these rules for *their* dog. However, disaster may result. Several years ago, in Moscow, a woman bought two first-class seats on a plane bound for Australia. She smuggled her Chihuahua aboard and kept it hidden until just before arrival in Australia, when she took the dog out of her carry-on bag and placed it on the seat beside her. The plane's crew was upset but could do nothing because she had paid for the second seat. The woman mistakenly assumed that Australia would not return the dog to Moscow. It didn't. Quarantine officials had the dog killed and fined the airline two hundred dollars for lack of vigilance.

The moral of this sad story is that if you are going to travel to a foreign country with your dog, find out the laws months in advance, and obey them to the letter.

Federal Regulations

Over a period of years, the Animal and Plant Health Inspection Service of the U. S. Department of Agriculture has formulated a set of rules for air travel by dogs. These rules are as follows:

1. Age. Dogs must be at least eight weeks old and must have been weaned for at least five days.

2. Cage. Cages or other shipping containers must meet rigid standards regarding size, ventilation, strength, sanitation, and handling. They must be large enough for the animal to stand up, turn around, and lie down in with normal posture and body movements. The cage must be strong enough to withstand shipping, must be free of interior protrusions that could cause injury, and must provide adequate access to the animal. It should be constructed with a solid, leakproof bottom and provided with litter or absorbent material unless a wire or other nonsolid floor separates the animal from the bottom. The cage must also be ventilated adequately on at least two opposite sides so that the air flows through both the upper and lower parts of the walls. There must be projecting rims or nobs on the outside to keep ventilation from being blocked by adjacent cargo. The cage must also be fitted with handles or grips for proper handling and marked Live Animals, with arrows indicating the upright position.

3. Scheduling. A dog must not be brought to the carrier for shipping more than four hours before the time of departure (six hours is permitted if shipping arrangements have been made in advance).

4. Food and Water for Long Trips. If puppies under sixteen weeks of age will be in transit for more than twelve hours, food and water must be provided, along with written feeding instructions. Older animals must have food at least every twenty-four hours and water at least every twelve hours.

5. Health Certificate. The new regulations require health certificates only for shipments by dealers, exhibitors, laboratories, and other agencies or companies licensed under the Animal Welfare Act of 1970. But airlines and state animal health officials may require health certificates under other applicable rules and regulations. It is a good idea to have a licensed veterinarian examine your pet within ten days prior to shipment and give you a certificate stating that the animal is in good health.

Boarding Your Dog

If you and your family go away on a trip and cannot take your dog along, the best solution is a boarding kennel. It is unwise to place your dog with friends. They may not have adequate facilities or may know very little about taking care of a dog — in case of illness, for example. Also, if the dog happens to run away from the strange home and gets lost, you will probably blame your friends and harbor a grudge against them.

People who run professional boarding kennels have experience in caring for dogs. All boarding kennels may not be of equal merit, but in most cases you will be able to inspect three or four and make an intelligent choice of which one is best for your dog.

Many boarding kennels will not accept dogs unless they are accompanied by proof that they have been recently vaccinated against distemper and have also had shots for infectious hepatitis and leptospirosis. The kennel you select may also want a health certificate from your veterinarian.

Kennels always have their own feeding plans, but most will allow you to bring your dog's own food and will feed it according to your system. However, if the kennel suggests that your dog be gradually switched to its plan, you should consider the matter seriously. Perhaps its feeding system is a better one.

For example, perhaps you have been spoiling your dog by giving so many between-meal snacks and so many meat handouts that it will not eat a standard dog food. You should tell the kennel operator this, and he or she will teach your dog to eat what you want it to eat. The dog will have to eat before its run-mate (if it has one) gobbles up the food. If it goes without a couple of meals, be assured it will not go without the third. When your dog comes home, keep it on a rigid schedule of proper dog food and no between-meal snacks.

Many dogs enjoy being in a kennel if they are allowed to share a run with another dog. *Gaines Dog Research Center*

Some kennels will require that you bring along something belonging to your dog, such as its sleeping rug or basket, or some clothing of yours. The theory is that the dog will smell your odor and not get too lonesome. You might also want to bring several of its toys.

You may specify that your dog be kept in a separate run (where it can eat and exercise) or that it be allowed to share a run with another dog. The other dog will help to maintain its interest, and many dogs enjoy the excitement of the kennel for this reason. If you have spoiled your dog outrageously, a few weeks in the kennel may help to correct the bad habits you have allowed it to develop.

Most kennels feed in the morning, and the dogs have bowel movements shortly after. This schedule allows the kennel operator to clean the runs and take care of the dogs before visitors come. Plan to take your dog to the kennel shortly after noon unless you arrange otherwise with the operator. By arriving at the kennel early in the day, your dog will have a chance to adjust before evening.

You should also give the kennel operator permission to take your dog to a veterinarian if it gets sick.

Do not board your dog at a veterinary hospital. Although most hospitals have excellent cage space, they have very small runs (if any), and they may need their cage space for sick animals.

chapter eleven
Care of an Old Dog

Pinned by the plague
Whimpering "good-bye"
His eyes a wounded brother's,
The dog wants to die.
The twisted body, shortened breath
Pray for an end, a refuge
in death.
"I did my best to help you live,
now help me die."

A man of few words, the vet
(concentration itself)
fills the syringe
with the mercy of death.
Galia leans into my shoulder
what a bitter pill!
the only way to be of help
is to be on hand to kill.

We and our dogs are programmed by our genes to grow old and to die. I think that dogs, like people, know when they are growing old, but I doubt that they worry about aging or death. Of course no one can know exactly what a dog thinks, but you can observe and draw conclusions. We can give aging dogs both special, intelligent care and attention, but this requires our being observant and knowing the symptoms of their aging.

"On the Death of a Dog," translated by Anthony Kahn. From *From Desire to Desire* by Yevgeny Yevtushenko, copyright © 1976 by Doubleday & Company, Inc. Used by permission of the publisher.

A Dog's Life-Span

Many people have asked me how to compare a dog's age with that of a human being. I do not think there is any true way to do so. One generally heard theory is that one year of a dog's life equals seven years of a human life.

In *The Health and Happiness of Your Old Dog,* Dr. George Whitney offers another theory, which I think comes as close as one can to approximating the age of a dog. We assume the prime of life for an adult male is between the ages of nineteen and twenty-five. Dr. Whitney considers that the first year of a dog's life equals age twenty-one for a man. After that Dr. Whitney adds four years. For example, the two-year-old dog equals a twenty-five-year-old man; at twelve the dog's age would be equal to that of a sixty-five-year-old man.

Genes program each dog differently, and no one can be absolutely sure what the life-span of an individual dog will be. Certain breeds age faster and die at a younger age than other breeds. For example, dogs of the giant breeds have a shorter life-span than medium-sized dogs; and tiny dogs, such as the Chihuahua, tend to live the longest of all.

With modern feeding, housing, and medical care, medium-sized dogs can live to be eleven to twelve years old, and giant dogs may average eight years, although occasionally one may live to be ten years old. I have been able to authenticate the records of two Chihuahuas that lived to be twenty and twenty-one; however, averages do not mean much to the person who is concerned about his or her own pet. Actually individual dogs often defy the averages. My Belgian Sheepdog lived to be seventeen years old.

Symptoms of Aging

Whether your dog lives to be twelve or twenty, and regardless of its breed, there are certain symptoms of aging that you should be able to recognize. First, a dog will begin to slow down, will be less eager to play, or will lose interest in games much more quickly. It will prefer shorter walks, and when it gets up, it will do so at a more leisurely pace and will stretch for a longer period of time.

Many dogs get gray around the muzzle, but this is not a sure sign of aging. This *muzzle frost* is a characteristic for certain breeds, such as the Belgian Sheepdog. Although my Belgian Sheepdog lived to be seventeen, she had gray around her muzzle at age three.

As a dog grows older, its luxurious coat may thin out a bit and lose its luster, and there may be less shedding. Again, however, each dog is an individual, and even a very old dog may have a luxurious and thick coat.

Another sign of aging may be foul breath. Teeth loosen, gum infections may occur, or food particles might putrify just under the gums. The dog's eyesight is not as sharp as it used to be, and the bright health of youth is gone.

Feeding

Some dogs tend to get fat as they get older. This is usually the owner's fault. Because the dog is less active, it should be fed less and not be allowed to gain weight. Gradual reduction in appetite and food consumption, however, may be the dog's own response to aging. A dog may also drink more water than it normally did and need to urinate more frequently. Incontinence (urinary leaking) may develop.

But feeding the older dog need not be a problem. In the case of my Belgian Sheepdog, I found that a self-feeding program worked. It stopped her diarrhea, and she ate and drank only as much as she needed. A swinging panel door permitted her to go outside to relieve herself as often as necessary.

There are now prescription diets that can be bought through your veterinarian to give to dogs with specific afflictions, and many commercial dog food companies make up special diets for generally healthy older dogs. Consult your veterinarian before changing your dog's normal diet.

Ailments

It is important to remember that if your dog seems to age suddenly, there may be two factors involved. Perhaps you have been slow to observe the symptoms of aging, or perhaps your dog has developed a disease that needs attention. Dogs are subject to the same kinds of aging ailments as their owners are, including heart diseases, diabetes, kidney disease, strokes, cancer, and benign tumors.

Here again, some breeds may develop certain types of heart disease more frequently than other breeds. If a dog contracts heart disease, it may also have trouble with its kidneys because the heart's ability to pump adequate amounts of blood to other parts of the body will be decreased. Heart disease may even affect a dog's temperament by injuring a section of its brain. Other diseases, such as diabetes, appear to be inherited; but in general, severe diseases during younger life may weaken the body of an aging dog so that it more readily succumbs to other ailments.

For example, I frequently hear this sort of complaint: "We have a wonderful dog, and she is healthy in every way. But lately she's begun to dribble urine. She's as upset by this as we are." Upon interrogation, the owner may say that the dog has been spayed (surgical removal of the ovaries) or has had an ovariohysterectomy (removal of the ovaries and the uterus). The surgery may have been performed while the dog was very young, and the loss of the ovaries has robbed the dog of a certain hormone. Consequently as the dog ages, it begins to leak urine. Your veterinarian can compensate for this by prescribing the proper hormone. Given these complications and the important role that the ovaries play in the growth of a puppy into a normal, mature dog, I have always recommended that the spaying operation be performed three or four months after a bitch's first heat.

It has been estimated that spaying an older dog cuts the chances of mammary and uterine cancer by two thirds. It also totally eliminates the possibility of ovarian cancer. If you do not plan to breed a thoroughly mature bitch, you should discuss spaying with your veterinarian.

A sudden severe change in temperament or sudden turning in circles in one direction could indicate a stroke in your dog. Other signs of a stroke are a drooping of the lip on one side, excessive salivation, and a greatly enlarged pupil in one eye. The latter symptom might also be an indication of a tumor. I once noted this in a dog at a dog show and called it to the attention of the owner, who later reported that a tumor was, in fact, involved.

If any of these signs appear, rush your dog to a veterinary hospital, but do not lose hope. Strokes are less severe in dogs than in human beings, and many a dog has recovered. One of my own dogs recovered and lived four years after a stroke that paralyzed one side of her face.

Female dogs often develop tumors in their mammary glands; these tumors appear as small lumps. If such tumors are excised early enough, recovery can be complete. However, uterine tumors are more difficult for the owner to detect, and bleeding from the uterus should be investigated immediately.

Older dogs of either sex may develop fatty lumps under the skin in various places. These are almost always benign and unless one interferes with a dog's activities, may be safely left alone. Small warts may also appear. Again, if there is no functional disturbance, let them be.

Euthanasia

Hundreds of people have consulted me on when and how to put their dogs to sleep. Some of these people have simply been looking for an excuse to have the dog destroyed and have consulted me in the hope that I will approve. In those cases I will not. A pet that has been a member of the family for years should not be destroyed as a matter of convenience.

It may be true that a dog does not understand death, does not anticipate it, and does not fear it. Yet, we cannot project ourselves into the dog's mind. My observations have led me to believe that dogs understand more than we think.

Sometimes a dog will approach the body of a companion, make a quick examination, and then turn away, recognizing that the companion is dead. Apparently the dog accepts the fact without grief and seems to understand that bodily death is irreversible. It is for this reason that I wish my own death to come at home so that my dogs can check the body and know the reason why I am no longer there.

There is another class of dog owners who refuse to let their pets die and who go to unbelievable lengths to keep the dogs alive. Perhaps they make such tremendous sacrifices on their dogs' behalf because they have some impulse to prove themselves martyrs. As far as I am concerned, these people are often practicing cruelty to animals. Although we cannot practice euthanasia in regard to other people, we can be merciful to our pets, and mercy often dictates a painless death for an animal.

I believe that hopelessly ill animals instinctively know their condition. They can probably see the disappointment and frustration in their owners' eyes when they have to turn down food. And many of them appear deeply distressed when they must be carried outside to relieve themselves or when they can no longer keep themselves clean.

Each owner should try to judge whether his or her dog is in serious pain or whether its bodily functions are so severely impaired that it cannot take care of itself. Even if its life could be extended for a little longer, would the dog remain in misery?

I have wanted my dogs to die at home, in the surroundings they have always known, and almost literally in my arms. When I have known that it was time, I have called the veterinarian and asked him to make a house call. With the dog's head in my lap, he has given the overdose of Nembutal or another barbiturate, and the dog has closed its eyes, relaxed. Only a slight shudder of muscles has indicated death.

There are dogs that like the veterinarians who have treated them. Almost certainly they recognize them as men and women who have cured their ills, and in such cases, the dog can be taken to the veterinary hospital. However, I still maintain that the owner should be present to give additional comfort to the dog.

I once wrote a column for The Cleveland *Press* in which I described the death of one of my dogs. Six months later I got a letter from a woman who wrote: "I read that column, and I said I could never do that. I wouldn't have the courage. But when the time came, I did as you had done. And I know I am a better woman for it."

Burial

Most people believe that a dog cannot be buried within the city limits, but a simple check of the statutes at the law department of your village or city may indicate that there is no such law on the books. You might even be able to bury the dog in your own backyard. If you do, bury it at a depth of four to five feet so that no animal can dig it up or dig down to it and so that no sanitary rules will be violated.

Veterinary hospitals can have the body cremated for you. However, if you want to save the ashes, it can be fairly costly.

I am opposed to pet cemeteries. Many are untrustworthy. You must pay for a plot and an annual rental or upkeep fee. But most plots are not kept up, and if you overlook the annual fee, the animal's body will be dug up and thrown out. In addition, pet caskets, pet monuments, pet funerals — with music and all the trappings — are expensive.

I suggest that you leave the disposal of your dog's body to your veterinarian. Or if you cannot bury your pet in your own backyard, do as I do; I bury our dogs in an unmarked, uncultivated area of our farm. You could make arrangements of the same sort with almost any farmer.

Finally, to honor your dog, make a research gift to a veterinary college or to a scholarship for a needy veterinary student.

part three
TRAINING

chapter twelve
Basic Training for Puppies

There are many lessons that you need to teach your puppy before it has a chance to pick up bad habits, habits you may be unable to correct. For instance, if you teach your puppy not to go out of your yard, or to stay by your side when you are outdoors, it will never become a roamer. You must teach it that it should not bite you, even while playing, or even get angry enough to bite. You should also teach your dog to come instantly when called, to walk at your heel, and to sit and lie down on command. These lessons should be taught before your puppy is twelve weeks old; it will learn far easier then than after it is sixteen months or older.

A dog's two collars and leashes (as suggested in Chapter 4) can play a part in training. If you want to take your puppy for a walk, use its leather collar and light leather leash. The puppy will very quickly associate these with going for a walk and will soon realize that it should leave the yard only with you. If you put a chain collar and leash on your dog, it should associate this with going outside to relieve itself.

Come

As a first training step to get your puppy to come when you call, put the small leather collar on your dog. Then get some venetian blind cord or an even lighter cord, attach it to the puppy's collar, and let it drag the cord around. You can start this training in the house, so the cord length can be about twenty feet.

While the puppy's attention is elsewhere, call it. At the same time begin pulling it toward you. The puppy's reaction will be to put on the brakes, but you should continue to draw it closer to you. All the while repeat its name and "Come." When your puppy has reached you, compliment and pet it, rubbing it on both sides of the neck.

Repeat this over and over again, even while the puppy is eating. Eventually it will learn two things: to listen for the sound of your voice and to come when called. It will also learn that obeying your command is a pleasurable experience that will be rewarded by petting and compliments. Never scold the puppy for not coming, even if you have to drag it to you. Just reward it with praise and petting when it does reach you.

If you started this training in your house, you should now repeat it outside. Always start the lesson when the puppy is playing or is otherwise distracted. When you think you have instilled the habit of its coming when you call, take off the line cord, and teach it to come when it is free. If you start when the puppy is young enough, this will not be a problem.

It has been my experience that it is futile to chase a puppy that deliberately runs away from you when you call. However, you can teach it that it cannot escape from you. Set up conditions so that if it does not come when you call, you can catch it and make it obey. That way the puppy gets the idea that it cannot escape, so it might as well obey.

For example, suppose your puppy is in another room in your home, not on the cord. If you call the pup and it does not come, you should rush into the other room, take it by the scruff of the neck, and half carry, half drag it to the place from which you called. Then praise and pet your puppy so that it learns that obeying you is a good thing to do.

Try this training lesson outside in an enclosed area. It won't be long until your puppy will obey your orders instantly.

Sit, Stay

There are many occasions when you will want your puppy to sit or stay where it is. For example, your puppy should never rush to its food dish, getting underfoot and perhaps making you spill the food. You must teach it to sit quietly, never to beg, and not to approach the food dish until told that it may.

When teaching your dog to sit, be very gentle. You are working with a puppy whose bones have not yet fully developed, and you do not want to risk injuring them. Kneel beside your puppy and put it in a sitting position. Then say, "Sit." Of course, the puppy will try to get up immediately, but make it sit again, repeating the command a little more sternly.

When you think the puppy will sit without your holding it in position, slowly remove your hands, keeping the palm of one hand in front of its nose while repeating the command "Stay." Then pet and compliment it. Now start to move away. If the puppy gets up, return it

If your puppy does not come when you call, be firm yet patient, and show it the place from which you called. *H. Armstrong Roberts*

to position, this time speaking more authoritatively, and tell it to "Stay." At this stage never call the puppy to you; always return to it, saying something like "All right," and then reward it with petting and compliments.

Lie Down

It is just as easy to teach a puppy to lie down as to sit down. Simply take the dog's forelegs and pull them forward gently, meanwhile pushing the dog's back down. Do this while using the command "Lie down." If this lesson follows the one for "Sit," you should be able to teach your puppy in a few lessons.

Pose

Every puppy should be taught to pose. You may never show your dog, but you will probably want to take its picture sometime. When someone shows you a picture of his family dog, it is often scrooched down in some awful position, and the owner apologizes, "Well, it's not a very good picture. He's a better-looking dog than the picture shows." If your dog knows how to pose, you will never have such a problem. Also, you will want your dog to stand still when the vet examines it or while it is being groomed.

To teach your dog to pose, set it in position facing to your right, putting its front legs perpendicularly under it and its rear up. Your right hand should support the dog under the chest, between its front legs, in such a way that your fingers keep its legs in position. Your left hand should go under the dog's abdomen to support its rear end. The command "Pose" can be given, followed by reassuring words. This can be repeated half a dozen times within a few minutes, with the puppy being required to hold the pose slightly less than a minute.

The next step is to remove your right hand from the supporting position. Give the command "Pose." If the puppy tries to drop its head or move, slap it very lightly upward under the chin, and place its head back in position. In a surprisingly short time your puppy will learn to keep its head still. It should also permit you to position its legs properly and should not move them once you have done so.

Next, remove your supporting left hand. Chances are that your puppy will immediately try to sit down. Repeat the command "Pose," and gently poke your thumb into its belly. Position each hind leg as you want it.

After these lessons, you may want to teach your puppy to relax while posing so that it is not awkward or stilted in its stance. Its tail should be put into position and stroked gently until the puppy holds it that way. You should also pick up each foot, finger the nails, and squeeze the toes and pads gently. While you are doing this, the puppy should learn to maintain its position.

Staying in the Yard

To teach your dog to stay in your yard, put it on a training cord, and have someone walk by along the sidewalk. The puppy will naturally run to greet the newcomer. However, when it reaches the sidewalk, jerk its cord back lightly and say "No" sternly.

Next, have people call your puppy from the street. Again, when it reaches the edge of the lawn, jerk its cord back. Repeat these lessons on all sides of the yard so that the puppy will recognize the limits of its territory and will not go beyond them.

A puppy is not thoroughly trained in this lesson until you have had friends with other dogs try to lure yours out of the yard. Only then can you be sure. However, there may be one exception. A female in heat may violate the rules you have taught it. Therefore, she should never be left alone in the yard.

Chasing Cars

If you have taught your puppy to stay in your yard, then you should not have to worry about its chasing cars or bicycles. Nonetheless, puppies do like to chase, and yours might chase children riding bicycles along the sidewalk in front of your home or children running across your yard.

One way to discourage this is to toss a small, empty juice can at your dog if it starts to chase down the street. Don't hit the puppy, just come close. You will be astonished with the results.

Although this lesson may seem barbaric or even dangerous to the dog, it need not be. You have to remember that you are giving training designed to save the dog from death under the wheels of a car or truck — or even to save the life of a child on a bicycle. If you throw the cans so that they strike just ahead of it, the pup will be so startled that it will quit the chase instantly. If you hit it in the back, you will scare but not hurt it. Sometimes water-filled balloons will work.

The training-line technique will also work, but it may not be as effective as the previous method. In this case, the puppy has a check line tied to its collar, although it is playing virtually free. The puppy will obey with the check line, but once that line is removed from its collar, it may dash after passersby. It may look to see if you are watching. Show your displeasure by scolding the puppy when you take it back into your yard. Naturally the younger the puppy is, the easier it will learn this lesson.

If your dog is grown and you have to teach it not to chase automobiles, the principle is the same, but the cure is far more difficult. First of all, a dog will not chase every car that goes by, and you may have difficulty trying to guess which one it will run after. It has been my experience that dogs usually chase cars that make a lot of noise on the road.

Try to enlist the help of the driver of such a car to drive past to see if your dog will chase after it. The people in the back seat can throw some small lightweight cans at the dog if it starts to run off. Again, it is only necessary for the cans to come close. This lesson should be repeated on different days and with different cars. You might even enlist the co-operation of the garbage collectors in your neighborhood.

Discouraging Other Misbehavior

If you sit on chairs, lounges, sofas, and beds, your puppy will see no reason why it should not do so, too. Slapping the chair with a rolled-up newspaper and firmly saying "No" should discourage a puppy from occupying that seat.

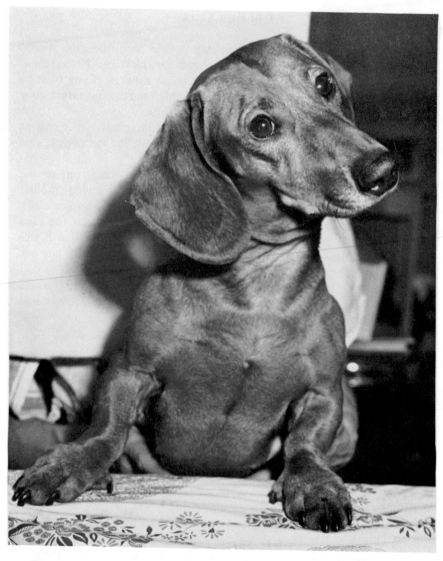

The best way to keep a dog off furniture is never to allow it on in the first place. *H. Armstrong Roberts*

A woman complained that her Kerry Blue Terrier would jump on chairs and sofas near windows and bark furiously at every passerby. The dog would stand on its hind legs to see out the window and, in its excitement, would tear down the curtains. She could do nothing to stop its crazy and continuous barking or the destruction of her furniture and draperies. Tossing small, empty juice cans at the dog cured it within two days. After that the dog would bark only when strangers came to the door and would stop on command.

Of course the best way to keep a puppy — or grown dog — off of furniture is never to allow it on in the first place, and keep him away by closing doors or putting in gates such as those used as barriers for small children. (I've discussed in Chapter 4 the use of crates to ensure a dog's safety and that of your belongings).

*

There are repellent sprays that are supposed to keep puppies from chewing on things. Some of them work; some do not. They also have a rather unpleasant odor, and they should not be used on fabrics. However, a repellent can be used on leather slippers. If a dog is chewing out of spite, it may ignore the repellent. Discipline your puppy if you catch it in the act by slapping it lightly upward under the chin and scolding it.

If these methods do not work, you might try putting a muzzle on its mouth. Dogs hate this, and it is a very effective punishment because a dog will not be able to chew. If you do not have a muzzle, wrap a two-inch-wide bandage around your dog's muzzle (jaw) twice, tying it under the chin and then tying the ends in behind its ears. Leave this on for half an hour. (Your dog will not smother; it can breathe through its nose. However, it will not be able to pant, which is one of its means of sweating, so keep it in a cool place.) The bandage system, by the way, is one method you can use to train a dog who bares its teeth to every person who comes near. Veterinarians also use it to keep from being bitten while treating nervous dogs.

*

Most puppies will get underfoot while you are preparing supper. Later they may hang around the table begging for food. Your puppy will not do this if you have taught it to obey the command "Sit" or "Lie down." It will be helpful if you give your puppy its evening meal before you have your own dinner. If it has a full stomach, it will prefer sleeping to begging.

*

Nothing can quite equal the joy a puppy has when it upsets and then goes through a wastebasket. A mousetrap set in the wastebasket will stop this. You can upset the wastebasket yourself, set the mousetrap in it, and then let the puppy go there to explore the rubbish. Be careful, though, that it does not get a toe caught. A firm scolding is also a good reminder that it should behave itself.

*

If you have a fenced-in backyard, your dog should learn not to race along the fence barking and snarling at all the dogs and passersby it sees. Sometimes, however, children or other dogs might tease your dog by racing along the fence and provoking it, in which case your dog's barking is not its fault.

Barking

It is not wise to discourage your dog completely from barking. In fact, having your dog alert you to the approach of people on your property is a definite advantage. However, your dog should learn to stop barking when you command it to. Be firm in saying "No" when it starts to make a racket. Slap the side of its crate, or slap it lightly upward under its chin, and scold it angrily.

If you see that your dog is very fearful during a storm, try to comfort and reassure it, saying, "Quiet" or "Good dog," or divert its attention if you can — to its toys, for example. It is important that your dog learn to obey you and be quiet when you want it to do so. As with other training your dog gets, the younger it is, the easier it will learn its lesson.

Kennel dogs have little to do but bark, and this they do furiously at times. An entire neighborhood may become infuriated with the noise. One man I know solved the problem by building an underground water system. Inside each fence post were sprinkler pipes directed toward the center of the area where the dogs could run around. Every time the dogs began to bark, he turned on the water. The dogs were sprayed from all sides and quickly retired into the kennel building.

Once I was called by a couple who lived in a two-story penthouse atop an apartment building; they had built a kennel on the roof. When deliverymen, garbage collectors, and meter readers climbed the stairs to reach the roof, the dogs would start barking furiously. So we set up some hoses, controlled from inside the house, and every time the dogs barked, strong jets of water would strike them from a second-story penthouse window.

Growling or Biting

I have heard many dog owners' complaints: A dog refuses to let its owner examine its teeth; it tries to bite the veterinarian; it nips the owner when he or she tries to trim its nails or pull a burr from its coat. Other common complaints are that a dog growls or bites when it is approached while it is eating or gets angry and bites during rough play. These faults are the owners'; the dogs have not been trained properly.

It is mandatory that you teach your puppy not to growl or bite, and you must be stern about it. I know of one case in which an infant was seriously injured when he crawled near a dog's food pan and was bitten. If the puppy will not let you near its food dish and growls when you approach, lift it off its front legs by the scruff or nape of the neck, scold it, and slap it lightly under its chin. Then return it to the food dish. The puppy will quickly learn that it should not growl at you and that it will be fed if it behaves itself.

Grooming is sometimes painful for a dog, particularly when you are trying to remove a burr from its coat or untangle a hair mat. A pup in pain may turn its head toward the source of its discomfort and try to bite. Such actions should be discouraged while you are grooming your dog or cutting its nails. Say "No" sternly, and slap the pup under the chin. Then straighten its head, and continue your work.

Teach your puppy to let you run your fingers between its lips and gums and to run your fingernail lightly down its teeth. The purpose of this is to accustom the dog to having your fingers in its mouth to scrape or clean its teeth. Later it will permit you to remove tartar along the gum line. This is done with metal tooth scalers similar to those used by dentists. Early training could save you a lot of trouble later, including a veterinarian's bill.

While you are playing with your puppy, it may growl and use its teeth. You have to show it how far it can go. If your dog growls, gets angry, and starts to use its teeth seriously, lift it by the scruff of the neck, and slap it under its chin. Then return to playing with it so that your dog will learn that play is all right but that anger and biting are not.

Contact with Other People

If your puppy is shy and afraid of strangers, it will not socialize readily. To overcome your puppy's timidity, allow it to get hungry, and take it some place where people congregate. Bring along a supply of small treat biscuits, and ask some people to give these to your puppy while speaking to it in a friendly manner.

Encourage your puppy to overcome its shyness and not be fearful when strangers approach. *H. Armstrong Roberts*

After a while it will realize that strangers do not represent danger and that most of them are friendly. It will not shun strange places or crowds. This is an absolute must if you intend to exhibit your dog in shows or have it compete in obedience trials.

This same principle can be used in teaching your puppy that such people as mail carriers, meter readers, and garbage collectors are its friends. Mail carriers usually try to befriend all the dogs on their routes. However, some meter readers and garbage collectors are hurrying and don't make an effort to make friends with a dog. Consequently it is difficult to blame the dog for being suspicious and eventually unfriendly.

Again, give a handful of small treats or puppy biscuits to the mail carrier. Ask him or her to approach your puppy with kind words, calling it by name and then offering it a biscuit. With some puppies this will require some coaxing and even some encouragement by you. However, after a few encounters the puppy will welcome the mail carrier, the two will be friends, and nothing more than petting and compliments will be necessary.

The same system can work with meter readers and garbage collectors. But because they come less frequently, they require more co-operation on your part. You must know approximately when they will come and be prepared.

*

Many people do not want their dogs to be overly friendly with strangers. In particular they do not want their dogs to accept food indiscriminately or to pick up bits of food on the ground when they are being exercised.

To teach this, you will need the assistance of another person, either a stranger or a friend. However, the person must not be a member of your immediate family.

Command your puppy to sit. Then have the other person show your puppy a biscuit, keeping it far enough away from the dog's nose so that the pup cannot grab it. Give the command "No." Repeat this action several times. Later, after the puppy knows that it should not take the biscuit from the other person, say "Okay," and give it to the puppy yourself. The puppy will quickly realize that it must not accept food from other people, that it will get its food from you. You should repeat this lesson with half a dozen different people.

(I mentioned earlier that you should have your mail carrier make friends with your puppy by offering it biscuits. These two lessons do not contradict each other. You should accompany your dog when the mail comes and allow your dog to accept the treat. It will soon learn that the person bringing the mail is an exception to the "no food from strangers" rule, that he or she is family.)

When your puppy has mastered this lesson, take the principle a step farther. Put some chunks of meat in your own backyard, and lead your puppy past them. When your dog tries to get the meat, jerk it away, and say "No" sternly. Repeat this a dozen times in your yard until the puppy always refuses to touch the meat. After each lesson compliment and pet your dog.

Ultimately, you will want your dog to avoid any food that it might come upon without your knowledge. This lesson may save your dog's life one day. Therefore, after testing your dog's willpower in your yard, tempt it outside its familiar boundaries. Prepare for walks by placing biscuits or meat along the route you will take. If the puppy starts to take the bait, jerk it away, saying "No" firmly. A few lessons should be sufficient if the puppy has learned the earlier ones.

*

Use one or all four of the following methods to train your puppy not to jump on people. The first is to put one hand on either side of your dog's neck, force it into a sitting position, look it in the eye, and say "No" sternly. If this does not work, grab your puppy by the fore legs and rush it backward until it topples over. Other methods are to grab its forelegs and step lightly on its hind toes, or to raise your knee and bump it lightly in the chest. You may have to use all four methods before the dog is cured.

A puppy's urge to mount people can be an irritating habit. Puppies of both sexes often show an instinct to cling with their front legs to a person's leg and then start the pumping motions of sexual intercourse. This is no indication that the puppy is oversexed or sexually perverse. It is an instinct that is present in many mammals.

To discourage this habit, place a hand on either side of your dog's neck. Shove the dog backward into a sitting position, thereby releasing its forelegs, and say "No" sternly. If the puppy persists, follow this with light slaps upward under its chin.

Closing Remarks

I would like to make several points in closing this chapter. *First,* do not give biscuits or tidbits as rewards for good performance. If you do, the dog will always be looking for them. Later, if you want it to obey your command and you don't happen to have any tidbits along, you will be betraying its confidence in you. Petting with both hands and verbal compliments are the only rewards it should need. Your dog is not a trained seal.

Second, no lesson should last more than three or four minutes. Never risk tiring or boring your puppy. Tests have shown that a puppy will learn faster and remember longer if it is given two three-minute lessons rather than one lesson lasting six minutes.

Third, from time to time I have suggested gently slapping a dog upward under the chin as a means of discipline. There is a good reason for this. Virtually all animals recognize the raising of an arm to strike as the first step in aggression, and their reaction may be to attack first. By striking under the chin and therefore beneath the dog's mouth, you will avoid the possibility of being bitten. Never strike or beat your dog with a newspaper or stick. Many dogs have a fear complex and may fight back as they are beaten. Use constructive means to discipline your dog, rather than destructive or physically harmful means.

Fourth, if you fence your yard, do not put a Beware of Dog sign up. Such a sign implies that you have a vicious dog. Under English common law, which the United States and Canada are governed by, the first

Do not put a BEWARE OF DOG **sign in your yard. It implies that you have a vicious dog.** *H. Armstrong Roberts*

wrongdoing of dog owners is possessing a vicious dog. If your dog bites a trespasser, even someone trespassing with criminal intent, you may be liable.

One solution is to put up several signs saying Keep Gate Closed, Dog at Large. These should convey the message to any intelligent person. If the trespasser ignores the message, at least you cannot be charged with owning a vicious dog. (However, if the dog has bitten a person before, whatever the reason, you may be liable for damages if it bites someone again. In that case consult an attorney.)

chapter thirteen
Tricks to Teach Your Dog

No one knows how much a dog can learn because there is no method to measure a dog's aptitude or intellectual potential. However, puppies do love to perform. The more you teach them, the more they can be taught and the faster they will learn. As I explained in Chapter 12, no lesson should be longer than three or four minutes. Three lessons for three minutes a day are better than ten minutes once a day. Puppies are like children: When a lesson is too long, the puppy will get bored, and its mind will wander. And if you cannot hold its attention, you will not be able to teach it.

Once you have given your dog the basic training described in Chapter 12, here are a few rudimentary tricks that should be in every dog's repertoire.

Speak

When you go out, your puppy will want to accompany you. Go out, leave the puppy in, and hold the door open just an inch or two. Then tell it to "Speak," demonstrating by barking yourself. A puppy will quickly get the idea, and when it performs satisfactorily, let it out. Later reverse the procedure, and teach your dog to bark when it wants to come in.

When you command your dog to speak, do not give it food rewards for obeying. You want your dog to obey out of a desire to please you, but if you use food rewards, the dog's attention will always be on food, not on your commands. The dog may even develop the unpleasant habit of barking whenever you are preparing its food.

There are times when your dog's barking can act as a special alert to you or a member of your family. For instance, if there is a person with a hearing impairment in your home, you can teach your dog to bark whenever the phone rings. Most dogs will bark when the doorbell rings or when someone knocks, but the telephone is a different matter. Have a friend call your number half a dozen times, three minutes apart, and have your dog on hand near the phone. As it rings, tell your dog, "Speak." After three or four days, it will get the idea, and sometimes only a couple of lessons are necessary.

You might also have a member of your household go into another room; then when the phone rings and your dog barks, command it to "Go get Joe," accenting "Joe." Then lead your dog to the room where Joe is. When Joe comes out to answer the phone, he should compliment and pet the dog.

Dead Dog

Have your puppy lie down. It will probably keep its head erect, so say, "Dead dog," and gently push its head to the floor. The puppy will probably react by trying to struggle to its feet.

Put it back into the prone position, repeat the command, and press its head down, repeating the process again and again until your puppy gets the idea. Use the palm of your hand in front of its face as a warning not to get up. After half a minute, remove your hand and say, "Okay." Finish with plenty of praise and petting.

Roll Over

While your puppy is in the "Dead dog" position, give the command "Roll over," and roll your dog over. Praise it, and then repeat the lesson until it gets the idea. Then give the command, at the same time moving your hand in a circle. Before very long the puppy will roll over on signal.

Catch

Remember that many tricks should start with the dog sitting, as in the case with this trick. Use a small piece of dog biscuit and stand about three feet from your puppy, in full view. Attract its attention by making short throwing motions. Then say, "Catch," and toss a biscuit toward its nose.

At first the puppy won't open its mouth to catch the biscuit; instead it will rush to grab the treat from the floor. You must pick up the biscuit before the dog reaches it. After a few attempts the puppy will realize that

Teach your dog to "speak" when it wants to go outside or come back indoors. *Ralston Purina Company*

it must catch the biscuit while it is in the air, and it will quickly become adept at this.

The dog can then be graduated to catching other things, such as a small rubber ball (*never* a hard ball). In fact, there are some dogs that learn to catch Frisbees with remarkable skill.

Carry

A dog should be taught to carry things before you try to teach it to retrieve. Both in field trials and in obedience trials, some dogs retrieve in a slinking or slovenly manner. If they have first been taught to carry properly and to do so proudly, they will retrieve beautifully as well.

Start with your dog in a sitting position. Then place the object to be carried — a rolled-up newspaper tied with string, for example — in front of its nose. Hold the object in your right hand, and command "Carry," at the same time using your left hand to open the dog's mouth. You can do this by placing your hand over its muzzle and pressing its lips against its teeth. Do this until the dog opens its mouth slightly, at which point you shove the newspaper in.

If the dog tries to spit the newspaper out, reprimand it, either with the command "Carry" or "Hold it." Meanwhile, keep the newspaper in the dog's mouth with your right hand. It may be necessary to slap gently upward under the dog's chin.

Make the puppy hold the paper until you take it away. Reclaim the paper with the usual command "Okay," and then give the puppy plenty of praise and petting. Never let the puppy drop the paper, and always make it place the paper or other object directly in your hand.

Next repeat all this with the puppy's leash on. Begin to back away while the puppy continues to sit and hold the object, using the extended palm of your hand, plus the command "Hold it." When the puppy will do this, you are ready for the first real lesson in carrying.

While repeating the command to "Hold it," take the dog by the leash with your left hand. Begin to move forward, tugging the puppy to come along. It may want to spit the paper out, but hold the paper in the dog's mouth with your right hand, repeating either the "Hold it" or "Carry" command. After a couple of lessons the puppy will understand.

These first lessons can be given in the house, but later you should take the puppy outside. Ask it to carry an object while it walks at your side; repeated commands will probably be necessary. If the dog drops the object, say "No" sternly, make the dog sit, replace the object in its mouth, and begin again.

Finally, use different objects — a small basket, a block of wood, a toy, almost anything. Soon you will find that the dog enjoys this and will carry a small basket with some item in it home from the store. The whole neighborhood will be delighted by this demonstration quite as much as the dog likes giving it. The pride that the dog displays will be carried over into its lessons in retrieving.

Retrieve

Most dogs retrieve instinctively, although spontaneous fetching is very different from retrieving on command. You must teach the dog to do the latter, which is to seize an article and return it to you. The difference is that many a dog will rush after a ball, only to scamper off with it rather than return it to you.

Start the retrieving lessons in your home or backyard. (Lessons are taught more easily in a home because the space is smaller and more restricted. Also, there are fewer distractions there.)

Tell your dog to sit; then throw a rolled-up newspaper or another object of your choice across the room and say "Fetch." The dog may not respond initially, in which case you should lead it to the *dummy* (a common word for a dumbbell or other object with which you are working) and draw the dog's head down to it. If necessary, force its

Part of a dog's basic training is learning to retrieve objects on command. *Gaines Dog Research Center*

mouth open as you did in teaching it to carry, and put the dummy in. Make the dog take the object back to the place from which you threw it, and insist that it hold the object until you take it away. The next step is to put your dog on a long leash or training cord. When it goes over to pick up the article, begin to draw the dog back to you, meanwhile complimenting it. Soon it will rush over, seize the dummy, and return it to you proudly at a gallop. Always make the dog sit before taking the dummy from its mouth.

Finally, take the dog into the backyard, and practice longer and longer retrieves. Try to practice in open fields so that your dog will learn to retrieve under all sorts of conditions and in many places.

Take Directions

To teach this trick, you will need some props: a stake in the ground in which a screw eye has been placed, either on top or on one side, and a thirty-foot-long venetian blind cord. Tie one end of the cord to the dog, and place the dog fifteen feet to one side of the stake. Then thread the cord through the screw eye, and stand in front of the stake, holding the other end of the cord.

Direct the dog with either arm outstretched, using the command "Right" or "Left." With the other hand, tug on the rope so that the dog has to go right or left. When it reaches the stake, command it to sit. Repeat this exercise from both sides of the stake.

When your dog appears to have mastered this, double the length of the cord and the distance between the dog and the stake. Your dog should learn to go in the direction signaled by your arm. The true test is to practice with the dog free. If it does not obey at first, use the cord and stake again until it does.

These Vizslas listen attentively to the directions given by their trainer. Photo of Ch. Bold Dog Rogi and Ch. Caesar, courtesy of Burnt Hills Boarding Kennel.

The most complicated application of this procedure involves using a dummy or dumbbell. With your dog sitting, place the dummy thirty feet to the right, and then stand twenty feet in front of the animal. Signal with your right hand, giving the command "Fetch." Repeat this on the left side, gradually lengthening the distance.

When these basics are quickly and skillfully performed, you are ready to go into the open fields with your dog. Practice sending it away from you and commanding it to sit. Then practice the right and left signals.

At field trials the best retrievers can be motioned out by an arm signal as much as a hundred yards away to retrieve an object, usually a dead duck or pheasant that they did not see placed. This is called a *blind retrieve*. If the dog gets off course, it can be stopped and redirected to the duck or pheasant by arm signals.

With time and patience a dog can learn hundreds of words and will be able to understand commands to get your slippers, carry your shoes to your bedroom, or even find hidden objects. All you will have to do is give an arm signal sending it into the room you choose.

Jump

This is an easy trick for your dog to learn. Erect a low barrier that you yourself can step over. Put your dog on a leash, walk to the barrier, command "Jump," and step over it yourself. The dog will follow, though a slight tug may be necessary. After a few tries, make the barrier higher so that you too must make a slight jump to clear it.

Next, place the dog in a sitting position a few feet in front of the barrier, and command "Jump." If it does not, use your training cord. Stand on one side of the barrier, command the dog, and pull it toward the jump. After a lesson or two it will jump on command when you are on the other side of the barrier. Now place the dog in front of the barrier while you stand beside it, and command it to jump. Sometimes an arm signal will help. Eventually the arm signal will be all that is necessary.

Make the barrier higher and higher until it is about one and a half times the dog's height at the shoulders. Use different kinds of items for it to jump over, such as an overturned chair, a low wall, a stick held out in front of the dog. This lesson proves extremely valuable when you are out in the fields because the dog may have to jump a fence.

If you are in the fields and reach a fence that is too high, show your dog how to run along it until it finds a place to crawl under. You should also show your dogs holes through which they can jump or edge their way.

After considerable training, a dog will be able to jump over a barrier that is much higher than it is. *Gaines Dog Research Center*

Say Your Prayers

The key word in this trick is *prayers*. Children delight in teaching a dog to do this and in watching other dogs perform it.

First, put your dog in a corner, and lift it by its front paws until it is sitting up. The dog will try to stand, but gently force it into a sitting position. Because it is in the corner, it cannot fall over backward.

When it has learned to sit up, take it to a chair and say, "Say your prayers," accenting "prayers." Make it sit in front of the chair; then lift its front legs, putting them on the chair. It should stay there until you say "Okay" or "Amen."

chapter fourteen
Obedience Training and Competition

Whether your dog is to be entered in competition or not, you should teach it the fundamental lessons of obedience training. This is simply an adaptation of the yard breaking, or special training, that has been given to hunting dogs for centuries and involves training a dog to obey, to respond to the orders of its owner. Dogs from the Sporting and Working breeds — including Golden Retrievers, German Shepherds, Poodles, Border Collies, Springer Spaniels, and Doberman Pinschers — do especially well in obedience tests.

Obedience training can be divided into two types. The first is the simple training of a dog to be a good citizen. Such training is given by responsible owners who recognize that they do not have the right to keep neighborhood nuisances. I believe that every dog should be given such training and that no one who is unwilling to give it should be allowed to own a dog. The lessons that are part of this type of training include teaching your dog to stop barking, to stay in your yard, not to chase cars or bicycles, and so on (see Chapter 12, "Basic Training for Puppies").

Another important primary lesson that you should teach your dog, whether you enter it in a course, obedience competition, or field trials, or just want to take it somewhere, is that it should relieve itself in a certain area when you want it to (see Chapter 5, "Housebreaking Your Dog"). No one wants to have a dog of which he or she is proud stop to drop a stool in front of a crowd or in the show ring. In the obedience ring a dog that stops to relieve itself is automatically out. I know one professional handler who fines his assistants twenty-five dollars if a dog ever relieves itself in the show ring.

A second kind of obedience training is an exciting form of competition during which dogs can win prizes, titles, a national championship, and even international titles. The American Kennel Club has established rigid standards for competition. A majority of dog shows held in the United States include obedience competition, as do the Canadian Kennel Club, the Asociacion Canofila Mexicana (Mexican Kennel Club), and the Bermuda Kennel Club. The rules for competition in all four countries are so similar that it is possible for a dog to win degrees in each of them without any additional training.

Obedience contests are divided into different classes, or levels, of increased difficulty.

By passing the Novice Class, a dog receives the designation of Companion Dog (CD). This abbreviation then becomes a suffix that is used after the dog's name. The next level of difficulty is the Open Class, in which a dog can receive a Companion Dog Excellent (CDX) title. The next class is the Utility Class, awarding the title Utility Dog (UD).

Classes are subdivided into A and B sections. An amateur trainer enters a dog in A classes; a professional trainer or an experienced amateur (one who has gained a title with another dog before) enters a dog in B classes. If an amateur has two dogs competing in a class, he or she must enter one in A and one in B, because the dogs do the Long Sit and Long Down in a group and each must have his own handler; and that handler in the A classes must be the same one who took him through the other exercises. In the B classes, someone else could take the dog in for these group stints.

Another class of competition is for the title of Tracking Dog (TD). With this designation and a UD title, a dog will be considered a thoroughly trained competitive winner. A new obedience trial championship title has been created, OT Ch. (Obedience Trial Champion), which can be won by dogs with a UD title. The prefix can be added to a dog's name.

Novice Class

The beginner or Novice Class for obedience dogs includes lessons in the following exercises: Heel on Leash, Figure Eight, Heel Free, Stand for Examination, Long Sit (one minute), Long Down (three minutes), and Recall (come when called). I will explain each of these in turn.

Heel. In *Heel on Leash,* a dog is expected to walk beside you, close to your body. The command is "Heel," and the dog is expected not to go ahead of you, hence to be close to your heel. It should walk on your left side, and when you stop, the dog must stop and sit. It should not move until you start forward. *Heel Free* is the same exercise except that the dog is not leashed.

In training my own dogs for the field, I expect them to learn to heel and sit when leashed in three evenings of training, with lessons not longer than five minutes. Sometimes several lessons can be given in an evening, but you should intersperse these with play periods lasting about fifteen minutes each. Heel Free should not require more than three more days.

To teach your dog to heel, you must first teach it to sit. Give the command "Sit," pulling back on the leash with one hand while pressing the dog's rear end down. Because a small puppy's bones may not be fully hardened, it is better to stoop over and push its hind legs under. In either case, keep some pressure on the puppy's body to hold it in the sitting position, letting it up with "All right" or some similar phrase, plus praise. Rubbing its neck with both hands and speaking words of praise are best.

After three or four lessons, have your dog sit at heel; then start forward, commanding "Heel." When the dog pulls ahead, many people jerk it back, but this seems to be unnecessarily hard on the dog. I prefer to use a cane, umbrella, or yardstick. If the dog goes ahead, I simply tap it lightly on the nose — *lightly,* not hard enough to be painful; just the touch causes the puppy to back up. Repeat the command "Heel" when you do this.

After several starts and stops to instill the command "Heel," give your dog the command "Sit," at the same time reaching down and making it sit. Then start to walk again, and command "Heel." Repeat this a dozen times, and then free the dog for a play period. Later on you can repeat the lesson.

When you feel that the dog has learned this lesson thoroughly, try it off the leash. However, you must be ready to grab it and make it sit when you stop or when you make a turn. Incidentally, be sure to practice turns and reverses both on the leash and off; if you do not, the dog will only heel when you walk in a straight line.

If the dog heels too far away from your body, you can reach down and draw it closer or touch it lightly with the cane or stick to get it to move closer. You can also accustom your dog to walk close to your body by walking along a curb or wall so that the dog has to stay close. In obedience competition the dog is expected almost to touch your body.

If you are teaching a field dog, you expect to use in hunting to heel, remember that heeling is simply to keep the dog under control. For instance, it may have to heel slightly behind you on a narrow path; or if you are teaching it to heel to a horse, it naturally cannot get too close to the horse's hooves. The main point is that wherever it is, the dog must be close enough to you to be under absolute control. I have watched dogs heel to a horse while going through a farmer's barnyard in which there were chickens and even the farmer's dog roaming about.

Figure Eight.   This exercise is an extension of the heeling on lead. You and your dog will be expected to walk a pattern around two "posts." These are people stationed about six feet apart facing each other. They remain absolutely still. You and the dog should come as close as possible without brushing a "post," and there should be no sniffing or jumping up. It's an exercise in concentration (on *you*), discipline, and maneuverability. You can practice with two chairs or between stakes or trees. But eventually the real test is live "posts."

Stand for Examination.   This test used to be part of utility work, or advanced training work for dogs. However, because the point of this exercise is to prove that your dog is not shy and will not bite, the exercise was moved to primary training.

Your puppy should have been taught to stand and pose when it was very young in order for it to be groomed or examined by a vet. This training will come in handy when the dog is being judged during obedience competition. If your puppy has already become accustomed to having its teeth examined and allowing you to run your finger along its teeth and gum line, it should not object if a stranger or a judge does so. In the show ring a judge should also be able to touch a dog's scrotum without the dog showing resentment or collapsing on the floor.

If your dog is inclined to bite or growl when strangers pet it, you can use several of the training methods described in Chapter 12. For example, allow other people to give your dog a biscuit snack in order to make it feel comfortable around strangers.

Long Sit.   This lesson should be easy for your dog to learn if you have already taught it to sit while its food is being prepared and to wait until you give an "All right" signal.

Here is another method you can use to teach your dog Long Sit. Drive a stake to which a screw eye has been added into the ground at the far end of your yard, and sit the dog in front of the stake. Tie one end of a long training rope (or venetian blind cord) to the dog's collar, loop the cord through the eye of the screw, and back away while warning the dog "Sit; Stay." At the same time keep a slight pressure on the training cord.

If your dog stays when you are thirty or forty feet away, duck behind a car or a corner of the house. Your dog will probably jump up immediately because it thinks you have gone away. Jerk the dog back into position with the training cord, come into view, and give the command "Stay" or "Sit" again. (In field trials, people use an upraised hand to command "Sit" and have the dog obey when it is a hundred yards away.)

When you think your dog has learned this lesson, remove the training cord, and repeat the same procedure while the dog is free. If it gets up, rush out, grab your dog, and take it back to the exact spot from which it broke. A thoroughly trained dog will stay for three or four minutes while you are out of sight. (Novice obedience dogs are required to stay only one minute with the handler in sight.)

Long Down. To teach this exercise, have your dog lie down, and repeat the format of the "Sit; Stay" lessons, using the training cord if necessary. In Novice Class obedience tests a dog is required to stay down for three minutes.

Recall. The procedure of teaching your dog to come when it is called is described in detail in Chapter 12, "Basic Training for Puppies."

Return to Heel. All training lessons must begin with the dog at the left heel, and they must end there as well. The dog may circle you to get to heel, or it may swing around and back up to heel.

It is quite easy to teach the dog to circle you to reach heel. Sit your dog in front of you, say "Heel," take the dog by the collar or use a short leash (which is easier), and move it around you. Eventually a circular motion of your arm accompanied by the command "Heel" will be sufficient. Another method is to reach down, turn your dog around, and back it up to heel. Regardless of the method you use, it is important to have the dog sit straight, and not with its hindquarters out of line with your body.

Open Class

The Open Class in obedience competition consists of the following exercises: Heel Free, Drop on Recall, Retrieve on the Flat, Retrieve over the High Jump, Broad Jump, Long Sit (three minutes), and Long Down (five minutes). Both the Long Sit and Long Down are held while the handler goes out of sight.

Drop on Recall. This is a valuable lesson for you to teach your dog. For instance, if you see a car coming that might hit your dog if it decided to dart suddenly into the street, you could prevent this from happening if your dog obeyed your command for it to drop to the ground.

To teach this, set up the stake and training cord as you did in the Long Sit exercise. Call your dog to you. When it is halfway there, command "Down," using a hand signal (arm raised and then lowered). At the same time, stop your dog with your left hand, which is holding the cord.

Do not repeat the lesson so many times in succession that your dog moves slowly, almost at a crawl, expecting the "Down" command. Vary this exercise with the Recall lesson, and try not to overdo it. Remember, you want your dog always to remain alert.

Retrieve on the Flat. Teaching your dog to retrieve is discussed in detail in Chapter 13. It is important to remember that a dog should retrieve enthusiastically, sit before you to deliver the object, and then return to your left heel to await your next command.

Retrieve over the High Jump. In this exercise a dog must retrieve an object, usually a dumbbell, after it is thrown over an obstacle jump. The high jump is one and a half times the dog's height at the shoulder; it is a minimum of eight inches and a maximum of thirty-six inches high, depending on the dog. An exception is made for Bloodhounds, Bullmastiffs, Great Danes, Great Pyrenees, Newfoundlands, and St. Bernards, who must clear just their own height, or thirty-six inches if they are taller.

This poodle has just retrieved the dumbbell and is returning to its handler after clearing the high jump.   *Gaines Dog Research Center*

Broad Jump.   In the broad jump a dog must clear four hurdles that are spaced to equal a distance that is twice that of the high jump. (Again the exact distance depends on the size of the dog.) Teach your dog to jump one hurdle, then two, and so on, gradually spacing them until the appropriate distance has been achieved.

I have known many dogs that have performed perfectly during both the High Jump and Broad Jump tests but that would refuse simpler jumps over other objects, such as ditches. If you decide to train your own dog, devise other tests so that the dog will learn to obey under any circumstances.

Utility Class

The tests in Utility Class are Scent Discrimination (two different articles), Directed Retrieve, Directed Jumping, Signal Exercise, and Group Examination.

Scent Discrimination.   In this test a dog must pick out an article bearing its owner's or handler's scent from among five identical articles placed before it. In one test the articles are metal; in another they are leather.

In the broad jump, a dog must jump over four boards. The distance it has to jump depends on the size of the dog.   *Gaines Dog Research Center*

In an advanced exercise, a dog is required to select the article bearing its handler's scent from among a group of identical articles. *Gaines Dog Research Center*

There are various ways to teach your dog to do this. One way is to start with two objects, being certain that you have not touched one of them. Rub the other object with your hands, and give the dog your scent by placing your hands over its nose. Place both articles a short distance away from your dog where it can see them. Lead your dog to them, and say "Fetch." If it selects the wrong article, pull the dog back slightly, saying "No." Let it smell your hands again. If your dog then picks up the correct object, praise it.

Continue this procedure, gradually adding items, so that your dog is eventually forced to sniff three or four items in order to find the right one. Then you should change to another material (such as metal, leather, or wooden objects). A way to make this lesson practical is to hide items such as your billfold or key chain and keys, and ask your dog to find them — first among a pile of objects, then hidden someplace less obvious.

Directed Retrieve. This is an exercise that all retrievers must perform in field trials, sometimes when they are seventy-five to a hundred yards from their handlers. In order for your dog to be successful with this test in obedience training, it must first know how to take directions (see Chapter 13).

As part of competition, this Papillon is retrieving a white work glove that its handler has commanded it to fetch. *Gaines Dog Research Center*

Place two articles at wide angles from you. Your dog should be sitting to your left, as always. With your left hand and arm, indicate the direction to one of the articles, and give the command "Fetch." If your dog starts toward the wrong object, stop it, return it to heel, and give the signal once again. If it still tries to go to the wrong one, bring it back, give it the direction, and then start toward that object with it. Praise your dog when it retrieves the right article.

In competition, three white work gloves are set far apart. The judge can order you to send your dog to any one of the three, so it is wise to practice with two items at first and work up to three. Practice this outdoors under all sorts of conditions until your dog always takes directions and goes to the right object.

Directed Jumping. In competition, the judge will tell you to send your dog to the far end of the ring and stop it there. The judge will then indicate either the high jump or the bar jump. Your dog must jump the correct one, return to heel, and then repeat the same procedure with the other jump.

Signal Exercise. For this exercise only hand signals are used to direct the dog. The judge will give you a series of orders during a Heel Free exercise, and you will have to make your dog obey without using your voice. For example, while the dog is heeling, the judge may order you to signal your dog to stay. You will then be ordered to leave your dog and use a hand signal to have your dog stay and remain standing. After specific signals from the judge, you will then have to signal your dog to drop, sit, or come.

Group Examination.   During this test the competing dogs are lined up at heel. If there are twelve or more dogs, they can be put into groups of six to fifteen dogs, at the judge's discretion. The dogs are then commanded to stand and can be posed by their owners or handlers. At the judge's order the handlers leave their dogs and go to the other end of the ring. The judge then examines each dog as he or she would do in the show or conformation ring. Handlers have to remain away from their dogs for at least three minutes during this exercise.

Tracking

This test is not given often because it cannot be performed in a show ring. It requires a large area with a trail covering 440 to 500 yards. A stranger makes the trail and stakes it out with flags, dropping a glove at its end. The trail must be at least half an hour old, but not more than two hours old. A dog is on leash as it works out the trail and finally reaches the glove.

Because all dogs have "nose brains," it is not difficult to teach a dog to follow a trail. You ask it to sniff at the beginning of a fresh trail and lead it along. If it gets off the trail, motion it in the right direction, and the dog will very quickly understand what it has to do. Practice with trails made by other people.

Teaching a dog to trail a person can be a lot of fun. Such a dog can sometimes be a great asset to a community. No section of the country is without annual incidents of children or older people wandering off and getting lost. Sometimes a dog skillful in "people-trailing" can actually save a life. If you have such a dog, inform the local police about it; there may be times when they will need to call your dog into service.

*

In the case of each of the preceding exercises I have simplified the procedure. Actually these exercises are extremely precise and complicated. If you are interested in entering your dog in obedience trials, you should join a class and go to dog shows that include such trials (not all do) to observe the entire procedure carefully. In addition, prospective obedience training competitors should get a book of rules and procedures from the American Kennel Club (51 Madison Avenue, New York, N.Y. 10010). A single copy may be obtained free of charge. Among other things, the booklet gives specifications for building a high jump, a bar jump, and broad jump hurdles for your dog.

In obedience training, a dog learns to pay close attention to its handler's commands. *Gaines Dog Research Center*

Scoring System

In obedience trials dogs are given scores of from 20 to 40 points, depending on the particular exercise. The top score would be 20 points for one exercise, 40 points for another. A perfect score for a complete set of exercises is 200 points. To win a leg on a title, a dog has to earn at least 50 per cent of the available points in all exercises and finish with at least 170 of the possible 200 points. A dog that fails any exercise loses its chance to win one of the three legs required for a title.

To win a Companion Dog (CD), Companion Dog Excellent (CDX), or Utility Dog (UD) title, a dog has to have three sets of passing scores (170 points or better); these scores must be won under three different judges; and at least six dogs have to compete in each class.

A dog that wins its UD title can compete for an additional title, Obedience Trial Champion (OT Ch.), which permits the usage of the prefix "Ch." (Champion) before its name.

Championship dogs must accumulate a total of 100 points, according to a complicated scale based on scores in Utility and Open B competitions and on the number of dogs entered. In other words the dog must win at least one first place in Utility with three or more dogs competing, one first place in Open B with six or more dogs competing, and another first place in either Utility or Open B. The remainder of the points (to equal a total of 100 points) can be won with second places. All first places must be won under different judges.

There is also a Versatility Class, in which dogs must complete six exercises taken from Novice, Open, and Utility Classes. The two scent discrimination tests (described earlier) are considered one exercise in this class.

Although breeds in the Miscellaneous Class cannot compete for championship points in dog shows, they may enter obedience competition and win titles. The Border Collie and the Australian Cattle Dog have scored high in this kind of competition.

Judges

If you are interested in becoming an obedience judge, you should apply to the American Kennel Club. Although the AKC does not publicize its qualifying standards for judges, it would obviously take into consideration the applicant's experience, that is, how many dogs the applicant has trained and handled, the scores that the dogs have earned, how many times the applicant has stewarded in various classes at licensed shows, and so on. It would also consider the applicant's character and stability.

If an applicant is approved, he or she is given a provisional license to judge Novice Classes. If the person judges with distinction, demonstrates a thorough knowledge of the rules, and judges a sufficient number of shows, he or she will be given a full license. Later, upon application, a judge might be granted the privilege of judging Open Classes and perhaps Utility Classes.

For a more detailed description of the application procedure to be a dog judge, see Chapter 34.

Training Clubs

At least a thousand cities and towns in the United States have obedience training clubs, most of which offer ten-week courses showing you how to train your dog in basic obedience. To find a class near you, ask your veterinarian, contact your local kennel club or animal shelter, and check newspapers. Here are several examples of how training clubs are organized.

For over a decade the Cleveland, Ohio, area had a club known as the Forest City Obedience Training Club. Its highly skilled trainers were all volunteers who gave ten-week courses twice a year in various parts of the city and its suburbs. There were eight locations, and classes averaged about thirty dogs for each trainer and staff, which meant that during those ten years, these volunteers trained some 1,480 dogs, and their owners as well, in the rules of good citizenship.

Training fees were not high, approximately ten to fifteen dollars for ten or eleven weeks. Because the trainers were volunteers and some of the locations were rent-free, the club was able to give scholarships and research grants of $10,000 each to the veterinary colleges of Ohio State University and the University of Pennsylvania.

Other groups and trainers in the area, such as the Cleveland All-Breed Training Club, trained dogs primarily for obedience competition and gave individual obedience shows.

Grace McDonald, a nationally known Canadian trainer in Winnipeg, Manitoba, is a prime mover behind an obedience training group in that area. Her group has fourteen instructors and gives eight classes a year, averaging 150 dogs per class. At least several trainers are necessary to handle each group of 150 dogs.

The classes are competition-oriented, although about 25 per cent of each class is composed of beginners, and another 5 per cent is made up of unregistered dogs that are being trained to become good citizens. The instructors are also geared to competition. If they have not been in competition for a year, they must return to it before they can continue instructing.

One problem in the United States, as well as in other countries, is that classes are sometimes given by people who have little or no experience in obedience training; they are doing it strictly for the money involved. Demands that the AKC should license instructors have gone unheeded because there is no way that such a licensing system can be worked out.

As a potential consumer you should first determine the qualifications of the instructor you choose for your dog. Ask him or her the following questions: How many of your own dogs have you trained to win obedience titles? How many dogs, your own or others', that you have trained have won UD titles? How long has it been since you were actively involved in training for an obedience contest and since your dogs won passing scores? Will you offer continuing courses working toward higher titles?

This type of screening system has been successful in recruiting trainers for Grace McDonald's school in Winnipeg. If you search for a training class with the same sort of instructors, you will have an excellent chance of obtaining proper instruction.

Even if you never intend to enter your dog in shows or obedience competition, the instructors who train dogs for that purpose are usually the best qualified. Your dog can take the first course leading to good dog citizen or Companion Dog status and skip the advanced training courses, or you may want to train your dog further with the advanced training, or your dog may require a second course in the primary, or Novice, work.

Hundreds of 4-H clubs also have dog training projects, and the instructors are likely to be well qualified. Many 4-H groups offer continuing courses designed to make your dog competitive in dog shows. You may discover that an instructor also has an occasional course for dogs owned by people who are not 4-H members.

Another alternative is to train your dog at home. However, the advantage of the ten- or eleven-week courses is that your dog will be trained to work in the presence of other dogs.

Benefits of Obedience Training

In closing this chapter, I would like to emphasize two points.

First, many people who show their dogs only in conformation classes (in which the overall quality of a dog is examined) say that obedience training ruins a dog for showing. That is totally untrue. The more you teach a dog, the more alert and observant it is — and the better show dog it is. Many dogs win both show championships and obedience titles. One dog, a Doberman Pinscher named Bengal von Grosshugel, a champion and holder of a UD title, competed in obedience and in conformation at a show in which he was judged both Best in Show and the highest-scoring obedience dog in the show.

Second, a dog that practices its obedience training in public will become the pride of the entire neighborhood. You will be considered a responsible citizen, and your dog will become the model by which all other dogs in the neighborhood are judged. Perhaps the example you set will inspire others to follow.

*

Obedience competition is only one element of dog shows. If you own a registered dog, you can participate not only in this form of competition but also in championship dog shows. These are discussed in detail in Part Five, "Dog Shows."

chapter fifteen
The Hunting Dog and Field Trials

The premise of this chapter is that you have bought a puppy belonging to one of the hunting breeds with the intention of training the dog to hunt or participate in field trials, that is, competitions in which a dog's hunting skills are judged. In either case the basic training is the same, but the goals are different. The dog that hunts with its owner a dozen times a year but is basically a house pet lacks the necessary experience to participate in a field trial, which places different demands on a dog.

Any of the hunting breeds, if properly trained, should make acceptable hunting companions. However, field trial dogs in particular

Although comparatively few Irish Setters are used for hunting, field trials are occasionally held for them. Photo courtesy of Dick and Pat Frost.

have usualiy been bred to establish specific traits. For example, the Labrador Retriever and the English Springer Spaniel are bred for speed; the Pointer and English Setter are bred for quick location of game over long distances.

Bench dogs (dogs seen in the show ring) and field dogs are so different in type that they might be referred to as separate breeds. A friend who has had both bench and field trial champion Basset Hounds says that the heavy-bodied Bassets for the show ring cannot negotiate satisfactorily in the woods.

Temperament is another consideration. Dogs bred solely for field trials may be so high-strung and nervous that they make poor house pets. Two breeds that are the most successful as both bench and field champions are the Brittany Spaniel and the German Shorthaired Pointer.

Trainers

Field trials are a fiercely competitive sport, and only a professional can give your dog the best possible training. The professionals have the ability, knowledge, facilities, and time to train a dog properly.

Many people use a professional field trial trainer even though they plan to use a dog only as a hunting companion. It is best not to hire a professional trainer during August or September because those are the months when trainers are already busy preparing a number of dogs for field trials.

Most serious field trial trainers prefer to whelp puppies of field trial ancestry. The length of training time is different for each dog, but a trainer is experienced in recognizing each dog's potential and has the good sense not to force, and possibly ruin, a good prospect. It is the trainer's responsibility to determine the dog's innate abilities, at what age they should be developed, and at what pace. However, a trainer may not accept a pup for training if it is over fifteen months old because valuable learning time will have been lost. Also, if your dog has not had a great deal of basic training, you should not expect it to become an accomplished hunter within two or three months.

Basic Training in Your Yard

If your dog is over fifteen months old and you cannot send it to a professional trainer, do not despair. Certainly your puppy can receive its basic training right in your backyard; you may even surprise yourself by developing a first-class hunting dog that will be a joy to you and the envy of your hunting companions.

Your first objective is to train your puppy to be totally dependent on you in order to capture its entire attention. You should be the only person to give food and water to the dog. It should turn to you for praise, and you should be generous with your compliments.

Many sportsmen train their dogs to obey whistle signals. A series of short, quick blasts might mean "Come" and a single sharp blast would alert the dog to stop, sit, and wait for directions. A friend of mine taught his puppies to respond to a command when they were playing at the far end of a run. He would give a signal, and when the puppies came, he would feed them. It was not long before they learned to listen for the signal and run to their owner.

Another teaching device is the training rope. It is tied to the puppy who then drags the rope around. While it is romping and playing, give a signal, and start drawing your puppy toward you. Praise it when it arrives.

The Brittany Spaniel is an excellent dog for hunting and for field trials. Photo of Ch. Millettes Dirty Harry, owned by Gary M. Tate.

In line with this suggestion, there is a trick that many professionals who whelp litters use to prepare the puppies for a training rope. They put a small rope collar on each puppy; to this they attach a lightweight cord, such as a venetian blind cord. It need only be six or eight feet long. The puppies learn to ignore the cord during training and play and romp in spite of it. This helps avoid the possibility of an inexperienced dog moving away from you when you attach a training rope to its collar later on.

I might mention here that a collar that is too loose, one that can slip over a dog's head, is as unsatisfactory as one that is too tight. A young puppy's rope collar should be loose enough so that there is space for one finger between the collar and the puppy's neck. For a dog that is going into the fields, there should be space for two fingers, never any more, between the collar and the dog's neck.

Training in the Field

Although you should make a puppy dependent on you in its early training period, it must teach itself by experimentation if it is to become field-wise. For example, never help a puppy up a steep bank or through a fence. Climb to the top of a bank or hill, and walk along the crest. The puppy will race back and forth at the bottom, wanting to follow but not knowing quite how. You should locate a spot that is not too steep for the puppy to climb and start walking out of sight. You will discover that after one or two attempts the puppy will be successful in climbing to the top of the bank. Eventually it will teach itself to accomplish many feats in different situations.

The same approach applies when training a puppy to cross a fence. You should walk along the side of the fence opposite the puppy and find a place where it is feasible for the puppy to either jump over or crawl under it. You may have to show the spot to the puppy the first few times, but after a number of lessons you will find that the puppy can handle the situation on its own. In the same manner, you should also be able to teach a puppy to jump through a hole in a fence.

In Chapter 13 I explained how to teach a dog to jump hurdles. Eventually a dog should be able to clear all sorts of barriers, including wire fences, to retrieve game.

Your puppies should learn to search for you without panicking when you are not nearby. A friend of mine often takes his German Shorthaired Pointer puppies to a heavily wooded area where there is also a steep bank and a stream. The pups love to play and explore, and while their attention is distracted, my friend hides. Eventually the puppies miss him and start searching for him. My friend always ends by returning to his car. After a certain amount of practice the puppies learn to return to the place from which they started.

This German Shorthaired Pointer has located some game. Photo of Ch. Adam Von Fuehrerheim, owned by Robert McKowen, courtesy of Nancy Conrad.

If a puppy has been properly trained, it is almost impossible for it to become lost. Teaching a dog to follow a trail is important for all hunting dogs, particularly in the case of American Foxhounds. A dog of this breed may follow a red fox long after its owner has given up from exhaustion. If the dog's master leaves his coat or the dog's blanket at the spot where the dogs were cast loose, he or she should be able to leave the area for a few hours and return later to find the dog lying on the coat or blanket, waiting.

Sportsmen, particularly those hunting quail in widely separated coveys, often follow Pointers and Setters on horseback. It will be necessary for your dog to learn to take orders from you while you are on a horse as well as to learn to heel (not too close) to a horse's hooves. A properly trained dog should heel whenever the circumstances necessitate the command. (The method for teaching a dog to heel is discussed in Chapter 14.)

When you are in the process of teaching your dog to hunt for quarry, the first rule is never to lie to your dog. It is important for your dog to find the game early on, so that it understands the purpose of the training. As time goes by, the dry periods (those during which it will not find game) can be extended so that the dog develops endurance, but it should never become discouraged by not eventually finding the game.

Two examples immediately come to mind. Once I was permitted to watch some dogs that belonged to custom officials being trained to sniff luggage for drugs and guns. The trainers always included the evidence in one piece of baggage. This meant that the dogs always had a find. On accomplishing the task, they received a great deal of praise. Consequently they never gave up when hunting for the specific materials they had been trained to find.

I once owned a young English Springer Spaniel that I hoped would qualify for field trials or would at least be a good general hunting dog. During the time the dog was a puppy, it was very ill. Because of my concern for the dog's health, I kept its training lessons very short. I believed this would be practical when I trained it with actual game. (An English Springer Spaniel might hunt for only fifteen minutes at a field trial and flush two pheasants.) Unfortunately, this dog never made it as a hunting or field trial dog. If it could not find game in seventeen minutes, it simply quit and came to heel. I think I made a mistake in never lengthening the time between flushes. In a sense I had lied to the dog.

It can be difficult to break your dog of the habit known as *hard mouth*. Dogs often seize a felled bird or rabbit and crush it between their jaws or start to chew it. Before taking a dog into the field, you should first teach it to carry an object, such as a piece of wood, in its mouth. In order to teach your dog not to bite down on retrieves, attach some feathers or pheasant wings to the object. This will also familiarize your dog with the smell of game.

This Vizsla is trailing pheasant in a special game area. Photo of Szekeres' Kis Bohoc, owned by Max E. Holland, courtesy of Burnt Hills Boarding Kennel.

Gun-Shy Dogs

I have known dogs that were gun-shy, noise-shy, or storm-shy; they ran whenever they heard a loud sound. If a dog has all these problems, the situation is probably hopeless.

Few professionals will take the time to try to cure such a dog, and many do not want to risk failing. To overcome shyness in a dog, the owner or handler should try to instill confidence in it through regular training and rewarding it for improvement. This is most effective when the dog is still a puppy.

Friends who have well-trained hunting dogs can be helpful in teaching your dog not to be gun-shy. Have them include your dog in a stakeout with a group of their trained dogs. A dead bird is thrown into the air, and a gun is fired. At the sound of the gun, the trained dogs will instantly start barking and struggling to make the retrieve. One by one they are released, and as your dog watches, it will get the urge to participate in the excitement. Eventually the sound of the gun will be a signal to your dog that a splendid game has begun.

Another way to try to cure your noise-shy or gun-shy dog is to fast it for thirty-six hours. Next, place the dog's food dish far enough away so that the dog cannot see it. Then fire a small cap pistol, and allow the dog to go to its food dish. After this, feed your dog lightly and only once a day. In that way the dog will be hungry when the gun is fired, and the sound will become a welcome signal that food is close by. After several weeks, change the procedure. Make the dog fast for thirty-six hours, but this time place the dog in a sitting position. Set the food dish at your side and then shoot the cap gun, which is the signal for the dog to come to you for the food.

Once the dog accomplishes this act, you can fire noisier guns. By repetition the dog learns that the sound of the gun always means food. The next step is to put the dog among other thoroughly trained dogs in a stakeout. You should notice a markedly reduced fearfulness in your dog in response to loud noise or gunshots.

Swimming

A hunting dog will have to swim at some time in its life. It makes no difference whether the dog is a waterfowl Retriever, a Spaniel, or a trailing Hound. Many people believe that dogs enjoy swimming and will begin to swim automatically if they are put into water. But this is not necessarily true; many dogs refuse to go into the water.

A noted trainer of Retrievers has often remarked that the first thing he must determine is whether a dog can swim. It is easy enough to teach a puppy to swim, but with an older dog the task is more difficult. On two occasions I have taught adult Retrievers to swim. Both dogs appeared to

A hunting dog should know how to swim in case it ever needs to cross a stream or retrieve an object in water. Photo courtesy of William and Carole Mader.

like the water, but both might have drowned within minutes if I had not trained them.

When I was actively involved in breeding English Springer Spaniels, I would often take seven- or eight-week-old puppies to a creek. I did this even in the winter unless the creek was completely covered with ice. I would find a place where there were shallow riffles and start walking across the stream. It was interesting to watch the puppies' responses. Some would follow without hesitation; others would run back and forth along the bank of the stream, eventually finding the courage to enter the water; others would absolutely refuse to go into the water. I was able to determine from this test which puppies would willingly retrieve in water and which would object to cold water.

There are a number of ways to encourage a puppy to enter water. You can pick the puppy up, carry it across the stream, set it down on the other side, and return to the original side. Chances are that the puppy will follow. If it does not follow, start walking toward home. Most likely the puppy, not wanting to be left alone, will decide to cross the stream.

Or you can attach a training cord to the puppy, enter the stream, gently pull the puppy closer to you, and continue to move toward the opposite bank. These lessons should be continued until the time when you are able to take the puppy into water that is deep enough for it to swim in.

It is wise not to make the lessons too long, particularly in cold weather, when a puppy will become cold quite quickly. A puppy has a thick, almost waterproof coat until it is nearly five months old; but no matter how young it may be, there is always the possibility it will become chilled. After a puppy has had its swimming lesson, you can either dry it with a towel or see that it receives adequate exercise on land.

Your dog should feel comfortable around other animals, especially while it is being trained in field work. Photo of Ch. Caesar and friend, courtesy of Burnt Hills Boarding Kennel.

Conduct Toward Other Animals

One of the most important lessons to teach your dog is not to harm or molest farm animals. I shall never forget the time a friend and I, along with our dogs, went to ask permission of a farmer to hunt on his land. Three small kittens were playing in the barnyard. My friend's dog spotted the kittens and attacked and killed them without warning. This incident proves how important it is for a dog to be familiar with, not hostile to, all types of farm animals: cattle, sheep, pigs, goats, chickens, and so forth.

A training rope can be extremely helpful in teaching your dog to accept and respect farm animals. You should take your dog to a farm whose owner will permit you to give training lessons. Each time your dog has the urge to chase one of the animals, give a severe jerk to the rope and sternly say "No." The lesson may have to be repeated many times, but eventually the dog will lose interest in the animals to the point of ignoring them.

Hunting Experience

About twenty years ago I interviewed the owner of a national champion Coonhound, and he told me this story.

"I had a great bitch, and I bred her to the finest male Coondog that I could find. That bitch had seven pups. When my friends heard about it, they started coming around to see them. I had made up my mind not to sell any of those pups until I had fully tested them all. But those friends would come around with a bottle of moonshine, and we'd sit under the apple tree for a drink or two. They'd tell me what wonderful friends they had always been to me. So one by one they got my pups. All except the one nobody wanted. Well, that pup grew up to be the national champion, as you now know. What made him a champion? Mister, I'll tell you. That dog was on coon 365 days a year for nearly three years."

In the long run no dog becomes a great hunting dog until it has gained wide experience in the field under actual hunting conditions. If a dog is to become a good bird dog, it must spend many months gaining this experience. It has to work out wind scents and learn the habits of the game it is to hunt, whether quail, partridge, grouse, or pheasant. If your dog is a Foxhound, it must learn the tricks and habits of the wiliest of game animals. A Coonhound must learn to ignore foxes and opossums. A Coonhound that leads its owner through a dark swamp at night, stumbling over logs, falling into bogs and creeks, only to find that the quarry was a fox or opossum is a dog that is likely never to enter the hunting fields again.

The coon hunter must find an area where there are raccoons and where hunting them is permitted. (Coons cannot be killed during most of the year.) The dog must be praised and encouraged to bark when on scent. An owner might buy coons raised on a game farm to aid in teaching a dog to follow a coon trail. He or she might also allow the dog to kill an occasional coon to further strengthen the dog's urge to trail and kill wild coons. Hunters can lay trails using a sack filled with coon droppings, and they might also want to lay or find fox trails so that they can teach their dogs to ignore all trails except the raccoon's.

Field Trials

A field trial is a kind of competition in which a dog and its handler work as a team. Several judges evaluate a dog's performance and style in a number of tests related to hunting skills (such as retrieving game or following a game trail). Dogs can vie for championship points in AKC field trial competition or can participate in less formal field trials, with one or more breeds in competition.

There are approximately one thousand field trials each year in the United States, which attests to the popularity of this sport. Breeds for which field trials are held include Beagles, pointing breeds, Basset Hounds, Retrievers, English Springer Spaniels, Foxhounds, Coonhounds, and Dachshunds.

Beagle field trials are the largest single activity of the American Kennel Club, and they account for half of all the field trials held in this country. If you are interested in this kind of activity, join a field trial club, such as a Beagle club, or else an outdoor or sportsmen's club in your vicinity.

Field trial clubs usually have heavily fenced areas in which game is stocked. Often you and your puppy can tag along with a person who has a thoroughly trained dog, and the older dog can help your puppy. But do not spend too much time with other dogs; you will want your puppy to strike out on its own, not to be just a follower.

A majority of the bird dog (pointing breeds) trials are given under the rules of the Amateur Field Trial Clubs of America. Foxhound trials are given under the rules of the National Foxhunters Association, and Coonhound trials are under the rules of the United Kennel Club.

Happy hunting!

part four
GROOMING

Proper grooming will keep your dog healthy, attractive, and clean. Photo of Ch. Blu-N-Tan Shadow Magic, owned by Mr. & Mrs. Lambert G. Schneider.

chapter sixteen

Basic Bathing and Grooming Instructions

It is important to learn to groom your dog properly, making sure that it is clean, neat, and well kept, and that it conforms to the style for its particular breed. Also, for the sake of its health make sure your dog is bathed regularly and kept free from fleas or other parasites.

If you let your dog become smelly or unkempt, with mats in its coat or nails so long that it cannot stand properly, not only will the dog feel uncomfortable but you will be constantly apologizing for its appearance. People will tab you for what you are, an irresponsible dog owner who does not take the time to keep his pet clean and looking reasonably well. Regular grooming and brushing at least several times a week will keep your dog healthy, attractive, and clean.

If you attend a dog show at which there is a professional handler showing your breed, you might ask if he or she can recommend someone to whom you can take your dog for grooming. If you do take your dog to a professional, watch carefully so that you can learn to do the grooming properly yourself. You might need to take your dog back to the professional several times before you fully master the correct grooming procedure.

Your Dog's Bath

One hears all kinds of nonsense about bathing dogs. For example, a common bit of bad advice is that a puppy must not be bathed until it is a year old. Another is that a dog can be bathed only twice a year.

A washbasin can be filled with several inches of lukewarm water for your dog's bath. *H. Armstrong Roberts*

I once rescued a litter of puppies that, at ten days of age, were so covered with lice that not a single bit of flesh could be seen. These puppies were bathed with a liquid insecticidal soap, rinsed with warm water, then dried with an electric hair drier. Their mother was given the same treatment. No harm resulted either to her or to her puppies. To be sure, this was an extreme case. But if the puppies had not been bathed, they would probably have died from the louse infestation.

Every puppy owner will face those times when his or her puppy needs a bath even though it had one only yesterday. Although bathing your dog too often will tend to dry out the oils in its skin, too little bathing is equally unsatisfactory. A dog that is exposed to dirt, grime, or any parasites should be bathed more frequently than a dog that is not kept out-of-doors.

If you ask a half-dozen people how to bathe a dog, you may get a half-dozen answers. In most cases you can use a washbasin or washtub or even your own bathtub. However, I would recommend placing a rubber mat in the basin or tub so that your dog doesn't slip and so that its toenails will not scratch the surface. Finding a suitable place in which to wash a large dog, such as a St. Bernard or Great Dane, is not so simple. A convenient location would be a basement that has a floor drain.

For bathing your dog you can use your own kind of bath soap. If you prefer, you can choose from a variety of soaps and shampoos made especially for animals. Many are designed to kill fleas as well as to bathe a dog. All should be used with caution because some contain insecticides that can irritate the dog's skin.

Cake soap has some advantages because it can be lathered into a dog's coat with a scrubbing motion. For this purpose the mildly antiseptic deodorant soaps can be used occasionally. Some dermatologists say that continued daily use of such soaps by people can cause dermatitis and other skin irritations, but it is doubtful that twice-monthly use would be harmful to dogs.

Mild liquid shampoos penetrate the coat easily and lather quickly. Except for use on very dirty legs and feet, they are more than satisfactory. Cake soap and a scrubbing brush, if necessary, will do the job on the dog's legs and paws.

Washing Your Dog

When you are ready to bathe your dog — after you have carefully brushed and combed it — fill the tub with several inches of lukewarm water. Lift your dog into the tub, and wet it with a spray or simply by pouring water from a large cup through the dog's coat.

Soap your dog thoroughly, but take care not to get soap in its eyes or ears. *H. Armstrong Roberts*

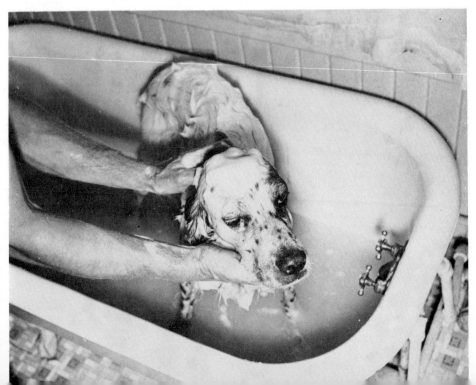

You should start washing your dog at the top of its neck just in back of the ears. Leave its face and ears until last because this is the part of the bath that the dog finds least pleasant. Soap your dog thoroughly, making certain the lather reaches through to its skin. If you do not have a spray with which to wash off the soap, fill a pan with lukewarm water, and pour the water over the dog while ruffling its coat to make sure all the soap is removed. Rinsing should be very thorough because it is most important not to leave a soapy film in your dog's coat.

Next, wash your dog's legs and feet. Lift each foot, and soap it thoroughly. Follow the same procedure for rinsing. Use a fresh pan of water if a spray is not available.

Work around your dog's rectum and prepuce with a soft sponge. Wash its tail carefully, soaping it well and then rinsing it with lukewarm water.

Take special care in washing a dog's ears. The outside flaps should be soaped lightly and rinsed clean. The same procedure should be followed for the insides of the ear flaps if the dog has folded-down ears. Be very careful not to get water in your dog's ears (many experienced people working in kennels plug a dog's ears with cotton so that water does not get into them).

Use a soft sponge to wash your dog's face, taking care not to get soap in its eyes. Many people put Vaseline or an oil, such as olive oil,

Lift each of your dog's paws and rinse it thoroughly.   *New York School of Dog Grooming*

around the dog's eyes before its bath so that any water inadvertently sprinkled near its eyes will fall away from its face.

At the end of the bath, wash out the dog's eye sockets with clear, warm water or with an artificial tear solution (the kind used by wearers of contact lenses is perfect for this purpose).

Drying Your Dog

Before lifting your dog out of the tub, you can remove a lot of water from its coat by using a fine comb. Wrap a large towel around the dog before taking it from the tub; otherwise it will shake itself and splash water everywhere.

Bathing destroys an insulating blanket of heat that dogs have stored in their coats. Therefore, after rubbing the dog as dry as possible, you might play with it awhile until it is warm once again. The same purpose can be accomplished by using a hair dryer or wrapping a dry towel around your dog, pinning it closed under your dog's belly. Be careful not to allow the dog to roll on rugs or in dust or grass until it is completely dry.

Bathing Your Dog at a Dog Show

At times it may be necessary to bathe your dog at a show, perhaps only an hour or two before it is to be judged. When this is the case, the bathing procedure is different. You will need a pail of warm water and a liquid shampoo of the no-rinse type. (Several such shampoos are made with dog shows in mind.) Use an ordinary washcloth to apply the shampoo.

Dry your dog off as much as possible with a towel. Follow this by using a drying powder or chalk, which can also be used to whiten white coats. Powder is preferred for use on breeds with short, smooth coats. Chalk, when used too often, tends to dry out the skin. Whichever you use, it must be thoroughly brushed out. The presence of any powder in the dog's coat when it is in the judging ring can cause its dismissal.

After a bath it may be necessary to restore your dog's coat luster by means of one of a number of coat dressings used for this purpose. Remember that the excess must be brushed out before a dog enters the show ring.

Early Conditioning for Grooming

Between the ages of six and fourteen weeks the puppy's automatic reflexes are being trained, and it seeks to adapt to its environment. This is the period for basic conditioning. What a puppy learns during this period will probably stay with it the rest of its life.

These are the basic lessons your puppy should learn that will prove invaluable when it is being groomed, treated by a veterinarian, or entered in a show:

To pose, as your dog would have to in a show ring, that is, to stand quietly in the position in which it is put by its owner.

To stand still on a table.

To lie quietly on a table. Older puppies of giant breeds should be taught to lie quietly on the floor or on a low bench.

To permit its teeth to be examined, its ears to be cleaned, and work to be done around its tail.

To permit its toenails to be filed, clipped, and shaped.

Again and again one hears dog owners complain that their dogs won't permit anyone to touch their ears or teeth, that they'll bite if anyone tries to work on their feet or tail. Others say that their dogs can't be forced to lie down, either on a table or on the floor. Quite apart from grooming and the show ring, imagine the problem confronting the veterinarian when such a dog is sick.

None of these things will occur if your puppy has been properly trained and conditioned when it is very young. Such training can begin by the time the dog is around six weeks old or as soon as it is purchased.

Care of Ears, Eyes, and Nails

Special care must be taken when you wash your dog's ears. Long-eared dogs, particularly heavy-coated dogs, such as Poodles and Spaniels, very often contract ear infections. The problem occurs because air circulation to the inner ear is cut off by the heavily furred inside ear flaps. To try to prevent such infections, clip the hair on the dog's inner ear flaps at least halfway down.

Earwax can be removed with a cotton-tipped safety swab. A paper stick, rather than a wooden or plastic one, is preferable. There are also preparations available at pet shops for softening earwax in dogs. Cleaning your dog's ears must be done with great care, or else serious irritation will result.

Long-eared dogs are prone to contract a rather severe infection caused by a bacterium known as *Escherichia coli*. This is usually an intestinal bacterium that requires an alkaline medium in which to live and reproduce. However, if an *E. coli* infection develops in a dog's ears, a few drops of white cider vinegar placed in the ear twice a day can cure the infection almost magically.

To keep your dog's eyes clean and free from foreign matter, wipe the corners of its eyes gently with cotton dabbed in warm water. If your dog has a mild eye discharge, try a few drops of boric acid. If the discharge does not clear up within a day or two, make an appointment with a veterinarian.

Some moderately to heavily coated dogs, such as Chow Chows and Golden Retrievers, suffer from entropion or trichiasis. Entropion is a disease in which the dog's eyelids turn inward. Trichiasis is a condition in which the eyelashes turn inward and brush against the eyeball. Both conditions are painful for a dog and cause weeping. If your dog has either condition, discuss the situation with your vet; an operation may be necessary to rectify the problem. Certainly it is unfair for any dog to go through life with these kinds of afflictions.

Whether or not you show your dog, its toenails should be trimmed. Veterinarians should not be expected to spend valuable time on this, so ask yours to show you how to do it. There are two types of nail trimmers: a guillotine clipper, whose blade slides along a track, and a heavy-jawed clipper, such as people use. Blood vessels can be seen in light-colored nails quite easily. Nails should be clipped back to this vessel, but *not* into it. If your dog has dark nails, proceed more carefully. If you cut into the quick, there are two simple ways to stop the bleeding: apply ferric subsulfate (Monsel's solution), or dab on a styptic agent such as iron sulfate powder, which you can obtain at a drugstore or pet supply shop.

Grooved pet nail files can be used to shape the dog's nails after they have been clipped. Press the nail with your thumb and finger to hold it steady when using the file. As a final touch the nails can be oiled to give them luster. Do this with one drop of a coat oil on your finger; this amount is sufficient to oil at least ten nails. If you use too much oil, you will make a greasy mess of the hair between your dog's toes.

Clipping and Trimming

Although the grooming of specific breeds will be discussed in detail in Chapters 17, 18, and 19, here are some general suggestions for clipping or trimming your dog properly. Actually many dog owners do not have the patience or know-how to do a good job of grooming their pets. So unless you are willing to devote the time and effort necessary to learning about the breed standard for your dog and the correct clipping and trimming techniques, the job should be left to a professional. That person may, in turn, be able to pass along some easy grooming techniques to you.

Study the standard of your breed (see Chapters 35 to 42). Note the correct placement of its ears. Use clippers to trim away excess hair on the skull so that both the shape of the skull and the proper set of the ears can be seen. Remember, a head covered with excessive hair spoils the look of the most important part of your dog.

This scene at a professional dog grooming school shows a poodle having the hair clipped from the pads of its feet and a terrier having mats removed from its coat. *New York School of Dog Grooming*

To prevent your dog from tracking mud or dirt into your home, trim the hair on its feet. This can be accomplished by pushing the hair between its toes upward and cutting it off. Trim around the foot to shape, and cut off the hair on the top. You may also trim the hair around the dog's pads.

In shaping the hair on the foot with scissors, be sure that the nails have been shortened first. If you do not shorten the nails first, you will be shaping the dog's foot to the nails, not to the toes. The foot will then appear to be too large, too flat, and possibly splayed.

You may need to trim excess hair from your dog's ears. Be certain to trim or clip the hair on the inside of the leather (flesh of the ear flap). This will make the ear hang closer to the dog's head. Also, clip the part of the neck that is in the area of the ear; this will allow as much air as possible to get into the ear, which is important in maintaining good ear health.

If your dog is a breed, such as an English Springer Spaniel or English Setter, whose body hair tends to get long and curly, it should be trimmed out. A very good instrument to use is the Duplex Dog Dresser, which will cut away the longer, curly hair, leaving a proper amount of flat, healthy hair. Essentially a safety razor with a handle, this instrument is also ideal for untangling mats that form in the undercoats of long-haired dogs and for removing burrs from a dog's coat. It catches and lifts out the burr; whereas a comb simply tangles the burr into more hair.

Feathering on the breast, neck, throat, belly, back of the legs, and tail needs to be combed out regularly to prevent mats. Before this hair becomes too long and unsightly, it should be shaped with scissors. Long-coated dogs, such as the Skye Terrier, Yorkshire Terrier, and Maltese, should be combed at least twice a week.

Study pictures of great show dogs of your breed, and try to shape your dog's coat in a similar manner. You could even shorten your dog's coat and still maintain the correct pattern for its breed. For example, you may not have the time and patience or even the knowledge to develop a flat, hard, show-quality coat on your Terrier. Nonetheless, you can cut its hair down to a reasonable length so that it does not look like a woolly mop.

There are two good tools you can use to groom rough-coated and wire-coated dogs. The first is an electric clipper. However, you must be very careful not to clip the hair too close to the skin; you don't want your dog to look scalped. The alternate and preferred method is shortening your dog's hair with a Duplex Dog Dresser. Scissors should be used on the forehead and on parts of your dog's neck under the ears.

Chapters 17, 18, and 19 will describe in greater detail the amount and type of grooming necessary for the different breeds — those that require little care, moderate care, and extensive care. Some of the finer points are necessary only if you plan to show your dog or simply want it perfectly groomed.

Grooming Equipment

There is a wide variety of grooming equipment for the family pet as well as for the show dog: combs, brushes, snub-nosed scissors, pet nail file and clippers, thinning shears, trimming shears, mat splitters, clippers, and a reasonably sized sturdy grooming table. Owners of dogs that require little grooming attention do not need this much equipment, of course; a brush, snub-nosed scissors, nail clipper and file would suffice. However, proper grooming of breeds that need moderate to extensive grooming care and of dogs that will be entered in shows requires more grooming tools and attention. Here's what to look for when purchasing this equipment.

Today most combs are either nickel- or chrome-plated. Whichever you buy is a matter of personal preference only. Combs come in coarse, medium, or fine spacing. Some will be coarse-spaced at one end and medium-spaced at the other. As a rule these do not have handles. Combs with handles will have only one type of spacing.

A flea comb, which has ultrafine spacing, is useful in working with the undercoat on many breeds.

The type of brush you use is also a matter of choice. Some brushes are double: One side has wire pins; the other side has fiber bristles. Pin brushes

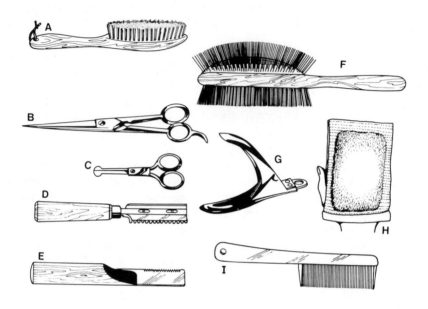

Basic grooming equipment: A) bristle brush; B) scissors; C) snub-nosed scissors; D) Duplex dog dresser; E) stripping knife; F) combination slicker and bristle brush; G) nail clipper; H) hound glove; I) comb.

are excellent for use on damp coats. Grooming gloves and slicker brushes have their advocates. The so-called mink brushes are used by many Poodle fanciers.

A slant-tooth comb and a mat splitter are useful in straightening out tangled hair that is in the process of matting. The Duplex Dog Dresser, essentially a razor with a handle, is the best of all burr removers and can shorten the coat as well.

For hard-coated Terriers, a stripping comb is necessary to remove dead hair and stimulate the growth of new hair. Both a dull-blade, coarse stripping comb, and one that is sharper and finer are useful for this purpose. Fingerstalls, such as those used by bookkeepers, also come in handy in grooming Terriers; they also keep your fingers from getting sore.

Unlike a stripping comb, which removes dead hair, clipping merely shortens a dog's hair. However, a dog owner who does not wish to go through the long process of using a stripping comb on a wire-coated dog may choose to clip it instead. But keep in mind that the effect is not the same and that wire-coated show Terriers are not clipped.

Shedding

Here is some advice on how to avoid the problems that result when your dog sheds and its hair clings to clothes, upholstery, or rugs. The best solution is to massage your dog's skin with your fingers, stroking from head to tail with the palms of your hands. The massaging loosens the bristles in its coat so that you can remove them. After you are finished, brush your dog so that oil is brought to the surface of its coat.

Another kind of shedding problem occurred with my Curly-Coated Retriever, which has a genetic thyroid disease that has left nearly half its body bare. Dense curls remain around its head and neck, but in some areas, its hair has grown back straight. The shedding problem is steady and severe. I use two grooming tools on this dog: a mink brush or comb on its straight hair and a regular comb with average-spaced teeth on its heavy curls. I then gently massage places where the skin is nearly bare and follow with a light brushing.

I have also found that a mink brush works well on the long, silky hair of my Borzoi. Long-coated dogs, such as Belgian Sheepdogs and Shetland Sheepdogs, also benefit from finger massaging, hand rubbing, combing, and brushing.

Anal Glands

Dogs the size of Cocker Spaniels and smaller sometimes suffer from anal gland impaction. Although it is not as common in the larger breeds, almost any dog can have this problem, especially fat and lazy dogs. It is my experience that a dog that suffers an impaction will probably have new impactions periodically.

A dog's anal glands may need to be emptied occasionally, especially if the dog drags its rectum along the floor, continues to lick the area, or has a strong odor. The veterinarian can do this for you when you take your dog for its annual visit. Or you can empty the glands yourself. To do this, locate the glands just above the rectum; then squeeze them, and remove the excretion with a paper towel. But be sure to ask your vet to show you the correct procedure first, before you try it yourself.

chapter seventeen
Breeds that Are Easy to Groom

There are many breeds that require little grooming except for occasional whisker and nail trimming and, of course, bathing. They are listed here in the order of their classification by groups.

Sporting Breeds: Pointer, German Shorthaired Pointer, Labrador Retriever, Vizsla, Weimaraner

Hound Breeds: Basenji, Basset Hound, Beagle, Bloodhound, Black and Tan Coonhound, Smooth Dachshund, American Foxhound, English Foxhound, Greyhound, Harrier, Ibizan Hound, Rhodesian Ridgeback, Whippet

Working Breeds: Akita, Australian Cattle Dog, Belgian Malinois, Boxer, Bullmastiff, Smooth Collie, Doberman Pinscher, Great Dane, Mastiff, Rottweiler, Shorthaired St. Bernard, Pembroke Welsh Corgi

Terrier Breeds: Border Terrier, Bull Terrier, Smooth Fox Terrier, Manchester Terrier, Staffordshire Bull Terrier

Toy Breeds: Smooth-coated Brussels Griffon, Smooth Coat Chihuahua, Italian Greyhound, Miniature Pinscher, Pug

Non-Sporting Breeds: Boston Terrier, Bulldog, Dalmatian, French Bulldog, Schipperke

Miscellaneous Breeds: Australian Kelpie, Border Collie, Miniature Bull Terrier, Pharaoh Hound

The simple instruments that you can use to groom these breeds are a short-bristled fiber brush, wire-bristled brush, or a hound glove for polishing a short, smooth coat; snub-nosed scissors; nail clippers and nail file.

The snub-nosed or curve-bladed scissors should be used to trim your dog's whiskers. (To avoid accidents, do not use sharp-pointed scissors.) For showing, you will want eyebrows, cheek and muzzle whiskers trimmed as flat as possible on some of these breeds to give the head a "clean" appearance. Be very careful when trimming under the chin, however, as any nick or pull could cause irritation and possible infection. Some people claim that too close trimming under the chin may cause early graying or whitening in non-white dogs, but that has not been proven.

A dog with a very thin coat will probably need little grooming attention other than an occasional brushing or polishing and then a wiping with a dampened cloth. Certain smooth-coated breeds, such as the Pointer, Dalmatian, and Smooth Fox Terrier, have short, bristle hair and need to be groomed differently. Massage the dog's skin with your hands to loosen the bristles of its coat. Then rub it with the palms of your hands from its head to its tail, and finally rub the dog with a dampened cloth.

chapter eighteen
Breeds that Require Moderate Grooming

Grooming problems differ for different breeds. This is true for those requiring only moderate grooming as well as for those requiring more extensive care. However, because you can learn helpful hints if you study the grooming of breeds other than your own, you may want to read the instructions for the other breeds given in this chapter.

Some of the finer points of these instructions are addressed particularly to the owner who plans to show his or her dog or keep it perfectly groomed. Of course, all owners should want to keep their dogs in fairly good trim, and suggestions for this are given. An occasional touching up with a blunt-tipped scissors can definitely benefit a dog's appearance. For more heavily coated breeds, be sure to brush the coat vigorously each day if possible.

Sporting Breeds

German Wirehaired Pointer. The outer coat should be straight, harsh, and 1½ to 2 inches long. If it is longer, it should be trimmed slightly. If the dog is to be shown, bathe it several days beforehand. Do not rub the dog dry with a towel because this may fluff out the coat. If the dog is bathed at the show, fasten a towel around its body to keep its hair flat. Leave eyebrows and beard long. Trim away tail feathers and hair between the toes and between the pads.

Wirehaired Pointing Griffon.   Follow grooming instructions for the German Wirehaired Pointer. Do not remove the beard or eyebrows. Leave the hair on the tail. Trim the feet to show the arch of the toes.

Chesapeake Bay Retriever.   If you are preparing your dog for a show, bathe it three to four days before so that natural oil can be restored to its coat. Towel the dog after bathing to prevent its coat from curling. If the coat is more than 1½ inches long, trim it. Tail feathers should not be more than 1¾ inches long.

Curly-Coated Retriever.   After bathing the dog, especially if you are going to show it, rub its hair dry with a towel to stimulate curling. Trim away mats or any hair that has formed cords. Remove straggling hairs around the face.

Flat-Coated Retriever.   Do not trim away feathering. Towel the dog after its bath to keep its hair flat. Trim out excess hair from between its toes and between the foot pads. Trim away scraggly hair on the skull and ears.

Golden Retriever.   Keep heavy feathering on the front of the neck. The ruff may be thinned out to blend the neck into the shoulders and to prevent the dog from seeming short-necked or steep-shouldered. Tail feathering should be kept moderate to heavy and can be trimmed to make a pleasing triangular outline. Trim hair from between the toes.

American Water Spaniel.   Keep curls or waves on the feet. Leg curls can be shaped to round out at the dog's elbows and knees. Do not touch heavy tail feathering other than to shape it.

Brittany Spaniel.   Trim until there is very little hair on the front legs and belly and only slightly more fringe on the hindquarters. Remove straggling hair on the head. Clip the cheeks to give the appearance of a narrow skull and to permit the ears to lie flat. Thin the ruff hair so that the shoulders and neck blend. Trim the feet if necessary. Towel the dog after bathing to prevent the hair from curling.

Irish Water Spaniel.   Shape around the head with scissors and thinning shears. Trim directly under the ears with No. 10 blade clippers. Thin the ear hair so that the ears lie flat. If you are showing the dog, bathe it three or four days before. Lightly apply coat oil and rough comb. Use scissors to snip out any fuzz. Comb it out at the show. On a puppy, pluck the hair under the tail (it won't grow back). On an older dog, pluck or strip the hair three days before showing.

Hound Breeds

Borzoi.   If you are preparing a Borzoi for a show, bathe the dog three days ahead, using a nylon-bristle brush to work up a lather. A cream rinse will keep the hair soft and silky. Trim away any fuzz around the head and ears and any tufts below the hock joints. The nails should be trimmed short enough so that they do not quite touch the floor. Brush the coat with and against the grain.

Longhaired Dachshund.   Shape around the head with clippers, particularly on the cheeks and on the inside of the ears. Trim the feet to show the toe arch, and cut away the hair around the foot pads. If you are going to show the dog, bathe it a day or two in advance.

Norwegian Elkhound.   If the dog is being prepared for a show, shampoo it three or four days before. Silver gray color-rinse shampoo of the type used by women works well. Loose hair should be pulled out by hand. Do this carefully, otherwise the coat will appear blotchy. Follow the instructions for grooming the Siberian Husky.

Irish Wolfhound.   The long hair on the dog's front legs can be shaped and boxed (to give a straight, squared outline), as is done with Terriers. Trim the feet to a round pattern; trim out any scraggly hair, and shape the hair to make the feet look deep and even. Use a stripping knife from the eyebrows to the back part of the skull to even the head area. Trim the cheek hair to accentuate the length and narrowness of the skull. Occasionally eyebrows will need slight thinning.

Otter Hound.   Do not thin out the neck ruff; the neck should look somewhat short. Do not trim tail feathers, which should be thick. Leave some hair on top of the feet, but not so much that their outline is hidden. Trim around the feet with scissors to give a clean outline.

Saluki.   To prepare a black Saluki for a show, bathe the dog three to four days in advance. Bathe a Saluki of any other color one or two days before a show. Wash the external ears and the tail the day of the show. Tidy up the sides of the neck, the cheeks, and under the throat with clippers a week ahead. Cut away heavy feathering around the pads, but otherwise leave the feet alone.

Scottish Deerhound.   Follow the instructions for grooming an Irish Wolfhound. Leave hair under the chest to accentuate its depth.

Working Breeds

Alaskan Malamute. Follow the instructions for grooming the Siberian Husky.

Bernese Mountain Dog. If you are preparing the dog for a show, bathe and towel down its coat three days in advance. Use clippers on the cheeks and on the inner ear flaps so that the ears lie flat. Use thinning shears to mold the neck into the shoulders, taking care to follow the grain of the coat. Clean up the feet to accentuate the arch of the toes. Chalk and brush out white areas.

Rough Collie. Brush and comb the dog's coat once a week, brushing against the grain. Clip the nails every other week. Every other week trim the hind legs up to the hock joints, and trim around the ears. If the dog is to be shown, cut its nails the night before, and trim away the hair up to the hock joints and around the ears. Use a nylon hairbrush with stiff bristles that can get down deep to straighten the hair. Use a stripping comb to eliminate any curl from underneath the chin down to the throat. Thin out the hair on the cheeks with thinning shears. Chalk white areas. Trim whiskers at the show, brush out the chalk, clean out the eyes and ears, and brush the dog's coat against the grain.

German Shepherd Dog. If you are showing the dog, bathe it two to three days before the show. Then brush the coat twice daily to restore the hair's gloss. Clean out the dog's eyes and ears before entering the show ring. Trim whiskers at the same time.

Great Pyrenees. To prepare the dog for a show, bathe it three days in advance. Brush and comb the coat to flatten it. Thin hair on the cheeks and inner flaps of the ears. Clean up the feet to show the toe arches. Clean out the eyes and ears.

Newfoundland. If you are preparing the dog for a show, bathe it three days before. Thin or remove the longer hair below the neck on the chest or apron. Mold the hair slightly at the junction of the neck and shoulders, using thinning shears.

Long-haired St. Bernard. If the dog is thin, bathe it the day before a show so that the fluffed coat will make it look heavier. If the dog is heavy, dry clean its coat with a towel to keep the hair flat, or bathe it a week in advance. Trim the feet to a cat's-paw outline. Push up the hair between the toes, and cut it off. Use thinning shears to trim the hair over the cap of the ear and 2 inches down. Clip the hair on the inner flaps of the ears so that the ears lie flat against the head.

Samoyed.   For bathing, use a mild detergent. Dry with a blow dryer if possible. Some owners mix vinegar with the detergent, rub it into the coat and down to the skin, and then rinse the dog carefully. Then follow with a gentle shampoo. A vinegar rinse (4 tablespoons to 1 quart of water) restores hardness to the coat. If you are going to show the dog, bathe it two days ahead of time. Clip its face with a No. 10 blade a week before the show. Cut the hair away from the tops of the feet, from between its foot pads, and shape around the foot. Brush steadily, using a pin brush to remove the dead undercoat.

Shetland Sheepdog.   Follow the instructions for grooming the Rough Collie.

Siberian Husky.   After bathing the dog, allow it to shake the water out of its coat. The outer coat dries immediately. Keep the dog warm by wrapping it in a towel until the undercoat dries. Clip the whiskers, including those at the lip line. Trim out the excess hair at the eye corners and any ragged hair around the head and ears. Cut away the hair from between the foot pads and trim the ragged hair on the tops of the feet. Clear the eyes, and clean the teeth. Comb the coat and finish by going over it with a soft brush, working with the grain of the coat. Comb the tail, working against the grain to fluff it. Comb out the ruff to frame the muzzle and face. If you are going to show the dog, bathe it the night before.

Cardigan Welsh Corgi.   When bathing the dog, use a small amount of vinegar in the shampoo. Use a vinegar rinse (4 tablespoons to 1 quart of water) to restore hardness to the coat. If the dog is to be shown, bathe it a week ahead of time. Shape its face and head hair with a bristle brush to give the desired foxy appearance. If the occiput is prominent, leave the hair long at that point to cover it. Trim the feet to give them a rounded appearance. Clip away hair from between the pads.

Terrier Breeds

Australian Terrier.   If you are going to show the dog, bathe it a week before the show. Use a vinegar rinse (4 tablespoons to 1 quart of water) to restore hardness to the coat. Brush the coat carefully each day. Pluck the coarse, dead hair only. Use a slicker brush, but do not work down to the skin. Trim the feet to make them appear as small as possible. Never use clippers. Shape the hair slightly around the ears.

Cairn Terrier. This Terrier has a hard coat that is often allowed to grow fairly shaggy. The length of the coat is a matter of the owner's choice. For a showlike appearance, pluck the hair on the dog's ears to one third of the way down, and pluck out the dead hairs on the body. Trim the tail to resemble an inverted ice-cream cone. Smooth out the belly hair. Use scissors to shape the feet. Other grooming instructions are the same as those for the Australian Terrier.

Dandie Dinmont Terrier. Brush and comb the dog's coat daily. If you are preparing the dog for a show, bathe it one week ahead of time to allow the coat to regain moderate harshness. If the coat is naturally too wiry, bathe the dog the night before the show. Fluff up the topknot and ear points. Leave cheek hair untrimmed to accentuate the power of the jaw muscles.

Soft-Coated Wheaten Terrier. There is a rule in the breed standard for this dog that for show purposes the coat "may be tidied up merely to present a neat outline but may not be clipped, plucked or stylized." Despite this rule, these dogs are given some scissoring to give a correct outline. Ear fringes are usually cut away. The coat is fluffed out but shaped to give a level back.

Toy Breeds

Affenpinscher. The dog's coat should have a rough appearance, but some trimming may be necessary around the face. If the coat is too soft, silky hairs should be plucked. This requires a light but steady touch. A vinegar rinse (4 tablespoons to 1 quart of water) will help to restore harshness to the coat.

Long Coat Chihuahua. After bathing the dog, dry with a blow dryer or hair dryer. Trim the whiskers, and shape the hair around the skull and ears to give a clean appearance. However, the ears must have some fringe. Do not trim the neck ruff. The feet may be trimmed slightly to show the arched toes, but if the feet are flat, do not trim them. If you are going to show the dog, bathe it one day ahead of time.

English Toy Spaniel. This dog requires little grooming except for bathing, combing, and brushing. However, if you are going to show it, trim its whiskers on the day of the show. Use thinning scissors to remove scraggly hair at the junction of the ears and skull.

Japanese Chin. Although the Japanese Chin's coat is not as profuse as that of a Maltese or a Yorkshire, many of the tips on grooming those

breeds will apply to this breed. If you are going to show the dog, start
months ahead with grooming because the dog's profuse coat will need a lot
of attention.

Papillon.   Do not trim away ear fringes or tufts of hair growing
between the toes. After bathing the dog, fasten a towel around it to keep its
hair flat. Do not trim or thin the collarette or neck ruff. If you are showing
the dog, fluff out the tail plume by brushing the hair against the grain
before entering the ring.

Non-Sporting Breeds

Chow Chow.   Trim the hair under the tail and the long hair on the
dog's belly to give an even appearance, that is, with no tuck-up. Trim the
hair around the feet, and remove the tufts between the toes by pushing them
up and cutting them off. A wire pin brush can be used to keep mats from
forming. Use a soft-bristle brush to brush the dog's coat, working against
the grain of the coat. Clear the eyes of matter, and dry the hair under the
eyes if they have a tendency to weep. If the dog is bathed before a show,
follow the instructions for the Samoyed.

Keeshond.   Follow the general grooming instructions for the Siberian
Husky, Samoyed, and Norwegian Elkhound. Keeshonden usually need
somewhat less grooming, but the tail plume should be fluffed out for best
appearance.

Miscellaneous Breeds

Cavalier King Charles Spaniel.   Follow the grooming instructions for
the English Toy Spaniel.

Spinone Italiano.   Trim and shape the hair on its feet. Tidy about the
head to show the shape of the skull and proper ear placement. Some tidying
around the vent may be necessary.

chapter nineteen

Breeds that Require Extensive Grooming

This group of dogs requires more extensive grooming care than those discussed in Chapters 17 and 18. It is important to brush longer-coated dogs carefully every day in order to keep them attractive and neat-looking. Many of the grooming details in this chapter are necessary only if you plan to show your dog or want it to look as beautifully groomed as a show dog. However, even if you want your dog to have only a moderately neat appearance, these breeds still require frequent attention.

It will be helpful to study the grooming instructions in this chapter for breeds other than your own in order to pick up additional pointers. Seek professional assistance if you feel that you do not have the time or the know-how to master the proper grooming techniques for the breed of dog you own.

Sporting Breeds

English Setter. Clip around the skull and the top of the ears for the first third of their length. Clip around the throat and front of the neck to about halfway between the jawbone and the forward point of the chest. Clip the hair on the sides of the neck down into the shoulder area and underneath the ear flaps. Clip the hair at the top of the neck down to the top of the shoulders; then mold the hair on the neck into the shoulders, using thinning shears and cutting with the grain of the coat.

Brush the coat daily with a soft-bristle brush or with a hound glove. Thin out the scraggly hair growing on top of the ears, particularly at the junction with the skull. Use thinning shears to remove scraggly body hair.

Trim hair from the feet. Shove up the tufts between the toes, and cut them off. Cut around the feet to shape them. Do not touch the leg feathers, other than to brush and comb them lightly. Leave hair under the chest and belly. Trim the hair from the hock joints to the feet. Tail feathers should be in the shape of an inverted pennant, about 8 inches long at the junction of the tail and body.

If you are preparing the dog for a show, bathe it the week before, and fasten a towel around its body so that the hair will dry flat or in a slight wave. If the dog must be bathed at the show, towel it dry afterward. Grooming for a show should begin two months beforehand.

Gordon Setter. Most instructions for grooming the English Setter apply to the Gordon Setter. However, because Gordons seldom have as much feathering, what they do have should be guarded carefully. Trim the top of the ears to accentuate the placement of the ears opposite the eyes. Keep the cheeks and inner flaps of the ears trimmed sufficiently so that the ears will lie close to the face. Do not leave heavy, scraggly hair at the junction of the neck and shoulders, particularly on the sides. Mold the hair on the neck into the shoulders by clipping. Then, if you will be showing the dog, use thinning shears to give it a neat appearance.

Irish Setter. See the general grooming instructions for the English and Gordon Setter. For Irish Setters that are going to be shown, the first clipping should be at least three months beforehand. Keep the dog out of the sun to prevent bleaching. Clipping should be done far enough in advance so that the clipped areas will regain their natural color. After that, trimming should be done with thinning shears to prevent the lighter color from showing through. If the tips of the hair show bleaching just before the show, use the Duplex Dog Dresser to snip off the ends, but do this very carefully to prevent the color of the coat from appearing blotchy.

Clumber Spaniel, English Cocker Spaniel, Field Spaniel, Sussex Spaniel, Welsh Springer Spaniel. If the dog is to be shown, see the instructions for show preparation of the English Springer Spaniel. A special note on the English Cocker Spaniel: A modern tendency is to trim these dogs Cocker-style. This is wrong and should be discouraged. Some people leave the dog's feet covered with hair. However, the feet should be cleaned to show the arch of the toes and shaped to prevent the appearance of flat feet. Trim any unruly hair in the coat.

American Cocker Spaniel. American Cockers are shown with hair reaching close to the floor or, in come cases, touching the floor. Although this is a contradiction of the breed standard (which says that excessive coat

An Irish Setter's coat should be brushed daily with a soft-bristle brush. *New York School of Dog Grooming*

will be penalized), it is the way the exhibitors choose to have the breed shown.

This practice would be impractical for a house pet because its long hair would probably become tangled and matted easily and pick up dirt both indoors and outdoors. You and your Cocker Spaniel will be happier if you clip its body fur to 1 inch or slightly less in length. Also cut away excess feathering from the legs and feet. Regardless of how meticulous you are in clipping, your dog's coat will have to be checked regularly for mats on the legs, lower throat, and chest.

If you show your dog, grooming should start several months ahead cf time. Use a fine-blade clipper. Work against the grain of the coat, trimming the hair from the breastbone all the way under the chin, under the ears and on the sides of the head to the corners of the eyes, and to the back corners of the mouth.

On both the inside and outside of the ears, clip against the grain from where the ear fold ends to the junction of the ears and the head. Then clip from the inside corners of the eyes down the cheeks to the nose. Clip the area at the top of the nose, working against the grain.

Hold the ear up. Use clippers to go down the seam and side of the neck almost to the elbow. Use thinning shears to make a gentle, rounded curve from the stop to the back of the skull. Many fanciers of the breed leave long eyebrow hairs.

Hold up the tail and trim down the rump, using thinning shears, working with the direction of the coat, never against it or across it. Also use these shears to blend the hair on the neck and shoulders together.

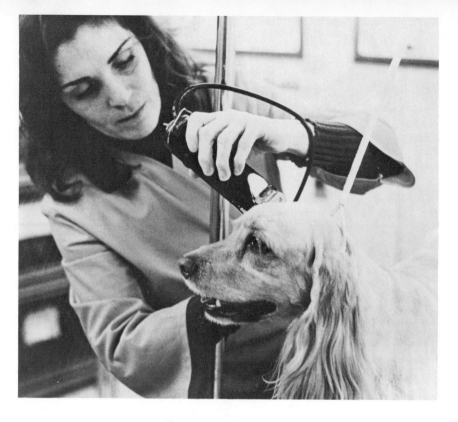

Carefully trim the hair on both the inside and outside of a Cocker Spaniel's ears. *New York School of Dog Grooming*

Clip around the vent and to the point of the tail. Round off the outline of the feet, going as close to the nails as possible, but leave hair on top of the feet. This helps to hide flat or splayed feet.

Some Cocker owners clip the hair on the dog's back and partially down its sides to the widest point of the ribs, using a medium or coarse clipper head. If this is done several months in advance of a show, the hair grows back slowly and can be shaped as it does. If this system is not used, it may be necessary to use thinning shears to keep the hair from growing curly. Feathering that touches the floor should be trimmed slightly to prevent this. Do not trim the breeches hair, but keep it clean.

English Springer Spaniel. Clip the hair around the head and neck with a medium clipper blade. Mold the hair on the neck into the shoulders. If the body coat is too profuse, clip the dog all the way to the end of its tail. Clip down the sides of the body, but leave the hair gradually longer from the midpoint of the ribs down. Under the chest, the hair should be long enough to square off the body. Because the English Springer Spaniel is a Sporting Dog, too much coat is objectionable. Leave the feathering on the underside of the tail.

As the coat grows back, eliminate any rough spots with thinning shears. Work the coat with a hound glove or soft brush that will not break the hairs. Clip away the hair on top of the feet and between the pads. Push up tufts between the toes, and cut them off.

If you are going to show the dog, trimming should begin at least two months in advance. Bathe the dog two or three days before the show. Wrap a towel around the dog so that its hair will dry flat or slightly waved. White areas should be chalked, then brushed out just before the dog enters the ring.

If you are preparing the dog for a show, begin two months beforehand: Clip the hair on the dog's ears about one third the length of the ear. As show time approaches, use thinning shears to keep out straggling hair at the junction of the ears and skull. Keep the hair on the inside flaps of the ears fairly short. Allow a gradual lengthening of the hair from the top to the bottom of the ear flap. Just before taking the dog into the show ring, comb out the ear fringes, and shape them nicely with scissors.

Hound Breeds

Afghan Hound. Afghans are not supposed to be trimmed, but many are. The hair on the neck and loins is shortened to give more even lines. The Afghan's coat should be oiled once or twice a week, if the dog

A slicker brush is being used to disentangle any mats before this Afghan is bathed. *New York School of Dog Grooming*

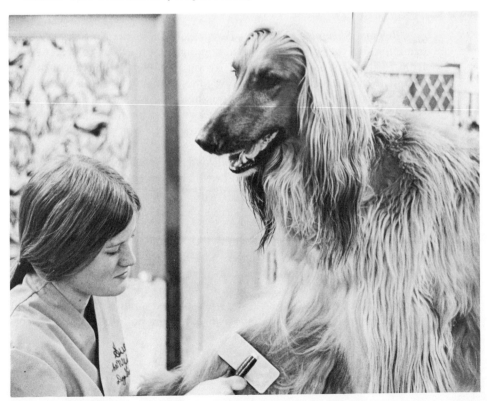

is being prepared for a show, to prevent it from breaking. A snood is sometimes put on the dog's head to keep the ear hair from breaking.

Brush the hair on the feet to prevent mats from forming. If there is excessive hair between the toes and on the pads, it should be clipped off. If you are going to show the dog, the toenails should be clipped every other week.

Use a cream rinse when you bathe the dog. Brush your dog carefully with a soft brush.

Wirehaired Dachshund. You should work with a Wirehaired Dachshund from the time it is weaned, to accustom it to having its hair plucked and stripped. If you do this, your dog will have a tight, short, uniform coat.

The best coat comes from constant care to keep the hairs from growing too long. If the dog was not stripped when very young, a complete stripping may be necessary every six months. It should take about six hours to strip the average Wirehaired Dachshund by hand, which is the preferred way. It will require four to six weeks for the coat to come into good shape. Then, if you show your dog, work with the coat every two or three days, and not less than once a week. Keep the dog's pads clean, and bathe the dog the day before a show.

Working Breeds

Belgian Sheepdog, Belgian Tervuren. These dogs need very little trimming, but they do need constant combing and brushing to prevent mats from forming. Work from the tail forward, lifting the hair and brushing against the grain with a pin brush. At times, a medium-toothed steel comb can be used. For mats that form on the legs, use special mat-softening shampoos and mat splitters. Simply cut away mats on the inside of the legs. Break up the other mats; if you do not, the dog's coat will have a blotchy appearance.

Some slight shaping on the skull and at the base of the ears may be necessary. The feet seldom need to be touched except for nail trimming. If you are showing the dog, bathe it a day or two ahead of time. Brush to restore the coat's sheen.

Bouvier des Flandres. Follow the grooming instructions for the Australian and Cairn Terriers unless a harder coat is desired. For a harder coat, the dog should be stripped down, according to the same procedures used for the Wirehaired Dachshund or some of the wire-coated Terriers. The legs can be boxed (to give a straight, squared outline) to accentuate the bone and shaped so that weak elbows or knees are not prominent. The coat should be heavy on the legs. Shape the foot to show roundness. Clip between the toes if tufts are sufficient to spread the toes. After bathing the dog, use a vinegar rinse (4 tablespoons to 1 quart of water). Do not touch the rough coat on the ears.

Briard.   Brush the dog's coat carefully to prevent mats from forming in the undercoat. Brush so that the eyebrows do not lie flat, but arch upward and out in a curve over the eyes. Trim the feet to a round outline. Use a vinegar rinse (4 tablespoons to 1 quart of water) after bathing the dog to restore the outer coat's harshness. Box the hair on the front legs to give the impression of heavy bone.

Giant Schnauzer, Standard Schnauzer.   Start plucking your dog's coat when the dog is four to six weeks of age. Your dog will become accustomed to it, and its coat will never get as woolly and silky as the coat of a dog that is not plucked until it is seven or eight months old. If you completely strip the coat, about three months are required for it to grow to perfect show condition.

During the final month before a show, pluck out the long guard hairs and silk. Avoid a skinned condition or appearance. The coat must appear rough and standoff. The hair on the front legs can be boxed. Trim the feet to accentuate roundness and strongly arched toes. Bathe a week before the show, then pluck out any ffuzz that appears during the week.

Kuvasz.   After bathing the dog, fasten a towel around its body to keep the hair down. When the hair dries, it should be wavy on the sides. The longer hair on the neck and croup should stand off slightly more and can be dampened and shaped later. Bathing should be done three or four days before a show. Trim the feet to show strongly arched toes. To restore the coat's gloss, chalk the dog thoroughly, then brush out the excess. Trim the tail to form an inverted pennant form. (See instructions for grooming the English Setter.)

Komondor, Puli.   The Puli can be shown either with a combed out coat or a corded coat. When it reaches two years of age, the Komondor must have a corded coat. Cords require no care except for bathing.

The center of the cord consists of a straight guide hair surrounded by hairs from both the undercoat and the outer coat. Cording begins when the dog is four to eight months of age, when the hair has reached sufficient length and density. Separate the coat into fairly large tassels, and allow the dead undercoat to fall out. If the hair starts to mat, use a mat splitter, and cut from the skin outward. Do not brush or comb the coat. The dog may be bathed when necessary, but a corded coat is easily kept clean because dirt does not enter the cords.

In grooming the combed out coat, use a slant-tooth comb. Lift the hair and work from the feet up and from the tail forward. A slicker brush can be used afterward. If you are going to show the dog, reverse the process to fluff out the coat. Bathe the dog a day before the show. With a combed-out coat, daily grooming is a must; otherwise mats will develop.

Old English Sheepdog. The secret of grooming an Old English Sheepdog is daily care. The dog should be brushed and combed out each night without fail. Use both wire and bristle brushes, and finish with a steel comb. Always comb and brush with the grain of the coat, never against it. Combing the coat after you have groomed it will fluff out the hair.

If you let the coat go for a few days, mats will tend to form. You can break these up by separating the hairs with your fingers. In case of truly serious mats, you can use a mat splitter. Cut through the center of the mats, always from the skin outward. Then break up these smaller mats with your fingers. The Old English Sheepdog needs little grooming in the way of barbering except for the feet. Press the hair down; then cut around the foot to shape it, but do not let the nails show.

Bathe the dog with a gentle shampoo. Use a Turkish towel to dry the dog. When the coat is almost dry, comb it gently until it is thoroughly dry and fluffed out. The dog can be bathed the night before a show.

Wire-coated Dogs

Most of the dogs discussed in this section are Terriers. They are the *Airedale Terrier, Wire Fox Terrier, Irish Terrier, Lakeland Terrier, Miniature Schnauzer, Norwich* and *Norfolk Terriers, Scottish Terrier, Sealyham Terrier,* and *Welsh Terrier.*

Owners of a Standard or Giant Schnauzer, Bouvier des Flandres, Wirehaired Dachshund, Wirehaired Pointing Griffon, or rough-coated Brussels Griffon can also learn a great deal about the care of their dog's coat by studying this section.

The breeder, owner, or handler can often do a far better job of producing a truly hard wire coat than a professional groomer can. The reason is that he or she can work on the dog's coat from early puppyhood, whereas the professional may not get the dog until it is mature and then may not have it long enough to do a perfect job.

It is possible to give only the rudiments of successful grooming here. Experience and competence, plus a true eye for your dog's breed, must do the rest. To see the final results of how show dogs are groomed, you should attend dog shows in your area and watch and listen in order to pick up pointers.

Although some people do not care whether their dog's coat is neatly groomed or woolly and disheveled, a knowledgeable owner will want his or her dog to be properly groomed. Therefore, get your dog used to being plucked while it is still young.

An owner should start grooming a wire-coated puppy when it is three or four weeks old. By that time small tufts of hair will begin to appear around its knees and throughout its coat. Plucking out the long hairs from a wirehaired dog's coat removes the dead hair roots and allows a new undercoat to grow out. Clipping will not produce the same effect on a dog's coat and is not used for most show Terriers, but it is a quicker method and will keep your dog's coat looking neat. If you have plucked your puppy's coat since it was small, allow about three months for its new coat to be ready.

One method of plucking a wirehaired dog's coat is with the thumb and fingers. This is the way preferred by people who take the time to do a careful job. If you rub your thumb and fingers with resin or chalk, you will be able to grip the dog's hair easier. Pull each small tuft of hair with a sharp, upward jerk. The dog should experience only a slight discomfort. Some people use bookkeepers' fingerstalls to keep their fingers from getting sore.

You can also groom Terriers with a stripping knife. Hold the knife in the palm of your hand with your thumb placed next to the edge of the blade. Press the blade against a small tuft of the dog's hair, and with your thumb held firmly against the blade, pull sharply.

Early grooming will indicate how fast your puppy's coat grows and whether it grows faster in some areas than in others. If young dogs are plucked from early puppyhood, they seldom (if ever) develop the very heavy, shaggy coat seen on some unkempt wirehaired dogs. As a result these dogs will always be easier to groom than those who were not plucked until they were at least a year old.

What if you have purchased a dog that is more than a year old and you want either to enter it in shows or to keep it in a showlike condition? If the dog has not been plucked before, it will take about six months with this kind of grooming for its undercoat to grow out to show quality.

You can get even better results if you strip the dog during its shedding periods, when it is casting off dead coat, which happens approximately every six months. With many of the wire-coated breeds, the dog is plucked practically naked, oiled, and then given a blanket coat to keep it warm until its new coat has grown.

After you have stripped the dog's coat, keep working on it and shaping it. By shaping I mean that you can allow it to grow thicker or keep it shorter as needed. For example, if your dog is swaybacked, you could allow the hair on its back to get thicker. Or you might have to pluck the cheek hair several times for it to be the correct length for a show because the hair in that area tends to grow quite shaggy rather quickly.

The hair on the neck, shoulders, and hindquarters, which also tends to grow rapidly, should be kept short. But proceed carefully so that you remove only the amount of hair you want to. Brush these areas regularly.

Do not forget to remove the hair on the inner flaps of the dog's ears. If the dog is to be shown, this should be done three to four days before the judging so that your dog is comfortable and has gotten used to the plucking. Otherwise the dog may not hold its ears properly when in the ring.

When working and shaping the dog's coat, work on one area for a few minutes; then stand back and survey your work, studying the dog from different angles. Only in this way can you achieve perfect balance, with all parts of the dog flowing into each other as they should. This is particularly important in shaping the hair on the face, skull, ears, and neck.

If showing, begin some months ahead of a show to cut the dog's nails back. Thereafter, file them a little twice a week.

To gain perfect coat bloom, many owners oil a dog's coat occasionally; some use just pure water to dampen it. The method used by an owner varies with the breed of dog, and styles change from area to area and year to year.

The grooming instructions for several breeds vary slightly from those I have just outlined, so here are some special hints for them.

For Scottish Terriers strip their legs, underbody, and tail first. Six weeks later, strip the loins, sides, and the back from withers to tail. In another three weeks, pluck the back of the neck and shoulders. Then days later, pluck the head, ears, throat, front of the neck, and under the tail.

Some Scottie owners use clippers for around the head and throat and on the underside of the neck. This is quicker than hand plucking but does not do quite as good a job. A Scottie's ears can be made to look smaller and set higher by leaving tufts of hair in front of them.

Many Scottie breeders believe that a Scottie should never be entirely stripped or that it should be stripped only once in its show career. Some owners of West Highland White Terriers feel the same way. They believe that total stripping tends to bring out cream-colored hair.

In both breeds, when complete stripping is not used, the coat must be worked constantly. Fuzz, ragged stray hairs, and dead hair must be removed two or three times a week.

The owner of a West Highland White Terrier must be careful not to take away too much facial hair. Facial hair contributes to the breed's distinctive appearance. Daily shaping of facial hair for two weeks before a show is necessary for it to be just right. Both Scotties and Westies should have their tails shaped to resemble an inverted cone.

Scissored Terriers

The **Bedlington Terrier** and **Kerry Blue Terrier** are groomed chiefly with scissors. Daily trimming and molding are necessary for these breeds.

Clip the hair on 3 to 4 inches of the tail, starting at the tip of the tail, and then do the underside; cut the balance of the tail hair gradually longer until it blends into the body. Leg hair should be combed outward at right angles to the ground, then cut to the desired length.

In most cases the hair can be combed over most of the legs and body into ridges either horizontal or perpendicular to the ground, depending on the body area. The ridges are then shortened. When the coat is fluffed out, no ridges will appear.

Clip the hair on the dog's ears, cheeks, under the jaw, and the throat. Comb the skull hair into a central peak, then trim. The topknot is cut so that it blends into the sides of the head.

Some breeders prefer to singe the hair to shorten and mold it. A patented singer is available at some pet stores. When used with care, it can do a good job, and it is a great time-saver.

The hair around the skull should be clipped so that it lies in flat waves. Clipping the cheek hair seems to give added length to the skull. The hair on the ears, both inside and out should also be trimmed. Gradually blend the hair on the back part of the skull and neck into the hair at the shoulder line by using thinning shears. Remember to cut with the grain of the coat.

The body hair should be 2 inches long. Clever groomers vary this slightly according to the dog. For example, if your dog has a shallow, thin chest, leave the hair slightly longer along the sides and under the chest. Trim away elbow tufts, and scissor closely under the tail to give a flattish look.

Skye Terrier

The Skye Terrier does not quite fit into any classification; it is neither a hard-coated nor a scissored dog. Some owners say that the Skye is the easiest of breeds to groom, although its coat does need careful and constant attention.

Oil the coat of your Skye occasionally to promote growth and to prevent breakage of the hairs. Keep its coat looking neat and clean. Take out mats and tangles by hand; do not comb or cut them out. Use nylon and slicker brushes on the dog's coat. Shape the hair on its feet with a scissors, and remove the hair from around the pads and between the toes.

Use the end tooth of a coarse-toothed comb to part the Skye's hair, first from the back of the skull to the tail, then from the back of the skull to the nose. The hair on the ears should fall forward in a natural manner.

Toy Breeds

Maltese.   A Maltese should be groomed with a soft-bristle brush. Part its skull hair evenly down the middle, and extend the part down the dog's back to its tail. The long hair will fall naturally down its sides. If the dog is to be shown, you might wish to gather each fall of hair from the skull, secure it with freezer rubber bands, and add a colored bow to each. Oil the dog's coat occasionally to promote growth and prevent breakage of the hair.

The Maltese, like many other Toy breeds, gets tearstains on the fur around its eyes. In this condition the dog's tear ducts are blocked because of heredity or other causes. Tears overflow, track down the face, and eventually leave brown stains. To remove this stain, wet the dog's hair and rub in a weak boric acid powder solution. Be careful not to get the solution into the dog's eyes. Once a month you can mix a name brand of bleach (the kind that is used on hair, not laundry bleach) with peroxide and allow it to remain on for fifteen minutes.

Bathe a Maltese the day before it is to be shown. Do not oil or powder its coat at that time. Brush its hair carefully an hour before going into the ring.

Pekingese.   Grooming should start at weaning or before. The puppy should learn to be groomed on a table and while lying on its back so that you can brush the hair on its belly and under its limbs. Use a soft, single-bristle brush, and work the coat upward, outward, and toward the nose. Spray the coat lightly with coat dressing or water while working. Brush its legs carefully. If there are tangles, separate them with your fingers.

Brush the head hair so that it will lie flat. Spray it lightly, and when it is nearly dry, dust it with talc. Work the talc with your fingers; then brush it out. Use the same procedure for the tail.

Brush the foreleg feathers so that they lie tight against the body. Brush hind leg feathers down to shape the coat. The body coat should be brushed upward and forward. If the dog is to be shown, do not use powder on its coat for at least two days beforehand. If you must use powder, follow it with a coat dressing. For dealing with tearstain problems, see the instructions for grooming the Maltese.

Pomeranian.   If possible, begin grooming before the dog is weaned. Brush the dog's coat twice a week with a single-bristle brush (pin brush). The primary reason for trimming a Pomeranian is to keep it neat. Trim the hair on the inner flaps of the ears to half the length of the hair on the outer side.

Cut away straggling hair around the vent but not to the base of the tail. Do not thin or scissor the croup hair in an effort to make the tail plume lie flatter. Brush the tail. Put your dog on its back, and brush its legs and belly.

Do not clip your Pomeranian's muzzle. You may leave the whiskers on, but many owners of show dogs prefer to cut them off.

Shih Tzu.   For coat care, follow the instructions for grooming the Pekingese. Train your dog as early as possible to lie on its back so that you can brush the hair on its belly and under its limbs. Oil and protect the beard and whiskers. Brush the nose hair upward. If you are going to show your dog, tie its topknot with a freezer rubber band and add a bow.

Silky Terrier.   For general coat care, follow the instructions for the Maltese. Your Silky will have little undercoat and therefore presents few problems. Be careful not to break the hairs in grooming, and use oil on the coat occasionally. Trim and shape the ears; remove whiskers and any straggling body hairs.

Yorkshire Terrier.   The grooming instructions for the Maltese apply to the Yorkshire. In addition, note the instructions for grooming the Skye Terrier.

Use only a soft-bristle brush on your Yorkie; otherwise the hair may break. Clip the hair inside the ears about a third of the way down. You may want to gather the topknot, secure it with a freezer rubber band, and add a bow.

Non-Sporting Breeds

Bichon Frise.   This dog is scissored to show its eyes and to give a full, rounded appearance to both head and body. Foot hair is trimmed to a rounded shape. Brush the dog's coat to give it a powderpuff appearance.

Lhasa Apso.   Follow the grooming instructions for the Old English Sheepdog and the Skye Terrier. Try not to comb out all the undercoat. Clip the nails before shaping the feet. Keep the hair around the eyes clean, and if there are tear stains, remove them using the method described for the Maltese.

Poodle.   The three varieties of Poodles—Toy, Standard, and Miniature—are all groomed in the same fashion. For obedience only, the dog can be scissored into any desired manner. For conformation, the only allowed clips are Puppy (dogs under a year old), Continental, English Saddle, and Corded. The latter is the Continental with the hair allowed to cord.

The Puppy clip can be used if you want your Poodle to be nicely groomed but not have an elaborate show appearance. It is also used for show dogs until they are a year old.

For this style of grooming, the dog's face is clipped but a fringe of whiskers is left. Move the clippers very slowly, particularly around the face, and do not put pressure against the skin. (If you press the skin, clipper burns may result.) The topknot is rounded, the feet are clipped clean, and the tail is clipped except for a pompon on the end. If your Poodle has well-arched toes, you will want to accentuate this as much as possible. Clip the underside of the foot and between the pads. To finish off the Puppy clip, trim straggly hairs with your scissors. Brush the coat forward for a few days so that the hair stands away from the dog's body.

If your Poodle is over a year old and you want to enter it in show competition or want it to look like a show dog, you should give it either an English Saddle clip, a Continental clip, or a Corded clip. The choice of clip should not be made impulsively. As with so many breeds, grooming can hide a lot of faults or imperfections, or it can accentuate them. For example, only a Poodle with superb hindquarters should be given the Continental clip because in this clip the dog's hindquarters are almost completely naked. A true connotation of naked is "defenseless"; your dog will have no defenses against the searching eyes of a judge at a show.

The English Saddle clip gets its name from the thick saddle of curly hair behind the dog's rib cage. The dog's hair is shaped just as it is for the Continental clip until you reach the end of the rib cage; the back and hindquarters of the dog are trimmed differently.

The Puppy clip is preferred by owners who want their Poodles to be nicely groomed but not to have an elaborate show appearance.

In the Continental clip a Poodle's hindquarters are shaved all the way down to the skin, except for the pompons on its hind pasterns.

The English Saddle clip gets its name from the thick saddle of curly hair behind the Poodle's rib cage.

Champion The Acrobat, shown in the early 1900s in England, was famous for the length of its corded coat. This style of grooming is now recognized in AKC dog show competition. *The Kennel Encyclopaedia,* **Volume 3, England, 1910.**

The diagrams on pages 184–185 show the general shaping for different show clips and should help you to decide which style you prefer for your dog.

Use a bristle or soft nylon brush to groom your Poodle. Steel combs are satisfactory if they have no rough edges to catch and tear the hair and if no teeth are missing. The clipper-blade sizes that are least likely to create burns or sores are No. 10 and No. 15.

Cold water will help to curl the saddle hair on a Poodle's back, although hot towels are sometimes used. Coat creams also help.

Many Poodles, particularly Toy Poodles, get tearstains around their eyes. To remove these stains from the dog's hair, follow the instructions given for the Maltese.

Tibetan Terrier. Follow the grooming instructions for the Shih Tzu, Lhasa Apso, Skye Terrier, and Pekingese. Be careful not to comb out the dog's undercoat. The dog's hair can fall over its eyes or can be combed back.

Miscellaneous Breeds

Tibetan Spaniel. Follow the grooming instructions for the Tibetan Terrier.

part five
DOG SHOWS

The famous Westminster dog show is held annually in New York's Madison Square Garden. *Gaines Dog Research Center*

chapter twenty

The Growth and Function of Dog Shows

The exhibiting of purebred dogs has become a worldwide sport that has grown at a rapid rate. In North America alone there are over one thousand championship dog shows annually and roughly three times that many match shows (which do not award championship points), puppy matches, and informal shows in which dogs, whether purebred or not, can be entered. Hundreds of thousands of people attend. Among the many spectators are dog owners and handlers; people in the businesses of dog foods, vitamin products, or various merchandise for pets; and many others who are just dog fanciers or attending out of curiosity.

Sportsmanship

Like so many other sports, dog shows teach valuable lessons in good sportsmanship. But whereas in a spectator sport such as football there will only be one loser in a game, in a dog show class, there might be up to twenty entries. In that case there will be one winner and nineteen losers, each of which will feel a direct individual loss. A participant centers a lot of dreams and hopes on his or her favorite dog and will certainly take it hard if a judge puts the dog last in its class. People are not automatically good losers. It takes time and victories, as well as losses, to teach graceful acceptance of the judge's placements. Dog shows teach this to a majority of the participants. There may, of course, be a few chronic poor sports, but on the whole those people who do not learn good sportsmanship do not continue to enter their dogs in competition.

Dog Care

Although you may not intend to make dog show competition a career, there is much you can learn from dog shows about your dog and how to care for it.

Novices who think that their dogs are in excellent condition and are perfectly groomed usually get a rude shock when they note the superior condition of most of the other dogs. If you are an exhibitor, you will soon discover that feeding and grooming methods are discussed among the participants. Former participants whose dogs have since become house pets probably find that their pets benefit all their lives from the better feeding and grooming methods learned at the dog shows. And even if you only attend shows as a spectator, you will come to understand more about grooming and conditioning your own pet.

Understanding Your Dog

An owner can learn a lot about a pet's disposition as a result of the dog's participation in a show. For example, an owner who thinks his dog is the dearest and gentlest animal that ever lived may find that the dog tries to bite every passerby, both canine and human, when it is entered in a bench show. Another dog, whose owner thinks it is a model of courage, may have a slinking posture in the show ring or refuse to pose at an outdoor show (although the dog poses perfectly at home).

Such behavior is sometimes caused by lack of proper training, but usually it indicates character faults. Exhibitors learn dozens of such things about their dogs. This is important because to understand your dog is to have a happier relationship with it.

Breeding

Many exhibitors who plan to breed their dogs become conscious of the character faults of certain individual dogs and may either try to breed away from these faults or choose not to breed the dogs at all. Dog shows sort out both the better and the best dogs in each breed — for character, as well as for intelligence and conformation. (Conformation is the structure, or the balance of parts, that gives a dog its individuality in terms of breed.) The shows also help owners understand the faults in their dogs; in no other way can comparisons between dogs be made so clearly. Character faults in a dog, such as shyness and fear biting, will make it virtually impossible for that dog to win a championship.

Obedience contests, which are a part of most dog shows, are valuable tests of a dog's character. They also demonstrate trainability, which is a totally different quality from intelligence. For instance, a very intelligent dog may refuse to give you its attention or may be attentive for only a few minutes during a training session. Obedience trials demonstrate a dog's willingness to work, to co-operate with its master in performing a certain exercise. Knowing whether a dog is enthusiastic and alert or slow and listless can help an owner decide whether or not to breed a certain dog in order to produce high-quality offspring.

Interest in Purebred Dogs

After a dog show the demand for quality puppies inevitably rises. Many people who want to get just an ordinary puppy for a household pet change their minds after attending a show. They see beautiful dogs that are in perfect health, well presented, and well trained. Perhaps for the first time they realize how desirable it can be to own purebreds.

Veterinary Support

In a very real sense dog shows have made better dog care possible. For example, it is no exaggeration to say that dog shows have revolutionized the profession of veterinary medicine. Sixty years ago a city of five hundred thousand people would have had only one or two veterinary hospitals. In fact, the rural county in which I was born (which contained two cities of nine thousand people each) had only one vet in the area, a large-animal man who refused to treat dogs. In those days few vets knew much about the diseases of dogs, and veterinary colleges offered only a limited number of courses dealing with small animals.

The spectacular rise in popularity of dog shows over the years changed all that. Today a city of five hundred thousand people will have ten to twenty small-animal hospitals staffed by highly skilled veterinarians, many of whom may even be dog show competitors.

A large number of today's small-animal hospitals, clinics, and diagnostic laboratories have been made possible through the support and demand of people actively involved in dog shows. For example, dog shows and dog show exhibitors throughout the world paid for the basic research that resulted in a vaccine to immunize dogs against distemper. Further research by veterinarians determined the relationship between canine distemper and human measles viruses; they learned that fresh canine distemper virus could protect children from measles.

Improvements have also been made in modern dog foods. More and more dog fanciers demanded proper diets for their dogs, and nutritionally improved dog foods came on the market.

The Dog's Personality

A dog is first of all your pet. This means that you have a responsibility to it both as a living being and as a member of your family. That responsibility includes the development of the dog's personality — and, one should add, its personality as a dog. Many people jokingly say, "My dog doesn't know that he's a dog. He thinks he's a person." They are surprised and unbelieving when they are told that this can be quite literally true and is almost always a tragedy for the dog. There will always be times when you will have to treat your dog as a dog, not as a person, and then the dog won't understand. Character and personality problems may arise subsequently that will make both your dog and you unhappy.

Exhibiting purebred dogs has become a worldwide sport that has grown at a rapid rate. Pictured here, the Ravenna, Ohio, show. *Gaines Dog Research Center*

For example, a puppy is taken from a litter at two weeks of age and never sees another dog until it is mature. Such a dog will not recognize itself as a dog, and that may defeat even its sexual drive. Thus, if the segregated dog is a bitch, she may drive away all male dogs even when she is sexually ready for mating.

Dog shows offer an opportunity to develop a dog's personality. Show dogs learn that they must get along with other dogs that may be as big or strong as they are. At bench shows they discover that they must lie in stalls most of the day. They must permit people to pet them and must obey judges (total strangers) as well as their masters. In the show ring they must pose for five to twenty minutes at a time.

Because show dogs may have to travel a hundred miles or more to a show, they have to become good car riders. They also learn to stand or lie quietly while being groomed for a show. Moreover they will pose obediently at their owner's command, whether for a casual family snapshot or in the show ring while being judged.

Health

Finally, show dogs are less subject to disease than their more sheltered house pet cousins. In any congregation of dogs (such as a dog show) there will be a concentration of bacteria and viruses. If a dog has been properly immunized beforehand, it will not pick up any disease. The constant exposure of the show dog keeps its immunity level at a maximum, unlike dogs that are kept segregated and therefore do not have a high immunity against infection or viruses.

chapter twenty-one
How Dog Shows Are Run

A dog show is a huge elimination contest. It may begin with two hundred or even thirty-five hundred dogs entered, but it ends with one Best in Show winner. The procedure is complicated yet orderly.

Dog shows are a highly organized sport. The vast majority of American shows are conducted under the rules of the American Kennel Club (AKC). **Licensed or championship shows** (in which registered dogs compete for championship points) operate under AKC license. These shows may have all breeds entered (**all-breeds shows**) or only a single breed (**specialty shows**). **Sanctioned match shows** are limited to entry by registered dogs. The same basic procedures apply to both match shows and championship shows. However, a match show, which is usually sponsored by a local dog club, cannot give championship points to its winners. **Nonsanctioned** or "fun" **match shows** permit dogs to enter that are not purebred and are usually very informal events.

In Canada, shows are licensed by the Canadian Kennel Club. Those in Mexico are licensed by the Mexican Kennel Club. Bermuda is governed by the rules of the Canadian Kennel Club, but separate Bermuda championships are awarded.

Coonhounds and Toy Fox Terriers are exhibited under the rules of the United Kennel Club. With the exception of the Black and Tan Coonhound, these breeds are not recognized or registered by the AKC. Foxhound shows under the control of bodies other than the AKC are sometimes held, although both American and English Foxhounds are shown at AKC shows.

Breed Standards

The purpose of a dog show is to serve as an arena in which the quality of the many different breeds of dogs can be determined. Each breed has a *standard,* which is a written description of the breed (see Chapters 35 to 42). It includes a general description of the breed type and specific descriptions of the individual parts of the dog—for example, the length and depth of the muzzle, the color and placement of the eyes, the size and placement of the ears, the length and quality of the coat, the undercoat (if there is one), and the color or permitted colors for each breed. The length of the back, depth of the chest, type and carriage of tail, size and type of feet, and similar points are all given in the breed standard.

Judges compare the dogs in competition against the breed standard and against each other. In doing so, they are sorting out the best dogs for breeding and indicating the best characteristics for use in breeding these dogs.

Obedience Contests

Probably two thirds or more of all dog shows today include obedience competitions, in which dogs are judged on the precision with

In this obedience competition, dogs are being judged on how well they clear a series of hurdles. *Gaines Dog Research Center*

which they perform obedience exercises. These include walking at heel, standing for examination, executing the high jump and hurdles, and retrieving (see Chapter 14, "Obedience Training and Competition," for details).

In obedience contests, amateur entrants in "A" divisions compete only against other amateurs. But amateurs who enter their dogs in conformation classes must compete against professional handlers.

Superintendents

Almost all licensed American dog shows use professional superintendents who attend to the vast number of details involved in any show. Among their many responsibilities, superintendents arrange judging schedules, compile all the pertinent information for the list of entrants in the show catalog, and see that the show's entry forms and various brochures are printed. They also see that scales and measuring equipment are provided at shows.

Specialty shows, at which only a single breed is judged, often use a club member who will be licensed to superintend the show. Sometimes a member may serve as show secretary, and no superintendent will be used. Where a number of breed clubs combine into an association of specialty clubs, it is customary to use a professional superintendent.

Owners Who Show Their Own Dogs

Many breeders and many dog owners show their own dogs. What is more, they do a fair share of winning. A majority of the dogs that compete in obedience trials are handled by their owners.

In fact, in junior showmanship competitions (for boys and girls, ages eight to sixteen) many young exhibitors score spectacular victories. It is not uncommon to see their dogs win Best of Breed and then win in a variety group, such as Hounds or Terriers. In 1967 a black Standard Poodle was Reserve Winner for Best in Show at Cruft's, the world's most prestigious dog show, which is held in England. The dog was handled by a sixteen-year-old girl.

Keep in mind that the decision to show your dog on a regular basis means a commitment in terms of time, energy, and money. You need to pay constant attention to the proper grooming of your dog, as well as to all the other conditioning, exercise, and care it needs in preparation for future shows. In addition you will need to handle the necessary travel plans and expenses related to entries. However, the many devoted owners of dogs who also show them prove that participating in this competitive sport is both challenging and rewarding.

Here are some outstanding examples of amateurs who have been conspicuously successful in the show ring.

William T. Holt of Richmond, Virginia, was a breeder of English Setters. An English Setter of his own breeding, Rock Falls Colonel, handled by himself, won a hundred Best in Show awards.

Mrs. Patricia Craige of Monterey, California, is a schoolteacher who breeds and shows her own Norwegian Elkhounds. Mrs. Craige is one of America's most successful breeders, and she often interests her students in taking part ownership in her dogs. Mrs. Craige's dogs have won in the Hound Group at Westminster three times and have taken many Best in Show awards.

Ch. Aennchen's Poona Dancer, a Maltese, has broken all records for its breed. It is owned by Frank Oberstar and L. G. Ward of South Euclid, Ohio. Poona has been Best in Show more than twenty times.

These records indicate that there is a place for the amateur in the world of dog show competition and that he or she may be able to place higher in the victory columns than the professionals.

Handlers

At dog shows owners can show their own dogs, they can have friends show them, or they can hire a professional handler to do this. A show that has two thousand dogs may have eighty or more of these professionals.

It is the job of a handler to groom and condition dogs for shows, make entries, transport the dogs to the shows, and then care for and exhibit them. They charge a fee for their services in addition to the cost of the dogs' board, entry fees, and possibly transportation to the show. They may also charge an additional amount if the dog wins first place in its variety group and a still higher amount if the dog wins Best in Show.

Most professional handlers gained experience when they were young by showing their own dogs. They became so skilled that other people wanted them to handle their dogs at shows. Gradually these young people began to show breeds other than their own and then became professional dog handlers. Others gained their experience in handling dogs by serving long apprenticeships working at large breeding kennels. As kennel boys and girls they learned to groom, care for, and condition dogs of various types.

As a handler's reputation for competence and integrity grows, so does the selection of dogs from which he or she can choose. The best professional handlers have good judgment in picking out top-quality prospects to exhibit. They can quickly recognize the faults of various

This Toy Poodle is being posed after winning Best of Variety. *Gaines Dog Research Center*

dogs and then spend a lot of time practicing with the dogs to show off their good qualities. Handlers also study judges and try to learn their likes and dislikes. For example, a certain judge may be particularly fussy about sound hindquarters in dogs but may tend to ignore ear set. So for that judge a handler may select only those dogs with strong, sound hindquarters.

Until mid-September of 1977, the AKC licensed professional handlers. Then, by the overwhelming vote of its delegates, it discontinued the practice. The sport has grown so much, with so many licensed handlers and applications for licenses, that the AKC could not adequately monitor them and had no feasible plan for trying to do so. A license didn't actually mean very much anymore, so they decided to dispense with the whole procedure. The Professional Handlers Association tries to set and maintain standards, but it does not, of course, have the regulatory powers that the AKC has. The Canadian Kennel Club does not license its handlers.

Judges

Dog show judges may be professionals or amateurs. They may be licensed to judge one breed or ten, or all breeds. Amateurs may judge solely for the honor of being invited or to gain the additional experience that they will need to become licensed.

If a person qualifies as a multiple-breeds judge, particularly one who judges one or more groups (e.g., all Sporting Dogs, all Hounds) and demands a fee in addition to expenses, he or she has become a professional judge. Judges with three or four group licenses and all-breeds judges may be called upon to judge at least fifty weekend shows a year and as many as 175 dogs on a single day.

There is much hard work that goes into judging, and the glory of being a judge may wear off after being out in the hot sun all day or standing on a concrete floor for eight to ten hours at a time, sometimes without lunch. As compensation, a judge is paid a fee of about $1500 and up per day, plus expenses. (It often happens that the professional handlers who are exhibiting under a judge may make three or four times as much money as the judge does.)

Detailed information on the many aspects of judging is given in Part Six, "Judging Dog Shows."

Ring Stewards

A steward serves as a judge's assistant and is a necessary part of a dog show. Without stewards, shows would take three times the normal amount of time to be completed or might not be able to operate at all. No judge ever finishes an assignment on schedule without being thankful for competent stewards, for they, as much as the judge, keep the show moving.

Stewards are usually people who have exhibited dogs in the past and for one reason or another no longer do so, but they still want to be part of dog shows. Many of them make it a point of honor not to charge for their services. The only kind of reimbursement they will accept is a free lunch (if it is available) or a small payment to cover their expenses if a long trip is involved.

Among a steward's many responsibilities at a show is searching the grooming areas for exhibitors who have not shown up. Such a *ring runner* is of immense value, particularly if the person is well acquainted with exhibitors and professional handlers.

Aside from the exhibitors themselves, only stewards wearing a proper steward's badge are permitted in the ring with the judge, and they must see that all unauthorized personnel are kept out. Other people who are permitted to enter the ring at specified times are the superintendent, the veterinarian, and the measuring committee.

The most important job of the steward is to assemble each class before the judging. If judging is to start at 9 A.M., the steward should begin assembling the class for the first breed at least by 8:50 A.M. The first class should be ready to enter the ring at exactly nine o'clock, not a minute later. While a class is being judged, the steward should assemble the next class. For this purpose some shows have *waiting,* or *ready,* rings.

In assembling a class, the steward must check to see that each exhibitor gets the correct armband number for his dog and must make sure that the dogs are actually entered in that particular class. It has happened that owners who are showing several dogs have brought the wrong dog into the ring. On one occasion an owner did not learn of the mistake until months later, and then it was too late to make a correction.

A few minutes before judging begins, the steward should lay out the ribbons and assemble any trophies that are to be awarded. If a listed trophy is not present, the steward should make a note of this for the trophy chairman and assure the winner that it will be sent to him or her. Sometimes there are no entries in a particular class for which a trophy or money prize is offered. In that case the steward should mark "void" on the trophy and return it to the trophy chairman or mark "void" on the money envelope and return it to the show superintendent.

A steward should also see that the ring arrangements are suitable to the judge. For example, the ring numbers may have been placed across the ring from the judge's tables, but the judge might prefer to have them placed closer in order to save time and steps.

Another important responsibility of the steward is to report the absence of any dogs entered in the show. When someone reports a dog absent to the steward, the steward should question the person making the report to make sure that that person has the authority to do so. It has happened that a dishonest exhibitor has reported his major competitor absent in the hope that the dog's presence will not be discovered until after the class has been judged. The steward can avoid this by demanding to know whether the person making the report is the dog's owner or handler.

At each show the steward is provided with a catalog containing information about the show's entrants. Except for the question of age in certain breeds, the judge cannot be told information that is in the catalog. If the steward tries to point out something in the catalog to the judge, a host of ringsiders will report that the judge was studying the catalog.

Because both stewards and judges can and do make mistakes, stewards should be careful to mark their catalogs as they go along. They should first list the absentees and then list the placings of the winning dogs. A final check should be made later to see that the steward's record is identical with the judge's.

Stewards can also render the judge some considerate service when the club that sponsors the show fails to provide coffee or lunch. They can see to it that the club provides this.

Sometimes an exhibitor will ask a steward, "How did Judge So-and-So place the dogs in that class?" The steward will answer "I don't know. I was too busy tending to my job to pay attention." Therein lies the proof of a good steward.

Veterinarians

Today it is very rare for a dog show to require a veterinarian to examine each dog before admission. For many years this was required, but it is no longer practical because of the large number of entries and because if a dog has a slight temperature, it is sometimes difficult for the vet to determine whether this is caused by illness or by the excitement of being in the show.

In 1977 the American Kennel Club ruled that a show could elect to have a veterinarian in attendance or on call. Canada also uses this system, and it has worked well. A veterinarian in attendance at a show must be provided with suitable quarters. If it is an outdoor show, a tent should be provided to offer protection and a telephone should be handy if the doctor is on call.

The AKC rules state that "show veterinarians are not to be called on to treat dogs for physical conditions that existed before they were brought to the show. Their duties are to give advisory opinions to Bench Show Committees when requested, to examine the health of dogs at the request of exhibitors and handlers, and to render first aid to dogs in cases of sickness or injury occurring at the show."

If the show committee elects to have a veterinarian present or on call during the show's hours, it must list the doctor's name and address in the premium list (the brochure sent to potential exhibitors before a show) and in the show catalog.

chapter twenty-two
Classes of Competition at a Championship Show

Regular Classes

The regular classes in which dogs are judged at a championship show are: Puppy, Novice, Bred by Exhibitor, American-bred, Open, and Winners. These are divided into sections according to sex—for example, an Open Class for dogs and an Open Class for bitches. Regular classes lead directly to the award for Best in Show.

In each of these classes, except Winners, the dog that wins first place gets a blue ribbon; second place, a red ribbon; third place, a yellow ribbon; and fourth place, a white ribbon. The first-place award in the Winners Class is a purple ribbon and championship points. In the final rounds of a show's judging, trophies and special decorations are awarded.

Puppy Class. The junior Puppy Class is for puppies over six months and under nine months old. The senior Puppy Class is for puppies nine months and under twelve months old. In considering eligibility, the age of the dog is calculated up to and including the first day of the show or, if it is a one-day show, up to and including the date of the show.

At American shows the Puppy Class is limited to dogs whelped in the United States or Canada. Puppies born in other countries must compete in the Open Class. No puppy may be entered whose date of birth, place of birth, name of breeder, or sire or dam are unknown or are not set forth in full on the entry form.

Novice Class. The Novice Class is for dogs six months old or older that were whelped in the United States or Canada and that have not won (prior to the date of the closing of entries) three first prizes in the Novice Class, a first prize in any class other than the Puppy Class, or 1 or more championship points.

Bred by Exhibitor Class.   The Bred by Exhibitor Class is limited to dogs registered by the American Kennel Club that have been whelped in the United States or Canada, are six months old or older, and are not champions. The dog must be owned wholly or in part by the person (or the spouse of the person) who was the breeder or one of the breeders of record. Dogs entered in this class must be handled by an owner or by a member of the immediate family of an owner.

American-bred Class.   The American-bred Class is for dogs that are not champions, are six months old or older, and were whelped in the United States as the result of a mating that took place in the United States.

A problem sometimes arises when an American goes to a foreign country with a dog that gives birth to a litter of puppies in the foreign country. In such cases the AKC has usually refused registration of the

Regular Classes at a Championship Show

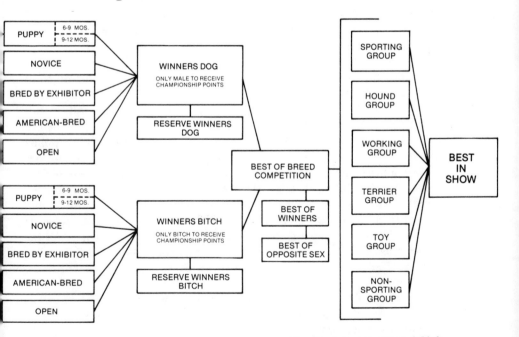

Credit: American Kennel Club

puppies, ruling that these dogs were born outside the jurisdiction of the AKC.

However, in at least one such case the AKC yielded. The litter was born in a United States embassy, and the puppies were considered American-bred.

Open Class. The Open Class is for all dogs six months old or older, including champions. It is the only class in which most foreign-bred dogs may enter. There is, however, one exception: If a member club of the AKC (the American Boxer Club, for instance) wished to hold a specialty show for American-bred dogs only, it would be permissible for the Open Class to consist of only American-bred dogs.

The Open Class at a dog show may also be divided by weight or by color. This occurs for breeds in which there are several sizes or allowable colors and where the number of entries is large enough to warrant this division. Such divisions prevent classes from becoming too large to be handled in a normal-size ring. Instead of twenty or thirty dogs in one class there would be two or three classes with eight to ten dogs each. For example, the Open Class for Dachshunds would be divided into a class for Miniatures weighing under ten pounds and a class for Standards weighing ten pounds or over. In terms of color the Open Class for a breed such as the Great Dane would be divided into brindle, fawn, harlequin, or another color specified in the breed standard. This division of the Open Class enables two or three more dogs to win a first prize and blue ribbon. There would also be equal sets of second-, third-, and fourth-place winners.

Dogs of various colors and weights must compete against each other in all the other previously mentioned classes, and they also must do so in the Winners Class.

The Open Class has always been open to champions and to un-confirmed champions (sometimes a lag of several months occurs before the AKC confirms that a dog has won the fifteen championship points necessary to win the title of Champion). However, many owners consider it poor sportsmanship to enter champions in the Open Class because they feel that this might rob other dogs of a chance to gain championship points. (An AKC rule also says that an owner may show his or her unconfirmed champion in Best in Breed competition for ninety days. If the dog has not gotten its championship confirmation by that time, the owner must withdraw the dog from further shows until confirmation has been received.)

Winners Class. Each of the first-place winners in the previous classes is automatically eligible to enter the Winners Class to compete against the other first-place winners. The winning dogs compete for the

The highest honor at a dog show is to win Best in Show. *Gaines Dog Research Center*

title of Winners Dog, and the winning bitches compete for the title of Winners Bitch. Each will be awarded a purple ribbon and championship points.

After they are chosen, a contest occurs in which the Winners Dog and Winners Bitch compete against champions (male and females) and winners of certain special classes (such as Veteran's) for Best of Breed. A purple-and-gold ribbon is awarded for this event.

If either Winners Dog or Winners Bitch is chosen Best of Breed, then the next judging category, Best of Winners (Winners Dog versus Winners Bitch), is automatically eliminated. However, if a champion is named Best of Breed, then Best of Winners is judged. The breed judging is completed with a Best of Opposite Sex selection (the dog or bitch of the opposite sex of the Best of Breed winner).

If for any reason the Winners Dog or Winners Bitch is disqualified, the Reserve Winner — either male or female — is moved up to the first-place spot. (The second-place winner in the earlier class would have competed against the other first-place winners in the previous classes for the Reserve designation.)

The Best of Breed winner then competes in variety group judging. In this event, a best Sporting Dog, best Hound, best Working Dog, best Terrier, best Toy, and best Non-Sporting Dog are given Best of Group awards. Four placings are made in each group, but only first-place winners continue to compete.

These six group winners are shown in the ring for the last time to decide which will receive the final and highest honor, Best in Show, for which a red, white, and blue decoration and a trophy are awarded. In this way a show that may have started out in the morning with four thousand entries will end with a single dog as Best in Show after all the judging is over.

Nonregular Classes

Nonregular classes give added sport to dog shows. One of these, the Veteran's Class, can also lead to Best in Show. In all nonregular classes these ribbons are awarded: first place, rose; second place, brown; third place, light green; and fourth place, gray.

Local Class. In this kind of competition the entrants compete for Best Local Dog of Breed, Best Local Dog in a Variety Group, and Best Local Dog in Show. The show-giving club must specify what county or counties are permitted to enter dogs.

The Local Class can be divided by sex, but more often the sexes are combined (local dogs and bitches). An additional entry fee is charged for each dog, and the class is judged after Best of Breed. The Best Local Dog in Show ribbon is blue and gold.

Brace and Team Classes. Many shows also schedule Best Brace and Best Team Classes, which have strong audience appeal and have helped to popularize both dogs and dog shows.

In this form of competition, the dogs are shown and judged as units. A brace is two dogs; a team is four dogs. Owners try to match the dogs as closely as possible in size, color, and conformation. If the dogs are entered for brace or team competition only, a regular entry fee is charged for each dog, plus a smaller fee for the unit. If the dogs are also entered in regular competition, the additional charge is usually only the unit fee.

Perhaps the most famous teams in the history of American dog shows were those developed by Dr. Vincenzo Calvaresi. His Villa Malta Kennels of Maltese were internationally famous, and Dr. Calvaresi drilled his teams to military perfection. Thousands of people went to the Westminster Show at Madison Square Garden every year just to see the Villa Malta team. His great teams were a major factor in the rise of the Maltese's popularity to its present level.

Miscellaneous Class. This is a nonregular class that is given at all-breeds shows for breeds that, though purebred, are not sufficiently numerous in the United States to have complete stud book registration.

The males from the Miscellaneous Breeds compete against each other, and the bitches do the same. Although there is no Winners Class, and no Best of Breed, Best in Show, or championship points awarded, the Miscellaneous Class is a step toward complete AKC recognition of the breeds that compete and enables those breeds to appear before the public.

William F. Stifel, executive director of the AKC, explains the entire process that precedes recognition of a breed in the following way:

"The admission of a new breed to our Stud Book has, in all recent cases, been the result of work that has extended over quite a period of years. In the case of each new breed, a specialty club has first been formed for the advancement of the interests of its particular breed in the United States. This specialty club has no official connection with the American Kennel Club.

"One of its main functions has been to keep its own stud book records for the breed in this country. Our correspondence with each of these clubs has extended over a period of eight to ten years or more. What is at stake as far as a club is concerned is when our Board of Directors sees its way clear to take over the keeping of their stud book records.

"Before taking this step, our Board must be convinced that the dogs have been purebred for a good many generations, that accurate stud book records have been kept on them in the United States, that there are a good many specimens of the breed in this country (well up in the hundreds at least) and that they are owned by a good many different people in various parts of the country who are seriously interested in breeding and exhibiting them in AKC shows, as well as registering them in the AKC Stud Book.

"At some point prior to admitting a new breed to the Stud Book, the Board of Directors may declare the breed eligible for entry in what we call the 'Miscellaneous Class.' However, this step is not taken unless the situation looks quite favorable and our Board is convinced that the breed will continue to develop to an extent that will warrant admitting it to the AKC Stud Book within a reasonable period of time."

At present, the dogs eligible to compete in the Miscellaneous Class are the Australian Kelpie, Border Collie, Cavalier King Charles Spaniel, Miniature Bull Terrier, Pharaoh Hound, Spinone Italiano, and Tibetan Spaniel.

Junior and Novice Classes. Most dog shows include Junior Showmanship competitions. These are classes for children between the ages of eight and sixteen.

The Novice A Division is for boys and girls eight to twelve years old who have never won a Junior Showmanship competition. The Novice B

Division is for youngsters thirteen to sixteen years old who have not won previously. The Graduate Novice Division is for boys and girls eight to twelve who have won in competition one or more times. The Open Division is for youngsters ten to sixteen years old who have been previous winners. These four class winners compete for Best Junior Showman. These classes are often judged by professional judges or handlers, who base their selections on how skillfully the competitors gait and pose their dogs.

Specialty Shows

A specialty show is another type of championship dog show that is given for a particular breed by a club made up of fanciers of that breed. The breed club is often called a *specialty club.*

Both all-breeds and specialty clubs can become members of the AKC and give one show a year without a license charge. If the club is a nonmember, it must pay a license fee.

The breed club can give its own show, or it can consider the classes at an all-breeds show to be its specialty show. In that case it does not pay a special license fee, the judges are hired by the all-breeds club, expenses are reduced, and there will probably be a larger entry than if the breed club gives its own show. However, at an all-breeds show, the all-breeds club absorbs the revenue; whereas if the breed or specialty club gives its own show, it will absorb the revenue. Many specialty clubs arrange to hold their shows the day before an all-breeds show, so their dogs can compete in two shows on a weekend with a larger than normal number of entries in those breeds.

Additional classes that may be given at a specialty show are Veteran Dog and Veteran Bitch, Stud Dog, Brood Bitch, Field Trial classes, and 12 to 18 Months Class.

Veteran Bitch and Veteran Dog Classes. A club can specify how old a dog or bitch must be before it can be entered in the Veteran's Class. This might be five, six, or even seven years old. The competitors are often champions, but they need not be. The Veteran's Class is the only nonregular class in which the winner can go on to Best in Show. Thus, the winner of the Veteran's Class has the right to compete for Best of Breed and if it wins, then automatically enters group competition.

Stud Dog and Brood Bitch Classes. The Stud Dog Class is for a sire and his offspring, and the Brood Bitch Class is for a dam and her offspring. The offspring have to be entered in the regular classes; their parents may or may not be. Only the names of the stud dogs and brood bitches appear in the catalog in these classes.

The winners of these classes do not compete for Best of Breed. This is because the judge's decision is based on the merits of the offspring as well as on those of the parents. These classes are judged after Best of Breed has been selected.

The rule barring castrated males and spayed females from entering shows (see Chapter 23) is waived for stud dogs and brood bitches because it is their offspring conceived before surgery that are being judged.

Field Trial Class. The Field Trial Class is occasionally seen at specialty shows or at all-breeds shows in which a specialty club considers the classes its specialty show. The Field Trial Class is limited to those breeds (Sporting Dogs and Hounds) that give AKC-licensed field trials. To be eligible for this class, a dog must have placed first, second, third, or fourth at a licensed field trial.

The breeds for which field trials are conducted are Pointer, German Shorthaired Pointer, German Wirehaired Pointer, Vizsla, Weimaraner, English Setter, Irish Setter, Gordon Setter, and Brittany Spaniel; Chesapeake Bay Retriever, Curly-Coated Retriever, Flat-Coated Retriever, Golden Retriever, Labrador Retriever, and Irish Water Spaniel (which competes as a retriever); American Cocker Spaniel, English Cocker Spaniel, and English Springer Spaniel; and Beagle, Basset Hound, and Dachshund.

12 to 18 Months Class. This class has several advantages. It provides four additional ribbon winners in each sex and cuts down the almost unmanageable size of other classes. It also provides for dogs that, while not strictly puppies, are still not mature.

chapter twenty-three
Entering a Dog in an AKC Show

Recognized Breeds

The American Kennel Club currently recognizes 126 breeds, or 137 breeds and varieties, of dogs for registration and showing. These fall into the major categories of Sporting, Hound, Working, Terrier, Toy, and Non-Sporting breeds. (See Part Seven, "Breed Standards.")

Unless a dog is a member of one of these breed groups, it cannot enter an AKC dog show. For example, the English Coonhound and English Shepherd are purebreds that are recognized by the United Kennel Club but not by the AKC; therefore, they cannot be entered in AKC shows.

There are also the Miscellaneous breeds, which are entered in the Miscellaneous Class at all-breeds shows. These dogs, although purebred, are not sufficiently represented in the United States to warrant complete stud book registration.

Pedigrees

To enter an AKC dog show, a dog must be registered in the American Kennel Club *Stud Book,* or it must be a part of a previously AKC-registered litter. If a dog is imported into the United States, it must be registered with a foreign registry organization whose pedigrees are acceptable for AKC registration.

Local dog clubs sometimes give shows that are not under the sanction of the AKC. Usually the rules of these informal shows are much more flexible, and dogs may be entered, whether purebred or not.

Health Regulations

No dog of any breed may enter a licensed dog show unless it is six months old or older on the first day of the show. A dog may not be entered if it has a communicable disease, has been exposed to one, or has come from a kennel in which such a disease has existed within the preceding month.

Of course, there is really no way in which show officials can check up on exposure to, or the presence of, disease in a kennel unless some other exhibitor lodges a protest against an entry. However, your own integrity is at stake in entering your dog into competition. It is your responsibility not to expose other dogs to disease, and it is your responsibility to protest if another owner is doing so.

Showing an Unregistered Dog

As mentioned earlier, an unregistered dog may be shown at an informal dog show that is not sanctioned by the AKC.

If your dog is not registered with the AKC but has an acceptable foreign registration, it can be shown at three AKC shows within a period of thirty days. After that it is ineligible to be shown until registered. An exception is made when circumstances beyond the control of the owner hold up registration of a dog. If the owner can prove this in writing to the satisfaction of the AKC's Show Records Department, then an ILP (indefinite listing privilege) number can be granted for the dog and will appear on its entry form.

For example, sometimes a fond owner may give his or her still unregistered dog a certain name and uses that name while showing it. However, the AKC may find the owner's choice of name unacceptable, in which case the dog must be registered under another name in order to compete. For example, a dog may first be shown as Donna's Bright Angel and later be registered as Delightful Donna. To prevent later confusion, the entry form must read "Delightful Donna (formerly shown as Donna's Bright Angel)." This must be done until the dog has won a first-, second-, third-, or fourth-place ribbon in a regular class at a licensed show. After that it can be shown simply as Delightful Donna.

Or suppose that you have bought a dog but its registration papers have not yet been transferred to your name. (The dog is still officially registered in the name of the former owner.) The AKC rule is that a dog must be entered in the name of the person who actually owns the dog at the time entry is made. The application for transfer of ownership should be made immediately and must be sent to the AKC within seven days after the conclusion of the show. Also, the entry blank for the show must state that the transfer application has been, or will be, shortly applied for. If there is an unavoidable delay in getting the transfer made, the new owner should apply to the AKC for an extension of time in which to have the transfer completed.

Entry Forms

It used to be that an entry for a dog show could be made on a scrap of paper or that the superintendent of a show could be telegraphed with instructions to enter a dog using the same information given for entry to a previous show. But these methods can no longer be used.

For an AKC show a dog must be entered on an official AKC entry form, and all pertinent data must be included. The entry form should be the official form for that specific show, although an entry form for another show can be used if the name, date, and place of the show are scratched out, the correct data is added, and the proper entry fee accompanies the form.

As a rule, entries for Saturday and Sunday shows close at noon on the Wednesday eighteen days before the show. For midweek shows a similar time stipulation is made. Because mails are sometimes delayed, entries should not be held off until the last minute. The entry form must be received in the superintendent's or show secretary's office before the closing date for the show; the date stamped on the envelope by the post office is not considered. It is also wise to file your entry promptly in case there is a limit to the number of entries being accepted for a certain show.

Hundreds of exhibitors get shut out of shows because their entries are received too late. Sometimes novice exhibitors have threatened superintendents or offered to pay double fees, but the AKC rule is enforced. A superintendent who accepts late entries will be heavily fined.

A superintendent may not accept conditional entries. Sometimes a dog will have won all its championship points except for one victory with a rating of 3 points or better (which is necessary for it to win a championship). Formerly an owner could instruct a superintendent to return his or her entry if the competition did not give the event a 3-point rating. Today superintendents are not permitted to do this. (A superintendent who does will be fined by the AKC.)

Owners cannot change entries or correct errors after the closing time for entries. However, there is one exception: If an owner lists the wrong sex for his or her dog, the entry can be changed in the judge's book at the show.

If a dog is incorrectly entered in a class, this cannot be changed after entries close. For example, an exhibitor may enter a Miniature Dachshund in the Open Class for Miniatures, in which a dog must be under ten pounds. The judge may weigh the dog, find it to be exactly ten pounds, and therefore rule the dog ineligible to compete in that class. The entry cannot be changed to put the dog in the class for standard-size dogs, and thereby the dog is disqualified from competition in the show.

It should be emphasized that dogs that are disqualified, that have been ruled ineligible to compete, or from whom ribbons have been withheld because of lack of merit (the dog is not, in the opinion of the judge, a good enough specimen of the breed to receive *any* award), cannot be counted as competitors. That can affect the number of championship points that can be awarded. For example, the loss of one entry may reduce the championship rating of an event from 1 to 0, or from 5 to 4. (For an explanation of the championship point system, see Chapter 24, "How a Dog Becomes a Champion.")

Kennel Registration

Novice exhibitors sometimes become enthusiastic enough to want to establish their own kennel. For example, a couple — let's call them Mary and John — decides to call their establishment Marjon Kennels. They name their dogs with the prefix "Marjon" and make their entries in the name of Marjon Kennels.

Whereas the prefix "Marjon" may be all right in naming the dogs, "Marjon Kennels" cannot be used unless the name has been officially registered with the AKC and a registration fee has been paid. This license must be renewed every five years.

Registration gives a kennel exclusive right to that kennel name. If Mary and John send in their entries under the name of Marjon Kennels without having registered that name, their entries will be disqualified or cancelled.

Also, if Marjon is already a registered kennel name, then Mary and John cannot name their dogs with that prefix. In that case the name will be prohibited at the time of the dog's registration.

Disqualification for Physical Reasons

There is a rule at dog shows that the novice may be unaware of. Every male dog is required to have two normal testicles normally descended into the scrotum. A dog having only one testicle descended into the scrotum is called a *monorchid;* one with neither testicle descended is called a *cryptorchid.* (These terms are not biologically accurate, but they are in general use.)

If a judge cannot find one or both testicles or thinks that the testicles are abnormal, the dog must be disqualified. The disqualification is permanent unless the owner decides to appeal.

A formal appeal may be made to the AKC, along with a deposit fee. An AKC committee, consisting of a chairman and two veterinarians, will review the case. If the original disqualification is sustained, the dog is permanently disqualified, and the fee is forfeited. If the dog is reinstated, the fee is returned. If the dog that has been disqualified at the show is still a puppy, no appeal will be acted on until the dog is at least a year old.

Castrated and spayed dogs cannot compete, nor can dogs whose appearance has been surgically altered in ways other than those specified by the standards governing those breeds. For example, a Saluki would be disqualified if its ears had been cropped, as would a Chihuahua whose tail had been docked. In most breeds it is considered desirable to remove the dewclaws (the extra toes on the front and hind legs), but a Briard would be disqualified if it did not have them. A Manchester Terrier may have cropped ears, but they would disqualify a Toy Manchester.

Another rule requires that a dog's natural color may not be changed either by coloring or dyeing. It has happened that youngsters have entered their white Poodles after coloring them pink or putting red nail enamel on their nails. Such dogs will be disqualified. Powders used to clean dogs and to whiten their white hairs must be removed before a dog is taken into the ring. If white chalk comes off on the judge's hands, or if a cloud of white dust arises during examination, the dog will be disqualified.

It had been common practice for owners to spray their dogs with hair spray before they entered the show ring. But in 1977 the AKC ruled against the use of hair sprays or hair lacquers on dogs being entered in shows. The same ruling applies to using water to set a dog's coat or disguise a dry, unhealthy coat.

This decision became necessary after judges and dog show authorities complained that it was virtually impossible to tell whether a dog's coat was in its natural state or whether spray, lacquer, or water had been applied shortly before the dog entered the ring. Take, for example, a Standard Poodle, which is supposed to have a naturally harsh coat. If the exhibitor of a soft-coated Poodle were to be permitted to put lacquer on the dog's coat, once the lacquer dried it might be impossible for a judge to determine whether the coat was in its natural state. Under the old rules, if the judge decided that the coat had been conditioned, the dog could not be dismissed; it would only be put at the end of the line. It hardly seemed fair for a dog whose coat had been glossed to be allowed to compete for Best in Show.

Unentered Dogs at the Show

Sometimes an owner may want to bring along a second dog — so that it will not be left at home alone or will serve as a riding companion for the dog appearing in the show. However, rules prohibit having a dog on the show grounds unless it is actually one of the entrants. One reason for this is the possibility of theft, particularly at bench shows. Guards may ask departing exhibitors to show the identification they were sent before the show, so keep it handy.

There are several exceptions to this rule. An exhibitor may deliver a dog to its new owner at a show or bring a bitch in season to turn her over to the owner of a male. Professional handlers may also bring dogs that are not entered at that show. For these reasons the superintendent or show secretary is required to set aside an in-transit area, apart from the main show. In some cases it might even be the superintendent's office. Here unentered dogs may be kept in their crates, with In Transit signs on the crates or around the area.

chapter twenty-four

How a Dog Becomes a Champion

A dog cannot win championship points simply by winning a blue ribbon at a show. These first-prize winners then compete in the Winners Class, in which they are eligible to win a purple ribbon and a certain number of championship points. Only purple-ribbon winners can win these points.

Schedule of Points

Points at championship shows are won under a rather complicated system called a *schedule of points,* which has been worked out by the AKC. The AKC bases its ratings on the total number of dogs of a given breed registered annually and the number exhibited annually in a given area. It also considers the number of dogs and the number of bitches competing in the Winners Class of the show.

A dog must win 15 championship points to receive the title of Champion. There are no fractional points. Thus, the lowest number of points that can be won by a dog at a single show is 1; the highest number is 5. However, a dog cannot become a champion by winning 15 single points. It must win at least twice in Winner Classes with a rating of 3 points or better. At least two of these *"major"* shows (worth 3 or more points) must be won under a third judge. This prevents a dog from winning its championship because of a single judge's decision or inadequate competition (as there might be in small shows).

The AKC divides the nation into zones. Fewer dogs in a given zone will mean that fewer entrants will be required for competition in the point ratings. For example, let's consider Zone One (which includes the states of Connecticut, Delaware, the District of Columbia, Illinois, Indiana, Maine, Maryland, Massachusetts, Michigan, New Hampshire, New Jersey, New York, Ohio, Pennsylvania, Rhode Island, Vermont,

Virginia, and Wisconsin). With a rare breed, such as the Sussex Spaniel, two competing dogs would yield 1 point to the winner, three dogs would give 2 points to the winner, and so on, until with six dogs competing, the winner would earn the maximum of 5 points. On the other hand, for German Shepherds it takes two dogs competing to win 1 point, twenty-eight dogs and twenty-nine bitches to win 3 points, and sixty-two males and seventy-six bitches to win 5 points. (A higher requirement for bitches indicates that more bitches are shown than males.)

These schedules are subject to change because the AKC constantly alters them to fit rising or falling levels of both registration and exhibition of dogs in each breed. All clubs which give shows that are licensed to award championship points must print a complete schedule of point ratings for the zone in which the shows are held. This is always given in the front of the catalog. All breeds are listed except rare breeds, which are covered by the heading "All Other Breeds and Varieties."

Suppose that the points are unevenly divided between the Winners Dog and Winners Bitch. For example, the Winners Dog for German Shepherds may have defeated sixty-two of his sex, and the Winners Bitch may have defeated only seventeen in hers. The male would win the maximum number of championship points, 5; the bitch would win only 2 points.

If the Winners Bitch then defeated the Winners Dog for Best of Winners, she is entitled to the same number of points as the male — in this case 5. She cannot add the male's points to hers because 5 points is the maximum that can be won at one show. This means that the Best of Winners is entitled only to the higher point rating of the two sexes.

The number of championship points that can be won at a show is figured according to the number of dogs that compete, not the number of dogs that are entered. In the example of the German Shepherd, suppose that there were sixty-two males entered but that only sixty-one dogs competed. The point rating for that contest would drop from 5 to 4. Also, dogs that are disqualified or excused because of shyness, viciousness, or lack of quality cannot be considered in figuring the championship rating. This ruling prevents an owner from loading a show with dogs of poor quality in order to allow a higher number of championship points for another dog.

Here is another example. Suppose that a judge decides that the best dog in a class of poor entries is not good enough to win a first prize or blue ribbon. In that case the judge can withhold the first-place award, and none of the dogs in that class will be counted in computing the point rating for the Winners Dog or Winners Bitch.

In the case of a rare breed such as the Sussex Spaniel, a dog may compete in fifty shows without ever facing another of its breed. However, if the dog is good enough to become the winner in its variety group (Sporting Dogs, Terriers, and so on), it is entitled to the highest point rating in any Winners Class in that group. For example, if there is a 5-point rating for Irish Setter bitches, a Sussex Spaniel that has won the Sporting Group would get 5 points. In this way, a dog that has never defeated a single dog of its own breed can still win a championship.

However, this same point system does not apply to tabulating points for Best in Show. Suppose that a Sussex Spaniel earned only 3 points by winning the Sporting Group and that it went on to win Best in Show by defeating a Doberman Pinscher that won 5 points by winning in the Working Breeds group. The Sussex Spaniel cannot claim 5 points for winning Best in Show, only the 3 points it won in the Sporting Breeds group.

AKC Certification

It is common practice for owners to make premature announcements that their dogs have *finished,* that is, become champions. However, no championship has been won until the AKC issues a championship certificate for a dog.

Sometimes errors are made because owners fail to account for absent, dismissed, or disqualified dogs. Sometimes the AKC makes a disqualification weeks after the show, and the owner of the newly proclaimed champion does not know about this disqualification. However, an owner can check on official results by consulting the American Kennel Club's official magazine, *Pure-bred Dogs: American Kennel Gazette.*

When a dog becomes a champion, the title of Champion becomes an official part of its name. This is usually listed as "Ch." The dog also receives an AKC championship certificate.

If a champion from outside the United States comes to this country to compete, it must be entered in Open Classes, but it may not be registered or shown as "English Ch. So-and-So." The AKC recognizes only its own championships. The dog can, of course, be advertised in magazines as an English champion. If it then wins an American championship, it can be called an "international champion." (Although this term is in common usage, it is incorrect in its implication that the dog has numerous championship titles around the world.)

There is an international federation of kennel clubs, called the F.C.I. (Fédération Cynologique Internationale), in which many European countries (excluding England) and some South American countries participate. This group licenses certain shows to award international championships. A dog must win a certain number of challenge certificates (called *cacibs*) in order to become an FCI international champion.

The AKC does award dual championships to dogs that win both show and field championships. However, it does not issue dual championship certificates.

chapter twenty-five
Sanctioned Match Shows

Match dog shows in the United States are sometimes incorrectly referred to as *puppy matches*. Their correct title is *sanctioned match shows*. They are sanctioned by the American Kennel Club and are run like other AKC conformation or obedience shows, with only registered dogs in competition. Match shows are not entitled to award championship points. *Nonsanctioned match shows,* which are usually less formal events, permit dogs to enter that are not purebred.

Entry fees for match shows — two to three dollars — are considerably less than those for licensed "point" shows, which helps to advance their purpose: to provide experience for young dogs and novice handlers. Most breeders and successful exhibitors will start puppies out at matches, so there is plenty of challenging competition, but the cost of "learning" is reasonable.

Most match shows have classes for puppies from the ages of two months to a year old, as well as classes for older dogs. Champions are barred from participating in match shows, and many shows bar dogs that already have some championship points. Judges must be approved by the AKC but do not have to be licensed for the breeds they are to judge. All-breeds and specialty clubs usually give obedience trials at these shows. Professional handlers can exhibit at match shows, but most clubs limit them to the handling of their own dogs.

There are two types of sanctioned match shows: Plan A and Plan B. In shows which consist only of obedience trials, there are Plan OA and Plan OB.

Applications to the AKC to hold match shows must be made at least four weeks before the scheduled event, but applications for Plan A and Plan OA will not be considered earlier than three months in advance. Plan A and OA matches must have a veterinarian present during the entire match or on call.

The ribbons awarded for match shows are: first place, rose; second place, brown; third place, light green; fourth place, gray; Special Prize, green with pink edges; Best of Breed, orange; Best of Match, pink and green; Best of Opposite Sex, lavender.

Plan A.   Newly formed kennel clubs must give two Plan A matches at least six months apart before they can apply to hold a licensed, or championship, show. Consequently this type of show is used to train club members in preparation for licensed shows and is called a *qualifying show.*

The rules for Plan A matches are quite involved and very strict. Entries must be made on regular dog show entry blanks; there must be premium lists for the entries; and regulation judging books must be used. Ribbons for such a qualifying show must bear the AKC emblem and give the name of the event, the name of the prize (such as "First Place"), the club, the date, and the city in which the show is held.

Because such a show is a practice event for licensed shows, dogs must be at least six months old to enter. Registered dogs are entered in Puppy, American-bred, and Open Classes. (Winners Classes are not offered.) A catalog and the entry forms for the competing dogs must be sent to the AKC along with an entry fee.

Plan B.   Shows under this plan are much simpler. Most Plan B shows take entries on the day of the event. Prizes other than ribbons are not permitted.

Puppies are eligible to enter when they are two months old. Classes are usually divided according to the age of the dogs: two to four months, four to six months, six to nine months, and nine to twelve months. Classes are also usually divided by sex. There is no fee to the AKC for a Plan B sanctioned match.

Obedience Matches: Plans OA and OB.   Obedience matches are usually given by an all-breeds club. Plan OA rules are about the same as those governing Plan A matches. An OA match is usually a qualifying one. If it is given by an obedience club, it is given in order to qualify the club to hold a show whose competitors can earn obedience titles.

OB matches have rules similar to those of Plan B matches. However, because two month old puppies are too young to compete in obedience work, OB matches do not accept dogs under six months old.

Dogs that hold the titles of Utility Dog (UD) or Companion Dog Excellent (CDX) may participate in obedience contests but cannot win prizes or ribbons.

chapter twenty-six
Canadian Dog Shows

The Canadian and the American Kennel Clubs enjoy a close relationship. As a result, registration procedures for both are very similar, extremely strict, and among the best in the world. Procedures for conducting their shows are also similar.

If an American dog is competing in a Canadian show, it must have a health certificate and a certificate of vaccination against rabies within the past year. It is then granted a temporary entrance permit, good for ninety days. A dog cannot win a championship in Canada without being registered there, and it cannot be registered unless it has been tattooed or noseprinted.

Dogs are registered by the Canadian Kennel Club, 111 Eglinton Avenue E, Toronto, Ontario. An application to register a dog from the United States must be accompanied by an AKC registration certificate (which is returned), the noseprint forms, and the registration fee. It is possible to list a dog for a small fee, and there is no limit to the number of times a dog can be shown as listed. However, it cannot win a championship until it is registered in Canada.

In Canada all winners of Best of Breed must enter group competition. Failure to do so brings cancellation of all awards the dog has earned at that show. There are a few exceptions to this rule. A Best of Breed winner can be absent without penalty if it is excused by a veterinarian because of illness, or if the show lasts an hour past the closing time given in the premium list, or if the show lasts past 10 P.M. (In the United States group competition is optional. A dog that wins Best of Breed can be declared absent from group competition.)

All Canadian shows are "examined" shows by veterinarians. (Each dog must be examined for signs of illness before it can enter the show.) Canada also has a rule which disqualifies a dog that has been administered drugs to stimulate, embolden, or tranquilize it.

To judge Best in Show in Canada, a judge must be licensed to judge all breeds.

Breeds Recognized in Canada

Canada recognizes all the breeds registered by the AKC, as well as some that the AKC does not recognize. These are the Pudelpointer, Nova Scotia Duck Tolling Retriever, and the Tahltan Bear Dog, all of which are included in the Sporting Dogs Group.

In the Hound Group, Miniature Dachshunds are given separate classifications according to coat. Therefore, there are six varieties of Dachshunds in Canada, instead of the three recognized in the United States, where Smooth, Wirehaired, and Longhaired standards and miniatures compete against each other. The Hound Group also includes the Drever, a breed unknown in the United States.

In Canada all breeds of Belgian Sheepdogs compete as one breed. (In the United States these dogs are classified into three groups: Belgian Sheepdog, Belgian Malinois, and Belgian Tervuren.) The Eskimo is also recognized by Canada.

In Canada the Lhasa Apso competes as a Terrier, whereas in the United States it is considered a member of the Non-Sporting Group.

These Vizslas won their awards during one weekend of showing in Canada. Photo courtesy of Burnt Hills Boarding Kennel.

Canada also recognizes the Cavalier King Charles Spaniel, a breed that at present appears in the Miscellaneous Class in the United States (although it may shortly be granted full breed status). Canada also recognizes the Mexican Hairless, a breed that has lost AKC recognition. The Shih Tzu has been given full breed status by Canada and appears in the Non-Sporting Group; it is placed in the Toy Group in U.S. competition.

Canada splits the Cocker Spaniel breed into four varieties. The fourth variety is the Black-and-Tan. (In the United States the Black-and-Tan must compete with the Ascobs, Any Solid Color Other than Black.) In Canada, when the four Best of Variety selections have been made, they must compete for Best of Breed. Only one Cocker variety enters the Sporting Group competition. In the United States there is no Best of Breed for Cockers except at specialty shows, and all the Cocker variety winners appear in the variety group competition.

Similarly, English Cockers are divided into two varieties, Solid Colors and Parti-colors, insofar as competition for championship points is concerned. One Best of Breed is awarded, and only one English Cocker enters the variety group. The same is true for Beagles.

Canadian Point System

To become a Canadian champion, a dog must win 10 championship points, compared with 15 points in the United States. Canada also uses a zone system and computes the scale of championship points in much the same manner as the AKC does. Because there are fewer competing dogs, the schedule of points is necessarily much lower. For example, in Canada's Zone 1, a German Shepherd would have to compete in an entry of nineteen of its sex to win 5 points. The point rating does not vary by sex. (In the United States, sixty-two males and seventy-six bitches must compete to earn a 5-point rating.)

Canada also grants points to a dog that wins Best of Opposite Sex. It would get the highest point rating of any dog of its sex for winning that designation.

A dog that wins Best in Show, if not a champion, is entitled to the highest point rating won by any dog at the show. To win its championship, a dog must win 10 championship points under at least three different judges. It must also defeat at least one of its breed, or it must win first place in its group against five or more breeds.

chapter twenty-seven
The World's Great Dog Shows

A number of dog shows have earned the distinction of being considered especially prestigious. These are not necessarily the largest shows. The reputation of the judges and the expertise of those organizing and managing the shows are considerations that are taken into account in an evaluation of a successful dog show. The location of the show and the time of year it is held are also factors, but they are of lesser importance.

The largest show in the world is the Birmingham, England National Show which in 1980 had 17,107 entries made for 10,970 individual dogs. The show has been held for more than 100 years.

The most prestigious show in the world is Cruft's. It is held in London and is actually given by the Kennel Club of England. It was formerly held at Olympia but has moved to Earl's Court.

Westminster is the most famous dog show in the United States. The Westminster Kennel Club, established in 1877, has been sponsoring a bench show over the years in various convention centers, and it is now held annually at Madison Square Garden in New York City. Like Cruft's, Westminster limits entries to dogs that have already won championship points. Three groups are usually benched each day, with about three thousand dogs entered in the show.

The Santa Barbara, California, dog show has been the largest in the United States for the last few years, with between thirty-five hundred and four thousand entries listed. (Actually the final number of entries at any given show is usually 8 to 10 per cent lower than the total entries processed because of absentees on the day of the event.) However, one factor in Santa Barbara's size has been the backing of Channel City and Ventura, within easy driving distance, and making three shows in successive days. However, Santa Barbara has had site problems because of its size. So in 1980, the other two shows have been given other dates. This could drop Santa Barbara from first place.

It is interesting to note that eight out of twenty of the largest shows in the United States are held in California. Factors accounting for this are California's large population, its superb year-round climate, and a high percentage of retired people who find breeding and showing dogs to be an excellent pastime.

The International Kennel Club of Chicago presents two dog shows a year, and these rank as the most prestigious ones in the Midwest. Both are held at Chicago's International Amphitheatre and are known to draw over 3,000 competitors.

Detroit's Cobo Hall and Cleveland's Convention Center have almost as much exhibition space as Chicago's hall. The Detroit Kennel Club's dog show is held in March, and the Western Reserve Kennel Club's show in Cleveland is held in mid-December. Both are prestigious events. The Kennel Club of Philadelphia show in November also ranks very high in quality.

It should be mentioned that the use of large exhibition halls has changed greatly in recent years. Week-long trade shows that have bookings in these halls take precedence over any one- or two-day events; consequently, many winter dog shows have had to be canceled. For example, Cleveland had to change the date of its March show to mid-December, a time when trade shows would not compete with it for booking exhibition space.

Many people feel that the most beautiful dog show in the world is the one held on the Grounds of Windsor Castle in England. Like the United States, England faces the problem of competition with trade shows for exhibition hall space. Some dog show locations have had to be switched; for example, the Richmond show was moved from the Olympia to Royal Ascot racetrack, where it is held in late summer.

Australia has two very famous "royal" shows: the Melbourne Royal and the Sydney Royal. The shows are held on the grounds of the Royal Agricultural Society, and each has entries totaling five thousand dogs. They are both extremely well-run shows, which is noteworthy because they last eight to ten days. At least six hundred to seven hundred dogs are judged and benched each day. A Best Dog and Best Bitch are picked for each breed. Best of Breed, Best of Opposite Sex, Group Winners, and Best in Show are not selected until the final day of the show.

Canada has a number of prestigious dog shows. Among them are the Midcontinent Show in Winnipeg, Manitoba; the Canadian National Sportsmen's Shows in Toronto; and the United Kennel Club Shows in Montreal. (I have said "Shows" because the same Canadian club might give two or three shows in the same building on successive days.) Canadian shows, although not very large, are extremely well run. They have an air of informality that always seems to delight American exhibitors.

American and Canadian exhibitors can attend a series of great dog shows held in Mexico City by the Asociacion Canofila Mexicana (Mexican Kennel Club). There are two shows during the last weekend of November and two shows during the first weekend of December. This allows visitors some time for sightseeing in Mexico during the festive Christmas season.

The Mexican show system permits foreign dogs to win both Mexican and international championships. Bermuda has the same system, with a series of shows running during one week. These shows have a delightfully informal atmosphere. Many of the best dogs from Canada and the United States compete in Bermuda, and it is considered a great honor to win a championship there.

New Zealand's great shows are Kumeu and the national show at Wellington.

The Japan International has drawn up to four thousand dogs and attracts judges from all over the world. This show has experimented a great deal with the different systems used by many foreign countries in an effort to make its show successful.

Both Colombia and Venezuela have excellent, well-run shows. Colombia, in particular, often has American dogs in the shows given by the Club Canino Colombiano. Brazil's Rio de Janeiro and São Paulo shows also have great prestige.

Sweden's National Show, with about 4500 dogs, is the largest in Scandinavia. The Paris, Madrid, and Seville shows have great prestige, as do those in Monaco.

part six
JUDGING DOG SHOWS

chapter twenty-eight
How a Judge Conducts a Ring

The way in which a judge conducts a ring (organizes the exhibitors and procedures) is of extreme importance. First, it should be conducted in an orderly manner so that both the gallery and exhibitors understand what is happening. Exhibitors and handlers should be able to tell the judge's progress at a glance. Also, a judge is less likely to forget to examine or gait a dog if the ring is conducted in an orderly manner.

Gaiting About the Ring

The standard procedure in conducting a ring is to have the dogs gait around the ring in a counterclockwise direction. The dogs are between the judge and their handlers, whose armbands (giving the entry numbers of the dogs) are visible to the judge. Normally a handler holds the leash in his or her left hand.

A judge may send the dogs around the ring once, twice, or three times, depending on the number of entries in the class and also on the breed. As a rule the larger the class entry, the greater the number of times the dogs will be asked to circle. This is the judge's first view of the dogs, from which he or she gets a general idea of their type, ring manners, and movement.

Because Toy dogs move more quickly and travel comparatively less far with the number of steps they take, the judge might find only one or two circles necessary for them. On the other hand, owners and handlers of German Shepherds and other large dogs both want and expect to be given very fast trotting work with their dogs, so the judge might require four, five, or six fast circles of the ring.

When a class is too big to handle easily in the ring provided, the judge has the right to split the class in two. He or she can send half the

Good gait is shown in this drawing of a dog (left), whose hind legs drive straight forward. Excellent movement in front is shown by this Terrier (right), whose legs move forward in a straight line.

The dog on the left has a straight stifle plus a lack of muscular strength in both the upper and the lower thigh. The dog on the right has a straight stifle and excellent muscular development.

dogs out, move the others in a circle, gait them individually, and then send those dogs out and test the second half in the same way.

A judge's first impression may be that a given dog is the best in the class, and so that dog may be placed at the head of the line. This is fairly standard procedure for judges. It is the judge's way of informing the gallery of his or her first impressions at the very beginning of the ring. It is important for the gallery to be given this kind of information. The spectators have paid their way in and are entitled to know, insofar as that is possible, what is going on.

Beginning judges sometimes seem to lose themselves in large classes. However, if they split the class in half and always try to keep the dogs in order, they are less likely to get confused and lose a dog somewhere in the shuffle.

At a show some years ago a certain English Springer Spaniel was Best in Show. The judge who had judged the breed the day before said to the handler, "Why didn't you show that dog under me yesterday? He's the greatest Springer I ever saw."

"I did," replied the handler. "You didn't even give him a fourth prize." The judge had put the dogs in two lines, side by side, and he had simply lost the dog in a big entry. If the judge had lined up the dogs in profile and kept their order in his mind, this would not have happened.

Lining Up

Where the judge lines up the dogs in the ring is important. Many experienced judges place the dogs for their convenience, which often is right in front of the judging stand. That is fine — *if* the gallery is outside the ring in back of the judge. A ring should not be held in such a way that the bodies of the exhibitors block the view of their dogs and the paying customers are unable to see the proceedings.

At one show the gallery seats in an arena began six feet above the floor level. The judge had a hundred or more Terriers lined up against an arena wall. None of the spectators could see any of the dogs. Even those in the front row could see only the backs of the dogs if they hung over the rail and looked down. Such carelessness and inconsiderateness on the part of judges — and on the part of show committees who do not instruct their judges — cause spectator interest in dog shows to wane.

Once the dogs are lined up, it is customary for the judge to take a careful look at them, to stand back and survey the entire class before examining the dogs individually. This may well confirm the judge's preliminary impression, which was formed while the dogs were being taken around the ring and perhaps gaited individually. However, there is also the possibility that this second look may cause the judge to change his or her mind about a given dog.

Individual Examinations

The judge is now ready to make an examination of each dog. The dog at the head of the line is usually examined first, although this is not an absolute rule. If, for instance, the judge spots a fault in the third dog, he (or she) might go to that dog first and check the fault, thus indicating to all that he (or she) has noticed it and dislikes it.

There are several dangers involved in starting individual examinations at any place other than at the head of the line. For example, the judge may somehow pass a dog by and fail to examine it. If the judge begins his or her examination by walking behind the dogs, the dogs may be upset. Unless the judge is checking for temperament, this procedure should not be used.

When a judge examines the heads of the dogs in line, what he or she looks for depends on the standard for that dog's breed. For example, in a Golden Retriever the judge would look for trichiasis (a form of inverted eyelashes), which is a disqualifying fault in this breed. In a Springer Spaniel, the ears should be set on at eye level; the leather or flap should reach the end of the nose; and the inside flap should be well covered with hair. In many breeds the ears should be set at eye level, but in many others they should be set higher. Clearly the judge must know the different standards and examine the dogs on that basis.

Similarly, eye color and the tightness of the lower lid against the eyeball are important. In some breeds, such as the St. Bernard, the lower lid is expected to droop so as to expose red flesh (the condition known as *haw*).

Dogs are subject to malformations of the jaw, and the most common ones are overshot and undershot. A dog is *overshot* if the lower jaw is so short that the outer edge of the lower teeth does not meet the inner edge of the upper teeth; it is *undershot* if the lower jaw is so long that the lower teeth are in front of the upper teeth when the jaw is closed. Most breed standards disqualify overshot or undershot dogs, but in a few breeds, such as the Boxer, an undershot jaw is considered proper and normal.

In certain long-jawed dogs, such as German Shepherds, some premolars may be missing. If more than four premolars are missing, this is a serious fault. When the outer surface of the cutting edge of the lower teeth meets the inner edge of the upper ones, the dog is said to have a *scissors bite*. When the cutting edges of the upper and lower incisors meet, the dog is said to have a *level bite*. Most standards specify the scissors bite; a few, the level bite; and some, either.

Most judges approach a dog from the front, put out a hand to show no harm is intended, and then open the dog's mouth to examine its teeth. Because this procedure is a means of spreading disease directly from dog to dog, the truly responsible judge will ask the exhibitor to show the dog's teeth. The rules of the Canadian Kennel Club specify that the exhibitor, not the judge, must open the dog's mouth; the American Kennel Club is silent on this point.

It is often difficult to get Toy dogs to show their teeth. One reason for this is that the timetable of growth of the different parts of Toy dogs' bodies never seem to be in balance. Quite often the dog's permanent teeth do not push out the milk teeth, which then have to be extracted. Consequently many Toy dogs are said to be *mouth-shy.*

Also, an occasional Toy dog may have what is known as a *wry mouth.* The lower jaw is twisted, so that one side is much lower than the other. The upper and lower teeth on one side may mesh, but the crooked or twisted jaw prevents those on the other side from engaging. Owners of such dogs may not attempt to train the dogs to open their mouths, hoping that the judge will miss the fault. To prevent this kind of deception, the judge may have to help an unwilling owner open the dog's mouth.

At its forward end, the lower jaw of the Bulldog should turn up in a rounded fashion rather than in a square or spade manner. It is often difficult for a judge to determine this without actually running his fingers along the jawbone.

The owner of a German Shepherd may not be anxious for the judge to see that his dog has some missing premolars, so he might open the jaw in such a way that the judge cannot tell whether all the teeth are there or not.

These are all instances in which the judge may have to help in order to make a proper examination of a dog's mouth.

Continuing the examination, the judge checks the angulation of the dogs' shoulder blades and leg assemblies. On long-coated dogs, trimming can do much to cover such things as straight shoulders, so the judge has to learn to feel and to check for this. The judge must also check under the dog's coat to determine whether a dog is swaybacked. For example, in the long months required to bring a Terrier's coat to perfection, it is possible to hide a swayback almost completely by means of grooming.

To the best of my knowledge all breed standards except that of the Pekingese call for sound feet. The Pekingese standard calls for flat feet. A sound foot is one that is strongly arched, with well-cushioned and padded toes. In heavy-coated dogs, or at least in those breeds with heavily furred feet and legs (for example, with Cocker Spaniels and Afghan Hounds), unsound feet can be disguised. Exhibitors simply do not trim the feet of these dogs. The judge has no way of telling whether or not the dog has strong, well-arched, and padded toes unless he or she feels for them. If the judge does not do this, dogs with flat feet, splayed toes, and paper pads may get by.

Today it is known that the lack of covering of the hip and thigh assembly by the secondary muscular structure is a probable cause of *hip*

In this drawing, dotted lines show the actual body outline; the solid lines show the terrier coat as groomed. A long swayback has been disguised by bringing the neckline coat farther down.

The facial hair on this terrier has been correctly "boxed," and the swayback has been properly covered. However, this dog is straight in stifle; the groomer made no attempt to give good stifle appearance by shaping the hair on the leg.

dysplasia, one of dogdom's great curses. When the above condition is not associated with true hip dysplasia, it may indicate probable future osteoarthritis. The careful judge will check for this. It is a hereditary fault that appears in all breeds except racing Greyhounds and Whippets. It is most prevalent in large breeds. The judge will know that the dog is lacking in this respect if the hip assembly is not covered with thick muscles and if the thighbone can be felt.

The examination is completed when the judge checks for such things as cow hocks, improper tail set, the presence or lack of dewclaws (which are required on some breeds), and in males, the presence of two normal testicles normally placed in the scrotum.

Sometimes the judge will want to turn all the dogs to face him or her in order to get the best possible view of their fronts. It is especially desirable to do this when judging Bulldogs.

If time permits, the judge may want to gait one or all of the dogs again and then line them up for a final survey or possibly make his (or her) choices as the dogs parade around the ring.

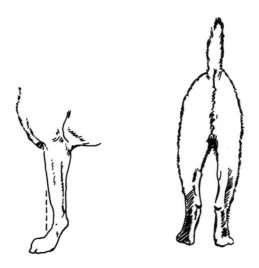

(Left). The dog pictured here has a badly fallen pastern. The dotted line indicates how grooming the leg hair can help to cover this defect.

(Right). A dog is said to have "cow hocks" if the hock joints are slightly turned in and the toes are turned out.

Placings

According to the official rules each ring must have numbered placing boards or cards. This is for the benefit of spectators. The judge must place the dogs before these numbers, to indicate placings, before marking the judge's book. The judge then gives out the ribbons. The boards are also used to indicate the dog that wins the categories of Best of Breed or Best of Variety, Best of Winners, and Best of Opposite Sex.

This procedure is also required in group and Best in Show judging, but one occasionally sees the rule violated, particularly in Best in Show judging. Sometimes a judge marks the judge's book first, hoping to add to the drama of the procedure, but the American Kennel Club does not approve of this practice.

chapter twenty-nine
General Considerations When Judging

Judging Methods

Three methods are used to judge dogs. The first method is to try to place the dogs on the basis of overall quality. The judge makes selections according to the general quality of the dogs, on the basis of their conformance to type and balance of parts.

The second method is to judge the dogs on faults. The judge tries to place the dogs in an order based on the fewest major faults. When judges use this method, a rather good dog may be ruled out because of a single fault that happens to be prominent. This is the method used in "ringside judging"; that is, the spectators can usually see the major faults, such as for poor ear set, loose elbows, incorrect length of coat, and inferior quality of color, from the ringside.

The third system is based on mathematics. Many breed standards contain what is known as a *scale of points*. For example, here is the scale of points for the Field Spaniel.

Head and jaw	15
Eyes	5
Ears	5
Neck	5
Body	10
Forelegs	10
Hind legs	10
Feet	10
Stern	10
Coat and feather	10
General appearance	10
Total	100

Some breed standards say that the scale of points is to be used only as a guide, but occasionally a judge follows it precisely. This method is also used by judges in some foreign countries. The difficulty in using this method is that dogs do not lend themselves to exact mathematics. Moreover, no two judges will allow the same number of points for a given part.

For example, some breed standards make an undershot jaw a disqualification (although it is desired in some breeds, such as the Bulldog). However, even when a standard does not call for disqualification, most breeders consider the undershot jaw an unforgivable fault. In this case the judge who tries to score dogs mathematically will be faced with a dilemma. In tabulating the points for a dog with an undershot jaw, the judge will have to decide how many points to give in the "head and jaw" category, whether both parts should be equal in point value, or how a penalty should be scored.

I once stewarded for a German judge who used the mathematical system, and it took him an hour and a half to judge two dogs. He would score points for a dog's eyes, ears, expression, and so forth; but when he returned to look at the dog a little while later, his ideas would change, and he would have to start scoring again.

Regardless of the method used, it is harder to judge a group of poor dogs than a group of very good ones. All the dogs in a poor group will have major faults. Conformation and type may be equally poor, making it hard for the judge to find any dogs he or she really likes. Inevitably questions will be asked, such as "How could you give a ribbon to a dog with such an outstanding fault?" The judge faces the difficult job of defending a choice with which even he or she might not be totally happy.

Type

In terms of dog shows, the word *type* has three closely related meanings. It can be defined as a class or group sharing certain characteristics, such as the kind of work the dog does: "He is a very good type of hunting dog." It can also have a meaning in terms of a breed. For example, when humane shelters try to describe the mongrels they pick up, they refer to a "Collie-Shepherd type," a "Spaniel type," or a "mixed Terrier type."

A dog's type can be examined in terms of their components. For example, almost all Spaniels have long, drooping ears; thick, heavy coats; heavy body and leg feathering; and docked tails. Greyhounds, Whippets, Borzois, and others share type as sight gazehounds and coursing Hounds. They have long, wedge-shaped heads, prominent eyes (set far enough apart to give them a very wide range of vision), and arched backs.

When we are dealing with a single breed, the components of type are the specifications in the standard of excellence for that breed. That standard, which is the sum of its components, is drawn up on the basis of a conception of the perfect dog of that breed.

The Ideal Dog

One frequently hears it said that a given breed standard "was written around that dog" or that a certain dog served as the blueprint for the standard. That is not quite true. When a group of breeders draws up a standard for their breed, presumably with expectations for having that breed at least eventually recognized by an official governing body such as the AKC, they may agree that a certain dog is the best specimen but not necessarily perfection on every point. The standard will reflect these idealizations.

At dog shows one also hears, "I wish he had So-and-So's head." "It's too bad he can't have So-and-So's stifle angulation." Again these are idealizations. They indicate a desire for perfection, which, of course, never is quite there. Otherwise there probably would be no need for dog shows or for dog judges.

Such an ideal dog cannot exist for another reason: The ideal is a subjective conception; no two people would ever completely agree on what constitutes it. If a dog were to be proclaimed the perfection of type, the ideal dog, a dissenting chorus would immediately ask, "Who says so?" "On whose authority?" "By whose standards?"

It might seem from this that there would be no popular or successful dog judges, but some are universally recognized as being competent. Such judges, whether or not they ever think it out sufficiently to put it into words, have a philosophy of judging. They also have a consistency about their judging that gives exhibitors confidence. Their judging philosophy is based on the concept of a dog as an entity, as something more than the sum of its parts. A dog is a living, moving being whose parts work together, functioning as a whole.

If a person looks at a dog as only a collection of parts, that person is in effect dissecting or destroying the entity. To idealize in this way — "I wish it had a shorter back" or "If I could put this dog's head on that one's neck" — is unfair and unrealistic.

Guidelines

The best judges have what is commonly called "an eye for a dog," that is, a sense of harmony, of a balance of parts in a functioning whole.

These judges know and understand the standards of the breeds. They follow the provisions of the standards very closely. When their innate eye for a dog combines with their experience, they are able to distinguish the best dogs in any class very quickly.

One of the great judges of the past — a noted artist, by the way — had this advice for a young judge:

"You have, or will gain, the experience. You know the standards and, above all, you have the eye. The answers will come to you rather quickly. Stand on them. Do not try to analyze them. Do not try to break down the dogs into their separate parts, saying: 'This dog has a better head than that one, but this dog has a better rib spring.' If you do this sort of thing, you'll more than likely change your placings. Also, more than likely, you'll be wrong. You will have talked yourself into being wrong. Remember, it is the harmony of all the parts that counts.

A judge must know and understand the standards of the breeds when he makes his selection of the best dog in a class. Photo of Vizsla, Hollandia's Arany Cigany (CD), courtesy of Burnt Hills Boarding Kennel.

"Of course, there will come those times when you must make a choice between two great and nearly perfect dogs. You'd like to call it a tie. But you can't. Then your decision will rest on purely minor points — often points so slight it would be unfair to the dogs to mention them. You will have heard it said: 'Pick the dog you'd like to take home with you.' But you would like to take both dogs. Then you will have to make your decision on dissecting the parts, so to speak. But you will do so humbly, knowing that while you are correct in your choice, another judge will be right if he or she disagrees with you.

"Finally, try not to be misled by 'flash,' by some point which is perhaps a crowd pleaser, but which is an over-accentuation of a part. This over-accentuation may even be a judge pleaser, but it is usually achieved at the expense of balance and harmony. That lack can destroy the dog as a stud or brood force."

Good though it is, this philosophy of judging is not the entire answer. The breed standards list disqualifying and major faults, and these may have little to do with the desired balance of parts. The judge might be forced to place a generally inferior dog over one that has better balance but that also has a major fault.

This brings up a final point. No judge likes to ignore the breed standards, and few will admit that they ever have; yet it is done continually. For example, the standard for American Cocker Spaniels says that they should have a profuse coat "but not so [excessive] as to hide the Cocker Spaniel's true lines and movement or affect his appearance and function as a sporting dog. Excessive coat . . . is to be penalized." Cocker breeders not only ignore this provision in the standard but actually try to increase the breed's coat from the abdomen to the pads of the feet. Cockers today are fantastically coated. Their lines are almost totally hidden, and it would be impossible for them to function as Sporting Dogs.

No judge likes to put down a superior dog for an otherwise inferior animal just because the superior dog has an excessive coat. The judge who makes such a choice may be obeying the standard, but that is not the way Cocker breeders want their dogs judged. It is easier for the judge of the variety group to enforce the coat provision because he or she may find superior dogs of other breeds that are also properly groomed. These dogs could then be placed above the Cockers without risking a bloodletting (the judge's own blood, that is).

Such problems caused one all-breeds judge to remark somewhat plaintively, "Show me any business executive who has to make as many tough decisions in a day as we dog judges must."

chapter thirty
Height, Weight, and Color Determinations

Some breed standards include height, weight, or color disqualifications. Some standards give desired heights or weights but do not make undesirable ones a disqualification. It is up to an all-breeds judge to remember which breeds and varieties carry these disqualifications.

AKC rules state that it is a judge's responsibility "to initiate a determination as to whether a dog is to be disqualified or declared to be ineligible for the class." Exhibitors also have the right to challenge any dog that is competing against them in the ring. Therefore, both judges and exhibitors are custodians of the breed standard. However, because many exhibitors seem to feel that it is poor sportsmanship to challenge the height, weight, or color of a competing dog, they remain silent.

Measuring Height and Weight

Show-giving clubs are expected to provide scales and measuring equipment at the show in case a breed has requirements for either height or weight. This equipment is always supplied by the superintendent except at those specialty shows for which the club appoints a member to act as show secretary.

The AKC now supplies wickets that have been accurately designed to determine height. These have extendible legs and can be adjusted to the correct height for a particular breed. (Dogs used to be measured with a guillotine-type instrument which often scared them so much that it was difficult to get an accurate measurement.)

The judge measures the dog in the ring. (In Canada a committee measures the dog at the secretary's office and then reports to the judge.) The dog is placed on a flat board (if the show is held outdoors) or on the floor (if the show is held indoors) so that the measurement will be taken on a level surface and under conditions in which the dog's feet will not sink into the ground. The owner is asked to place the dog in its natural standing position, exactly as it would be posed for showing. The judge, having preset the wicket at the exact height, should show it to the steward and to the owner, so that no questions arise later. The wicket is then slipped over the dog's back and placed on its withers (the highest point of its shoulders). If the dog is long-coated — a Poodle or a Shetland Sheepdog, for instance — the owner is allowed to brush the hair forward so that the wicket rests as nearly as possible on the dog's skin, not on half an inch of hair.

If the legs of the wicket do not touch the floor, it is obvious that the dog is too tall. But if the legs do touch the ground, the dog is either at the maximum allowed height or under it. The judge then marks the judging book: "Dog No. 2 — measured out." If a dog is measured out, it is disqualified from competition at the show.

If the owner feels that the dog was incorrectly measured, a written appeal can be made to the American Kennel Club. The appeal must be accompanied by a deposit of twenty-five dollars. The AKC will appoint an official measuring committee in the owner's home area, and a final measurement will be taken. If the dog is still a disqualifying height, the dog is disqualified from any further competition in licensed shows and the twenty-five dollar deposit is forfeited.

Today many exhibitors have their own wickets; consequently fewer ring measurements are required. However, there are always exhibitors with dogs that are so close to the standard in measurement that they hope to get by unmeasured. The wicket system does not provide an absolute height measurement, which is really impossible to obtain; it simply facilitates the determination of whether the dog is too short or too tall.

It should be noted that some breed standards have minimum as well as maximum heights. For example, the standard for Shetland Sheepdogs calls for a minimum height of thirteen inches and a maximum height of sixteen inches; the standard for Miniature Schnauzers calls for a minimum of twelve inches and a maximum of fourteen inches.

Weight determinations are not so approximate. If a proper and accurate scale is used, the exact weight of the dog can be obtained. Weighing must also be done in the ring. A club or superintendent that provides a scale that is inaccurate, unsuitable for weighing a dog, or broken in transit will be fined by the AKC.

Color Standards

Some breed standards have color disqualifications. For example, the Boxer standard calls for the disqualification of any dog with a white or black ground color, a coat entirely black or white or any color other than fawn or brindle, or a dog with white markings that exceed one third of the ground color. Dalmatians are disqualified if they have any markings other than black or liver or if they have both black and liver spots. French Bulldogs must be disqualified if they are black and white, black and tan, liver, mouse, or solid black (black without any trace of brindle).

The judge must determine these color questions. If he or she decides that the dog has disqualifying color or markings, then the judge disqualifies the dog and records this information in his judge's book.

chapter thirty-one
Temperament Problems in Show Dogs

A dog's temperament can be a major concern for its owner. This is true of mongrels, offspring of haphazard matings of purebreds, field trial dogs, and show dogs, but it is most serious in the last two categories because one expects more from carefully bred dogs.

It is not too difficult to determine the temperament of field dogs. Problems will become evident long before a dog reaches the field trials. Failure to take training, refusal to go out to hunt, and gun-shy or man-shy behavior are temperamental flaws in a field trial dog.

Good temperament is of great importance for show dogs. First, poor temperament can prevent an otherwise great dog from proving its greatness. Second, dogs of poor temperament produce their own kind. This may not matter to the exhibitor who is solely interested in winning, but it is of major importance to the serious breeder. The buyers of purebred puppies are paying for carefully bred, healthy, good-tempered dogs. If instead they get a puppy that is hysterical, shy, vicious, or a fear biter, they will have been defrauded and the breed will have received an undeserved black eye.

One should remember that for every great show dog, ten or more with comparable breeding do not make the grade. Nonetheless, exhibitors who care only about winning may try to make champions out of temperamentally unsound dogs. To do this, they may use frauds; for example, they may give stimulants to shy dogs or sedatives to highly nervous, hysterical dogs.

Some judges choose to ignore poor temperament entirely, or they may be careless in paying attention to it. For example, a certain Miniature Pinscher won Best of Breed and then went on to win in the

Good temperament is of great importance for show dogs. *Gaines Dog Research Center*

Toy Group. However, this dog was extremely shy, gaited poorly, and did not pose properly. Spectators were astounded to see it win even a first place in its class. Later I overheard the two judges discussing the dog, perhaps trying in a roundabout way to justify their decision. "There comes a time when you have to ignore temperament in favor of great type," one judge said. "You're right," the other answered. "When you get such supreme type as that, you just have to overlook ring manners." However, the judge who makes excuses for any dog or who accepts them from exhibitors will sooner or later be in deep trouble.

Shyness

An exhibitor may try to excuse a dog's poor performance by explaining "This is his first show" or "She doesn't like the table" (spoken of a Toy, which is always shown on a table). Such excuses are not valid. There are always some dogs that show with spirit at their first show or, in the case of Toy dogs, that stand at attention on a table. It is the duty of the exhibitor to train and condition a dog so that it will show well even at its first show.

One sometimes hears this excuse: "The dog doesn't like people." Maybe so, but the odds are great that the dog is suffering from a serious character fault. Moreover, how can a judge know that the exhibitor is telling the truth?

I am reminded of a professional handler who once complained to the judge that his dog had never been beaten in competition. An AKC field representative challenged the handler on this. "Well," said the handler, "it's true. This is the first time the dog has been shown."

What is shyness? Most of the breed standards either ignore the question or are so vague that neither breeders nor judges know what is meant. However, some standards are specific. The definition of shyness in the standard for Doberman Pinschers is valid for other breeds. It makes "shyness" a disqualification and defines it as follows: "A dog shall be judged fundamentally shy if, refusing to stand for examination, it shrinks away from the judge; if it fears an approach from the rear; if it shies at sudden and unusual noises to a marked degree."

A judge cannot disqualify a dog for shyness unless the standard for that breed calls for it. However, the judge can withhold ribbons from shy dogs or place an otherwise first-class dog second or third for "reasons of temperament."

Many judges seem to be afraid to withhold ribbons because of a dog's lack of temperament or lack of quality. Nevertheless, although the withholding of ribbons may make some exhibitors very angry, the majority will approve of the judge's courage.

Viciousness

A second temperament problem in dogs is viciousness. It is seen less often than shyness, but again it presents a problem to the judges at a show. Although a judge knows that a vicious dog should never be used for breeding, what is viciousness? In several breed standards it is defined in terms of a dog that attacks or tries to attack the judge or its handler.

As in the case of shyness, a judge's ruling is governed by the standard for each breed. For example, if a Standard Schnauzer is vicious, the judge can — indeed *must* — disqualify it, but there are other breed standards that do not call for this. A judge should disqualify *all* vicious dogs but is prevented from doing so by the rules of the American Kennel Club. Those rules state that if a breed standard does not make viciousness a disqualification, the judge cannot disqualify a dog of that breed for that reason.

In the case of Chesapeake Bay Retrievers the standard says that a judge must disqualify any unworthy dogs. A certain judge may feel that any dog which bites him or her is unworthy. However, the AKC has ruled that "unworthy" applies only to a dog's physical qualities, not to temperament. Therefore, such a dog cannot be disqualified on the grounds that it is unworthy. However, the rules do say that the judge can withhold any or all ribbons from a dog for lack of quality. It may be stretching a point to say that viciousness constitutes lack of quality, at least under the AKC's conceptions of quality, but the judge can give that reason.

If the judge writes in the judge's book: "Withheld for viciousness," the AKC will probably write a letter to the judge asking, "What do you mean? Did he try to bite you, or what?" The judge's explanation is likely to be as far as the matter goes; the AKC simply wants to complete the record.

If there is competition in the class, the judge can duck even that bit of correspondence by simply placing the dog last in the class. If the dog is an otherwise good specimen, the judge can give his or her reasons to the handler or owner, and that should end the matter.

Inexperience

A question sometimes comes up about whether a judge should make excuses for puppies or dogs in classes where the entries are obviously inexperienced. This question is a hard one to answer because judges can be understanding as well as unbending. Here are two examples from my own experiences as a judge.

At one show a puppy was so shy that it could not be posed. It struggled to get away from its handler. In its terror it urinated on the handler's shoe. All ribbons were withheld. The owner wrote a scathing letter saying that the dog was a puppy, and what could you expect? And yet a puppy from the same breed, but of another variety, not only won its class but went on to win Best of Variety.

At a show in a foreign country, a judge was suddenly faced with five bitch puppies, all from one litter, and all of extraordinary quality. However, they were not well trained, and the judge spent a long time trying to decide which of the five was best. Eventually he gave a first place (and later Best of Breed) to a certain puppy. Several years later this dog came to the United States to compete. It bit the first three judges it faced. The previous judge had obviously made a poor decision, mistaking poor temperament in the puppy for lack of training. By making excuses, he was guilty of poor judging.

chapter thirty-two
Other Problems that Judges Face

Judging Schedules

The problem of waiting for dogs to come to the ring is a vexing one. It happens at every show that both novices and experienced exhibitors fail to get their dogs to the ring on time. Yet it is their responsibility to be at ringside at the time given in the judging schedule, which each exhibitor receives about a week before the show. Many dog show premium lists state that a judge will not wait longer than ten minutes; others say five minutes. Some say: "The judge will not wait for any dog. It is the responsibility of exhibitors and handlers to have their dogs at ringside at the hour stated for judging."

Judging schedules are usually arranged on an hourly basis. Here is a sample from an actual schedule:

9 A.M.	3	Smooth Fox Terriers
	7	Wire Fox Terriers
	9	Cairn Terriers
	1	Sealyham Terrier
10 A.M.	22	St. Bernards
	1	Bullmastiff
	1	Rottweiler
	1	Giant Schnauzer
11 A.M.	2	Cardigan Welsh Corgis
	22	Pembroke Welsh Corgis
	1	Belgian Tervuren

The rules prohibit a judge from starting an assignment before the advertised time. He or she cannot start a 9 A.M. assignment before nine. Even if an assignment is finished early, the next one must begin on time. People pay to see dogs judged, and they do not want to arrive after the judging is over. Neither do exhibitors.

In the above schedule, ten Fox Terriers were to be shown at 9 A.M. Cairn exhibitors might figure that it would be nine twenty-five or nine-thirty before their own breed would be called, but they cannot rely on this. One or all of the Fox Terriers could be absent, and in that case the judge would start judging Cairns at nine or very shortly thereafter. When such a situation occurs very early in the day, the judge can afford to wait a few minutes because the second hour's work cannot start before ten o'clock.

To help minimize a judge's waiting time, capable stewards will notify the handlers in another ring that the judge in the next ring will be

The judge examines each dog individually on the basis of the standard for that breed. *Gaines Dog Research Center*

waiting for them shortly. The stewards may also search out exhibitors and give them their armbands well ahead of the judging time for that breed.

Handlers who see that they will be needed in two rings at once usually arrange for another handler, an assistant, or even a dog's owner, to take one of the dogs into the ring. After one ring is finished, the handler will then go to the other. However, the handler must obey a certain rule of etiquette and ask the steward to ask the judge to allow him or her to take over the handling of the dog. The judge should also obey a rule of etiquette by granting the permission. However, AKC rules permit this only if the judge has not already examined the dog.

If a judge has a large class and is delayed by the late arrival of handlers, other handlers in the ring may be holding up the judge in some other ring. One solution is to put a dot before the number of the missing dog and then start the judging. The judge should explain to the exhibitors that rather than hold up the class, he or she will begin and will allow the missing dog to come in later. The chances are that by the time the other dogs are examined, the handler with the missing dog will come into the ring. In this way the judge will not have held up the class or fallen behind in the judging schedule. There is, however, a danger that the judge may forget about the missing dog and judge and complete the class before the handler arrives.

Absentees are not marked absent until the actual judging has taken place, the dogs have been placed before their numbers, and the judge has prepared to mark the awards in the judge's book.

Catalog Information

A dog show catalog contains privileged information about the dogs that are entered in competition. After a judge's assignments are completed, the judge receives a catalog along with copies of his or her judging sheets from the superintendent. Both should be kept for at least eight months. The judge can then refer to these records in case of an inquiry from the AKC or from an exhibitor.

It sometimes happens that a show is the first of two weekend events, both of which are handled by the same superintendent. A given judge may be officiating at both. In that case discretion dictates that the judge should refuse to accept the first day's catalog until his or her judging for the second day is completed. In this way the judge cannot be charged with checking over the catalog to see what dogs will be judged on the second day.

Occasionally an exception is made, and catalog information is made available to a judge. For example, black is a disqualification in Kerry

Blue Terriers over eighteen months of age. However, at birth Kerry Blues are an "apparent black" in color. Therefore, if a blackish dog appears in any class but the Puppy Class, the judge has little clue to its age. Yet the judge must know this information before making a decision. Asking an exhibitor may produce a deliberately wrong answer or an "I don't know." Instead the judge should ask the steward to bring the catalog to the exhibitor's side. Then, in the presence and hearing of the exhibitor, the judge should ask the steward to check on the dog's age. There can then be no chance of misinterpreting the judge's action, and the judge will have the correct information on which to base his or her decision.

Here's another example: The Yorkshire Terrier is born black and tan. As it matures, the black should turn to steel blue within eighteen months, but sometimes it does not. Again, unless the dog is entered in the Puppy Class, the judge can get no real clue to whether the coat will ever turn blue. So again the judge should ask the steward, in the exhibitor's presence, to check in the catalog to determine the dog's actual age.

With Poodles, only puppies may be shown in a Puppy clip. Dogs over a year old must be shown only in the Continental, English Saddle, or Corded clips. Any other clip will result in disqualification. Again, if there is a question regarding the correct clip for a certain dog, the judge should ask the steward, in the presence and hearing of the handler, to check in the catalog for the dog's true age.

Reserve Winners

A common pitfall in judging is to forget to call back a dog chosen as a Reserve Winner. (A Reserve Winner is chosen in case the Winners Dog or Winners Bitch is disqualified for any reason.) Even experienced judges sometimes forget to do this.

In other cases the required dog cannot be found. This happens chiefly with inexperienced exhibitors (but sometimes even with professionals), who may leave the show building with the second-place winner before the competition is over.

When such a dog cannot be found, the judge should make a notation to this effect in the judge's book because the American Kennel Club needs to know everything that has happened at the show.

Rejudging

A class cannot be rejudged. Once the judge has marked the judge's book and handed out the ribbons, that class is completed forever. This applies regardless of circumstances which might suggest that the class be rejudged.

Here's a hypothetical case: There is a class of three dogs, but two cannot be found. The judge marks them absent, marks the other dog first, and gives out the ribbon. Just at that moment the other two dogs show up. They are out of luck.

At one show a handler's dog won the Puppy Class with five dogs competing. Seconds after the handler had left the ring, he returned in great embarrassment. He had shown his entry for the Open Class instead of his puppy. However, the Puppy Class had been judged. A note of this was made in the judge's book, and the superintendent also reported the incident. When results reached the AKC, it canceled the first-place dog's win, wrote letters calling in the ribbons given out in the class, and moved up the second-, third-, and fourth-place dogs one rank.

Explaining Decisions

A question that sometimes comes up is whether or not a judge should be expected to explain his or her decisions. One answer is that the judge should be willing to give the reasons for any decision that an exhibitor questions. However, this may take time that a judge cannot afford to lose. Moreover, if a judge explains decisions without having been asked to do so, many exhibitors may feel that the judge is trying to make excuses for having made wrong choices.

From a practical standpoint, explanations are difficult to make. The judge is, after all, looking at the dogs as entities. If a judge tries to give an answer other than "I liked the overall quality of the other dog," he or she will have to detail the criticisms of the dogs that did not win, and, as I just explained, there are several reasons why that would be unsatisfactory.

Novice exhibitors, especially, need to understand why a judge does not make such explanations. But sometimes a novice whose dog has been defeated may go out of the ring both mystified and hurt. At times like that a few words from a judge can make those exhibitors understanding losers and keep them enthusiastic about dog shows.

Owners of puppies are always eager to know the judge's opinion. Experienced breeders in particular know how easy it is to become kennel-blind (i.e., to oversell themselves on the qualities of a puppy). At least in Puppy and Novice Classes the judge should be ready and willing to give explanations and words of encouragement. When time permits, the judge should volunteer them.

However, explanations should be made only in the ring and only at the end of a class. It is unfair of exhibitors to ask a judge hours — and fifty dogs — later, "What didn't you like about my dog?" It is also unfair to the dog. In such circumstances the judge should say something like, "I'm sorry, but too many dogs have gone by for me to remember the details about your dog. I think it would be very unfair to make comments now, especially since I might have the wrong dog in mind." Sometimes, if there is time and if the exhibitor is a novice, the judge might say, "It would be unfair to discuss your dog without seeing him (or her) again. Why don't you bring your dog over? Then we can go over the dog together."

The Poor Sport

A problem for all judges is what to do about the poor sport. The majority of dog fanciers are decent, respectable people. They are reasonably good losers and can be considered good sportsmen. However, there are also exhibitors who are poor losers and always call the judge and the winning dog's owner dishonest and the winning dog a bum and "full of holes."

When such people ask a judge for an explanation, no answer will satisfy them because they simply want the chance to vent their frustrations. The simplest answer to a poor sport is the same as the one given to an exhibitor who asks for a clarification: "I simply liked the overall quality and balance of the other dog." But the reason for giving the answer is different: It is an answer for which it is difficult for the poor sport to think of a reply.

The judge does not have to take abuse from exhibitors, nor should poor sportsmanship be permitted in the ring. For example, the judge should not — and need not — permit an exhibitor to refuse to accept a ribbon. If an exhibitor walks out of the ring without his or her ribbon, the steward should be sent to order that person back to the ring to receive the ribbon in front of the placing number. If the person refuses, the bench show committee should be summoned and notified. The bench show committee should also be summoned if an exhibitor throws the dog's ribbon on the floor of the ring.

If an exhibitor makes remarks to the effect that the judge is crooked, incompetent, or political, the matter should also be placed before the bench show committee. The AKC demonstrates its confidence in judges when it licenses them, so it will defend them in such cases. The bench show committee represents the AKC in the field, as it were. It has the right to hear both sides, and it also has the right to recommend suspension of the exhibitor.

Unusual Occurrences

When the records of a show come into the offices of the American Kennel Club, officials there have the job of recording the results. They must be able, as nearly as possible, to reconstruct the events at the show. The judge should record in his or her judge's book any unusual occurrences that might help AKC officials understand what happened in the ring. The judge should note disqualifications, dogs ruled ineligible, or the refusal of an exhibitor to return his or her dog for Reserve Winners. Sometimes, as mentioned, a dog cannot be found when Reserve Winners is to be judged. The judge should note this in the judge's book. If the exhibitor later claims that Reserve Winners was not called, the record will indicate exactly what happened.

Sometimes an exhibitor will make unfair and dishonest remarks to the judge about a dog: "I could finish the dog with this win today." "He got Best of Breed yesterday." "He's won eleven points in three shows." Such remarks may not be strong enough to warrant bringing the exhibitor before the bench show committee, but they can put a judge in an unfortunate position. If the judge awards a ribbon to the dog, the exhibitor might think, "This judge can be had." If the judge does not award the dog a ribbon, the exhibitor knows that the judge does not tolerate such dishonesty. However, if that dog happens to be the best dog there, the judge will be dishonest if he or she does not give it a first place.

The solution for a judge is to record such an incident in the judge's book: "Handler of dog Number 16 whispered that the dog could finish its championship with this win. His remark has not affected my judgment." The AKC can then be depended on to write a scathing letter to that exhibitor or handler. If the person has a history of such conduct, a suspension might result.

chapter thirty-three
Judges' Code of Conduct

Before anyone applies for a license to judge dogs, he or she should think the matter over carefully. What is involved is far more than just the ability to tell which of a group of dogs is best. A judge's honesty is at stake, and that honesty or integrity will be challenged in many different ways.

For example, a judge must decide among the dogs of friends, enemies, and strangers. The oath to make impartial decisions is implied in the application to judge. Every applicant for a judging license probably understands this, though vaguely, but no applicant can understand the true pressure a dog judge is under until he or she has experienced it. At a judge's first show there may be a dozen of the judge's friends showing their dogs. Some will be intimate friends; others will pretend to be. Each will believe that he or she knows the judge's mind thoroughly and cannot lose.

A judge gradually learns to withstand this pressure, or most of it. The truth is, the pressure never lets up, and it will come in ways that the judge may never have faced before and that consequently hit him or her in tender spots.

Honesty

Conceptions of honesty vary; what one person considers honest, another may regard as dishonest. Let's examine some situations in which integrity is at stake during the judging at a show.

A judge who considered himself honest once said to an exhibitor, "I couldn't separate the two dogs. But I knew you wouldn't care, so I put up the other dog." Another judge, who also considered his integrity to

BEST OF
BREED

TROY
KENNEL CLUB

OCTOBER 1977

ASHBEY

A judge should be impartial when choosing which of a group of dogs is best and base his decision on the merits and faults of the dogs. Photo of Ch. Longcove's Golden Gemini, courtesy of Jeannie and Alfred Kinney.

be beyond question, had this to say: "Of course, when two dogs are equal, I'll give my friend a break. Who wouldn't?" In the first case the judge made his choice by penalizing a good sport. In the second case he favored a friend. But it is the judge's duty to study the dogs until he or she can reach a decision based on the merits and faults of the dogs.

If a judge gives in once, the next time it will be that much easier to do so. It is always easy to find your friend's dog superior to another's, or for a poor sport's dog to win over a good sport's dog because of intimidation. But this would be highly unfair.

At a certain show it was known that one of the most popular men connected with showing dogs was dying. His wife was crippled, but she loyally brought their dog to the show and bathed and prepared it. Then the man's sister showed the dog. The breed, group, and best-in-show judges knew the situation. The dog went all the way to Best in Show. The decision was immensely popular, and perhaps the owner died happy. Yet insiders knew that the show had been fixed and that the three judges had been dishonest. Perhaps those judges would argue that they were being so for a good cause, but having been dishonest once, it will probably be progressively easier for them to be dishonest with the rest of their judging.

It definitely takes an iron will to judge honestly under such circumstances. However, a judge is not there to make selections for sentimental reasons. A judge is there to pick the best dog.

A friend of an exhibitor once said to a judge, "So-and-so's dog only needs this win to finish its championship. And today she just learned that the dog is hopelessly ill with cancer." Nothing further was said, but the judge received the intended message. The dog won — and it lived to be fourteen years old. Eventually the AKC revoked the license of this judge permanently.

Here is another case: A dog that gets Best of Winners is entitled to as many championship points as were won by the dog it defeated. Suppose that the Winners Dog has won only 1 point but that the Winners Bitch has won 5 points. If the male then gets Best of Winners, he is given 5 points instead of 1. Because 5-point victories are rare, an occasional judge will give Best of Winners to the inferior dog so that both will get 5 points. This is dishonest judging. It is the judge's job to give Best of Winners to the better of the two dogs.

A judge can never afford to relax. The rule must always be that a judge is in the ring to pick the best dog regardless of friends, foes, politicians, the sick, or the dying.

Because people are only human, dog shows are always cauldrons brewing gossip and scandals. Judges can avoid most of this by their conduct. They must establish a code of conduct such that petty gossip about them cannot arise.

Conduct Before and After a Show

Sometimes dog shows are held in areas in which the judges will be dependent on the show-giving club for transportation to the show. Whenever possible, a judge should avoid riding to the show with an exhibitor or someone who will be showing a dog under him that day. (The Canadian Kennel Club has very strict rules governing this; judges who violate the rule are subject to severe discipline.)

Someone once said that there is no lonelier person in the world than a dog judge after a show. The exhibitors whose dogs have not won have no desire to transport the judge to an airport or into town, and the judge has no desire to ride with the handler or owner of the Best in Show winner. For these reasons it is often best if the judge rents a car to travel back and forth; in that way he or she will not be dependent on anyone.

The AKC recommends that a judge arrive at a show not later than half an hour before his or her judging is scheduled to begin. The judge should report to the superintendent upon arrival. Having done so, the judge should try to stay away from exhibitors. Many of them will come forward to try to promote their dogs. Many will stop by just to give a courteous greeting; others will interpret this as politics of some sort. Sometimes judges will wander about, watching dogs being groomed and talking to handlers or exhibitors. Nothing can start a scandal faster.

Many judges seem to wear their hearts on their sleeves. After a show they will make a minute study of the entries. They may feel offended because this or that exhibitor did not show under them. However, there are many reasons why an exhibitor will not enter a dog at a given show. Family, business or personal reasons may prevent them. The dog may be sick or out of condition. Judges should be mature enough to understand that such reasons are valid and that in most cases exhibitors did not intend to slight them.

A judge should not drink alcoholic beverages either before entering the ring or while judging. Otherwise, the judge may have his or her license revoked. Although an occasional drink may not interfere with a judge's ability and might even be a valuable stimulant for one who is very tired, it gives defeated and angry exhibitors a chance to challenge the judge's decisions.

Dress

A judge should dress like a judge and should carry himself or herself like a judge. This is a position of honor and respect. A judge expects to be treated with dignity and therefore must treat the job with dignity.

The show-giving club may have advertised the merits of its judges and may have spent a great deal of money to get a top-quality panel. It has the right to expect these individuals to look and act according to their positions.

A male judge should wear a pressed suit. It is preferable at indoor shows for him to wear a suit with matching trousers and jacket, a white shirt, and a necktie. There can be more informality at an outdoor show. Pressed slacks and a sport jacket will be acceptable, and sometimes even a sport shirt. Only on rare occasions, when the temperature is unbearably hot, should a judge remove his jacket.

A woman judge should also dress comfortably and should avoid anything too extreme in style. A pantsuit is practical for the occasion, although a simple dress or skirt and blouse in a color or pattern that is not too flamboyant is also fine. Remember to wear comfortable shoes; a judge may have to stand for eight to ten hours on a concrete floor.

chapter thirty-four
How to Become a Dog Judge

The American Kennel Club does not publish a set of rules and procedures for people who want to become dog judges. Consequently, interested people are always asking judges how they reached such a position. This chapter discusses the basic criteria for applying to be a dog judge. According to the AKC, the system presented here has been well tested and is subject only to minor and relatively rare changes.

Who Is Ineligible?

Certain people are barred by their professions from being dog judges. A professional handler or the spouse of a handler cannot be a judge. A handler who wishes to be a judge must resign as a handler and wait a year before applying for a judge's license. However, professional handlers can be licensed to judge at a specialty show, although the AKC may refuse to approve the appointment.

If a judge has a son or daughter who is a professional handler, the handler is not allowed to live in his or her parents' household. Presumably the handler would be asked to show some discretion in the matter of showing dogs under his or her father or mother.

A judge cannot be engaged in the business of buying and selling dogs because he or she could buy dogs for a low price and sell them for two or three times as much, with the understanding that they would get preferential treatment at coming shows. A breeder can be a judge only if that breeder's buying and selling is connected only with his own breeding kennel.

A judge cannot solicit kennel advertising for a magazine or newspaper because he or she might get lucrative advertisements in return for favoring dogs of a certain kennel.

A person who operates a professional grooming and boarding kennel is also ineligible to judge. In the past a judge might groom and board a client's dogs, who would then enter them at shows that he was judging. Now, the rule is strictly enforced by the AKC.

When the AKC turns down an applicant for a judge's license, it does so in a terse letter. Hundreds of disappointed applicants never learn why they were rejected and are embarrassed or hurt. I know of only one persistent person who did get an explanation. She was told that no one was being approved who had not bred and shown two or more championship dogs.

Formal Application

A person who wishes to become a judge must write to the American Kennel Club for an application, which is in the form of an extensive questionnaire. Questions concern family background, occupation, experience with dog shows, and breeds owned and shown. A second questionnaire is given to applicants to test their knowledge of the breed(s) for which they are seeking a judge's license. In the second questionnaire the applicant must describe his idea of an ideal dog of that breed and list both the major qualities and major faults of the breed.

People who have served steadily as ring stewards and have judged at sanctioned match shows have had many types of valuable experience. Both questionnaires ask for details of such experience. Prospective judges should therefore apply to serve as stewards at as many licensed dog shows as possible. Wherever possible, that stewardship should be under a judge who is judging the breeds in which the steward wishes to specialize.

Included in the second questionnaire are half a dozen hypothetical situations that might come up in the ring. These are always highly technical. The applicant answers these to the best of his ability, perhaps using the AKC *Rules Applying to Registration and Dog Shows* as a reference. An applicant should secure a copy of the rule book and learn its contents thoroughly long before applying for a license.

When the questionnaires are completed, the applicant has to swear that he or she has received no help from established judges in answering the questions. It can be presumed that those who cheat on this will not be particularly honorable judges.

The application then goes to the AKC, and the exact course it takes from there on is not definitely known by those on the outside. Presumably officers screen it. They may reject it or send it to the judges' committee. (Members' names are kept secret.) When challenged by a rejected applicant, AKC officers will say only that they have taken no part in the committee's decision and will refuse to divulge the names of any committee members.

The AKC files may contain information about an applicant. Such information is usually derogatory because people seldom take the trouble to write to the AKC in praise of other exhibitors. However, it can be assumed that AKC officials turn over any information they may have on the applicant to the committee.

Provisional Judges

If an applicant is given temporary approval by the committee, his or her name is then published in the official AKC magazine *Pure-bred Dogs: American Kennel Gazette*. Each month this magazine lists the names of applicants on the "Secretary's Page." They are listed under the heading "Judging Application, Provisional Judges," along with this wording:

"The Board of Directors is considering approval of the following persons as provisional judges for the breeds specified. Letters concerning these applicants should be addressed to [the attention of the] Secretary."

The person applying for the first time can expect that both friends and enemies will write those letters. On first thought one might guess that it might be difficult to pass this letters test because if the applicant had bred and exhibited a number of champions, he would probably have made some jealous enemies who would be sure to write in. As one exhibitor said, "You're a great guy or gal until you start to win. Then you become a progressively worse skunk until you produce a great champion. Then you haven't a friend left on earth."

However, enough do pass this test that one's faith in either humanity as a whole or the judges' committee is renewed. One must assume that the anonymous committee must have considerable experience and skill in recognizing the purely vicious letters that come in.

After the Board of Directors has had a chance to study the record of an applicant and any letters that it has received, the application is either denied or granted.

If it is granted, the applicant's name will appear in *Pure-bred Dogs: American Kennel Gazette* under the heading "Provisional Judges" and prefaced by these words: "The following persons have been approved as judges of the breed designated on a provisional basis in accord with the policy governing the Provisional Judging System."

This system enables a provisional judge to judge a breed (or sometimes breeds) at three or more shows, at which time his performance is evaluated by AKC field representatives. If a provisional judge has judged satisfactorily at these shows, the AKC will then consider granting a full license. But if the provisional judge's performance has been unsatisfactory, the AKC may order that person to judge at more shows (one person was required to judge six times), or it may deny approval of a license.

If approved, *Pure-bred Dogs: American Kennel Gazette* will list the judge's name under: "New Judges, Provisional Judging Completed. The following persons have completed their Provisional Judging assignments and their names have been added to the list of regularly approved judges."

Judging Additional Breeds

A somewhat similar method is used when a judge applies for a license to judge additional breeds. The applicant's name appears in the official AKC magazine under the heading "Judging Applications," together with the breeds for which application is made and the request for letters concerning the applicant. A fully licensed judge who has officiated at three licensed shows may apply to judge additional breeds.

Sometimes a judge will apply for a license to judge six more breeds. After studying the application, the Board of Directors may deny the request completely, grant permission for one or two breeds, or possibly grant a license to judge all six breeds.

The *Pure-bred Dogs: American Kennel Gazette* would carry this announcement: "The following persons who are presently on the eligible list of judges for one or more breeds have been approved for additional breeds as follows."

In this way, a judge might progress from one breed to all breeds in a group, then to breeds in another group, and so forth. The current policy of the AKC seems to be not to license future judges for all breeds and to limit those judges to only two groups of dogs (e.g., Terriers, Sporting Dogs). However, some experienced all-breeds professional handlers may be exempted from the "two groups only" policy.

The AKC will consider approving Canadians on a show-to-show basis for those breeds the Canadians are licensed to judge in their own country. Assuming that the Canadian can pass all the requirements that American judges must meet, the AKC could license that person to judge a few or all of the breeds he or she can judge in Canada.

Specialty Judge versus All-Breeds Judge

One of the most frequent subjects of contention around dog shows and in both individual breed and all-breeds magazines is the comparative merits of the specialty judge and the all-breeds judge.

The specialty judge judges the particular breed of dog that he breeds and exhibits. That person will probably have a more precise knowledge of a particular breed than an all-breeds judge and will know both the qualities breeders are striving for and the faults they are trying to eliminate in their dogs.

To some extent this may be a disadvantage, particularly on the latter point. Many breeder-judges are unbalanced in their judging because they are overly swayed by the presence either of a single quality for which they have been striving or of a fault that they have been trying to eliminate. It is not uncommon to hear specialty judges criticized for doing an uneven job.

The specialty judge may make mistakes because of a lack of judging experience. Because this person is more intimately involved with a particular breed than the all-breeds judge is, his or her judgments will also be more subject to pressures from friends and enemies than the all-breeds judge's would be.

On the other hand, the lack of association with a particular breed is to the advantage of all-breeds judges. They will not be influenced by the pressures wielded by members of a specialty club. The all-breeds judge also has had greater ring experience and probably makes fewer mistakes than the specialist. It should be emphasized, however, that both the specialty and the all-breeds judge are very dependent on competent stewards in order to do a really good job.

The all-breeds judge will tend to have a greater general knowledge of the goals of breeding and will have fewer breed prejudices than the specialist. He will also be less likely to be impressed by current, often temporary, fads within a breed or by the past record of a certain dog.

This problem is of more than academic interest to all-breeds clubs that are sponsoring shows and must select judges. They need all-breeds judges, if for no other reason than to judge the rarer breeds for which specialty judges cannot be found. But they also need specialty judges if the show is especially large. As a rule, all-breeds clubs will have to assign breeds with major entries to specialty judges. For example, if an all-breeds judge is assigned to two breeds that produce an entry of 150 to 175 dogs, that judge cannot be assigned other breeds at that show. A show-giving club probably could not find enough specialty judges to judge entire shows such as Westminster, Beverly Hills, or the Chicago International; and if it could, it might not be able to afford the tab.

Local specialty clubs do not always ask for specialty judges for their shows. Some clubs ask for all-breeds judges or say, "We'll take anyone you select as long as the individual is not from this area," in order to avoid any suspicion of favoritism.

Actually it is the duty of kennel clubs to use both specialists and all-breeds judges and to select and use them wisely.

part seven
BREED STANDARDS

This section contains the major points of the standards
of all breeds presently recognized by the American Kennel
Club, as well as the standards for many breeds that have
not yet received full AKC recognition. The breed
descriptions are selective, edited versions of the AKC
standards, prepared by the author.

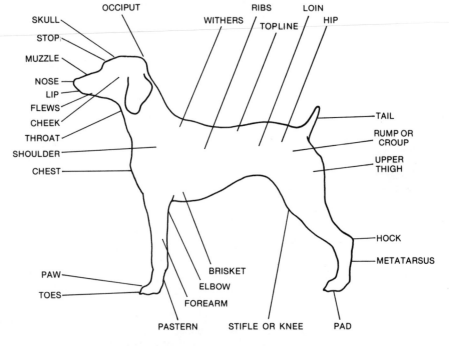

SKULL
OCCIPUT
STOP
MUZZLE
NOSE
LIP
FLEWS
CHEEK
THROAT
SHOULDER
CHEST

WITHERS
RIBS
TOPLINE
LOIN
HIP

TAIL
RUMP OR CROUP
UPPER THIGH

HOCK
METATARSUS

PAW
TOES

BRISKET
ELBOW
FOREARM

PASTERN
STIFLE OR KNEE
PAD

Diagram of a Dog's Anatomy

chapter thirty-five
Sporting Breeds

The Sporting Group is made up of those breeds whose instincts are to use wind-borne scents in hunting. Experienced dogs of all these breeds can track game, but they normally hunt with a high nose and locate their prey by searching the air currents for body scents.

Three classes of dogs make up the group. The first includes all the pointing breeds; the second, the retrieving breeds; and the third, the flushing breeds or Spaniels. It should be added that the Brittany Spaniel is a pointing dog and the Irish Water Spaniel is a Retriever.

In England and in those countries that follow its example, the Sporting Group is called the Gun Dog Group. Canada follows the American system.

POINTER

The development of the Pointer began in England as early as 1650. The dogs were first used to locate and point hares, and Greyhounds were then unleashed to course them. Pointers were later used to keep quail setting on the nest until nets could be cast over them. Then, as shotguns were developed, wing shooting as we know it today began.

European and particularly Spanish pointing breeds were used to perfect the breed. Foxhound crosses were also made. Today the Pointer remains a supreme specialist in locating and holding game birds until they can be flushed by the hunter.

HEIGHT: Males, 25 to 28 inches at the shoulder; bitches, 23 to 26 inches.

WEIGHT: Males, 55 to 75 pounds; bitches, 45 to 65 pounds.

GAIT: Free-striding, with strong drive in rear quarters.

COLOR: Preferred colors are white with liver, orange, lemon, or black. Nose dark or light to match color.

HEAD: Long rectangle; furrow between eyes, which are dark or light to match color of coat. **Skull:** Slightly rounded, but skull topline and muzzle in same plane. **Ears:** Set at eye level. **Bite:** Scissors or even. **Flews and throat:** Clean. **Neck:** Long, arched.

BODY: **Shoulders:** Sloping, angulated, blade tops close. **Forelegs:** Parallel from front view, perpendicular from side. **Chest:** Deep, reaching to elbows, ribs moderately sprung. **Topline:** Slight slope withers to croup, which falls slightly to root of tail. Slight belly tuck-up. **Tail:** Carried at back level when in motion, reaches to hock joint. **Hindquarters:** Well angulated at stifle joints. **Hocks:** Parallel viewed from rear; perpendicular from side. **Feet:** Deep, well knuckled up. **Coat:** Short, dense, with sheen.

FAULTS: Timidity, unruliness, apple head, snipy muzzle, pendulous flews, Roman nose, undershot or overshot jaws, hound ears, ewe (concave line) neck, straight shoulders, straight stifles, cow hocks, crossing over or crabbing in gait, thin pads, splayed feet, knuckling over at wrists.

GERMAN SHORTHAIRED POINTER

The goal in developing this breed was to achieve a fine, all-purpose sporting dog, one that could be used for waterfowling and that could track a variety of game. To obtain these qualities, the now extinct German Bird Dog, Spanish and other European Pointers, English Pointers, and even Foxhounds were used. The early offspring of these crosses were heavily built and rather slow.

The breed began to take its present form about 1871. It is now less heavy and faster afoot than its forebears. The German Shorthaired Pointer was admitted to the *American Kennel Club Stud Book* in March 1930. Except for the Brittany Spaniel, it has more dual (show and field) champions than any other breed.

HEIGHT: Males, 23 to 25 inches at the withers; bitches, 21 to 23 inches. Deviations of 1 inch above or below to be seriously penalized.

WEIGHT: Males, 55 to 70 pounds; bitches, 45 to 60 pounds.

GAIT: Free-striding.

COLOR: Solid liver and white spotted and ticked, liver and white ticked, liver roan. Nose brown.

HEAD: Skull: Reasonably broad, arched on sides, median line not deep; as in the Pointer, no pronounced stop or occiput. **Ears:** Broad, set above eye level. **Muzzle:** Length about equal to skull, not narrow, never Roman-nosed or dish-faced. **Teeth:** Scissors bite, level bite to be penalized. **Nose:** Brown, nostrils well opened, projects slightly over jaws. **Flews and throat:** Clean. **Neck:** Long, arched.

BODY: Shoulders: Sloping, blades close at withers. **Forelegs:** Parallel from front view, perpendicular from side. **Chest:** Depth to elbows, moderately sprung ribs, slight tuck-up. **Topline:** Short, sloped from withers to root of tail, arched over loins. **Hindquarters:** Well angulated at stifles and hocks. Hips broad. **Tail:** Set high, docked to two fifths of length, never carried over back. **Feet:** Round to spoon-shaped, deep, strongly knuckled up, toes close, pads hard. **Hair:** Short, dense, rough to the touch. Shorter and softer on the ears and head.

FAULTS: Ponderousness because of excess weight, too leggy, too large a head, heavily wrinkled forehead, dish-faced, snipy muzzle, flesh-colored nose, light eyes, excessive loose skin under throat, feet or elbows turned in or out, down in pasterns, swayback.

DISQUALIFICATIONS: China eyes or walleyes; flesh-colored nose; extremely overshot or undershot; a dog with any area of black, red, orange, lemon, or tan; a solid-white dog.

GERMAN WIREHAIRED POINTER

This breed was developed about a hundred years ago by German sportsmen who wanted an all-purpose sporting dog. They crossed the Griffon, Pudelpointer, and Stichelhaar with other European pointing breeds. The Pudelpointer was a cross between a Poodle and an English Pointer. The Griffon and the Stichelhaar were both mixtures of Foxhound, Pointer, Polish Water Dog, and Poodle.

The final result was a wirehaired dog made up chiefly of English Pointer, Foxhound, and Poodle. It was recognized as a distinctive breed in 1870. Although German Wirehaired Pointers, then known as Deutsch-Drathaar, were seen in America as early as 1920, the breed did not become well known until after World War II. It received American Kennel Club recognition as the German Wirehaired Pointer in 1959.

HEIGHT: Males, 24 to 26 inches; bitches, smaller but not under 22 inches.

WEIGHT: Males, 55 to 70 pounds; bitches, 45 to 60 pounds.

GAIT: Free and driving.

COLOR: Liver and white spotted, liver and white spotted with ticking, liver roan, solid liver. Head, ears, and nose brown, but white blaze permitted.

HEAD: Skull: Moderately long, broad, occiput not prominent, stop medium. **Eyes:** Brown, oval, eyebrows bushy. **Ears:** Rounded, close to head, set above eye level. **Lips:** Pendulous, close, bearded. **Teeth:** Scissors bite. **Throat:** Clean, free of dewlap. **Neck:** Medium length, arched.

BODY: Longer than tall, as 10 is to 9. **Shoulders:** Set obliquely. **Forelegs:** Straight, conforming to other pointing breeds, elbows close to body. **Chest:** Reaches to elbows, ribs well sprung. **Topline:** Slopes withers to croup, tuck-up moderate, skin fits tightly to body. **Hips:** Broad, croup rounded, tail docked to two fifths of length. **Hindquarters:** Moderately angulated at stifles and hocks. **Feet:** Round, strongly arched, webbed toes, thick pads. **Coat:** Dense undercoat develops in winter, nearly disappears in summer, outer coat partly water-repellent, lies nearly flat, is up to 2 inches in length.

FAULTS: Yellow eyes; overshot or undershot mouth; unsoundness of legs and feet; a short, smooth coat; soft, woolly coat; excessively long coat; black color in coat; spotted or flesh-colored nose.

CHESAPEAKE BAY RETRIEVER

This breed traces its origin back to 1807, when an English brig was wrecked in Chesapeake Bay. The crew was rescued along with two dogs of remarkable retrieving ability. They were a dog and a bitch and were said to have been of Newfoundland blood. They were mated with local fowling dogs, and the offspring had the same ability and extraordinary stamina in rough seas and cold water as their parents had. The present type was fixed by 1885, although the popular deadgrass color did not come until after World War I.

HEIGHT: Males, 23 to 26 inches; bitches, 21 to 24 inches.
WEIGHT: Males, 65 to 80 pounds; bitches, 55 to 70 pounds.
GAIT: Normal.
COLOR: Dark brown to faded tan or deadgrass; deadgrass varies from tan to dull straw color. White spot on breast, toes, belly permitted, but the smaller the better.
HEAD: Skull: Broad and round with medium stop and with muzzle pointed, but not snipy. **Eyes:** Yellowish or amber, set wide apart. **Ears:** Small, set high. **Lips:** Thin, not pendulous. **Bite:** Scissors or level. **Neck:** Medium length, muscular.
BODY: Medium length, neither cobby nor roached, flanks well tucked up. **Shoulders:** Sloping. **Forelegs:** Medium length, free and powerful in action. **Chest:** Deep barrel chest. **Topline:** Slightly hollow. **Hindquarters:** High hindquarters for swimming, powerfully muscled, stifles well angulated, pasterns and hocks medium length. **Tail:** Reaches to hocks, thick at base. **Feet:** Well-webbed harefeet. **Coat:** Thick, dense, not over 1½ inches, with dense undercoat. Both coats contain oil to protect from water. Outer coat is never curly.
DISQUALIFICATIONS: Black, dewclaws on hind legs, white except as specified, tail feathering over 1¾ inches, undershot or overshot jaws, curly coat or tendency to curl all over body, deformed dogs, or dogs without necessary breed characteristics.

CURLY-COATED RETRIEVER

The origin of the Curly-Coated Retriever is uncertain. One theory is that it is a descendant of a sixteenth-century English Water Spaniel crossed with a retrieving setter. It seems likely that it also has the genes of the Poodle and the Irish Water Spaniel. Another theory is that the Curly-Coated Retriever is descended from the now extinct St. John's Dog of Newfoundland.

The breed nearly died out, but as with so many English breeds a call was made to rescue it. The new Curly Retriever Club was organized in England in 1933. Since then the breed has made slow progress. Although it is a good water dog and is easily trained, it remains one of the rarest breeds fully recognized by the American Kennel Club.

HEIGHT: Not specified, but 24 to 26 inches for males is normal; bitches, smaller.

WEIGHT: Males, 60 to 70 pounds; bitches, smaller.

GAIT: Not specified.

COLOR: Black or liver. Nose color matches coat.

HEAD: Skull: Long, not too flat, jaws long and in proportion to the skull. **Eyes:** Black or brown, never yellow, rather large. **Ears:** Small, set at eye level. **Bite:** Usually level, but may be scissors.

BODY: Short. **Shoulders:** Sloping. **Forelegs:** Parallel when viewed from the front, perpendicular when seen from the side, pasterns slightly bent, elbows tight to body. **Chest:** Deep, reaching to elbows, not especially broad, ribs moderately sprung, carried well back, loins powerful, with only slight tuck-up. **Topline:** Level, or slightly sloping from withers to rump, slight arch over loins. **Hindquarters:** Strong, muscular, moderate angulation of stifle and hock joints, hocks well let down. **Tail:** Moderately short, carried at level of spine, covered with curls. **Feet:** Round, compact, strongly arched toes. **Coat:** Dense, crisp curls, though slightly more open curls permitted.

FAULTS: Yellow, very prominent eyes; large white patch on breast; saddle of uncurled hair on shoulders; snipy muzzle; ears set above eye level.

FLAT-COATED RETRIEVER

The Flat-Coated Retriever was developed in England. The first of the breed to be exhibited — a dog named Wyndham — was seen at the Birmingham show in 1860. Wyndham was of Labrador type but had a fairly long, flat coat. It is believed, therefore, that he was a cross between a Labrador and a St. John's Newfoundland. This seems likely both because of his Newfoundland coat and his larger-than-Labrador size. Later crosses with Irish and Gordon Setters may have been made. The breed has been making steady progress in the United States, and the present standard is being reviewed.

HEIGHT: Not specified, but about 24 inches.
WEIGHT: Between 60 and 70 pounds.
GAIT: Free-moving, not ponderous.
COLOR: Solid black or solid liver, with nose color to match.
HEAD: Long. **Skull:** Flat and moderately broad, stop deep, top skull and muzzle in parallel planes. **Eyes:** Medium size, brown or hazel, not set

obliquely. **Ears:** Small, close to head, set above eye level. **Muzzle:** Long. **Bite:** Not specified, but scissors normal. **Nose:** Nostrils large and open. **Neck:** Long, arched, free of throatiness.

BODY: Shoulders: Sloping, blades close at withers. **Forelegs:** Straight, with strong bone extending down to the feet. **Chest:** Deep, fairly broad, well-defined brisket, foreribs fairly flat, well arched at body center, loins or couplings strongly muscled. **Topline:** Level or slight slope from withers to base of tail, tuck-up not specified, but slight. **Hindquarters:** Moderate stifle angulation. **Feet:** Dog stands square on well-arched feet with toes close, pads thick. **Tail:** Short, straight, not carried above back line. **Coat:** Dense, fine in quality and texture, lying flat to body, legs and tail well feathered.

FAULTS: Dish- or down-faced; round, prominent eyes; out at elbows; open couplings; straight stifles; cow hocks; poor feet.

GOLDEN RETRIEVER

The actual origin of the Golden Retriever goes back to 1865, when Lord Tweedmouth bought a yellow puppy from a cobbler. The yellow puppy was the only yellow dog in a litter of black pups, and the cobbler had taken it in as payment on a debt. Lord Tweedmouth mated the dog to a bitch of a now extinct breed, the Tweed Water Spaniel. Three yellow puppies resulted.

Both linebreeding and outcrosses to Tweed Water Spaniels and to early Wavy-Coated Retrievers were made. The breed was called Wavy- or Flat-Coated Retriever until 1913, when it was given separate breed recognition under its present name. It is among the most popular of all breeds in the United States and Canada.

HEIGHT: Males, 23 to 24 inches; bitches, 21½ to 22½ inches.

WEIGHT: Males, 65 to 75 pounds; bitches, 60 to 70 pounds.

GAIT: At a fast trot, feet tend to converge to dog's center of gravity.

COLOR: Various shades of golden. A few white chest hairs permitted, but not desired. Nose black or dark brown.

HEAD: **Skull:** Broad, frontal and occipital bones not prominent, good stop, foreface deep, nearly as long as skull. **Eyes:** Dark brown, never lighter than coat, rims dark. **Ears:** Short, set at eye level. **Teeth:** Scissors bite. **Neck:** Medium length, untrimmed natural ruff.

BODY: **Shoulders:** Form ninety-degree angle with upper arms. **Forelegs:** Straight, pasterns short, sloping slightly. **Chest:** Extends to elbows, ribs long, not barrel-chested. **Topline:** Level whether dog is moving or standing, croup slopes gently. **Hindquarters:** Form ninety-degree angle at stifle joints, hocks let down. **Tail:** Reaches hocks, slight upward curve. **Feet:** Medium size, round, compact. **Coat:** Dense, water-repellent, neither harsh nor silky, lies flat, but may be wavy, feathers on legs and tail.

FAULTS: Hound ears, Dudley nose, weak chest, excessive tuck-up, tail curled over back, crossing over of feet in gait.

DISQUALIFICATIONS: 1 inch in height deviation from standard limits, undershot or overshot, trichiasis (abnormal direction or position of eyelashes).

LABRADOR RETRIEVER

In 1830 the British sportsman Colonel Hawker, a dog authority of the time, referred to a dog from Newfoundland that "is by far the best for any kind of shooting. He is generally black and no bigger than a Pointer, very fine legs, with short, smooth hair, and does not carry his tail so much curled as the other [a reference to the Newfoundland Dog]; is extremely quick at running, swimming and fighting . . . and their sense of smell is hardly to be credited."

From dogs of this type shipped to Great Britain, the Labrador was developed. The breed was recognized by the English Kennel Club in 1903 and in the United States and Canada after World War I. It is the most popular of field trial retrievers and one of the most popular all-purpose dogs as well.

HEIGHT: Males, 22½ to 24½ inches; bitches, an inch smaller.

WEIGHT: Males, 60 to 75 pounds; bitches, 55 to 70 pounds.

GAIT: Free, effortless, with legs on each side moving in parallel planes.

COLOR: Black (white on chest permitted), yellow (shades from fox red to light cream, with darker shadings on ears, underparts, and underside of the tail), chocolate (from light sedge to chocolate). Nose black in blacks, black or dark brown in yellows (may fade to pink in winter), liver or dark brown in chocolates.

HEAD: **Skull:** Wide, stop slight, muzzle long and deep. **Eyes:** Brown or black, but yellow permitted. **Ears:** Medium size, set well back and low. **Teeth:** Level bite. **Neck:** Medium length.

BODY: **Shoulders:** Long, sloping. **Forelegs:** Straight from shoulder to ground. **Chest:** Wide and deep, ribs well sprung, loins wide, strongly muscled. **Topline:** Not specified, but should be level, tuck-up not specified, but should be slight. **Hindquarters:** Stifles well turned, strongly muscled. **Tail:** An otter tail (very thick at base, rounded, tapering, thickly furred, but without feathering). **Feet:** Compact, toes strongly arched. **Coat:** Short, dense, without wave, gives a hard feeling to the hand, is free of feathers.

FAULTS: Snipy muzzle, overshot or undershot, fleshy cheeks, insufficient body substance, weak feet, short legs, thin tail, tail curled over back, lack of dark eye rims in yellows and chocolates, pacing or weaving in gait.

NOVA SCOTIA DUCK TOLLING RETRIEVER

This smallest of the retrieving breeds is gifted with remarkable intelligence and trainability. The breed standard is recognized by the Canadian Kennel Club but not by the AKC.

HEIGHT: Males, 20½ inches at the shoulder; bitches, 18½ inches.
WEIGHT: Males, about 50 pounds; bitches, about 35 pounds.
GAIT: True for a Sporting Dog.
COLOR: Red or fawn, but predominantly fox red. Although white is not desired, a white blaze, chest spot, and white toes and tail tip are common and are permitted.

HEAD: Resembles that of a Golden Retriever, about 9 inches from nose tip to occiput. **Skull:** Broad. **Ears:** Medium size, set high, rounded tips. **Eyes:** Golden brown, set wide apart. **Muzzle:** Not snipy. **Teeth:** Lower jaw thin, scissors bite. **Neck:** Medium length, partly hidden by heavy neck coat.

BODY: Shoulders: Sloping, elbows well under body. **Forelegs:** Straight, heavy-boned. **Chest:** Deep, belly fairly well drawn up. **Topline:** Level. **Hindquarters:** Broad at hips, hocks not set too low. **Tail:** 12½ to 13½ inches long, well feathered. **Feet:** Strongly arched, webbed. **Coat:** Double. Outer coat, straight and soft or silky; undercoat, dense and soft.

ENGLISH SETTER

The setters were once called *setting spaniels* because they kept the quail coveys pinned to the ground until nets could be cast over the birds. Probably the English Setter descends from a mixture of Spanish Pointer and English Water Spaniel. Around 1825 Edward Laverack developed the great beauty of the breed; later Purcell Llewellin developed a field strain from Laverack's dogs. Even today sportsmen are likely to say they have a Llewellin Setter, although all are registered simply as English Setters.

The breed may first have been brought to North America as early as 1874. At least that is the time when they first received national attention as superb gun dogs. Those registered by the *Field Dog Stud Book* are used chiefly for hunting and field trials; those registered by the American Kennel Club are used chiefly as show dogs and pets.

HEIGHT: Males, about 25 inches; bitches, 24 inches.

WEIGHT: Not specified.

GAIT: Free, graceful, high head carriage, tail not carried above back line.

COLOR: Black, white, and tan; black and white; blue, orange, lemon, or liver belton; lemon, liver or orange, and white; solid white. Dogs flecked all over, rather than with heavy patches of color on the body, preferred. Nose black, liver, or in harmony with lighter colors.

HEAD: **Skull:** Oval from ear to ear, long, lean, well-defined stop. **Eyes:** Dark brown, eyebrows prominent. **Ears:** Set at eye level, of moderate length. **Muzzle:** Long, square, lips square, and pendant. **Teeth:** Level or scissors bite. **Neck:** Long, lean, arched.

BODY: **Shoulders:** Sloping, close at withers. **Forelegs:** Flat bone, set well under dog, elbows tight to body, pasterns short, slightly sloping. **Chest:** Deep, ribs long, carried well back. **Topline:** Slightly sloping from withers to loin, slight arch at loins, hipbones set wide, slight slope to root of tail. **Hindquarters:** Upper and lower thighs well muscled, stifles well angulated, hocks wide. **Tail:** Straight, reaches to hocks or less, straight, silky feathers. **Feet:** Closely set and strong, toes well arched, pads thick and tough. **Coat:** Flat, good length.

FAULTS: Dish-face or Roman nose; muzzle not in proportion to skull; ears set too high; overshot or undershot; barrel chest; sharp tuck-up; elbows turning in or out; cow hocks; straight stifles; coat curly, soft, or woolly; stilted, clumsy, or lumbering gait.

GORDON SETTER

In 1620 a writer named Markham praised the "black and fallow setting dog" of Scotland as the "hardest to endure labor." This dog has come to be known as the Gordon Setter. It was the fourth Duke of Gordon who carefully developed the breed in the late 1700s. It has been used in crossings with a number of other breeds for reasons of color, stamina, and nose.

The Gordon is less swift than the English and Irish Setters and works closer to the hunter. This is especially advantageous in foul weather and for those who must hunt in small areas, where far-ranging dogs are at a disadvantage. For these reasons the Gordon has often been called the "meat dog."

HEIGHT: Males, 24 to 27 inches; bitches, 23 to 26 inches.
WEIGHT: Males, 55 to 80 pounds; bitches, 45 to 70 pounds.
GAIT: Smooth, free movement, with high head carriage.
COLOR: Rich black, with clearly defined tan or mahogany markings on eyebrows, sides of the muzzle, throat, chest, inside of hind legs from hocks to toes, pasterns and toes of forelegs, around vent. White spot on chest permitted.
HEAD: Rather heavy. **Skull:** Long, deeper than broad. **Muzzle:** Same length as skull, stop well defined. **Eyes:** Oval, dark brown. **Ears:** Set at eye level. **Teeth:** Scissors bite preferred, but level bite not a fault. Teeth pitted by distemper not a fault. **Neck:** lean, arched.
BODY: Short. **Shoulders:** Form ninety-degree angle with upper arms. **Forelegs:** Heavily boned, elbows turning neither in nor out. **Topline:** Strong, rather short. **Chest:** Forechest to back of thigh equals height, loins not arched, little slope to croup. **Hindquarters:** Well angulated, muscles long and flat, hocks perpendicular. **Tail:** Reaches to hocks, carried level, heavily feathered. **Feet:** Catlike, well-arched toes. **Coat:** Soft and shining, straight or slightly waved.

FAULTS: Dish-face or Roman nose, overshot or undershot, elbows or feet turning in or out, flat feet, cow hocks, straight stifles. Predominantly tan, red, or buff dogs are ineligible for showing and must be disqualified.

IRISH SETTER

The beauty and merry disposition of the Irish Setter have made it the fourth-most-popular dog breed in America. It has ranked among the ten most popular dog breeds for many years.

The breed's origin is in doubt; the most likely theory is that it evolved from crosses between English Pointers and English Setters, and perhaps Spaniels. In Ireland they were usually red and white, although solid-red dogs appeared in Ireland in the early 1800s. In the United States and Canada solid reds have been bred for many years. Ocassional red and whites are still seen in Ireland.

Comparatively few Irish Setters are used for hunting these days, although field trials are occasionally held for them. They do well in obedience competition and are popular as home pets.

HEIGHT: Males, 27 inches; bitches, 25 inches.
WEIGHT: Males, about 70 pounds in show condition; bitches, about 60 pounds.

GAIT: Swift, stylish, and driving.

COLOR: Mahogany or rich chestnut red, with no trace of black. Small amount of white on chest, throat, toes, or narrow, centered blaze on skull not to be penalized. Nose black or chocolate.

HEAD: Long, lean, at least double width between the ears, skull and muzzle same length and in parallel planes. **Skull:** Slightly oval, occiput prominent. **Eyes:** Almond-shaped, dark to medium brown. **Ears:** Set at eye level or below, leather reaches nearly to tip of nose. **Teeth:** Scissors or level bite. **Neck:** Moderate length, lean, arched, not throaty.

BODY: **Shoulders:** Sloping, blades close at withers. **Forelegs:** Straight, elbows moving freely, pasterns straight. **Chest:** Reaches to elbows, narrow in front, but middle ribs well sprung. **Topline:** Slopes gently from withers to root of tail, loins slightly arched. **Hindquarters:** Well angulated at stifle and hock joints, hocks nearly perpendicular from joints to ground. **Tail:** Reaches about to hocks, carried at back level, well feathered. **Feet:** Rather small, toes arched and close. **Coat:** Moderate length, flat, feathering on ears, forelegs, belly, thighs, tail.

FAULTS: Size variation of 1 inch up or down, elbows turning in or out, cow hocks, crossing or weaving in gait (but tendency to single track as speed increases not to be faulted), waved or curly hair.

AMERICAN WATER SPANIEL

This breed was originally known as the American Brown Water Spaniel, but because it breeds true to brown, the name was simplified. It seems probable that the breed developed from crosses of Irish Water Spaniels, Curly-Coated Retrievers, and possibly Poodles, but this cannot be definitely known.

After the Civil War the breed was developed for pothole shooting, in which men and their dogs had to crawl on their bellies to try to get within shooting range of the small ponds (potholes) along the great Mississippi flyway, where ducks might be sitting. For such a sport a small, brown water dog was needed. The breed received official American Kennel Club recognition in 1940.

HEIGHT: 15 to 18 inches at the shoulders for either sex.

WEIGHT: Males, 28 to 45 pounds; bitches, 25 to 40 pounds.

GAIT: Not specified, but conforms to typical Sporting Dog soundness.

COLOR: Solid liver or dark chocolate, a little white on toes or chest permitted. Nose dark.

HEAD: Skull: Rather broad, stop moderate, muzzle medium length. **Eyes:** Hazel or dark to harmonize with coat. **Ears:** Long, lobular, set slightly above eye level, reach to nose tip, covered with curls. **Teeth:** Scissors or level bite. **Neck:** Medium length, no throatiness, arch not accentuated.

BODY: Not too compactly coupled. **Shoulders:** Sloping. **Forelegs:** Reasonably straight. **Chest:** Deep brisket, but not barrel-chested. **Topline:** Not specified, but level, tuck-up not specified, but slight. **Hindquarters:** Well-bent stifles, hocks well let down. **Tail:** Length moderate, slight curve, carried below back level, covered with hair to tip. **Feet:** Toes closely grouped, well padded. **Coat:** Dense, closely curled or marcel wave, texture not coarse. Short, curly feathers on legs; short, smooth hair on forehead, without tuft or topknot.

FAULTS: Flat skull, snipy muzzle, undershot or overshot, rat or shaved tail, cow hocks, legs too short, weak feet.

DISQUALIFICATION: Yellow eyes.

BRITTANY SPANIEL

The Brittany Spaniel is the world's only pointing Spaniel. It was developed in the Brittany area of France from Spanish Pointer and Spaniel stock and from other French Spaniels. The local dogs were then apparently crossed with Setters brought over to Brittany by English sportsmen and left in France for the winter. These dogs were principally Gordon Setters, although both Irish and English Setters may also have been used. Many Brittany Spaniels are born tail-less. Black is an allowed color in France.

The Brittany is not particularly handsome, but its small size makes it an excellent dog for travel to hunting fields and for the home. Brittany Spaniels hold more dual championships (bench and field) than any other breed.

HEIGHT: Both sexes between 17½ and 20½ inches at the shoulder.

WEIGHT: 30 to 40 pounds for both sexes.

GAIT: A leggy dog with driving force and agility.

COLOR: Orange and white or liver and white in either clear or roan patterns. Some ticking is desirable. Orange and liver are found in piebald or parti-color patterns. Washed-out colors are not desired. Nose fawn, tan, light shades of brown, deep pink. Penalized for a two-tone or butterfly nose.

HEAD: **Skull:** Rounded, slightly wedge-shaped. For a 19½-inch dog, skull 4¾ inches long, 4⅜ inches wide, never apple-headed. **Muzzle:** Two-thirds skull length. **Eyes:** Medium size, dark to amber in color, set under protective eyebrows. **Ears:** Set above eye level. **Teeth:** Scissors bite. **Neck:** Arched. **Nose:** Open nostrils, never shiny.

BODY: Length from withers to rear of haunches equals height. **Shoulders:** Sloping, two thumbs' width apart at withers. **Forelegs:** Perpendicular, pasterns only slightly bent. **Chest:** Reaches to elbows. **Topline:**

Slight slope from withers to rump, four fingers' width from last rib to upper thigh, ribs well sprung, little tuck-up. **Hindquarters:** Stifles well bent, hind foot should step into print left by forefoot. **Tail:** Absent or cut to 4 inches. **Feet:** Smaller than in most Spaniels, halfway between harefoot and cat foot. **Coat:** Dense, flat or wavy, never curly, neither wiry nor silky, little ear fringe, a little feathering on legs. Profuse feathering or long hair on the body will bring elimination from competition.

FAULTS: Cow hocks; excessive feathering; crossing or weaving in gait; splayed feet; tricolors (liver, white, orange); large, prominent eyes; overshot or undershot.

DISQUALIFICATIONS: Size over or under standard; black in coat or black nose; tail longer than 4 inches.

CLUMBER SPANIEL

There is little known about the origin of the Clumber Spaniel. The breed takes its name from Clumber Park, the home of the Duke of Newcastle at Nottingham, England. The dog's long, low, and heavy body may indicate a cross between Spaniels and Basset Hounds; its head reminds one of the St. Bernard.

The dog made an ideal hunting companion for elderly retired English civil servants who had to hunt at a slow pace and in a small area. Clumbers first appeared at English dog shows in 1859, and this gives a true indication of the antiquity of the breed. Clumbers also appeared in the United States as early as 1883.

HEIGHT: Not specified, but about 15 inches at the shoulder.
WEIGHT: Males, 55 to 65 pounds; bitches, 35 to 50 pounds.
GAIT: Sedate, but not ponderous.
COLOR: Generally all-white body with lemon or orange head markings and leg tickings. Nose flesh- or cherry-colored.
HEAD: Massive. Round above eyes, flat on top, median furrow, and marked stop and occiput. **Eyes:** Hazel, showing haw, deep-set. **Ears:** Long, set low, slight feathering on front edge. **Muzzle:** Powerful, but not square, with overhanging lips. **Teeth:** Scissors bite. **Neck:** Long, powerful, carrying a ruff.
BODY: **Shoulders:** Immense, giving a heavy appearance. **Forelegs:** Short, straight, very heavy bone, elbows close. **Chest:** Wide and deep. **Topline:** Long, broad, level, only a slight arch over the loin, no tuck-up. **Hindquarters:** Less heavily boned than forelegs, moderately angulated, hocks well let down. **Tail:** Set at spine level, carried low. **Feet:** Large, compact, filled with hair between toes. **Coat:** Dense, silky, straight, feathers abundant, but none below the hocks.
FAULTS: Very pale eyes, crooked front legs, cow hocks, overshot or undershot, heavily marked coat, thin or harsh coat.

AMERICAN COCKER SPANIEL

The Spaniel goes back to at least the latter part of the fourteenth century. Some varieties were known as Land Spaniels; others, as Water Spaniels. The Cocker Spaniel, once called a Cocking Spaniel, got that name because of its proficiency at woodcock hunting.

There is a close similarity between Spaniels and Springers. In fact, before there was an official separation of these breed types, in a given litter one dog might have been dubbed a Cocker, another a Welsh Springer, and still another an English Springer. A dog might at first compete as a Cocker, then grow into a Springer — size became the differentiating factor.

Cockers were first exhibited in the United States in the early 1880s. By 1946 the variation between the English and American dogs had become so great that the breed was split into English Cockers and American Cockers. (In England the breeds are called Cocker Spaniel and American Cocker; in the United States and Canada they are called English Cocker and Cocker Spaniel.) The American breed was then split into three varieties: Blacks, Parti-colors, and Any Solid Color Other than Black (but including Black-and-Tans), for which the acronym Ascob is used.

HEIGHT: Ideal for males, 15 inches; for bitches, 14 inches.
WEIGHT: Not specified, but traditionally 22 to 26 pounds.
GAIT: Smooth, effortless Sporting Dog gait with strong rear drive.
COLOR: Black, any solid color other than black (Ascob), black and tan, parti-color. Black-and-Tans shown with Ascobs; roans with parti-colors. Nose black in Blacks and Black-and-Tans, black or brown in others.
HEAD: Well proportioned. **Skull:** Rounded, marked stop. **Eyes:** Round, full, black in Blacks and Black-and-Tans, black or brown in others. Prominent eyebrows. **Ears:** Lobular, set at eye level or below, leather reaches to end of nose, heavily feathered. **Teeth:** Scissors bite. **Neck:** Long, arches slightly, muscular, no throatiness.
BODY: Square, ribs strongly sprung. **Topline:** Sloping. **Chest:** Deep, ribs well sprung. **Forelegs:** Straight, well boned, muscular. **Hindquarters:** Strongly angulated. **Feet:** Large, compact, with thick pads. **Coat:** Heavy. Exhibitors normally ignore standard ban against excessive coat and feathering. In other respects dog conforms to normal Sporting Dog soundness.
DISQUALIFICATIONS: Males over 15½ inches tall, bitches over 14½ inches tall. Markings: On Blacks and Ascobs, white except on chest and throat; on Parti-colors, 90 per cent or more of a primary color or secondary color or colors limited to one area; on Black-and-Tans, more than 10 per cent tan, lack of tan over eyes, sides of muzzle, undersides of ears, on all feet and legs, around vent; white except on throat and chest. Tan not readily visible on Black-and-Tans.

ENGLISH COCKER SPANIEL

In England sportsmen used the larger Spaniels for springing game and the smaller ones for shooting woodcocks. In 1892 the English Kennel Club gave the smaller Spaniels separate registrations as Cocker Spaniels, something the Americans had done a decade earlier. One strain, the Marlborough, was slightly smaller than the other Cockers and a bit apple-headed. This style became popular in the United States and led to the development of the American Cocker. The larger strain, the present English Cocker, also had a longer muzzle.

In 1935 fanciers of the breed established the English Cocker Spaniel Club of America. An effort was made to search out pure strains in England that did not have the Marlborough crosses in them. Americans had, up to this time, often crossbred the two. This was stopped by the American Kennel Club in 1947.

HEIGHT: For males, ideal is 16 to 17 inches; for bitches, 15 to 16 inches.

WEIGHT: Males, 28 to 34 pounds; bitches, 26 to 32 pounds.

GAIT: Powerful, frictionless, true.

COLOR: Black, shades of red, parti-colors, black and tan, and blue, liver, red, orange, and lemon roans. A solid-color dog with white feet is not a parti-color. Nose black preferred, but may be brown in colors other than black.

HEAD: Skull and muzzle equal length, definite stop, lips square. **Eyes:** Medium, set wide apart, oval, dark brown; hazel in light parti-colors and light roans. **Ears:** Set low, lobular, reaching to muzzle, covered with long, silky, wavy hair. **Teeth:** Even. **Neck:** Long, arched.

BODY: Square from ground to withers to root of tail. **Shoulders:** Sloping. **Forelegs:** Straight, pasterns short. **Chest:** Ribs moderately sprung, reaching to elbows, carried well back. **Topline:** Sloping. **Hindquarters:** Well angulated. **Tail:** Docked, conforms to topline, merry. **Feet:** Medium size, catlike, deep pads. **Coat:** Flat or wavy, medium length, well but not profusely feathered.

FAULTS: Too short or snipy muzzle; skull too flat or rounded; lips snipy or pendulous; ears set too high; hair curled or ringlets; body too long, lacking depth; too low at withers; unsound forelegs, cow hocks; flat, splayed feet; white feet in a solid-colored dog; deviations in size.

ENGLISH SPRINGER SPANIEL

The English Springer Spaniel is the largest of the five British Land Spaniels that have a common origin. (The others are the Welsh Springer, the two Cockers, and the Field Spaniel.) The origins of the breed can be traced back to 1800. However, English recognition of this specific breed did not come until 1902. In 1924 the breed was sufficiently strong in the United States to have a breed club, the English Springer Spaniel Field Trial Association, sponsor it. The first licensed field trial was held in 1927.

Thereafter the breed rapidly became popular, both as a hunting dog and as a pet. At one time it was among the ten most popular breeds. The present tendency is to use much larger dogs than the original standard's size for show and pets and a much smaller dog for field trials.

HEIGHT: 20 inches ideal for males; 19 inches for bitches.
WEIGHT: 49 to 55 pounds, the males being heavier.
GAIT: Forelegs and hind legs move in parallel planes, but tend to move in to center of body when dog is at a fast trot.

COLOR: Black, or liver and white; tricolors; blue or liver roan. Nose black or liver to match coat.

HEAD: Well proportioned, not coarse or heavy. **Skull:** Medium length, flat top, slightly round at sides and back. Moderate stop. **Muzzle:** Half the width of skull. **Eyes:** Round, fairly deeply set, and dark brown to hazel. **Ears:** Set at eye level, leather reaches to tip of nose. **Neck:** Arches, moderate length, no throatiness.

BODY: Square from ground to withers to root of tail. **Shoulders:** Sloping, ninety-degree angle with forearms. **Forelegs:** Well boned, straight, elbows close to body, pasterns short, strong. **Chest:** To reach elbows, ribs not sharply sprung, carried well back, tuck-up slight. **Topline:** Gentle slope. **Hindquarters:** Hips broad, thighs well muscled, stifle and hock joints moderately angulated. **Feet:** Round or oval, compact, strongly arched, deep pads. **Coat:** Dense, flat or wavy.

FAULTS: Down-faced, Roman-nosed, or dish-faced; eyes showing haw; snipy muzzle; roach back or swayback; straight stifles; cow hocks; crossing over, weaving, or stilted gait; red, lemon, orange colors, which require judge not to award a ribbon; curly coat; faulty jaw formation; over-trimming.

FIELD SPANIEL

At one time size was the only difference between the Field Spaniels and Cocker Spaniels. The breed nearly became extinct, but it was revived by patriotic British breeders. To do this, crosses between purebred Field Spaniels and other Spaniels were made by interbreeding, which was permitted in England.

However, this procedure has held up the breed's development in the United States, where interbreeding is prohibited. Despite this, dedicated American breeders have slowly developed quite handsome dogs with excellent conformation and good hunting aptitudes.

HEIGHT: About 18 inches at the shoulder, either sex.
WEIGHT: From 35 to 50 pounds, either sex.
GAIT: Not specified, but sound and far-reaching stride.
COLOR: Black, liver, golden liver, mahogany red, or roan or any of these colors with tan over the eyes, on cheeks, feet, and pasterns. Nose black or brown.
HEAD: **Skull:** Well developed, prominent occipital crest. **Eyes:** Medium size, dark hazel or brown or nearly black to match coat color. **Ears:** Set low, moderate length, moderately feathered, lower parts curling inward and backward. **Muzzle:** Long, lean, never snipy or square-cut, lean beneath the eyes. **Neck:** Long, muscular.
BODY: **Shoulders:** Long, sloping. **Forelegs:** Good length, bone clean and flat. **Chest:** Moderate length, deep, ribs moderately sprung. **Topline:** Level, loins straight or arched. **Tail:** Carried low, never above topline. **Hindquarters:** Stifles moderately bent, not turning in or out. **Feet:** Medium size, round, thick, strong pads. **Coat:** Flat, slightly waved, silky, not curly, abundant feathering.
FAULTS: Yellow eyes; haw; lack of prominent occiput; short, snipy muzzle; swayback or roach back; straight stifles; cow hocks; weak pasterns; flat, splayed feet; parti-colors of black, liver, red, or orange and white do not disqualify, but are less desirable than others.

IRISH WATER SPANIEL

The Irish Water Spaniel appears to have been developed from an ancient breed known in Ireland as the South Country Water Spaniel. There was also a North Country Water Spaniel, and crosses with it may have been made. By 1859 the present breed had become firmly established, and the two earlier ones had died out.

The Irish Water Spaniel is well adapted to waterfowling but is less favored for hunting upland game because, like the Curly-Coated Retriever, its curly coat picks up burrs and is torn by briars. For a time the American Kennel Club listed it among the breeds that could compete in licensed Retriever trials, but this is no longer the case. The breed is both too rare and too scattered across the United States and Canada to make individual breed trials successful.

HEIGHT: Males, 22 to 24 inches at the shoulder; bitches, 21 to 23 inches.

WEIGHT: Males, 55 to 65 pounds; bitches, 45 to 58 pounds.

GAIT: Square and true on all four feet.

COLOR: Solid liver. Nose liver.

HEAD: Skull: Large, high dome, prominent occiput. **Topknot:** A distinctive breed characteristic. Long, loose curls, growing to a well-defined peak between the eyes. **Eyes:** Medium size, set almost flush, without eyebrows, dark hazel preferred. **Ears:** Set low, leather reaches to nose tip, covered with curls reaching 2 or more inches below leather. **Muzzle:** Square, long, deep. **Teeth:** Level. **Neck:** Long, arched.

BODY: Medium length. **Shoulders:** Sloping. **Forelegs:** Medium length, straight, well boned, elbows close. **Chest:** Deep, but not too wide between legs, ribs well sprung, pear-shaped at brisket, carried well back, slight tuck-up. **Topline:** Level. **Hips:** Wide and as high as withers or higher. **Hindquarters:** Not too straight, hocks set low, moderately bent. **Tail:** Set low, does not reach hocks, carried at back level, curls at base, tapering to fine, short hair and giving appearance of shaved or rat tail, which is a distinct breed characteristic. **Feet:** Large. **Coat:** Dense, tight ringlets on neck, back, and sides, free of woolliness, leg hair falling in curls, shorter in front than behind, short on legs in front of hocks.

FAULTS: Leggy, lack of Sporting Dog soundness, lack of distinctive breed characteristics.

SUSSEX SPANIEL

Competitions for Sussex Spaniels were first held at English dog shows as early as 1862, when the breed was exhibited at the Crystal Palace show in London. The breed is named after Sussex County, England, where a kennel owner developed the dogs' distinctive rich, dark golden, almost liver color. The breed was developed to hunt with men on foot and in fairly restricted areas, where a close-hunting dog was needed.

The dog is long and low and rather heavy-bodied. It has not fit into the American hunting scene, where hunting areas are larger, game is scarcer, and a wider-ranging, faster dog is needed. Sussex Spaniels do make excellent home dogs and have quiet, even dispositions.

HEIGHT: Not specified.
WEIGHT: 35 to 45 pounds, either sex.
GAIT: Free and merry, good tail action.
COLOR: Rich, golden liver. Nose liver.
HEAD: **Skull:** Moderately long and wide, with median line and deep stop, occiput full, but not pointed. **Eyes:** Fairly large, hazel, slight haw

often showing. **Ears:** Set at about eye level, thick, large, lobular, covered with soft, wavy hair. **Muzzle:** About 3 inches long. **Teeth:** Not specified, but level or scissors bite normal. **Neck:** Short, arched, not carrying head much above back level.

BODY: Long. **Shoulders:** Oblique. **Forelegs:** Bony, muscular, knees large, pasterns short, bony. **Chest:** Deep, round, loins broad, back ribs carried well back and deep. **Topline:** Level. **Hindquarters:** Stifles and hocks only moderately bent, hocks set wide apart. **Tail:** Docked, 5 to 7 inches long, set low, carried at back level. **Feet:** Large, round. **Coat:** Abundant, flat or slightly waved, moderate feathering.

FAULTS: Light eyes, weak muzzle, curled coat, ears set too high, topknot, short body, dark liver or puce color, flat sided.

WELSH SPRINGER SPANIEL

The development of the Welsh Springer Spaniel closely parallels that of the Cocker Spaniel and English Springer Spaniel. A litter of puppies might contain both red and white, and liver and white pups. The Welsh favored the red and white dogs, and red and white became the only color permitted in the breed.

The modern Welsh Springer is smaller than the English Springer but larger than the English Cocker. It is an excellent hunting dog, and there has been no attempt to make it a high-strung field trial race dog. While the breed has been slow to develop in the United States, it now has the sponsorship of an active national breed club.

HEIGHT: Not specified, but about 18 inches is average.
WEIGHT: Not specified, but 40 pounds is average.
GAIT: Merry and possessing Sporting Dog soundness.
COLOR: Dark, rich red and white. Nose dark or flesh-colored.
HEAD: **Skull:** Moderate length, slightly domed, clearly defined stop, well chiseled below the eyes. **Eyes:** Hazel or dark. **Ears:** Set low, comparatively short, narrowing at tips. **Muzzle:** Medium length, fairly square. **Teeth:** Level or scissors bite. **Neck:** Long, arched, no throatiness.
BODY: Square from ground to withers to root of tail. **Shoulders:** Long, sloping. **Forelegs:** Medium length, straight, well boned, moderately feathered. **Chest:** Deep, well-sprung ribs. **Topline:** Level from shoulders to slightly arched loin, well coupled up. **Hindquarters:** Stifles moderately bent, hocks well let down, strong and deep. **Tail:** Set low, not carried above back level. **Feet:** Round, thick pads. **Coat:** Straight, or flat and thick, silky.
FAULTS: Chubby head, haw, yellow eyes, long body, loose elbows, cow hocks, curly coat.

VIZSLA

This breed has been known under various names, such as Magyar Vizsla, Hungarian Pointer, and Yellow Pointer. It is definitely of Pointer type and reached its present development about a hundred years ago on the game lands of Hungary, Czechoslovakia, and Turkey.

The breed was admitted to the *American Kennel Club Stud Book* in 1960 and has gained rapidly in popularity in both the United States and Canada. Vizslas compete successfully in field trials limited to their own breed, in trials for all pointing breeds, and in trials for German pointing breeds, but including Vizslas. The Vizsla makes an excellent house dog and does well in obedience trials.

HEIGHT: Males, 22 to 24 inches; bitches, 21 to 23 inches.

WEIGHT: Not specified, but balance is more important than actual weight.

GAIT: Balanced, swift, and tireless.

COLOR: Solid, rusty gold or rather dark, sandy yellow of different shades, with the darker preferred. Small white spots on chest and feet not faulted. Nose brown.

HEAD: **Skull:** Moderately wide, furrow down the center of the skull, stop moderate. **Eyes:** Medium size, color harmonizes with coat. **Ears:** Thin, silky, set low, fairly long, rounded tips. **Muzzle:** Longer than skull, tapering, but well squared at the nose. **Teeth:** Scissors bite. **Neck:** Moderately long, arched, no dewlap.

BODY: **Shoulders:** Well laid back. **Forelegs:** Straight, muscular, elbows close. **Chest:** Moderately broad, reaching to elbows, the back is short, the withers are high. **Topline:** Slopes slightly, rounded over loins to tail, slight tuck-up, ribs well sprung. **Hindquarters:** Well-developed thighs, moderate angulation at stifle and hock joints. **Tail:** Set below back level, docked one third off. **Feet:** Catlike, round, compact. **Coat:** Short, smooth, dense, without woolly undercoat.

FAULTS: Black or slate gray nose, yellow eyes or eyes with whites showing, too much or too little angulation, dewclaws, harefeet, dark brown or pale yellow color.

DISQUALIFICATION: Deviation in height of more than 2 inches from standard either way.

WEIMARANER

This German breed (pronounced *Vy-mah-rah-ner)* is named for the Weimar region of Germany. It is related to other European pointing breeds, including the German Shorthaired Pointer, and to several breeds that are now extinct. The first Weimar Pointers came to America in 1929, when only sterilized animals could be sold to nonmembers of the German parent club.

After World War II the breed was the recipient of the most astonishing publicity campaign ever waged for a dog breed. Weimaraners were reputed to be able to do everything, including answer the telephone. Fortunately the breed has survived this publicity. Although its numbers and popularity declined for a while, the breed now is well established as an excellent hunting companion and home dog.

HEIGHT: Males, 25 to 27 inches at withers; bitches, 23 to 25 inches.
WEIGHT: Not specified.
GAIT: Free and far-reaching, conforming to gait of other Sporting Dogs.
COLOR: Mouse gray to silver gray, usually blending to lighter shades on the head and ears. Small white spot permitted on chest, but not elsewhere. Nose gray.
HEAD: Moderately long, skull and muzzle of equal length. **Skull:** Moderate stop, prominent occipital crest, trumpets set well back, slight median line. **Eyes:** Light amber, gray, blue gray. **Ears:** Long, set high, reach to within 2 inches of nose. **Lips and gums:** Pinkish flesh shades. **Neck:** Clean-cut, moderately long.
BODY: **Shoulders:** Well laid back. **Forelegs:** Straight, length from ground to elbow approximates length from elbow to top of withers. **Chest:** Depth to elbows, ribs well sprung, long. **Topline:** Back moderate length, straight, slight slope from withers, tuck-up moderate. **Hindquarters:** Well angulated. **Tail:** Docked to measure 6 inches at maturity. **Feet:** Arched, webbed toes, compact, nails gray or amber, dewclaws removed. **Coat:** Short, smooth, sleek.
MAJOR FAULTS: More than four missing teeth, back too long or too short, neck too short or throaty, poor gait, cow hocks, roach back or swayback, badly overshot or undershot. **Very serious faults:** White, except on chest; off-color eyes; black-mottled mouth; nondocked tail; dogs showing strong fear, shyness, nervousness.
DISQUALIFICATIONS: Deviation in height of more than 1 inch either way from standard, distinctly long coat, distinctly blue or black coat.

WIREHAIRED POINTING GRIFFON

This breed was once called the Korthals Griffon or Dutch Griffon. It was established by a wealthy Dutchman, E. K. Korthals. He began his breeding program about 1874, using a gray and brown bitch named Mouche, and in the next few years he purchased five other dogs to build his foundation stock.

Korthals moved to Germany, where he purchased further dogs to continue his breed development. He also traveled extensively in France, where the breed also happened to receive its greatest growth. The Wirehaired Pointing Griffon was developed to work with a man on foot, and it is a competent work dog.

HEIGHT: Males, 21½ inches; bitches, 19½ to 21½ inches.

WEIGHT: Not specified.

GAIT: Moves with legs in parallel planes.

COLOR: Steel gray with chestnut splashes, gray white with chestnut splashes, chestnut, dirty white mixed with chestnut, never black. Nose always brown.

HEAD: Harsh head coat forms a mustache and eyebrows. **Skull:** Long, narrow. **Muzzle:** Long, squared at the nose. **Eyes:** Large and full, iris yellow to light brown. **Ears:** Medium size, lying flat or slight curve at tips, set high, lightly furnished with hair. **Teeth:** Not specified, but scissors or level bite is normal. **Neck:** Rather long, no dewlap.

BODY: **Shoulders:** Long, sloping. **Forelegs:** Straight, rather short, furnished with short, stiff hair. **Chest:** Deep enough to reach the elbows, ribs rounded, but not barrel-chested, carried well back. **Topline:** Not specified, but normally level, tuck-up not specified, but normally slight. **Hindquarters:** Thighs long, well developed, furnished with rather short, stiff hair. **Tail:** Cut to one third of its length, carried gaily or level, hard coat without plume. **Feet:** Round, firm. **Coat:** Harsh as that of a wild boar, moderate length, unkempt.

FAULTS: Not specified.

chapter thirty-six
Hound Breeds

There are two types of Hounds in the Hound Group. The first includes those that hunt by tracking; that is, they use their noses to follow the trails or tracks left by moving game. Their quarry may be the rabbit, raccoon, fox, bear, elk, or other game. The second group are the gazehounds; that is, they are dogs that hunt by sight. They are the swiftest of all breeds. They may run singly, but as a rule, they course in pairs or even in packs. Their goal is to use their great speed to run down and capture their quarry or bring it to bay. Some Hounds are built long and low so that they will be able to enter small burrows; others are large enough to clash with wolves.

AFGHAN HOUND

The Afghan is said to have originated near the Jebel Musa, the Mountain of Moses, on the Sinai Peninsula some three thousand to four thousand years before Christ. The Egyptian name for the breed meant "monkey-faced" or "baboon" dog. Gazehounds spread out across the deserts, and one branch of the family moved into the mountainous area of Afghanistan. There the breed developed a longer coat and higher hip set, which enabled it to live in the colder climate and to run over rocky ground at great speed.

The Afghan reached England after World War I, and it came to North America in 1926. Since then it has become extremely popular as a show dog and as a beautiful and exotic home companion. It is also used in lure-coursing events that have become so popular in recent years.

HEIGHT: Males, 26 to 28 inches; bitches, 24 to 26 inches.

WEIGHT: Males, about 60 pounds; bitches, about 50 pounds.

GAIT: When dog is at a trot, hind feet step into prints of forefeet.

COLOR: All colors, but combinations preferred. White not desired, particularly on head. Nose black.

HEAD: Refined, little or no stop, nose to give slight Roman appearance. **Skull:** In balance with muzzle, occiput prominent. **Topknot:** Required. **Eyes:** Almond-shaped, dark. **Ears:** Set at eye level, of sufficient length to reach nearly to nose tip. **Teeth:** Level bite preferred, but scissors bite not penalized. **Neck:** Long, arched.

BODY: **Shoulders:** Well angulated. **Forelegs:** Set well under dog, pasterns straight. **Chest:** Deep. **Topline:** Level from shoulders to slightly arched loin, hipbones high, prominent, tuck-up pronounced. **Hindquarters:** Long from hips to hocks, excellent angulation at stifles and hocks. **Tail:** Ring at end, never bushy, never carried over back. **Feet:** Strongly arched, deep, broad pads, toes covered with hair. **Coat:** Short and close on neck and saddle, silky and profuse elsewhere.

FAULTS: Light eyes, snipy muzzle, overshot or undershot teeth, roach back or swayback, goose rump, tail set too high, elbows turning in or out, weak pasterns, straight stifles, sharp or shy temperament.

BASENJI

The present name for this dog is somewhat unfortunate because in some African languages *basenji* means "savage." Other names of the breed have been the Congo Barkless Dog and Dog of the Forest.

The Basenji does not bark, but it is not mute; it can make high whining or yodeling cries. However, Basenjis hunt silently. In type they are one of the oldest forms of the domestic dog. Another unusual characteristic of the breed is that the bitch is "in season" only once a year.

Basenjis reached England about 1930 and the United States in 1937. A British breed standard was drawn up, and this was accepted by the Basenji Club of America when it was formed in 1942. The American Kennel Club recognized the breed and approved the standard in 1954.

HEIGHT: Males, 17 inches; bitches, 16 inches.
WEIGHT: Males, 24 pounds; bitches, 22 pounds.
GAIT: Beautiful, flawless trot.
COLOR: Chestnut red, pure black, black and tan, all with white feet, chest, and tail tip. White legs, white blaze, white collar permitted. Nose black.
HEAD: Skull: Medium length and width, muzzle tapering, shorter than skull, skull flat, with wrinkles, which should also appear on sides of head. **Eyes:** Obliquely set, dark. **Ears:** Small, pointed, erect, set well forward on top of head. **Teeth:** Level or scissors bite. **Neck:** Long, arched.

BODY: Shoulders: Well laid back. **Forelegs:** Straight, with erect, flexible pasterns. **Chest:** Deep, with well-sprung ribs, moderate tuck-up. **Topline:** Level, short-coupled. **Hindquarters:** Long second thighs, hocks well let down. **Tail:** Tightly curled to either side. **Feet:** Small, narrow, well-arched toes. **Coat:** Short, silky.

FAULTS: Coarse or domed skull; snipy muzzle; overshot or undershot; splayed or flat feet; coarse, wide body; creams, shaded, or off colors to be heavily penalized.

BASSET HOUND

The Basset Hound belongs to a very old family of long-bodied, short-legged Hounds. It was originally related to the Dachshund, with the larger dogs being developed in France as Bassets, and the smaller dogs being developed in Germany as Dachshunds. Bloodhounds or the legendary St. Hubert Hounds of France were introduced to give the breed the Bloodhound type of head and ears and the loose skin.

Most American Bassets descend from Hounds developed in the kennels of Monsieur Lane and Count Le Couteulx in France. Lord Galway imported some dogs to England in 1866. He and others further developed the type of dog that is now found in Britain and America.

HEIGHT: Not to exceed 14 inches.
WEIGHT: Not specified.
GAIT: Slow, deliberate, but not ponderous.
COLOR: Any hound color, lips darkly pigmented. Black nose preferred, but liver nose permitted to match coat color.

HEAD: Skull and muzzle of equal length and in parallel planes. **Skull:** Domed, occiput prominent, moderate stop, head skin loose. **Eyes:** Deeply sunken, dark brown preferred, showing haw. **Ears:** Set low, almost on neck, fold over nose. **Teeth:** Level or scissors bite, pronounced dewlap. **Neck:** Massive, arched.

BODY: **Shoulders:** Well laid back. **Forelegs:** Elbows close to body; from deepest point of chest to ground should not be more than one third of total height at withers; legs powerful. **Chest:** Ribs long, well carried back. **Topline:** Straight, level. **Hindquarters:** Full, rounded, about equal to shoulders in width, hocks well let down, parallel, perpendicular to ground, stifles strongly angulated. **Tail:** Carried gaily, underside coarse. **Feet:** Large, deep, no dewclaws. **Coat:** Hard, smooth, short, dense.

FAULTS: High-set, flat ears; tight head skin; lack of elastic body skin; paddling, weaving gait; cow hocks; sagging or roach back; flat feet.

DISQUALIFICATIONS: Over 15 inches, legs knuckled over, distinctly long coat.

BEAGLE

The Beagle, a type of Foxhound in miniature, is believed to get its name from the French word *begle*. The breed dates back to at least the late 1500s, when large hounds called Buck Hounds were used to hunt stags and smaller dogs were used to hunt hare. Foxhounds as we know them had not yet been developed because the sport of riding with Hounds after foxes was still unknown.

Modern Beagle history began in England with Parson Philip Honeywood, who developed a pack of small Hounds about 1850 that he used to hunt hare. Just after the Civil War, General Richard Rowett of Carlinsville, Illinois, began importing English Beagles to America. The National Beagle Club was formed in 1888. Today field trials are the American Kennel Club's greatest single activity, and Beagle field trials form the major part of this.

HEIGHT: Two varieties, 13 inches and under or over 13 inches to 15 inches. This holds true for males and females.

WEIGHT: Not specified.

GAIT: Good foreleg reach, strong rear driving power.

COLOR: Any true hound color.

HEAD: Skull: Fairly long, slightly domed at occiput, broad, and full. **Eyes:** Large, set well apart, brown or hazel. **Ears:** Set low, nearly reaching to tip of nose. **Muzzle:** Medium length, square-cut, stop moderately defined, free of flew. **Teeth:** Level, scissors bite not specified, but permitted. **Neck:** Arched, light, medium length.

BODY: Shoulders: Medium length, not loaded. **Forelegs:** Straight, well boned, pasterns short, well boned, and straight. **Chest:** Deep, broad. **Topline:** Short, loins slightly arched and broad, ribs well sprung. **Hindquarters:** Hips and thighs strongly muscled, stifles well let down, hocks moderately bent. **Tail:** Set moderately high, carried gaily, slight curve, not carried over back. **Feet:** Close, firm. **Coat:** Close, hard, medium length.

FAULTS: Flat skull; excessive dome; small Terrierlike eyes; protruding muzzle; snipy; Roman nose or dish-face; thick, cloddy neck; upright shoulders, too heavy or loaded; long back, roach back, or swayback; out at elbows; cow hocks; straight hocks; long tail; rat tail; open feet.

DISQUALIFICATION: Over 15 inches at shoulder.

BLACK AND TAN COONHOUND

Coonhounds were developed basically from Foxhounds except that the Black and Tan has a strong infusion of Bloodhound blood. Coonhounds are night hunters and are particularly skillful at trailing raccoons. Some Coonhound field trials are held during the day, but the great championship events are at night. Water trials are also held for these dogs. Of the half-dozen Coonhound varieties, only the Black and Tan is registered by the American Kennel Club; the others are registered by the United Kennel Club.

HEIGHT: Males, 25 to 27 inches; bitches, 23 to 25 inches.
WEIGHT: Not specified, but body moderately heavy.
GAIT: Graceful, free, reaching with forelegs, good drive with rear legs.
COLOR: Coal black, rich tan above eyes and on sides of muzzle, chest, legs, buttocks, and feet, but with black penciling on toes. Nose black.
HEAD: Total head length, 9 to 10 inches in males, 8 to 9 in bitches; medium stop. **Skull:** Same length and in parallel plane with muzzle, prominent occiput. **Eyes:** Hazel to brown, deeply set. **Ears:** Set low, well back, to reach beyond the tip of the nose. **Teeth:** Level or scissors bite, flews well developed. **Neck:** Medium length, arched.
BODY: Shoulders: Sloping. **Chest:** Rounded, well-sprung ribs, chest depth to elbows. **Topline:** Back straight, sloping from withers to rump. **Hindquarters:** Heavily muscled, well angulated at stifle and hock joints. **Tail:** Set below back line, carried at right angle to back. **Feet:** Large, deep, hard pads. **Coat:** Short, dense.

FAULTS: Light eyes; short, high-set ears; undershot or overshot; flat-sidedness; swayback or roach back; loose elbows; cow hocks; splayed feet; undersize; shyness; nervousness.

DISQUALIFICATION: White anywhere on body if it exceeds 1½ inches in diameter.

BLOODHOUND

The progenitors of the Bloodhound are believed to have been brought to Europe before the Crusades. A northern black breed became known as the St. Hubert Hound. Most monasteries had Bloodhounds and kept the breed scrupulously pure. After the Norman Conquest, the dogs were brought to England. Only the blooded gentry could own them, hence the name Blooded Hounds, or Bloodhounds.

Bloodhounds have the finest scenting ability of any of the tracking Hounds. They have become world famous for their ability to follow man-made trails, hours and even days old, across highways. Consequently they are used by many law officers and in locating lost children.

HEIGHT: Males, 25 to 27 inches; bitches, 23 to 25 inches.

WEIGHT: Males, 90 to 110 pounds; bitches, 80 to 100 pounds.

GAIT: Elastic, swinging, free, tail carried high.

COLOR: Black and tan, red and tan, tawny, darker colors sometimes interspersed with lighter or badger-colored hair, sometimes flecked with white. Small amount of white permitted on chest, feet, tip of tail. Nose dark.

HEAD: Narrow, flattened, nearly equal in width for entire length; total head length for males, 12 inches; bitches, 11 inches. **Skull:** Long, narrow, in parallel plane with muzzle, occiput prominent. **Eyes:** Deeply set, dark, showing haw. **Ears:** Extremely long, thin, silky. **Wrinkle:** Formed by loose head skin, falls into wrinkles when head is lowered. **Teeth:** Level or scissors bite, lips square, deep, hanging flews. **Neck:** Arched, throaty, with loose skin.

BODY: Shoulders: Sloping. **Forelegs:** Straight, heavily boned. **Chest:** Deep. **Topline:** Strong, ribs well sprung. **Hindquarters:** Heavily muscled and angulated. **Tail:** Long, tapering, set high. **Feet:** Large, deep. **Coat:** Dense, hard, sometimes slight wave.

FAULTS: Unsoundness of legs and feet, quarrelsome with dogs or people, undersized, yellow eyes, swayback or roach back.

BORZOI

Prior to 1936, the Borzoi was known as the Russian Wolfhound. The dog is a true gazehound, believed to be descended from crossing the now extinct Steppe Greyhound with Arabian Gazelle Hounds and finally with Collies, from which it may have inherited its unusual coat.

The American Borzoi comes basically from dogs brought from Russia by Joseph B. Thomas, one of the all-time great masters of Foxhounds and a true authority on many breeds. Borzois have been used to hunt wolves and stags, and in the American West, coyotes. They are also used in the growing sport of lure coursing.

HEIGHT: Minimum for males, 28 inches; for bitches, 26 inches. Many Borzois reach 32 to 34 inches.

WEIGHT: Males, 75 to 105 pounds; bitches, 60 to 85 pounds.

GAIT: Great forward reach; when dog is at a fast trot, feet tend to move to center line of body.

COLOR: Any color or combination of colors acceptable. Nose black.

HEAD: Long, narrow. **Skull:** Slightly domed, almost no stop. **Eyes:** Dark, set obliquely, not full or staring, eyelids dark. **Ears:** Small, folded, lying back on neck, tips almost against occiput when in repose. **Muzzle:** Long, Roman-nosed. **Teeth:** Level or scissors bite. **Neck:** Arched, rather short.

BODY: **Shoulders:** Sloping, blades close at withers. **Forelegs:** Flat, straight bone, strong pasterns. **Chest:** Very deep, ribs only slightly sprung. **Topline:** Rises in curve over extremely muscular loins. **Hindquarters:** Well-bent stifles, strongly muscled second thighs, hocks well let down. **Tail:** Reaches below hocks, curved. **Feet:** Harefoot, toes strongly arched, close. **Coat:** Long, silky, flat, or wavy.

FAULTS: Curly coat, pig-jawed or undershot, missing teeth, weak pasterns, loose elbows, light eyes, straight stifles, cow hocks, dogs under 28 inches, bitches under 26 inches.

DACHSHUND

Fifteenth-century hunting scenes often showed long-bodied, short-legged dogs hunting the *dachs,* or Eurasian badgers. Because the badger has a body three feet long but only twelve inches tall, a dog of similar type had to be developed to follow the badger into its many-chambered den. Both the Basset and the Dachshund have this type of dog in their past. The smaller, shorter-eared dog, the Dachshund, came to be preferred for this type of hunting because the Basset's long ears could be easily torn and cause mortal bleeding.

About two hundred fifty years ago, the badger-hunting dog got its official name, Dachshund. There were three varieties: Smooth, Longhaired, and Wirehaired (a variety that was recognized in 1890). The dogs can be Miniature or Standard, in terms of size. Dachshunds reached America in the late 1870s, and the Dachshund Club of America was formed in 1895.

HEIGHT: Not specified.
WEIGHT: Standards, 10 to 20 pounds; Miniatures, under 10 pounds at 12 months of age.
GAIT: Not specified, but forelegs and hind legs move in line, back remains level.
COLOR: Red, red yellow, tan, yellow, with red preferred; black, chocolate, gray, white, each with tan markings; and dappled. Nose and nails black or chocolate to match coat, or gray or flesh color in grays and whites, but flesh color not desirable.

HEAD: Long, tapering. **Skull:** Slightly arched, no stop. **Eyes:** Medium size, oval, dark. **Ears:** Broad, rounded, set high. **Teeth:** Scissors bite. **Neck:** Arched, long.

BODY: Shoulders: Form right angle with upper arms, which are same length as shoulders. **Forelegs:** Straight, vertical, covering deepest point of chest. **Chest:** Deep, oval, long, breastbone prominent. **Topline:** Level, little tuck-up. **Hindquarters:** Strongly angulated. **Tail:** Set on line of spine. **Feet:** Well arched. **Coat:** Smooths: Short, thick, no bald patches. Longhairs: Long, silky. Wirehairs: Uniform, tight, short, wire coat with beard and bushy eyebrows.

FAULTS: Minor faults: Poor ear set, weak jaws, distemper teeth, too marked a stop, goggle-eyes, walleyes in dappled dogs, short or swan neck. **Secondary faults:** Long-legged, body hanging between shoulders, croup higher than withers, waddling gait, toes turned in or radically outward, splayed feet, sunken or roach back. **Serious faults:** Overshot or undershot, knuckling over, very loose shoulders.

FOXHOUND (AMERICAN)

The American Foxhound descends from English Foxhounds and, to some extent, French Hounds such as those given to George Washington by General Lafayette. (Washington rode to Hounds in the English fashion but the chase was for gray foxes which do not run well.) American Hounds are lighter and faster than English Hounds, and they tend to hunt individually. Their quarry is red fox.

A good deal of hunting with American Hounds is done at night, and the quarry is a red fox. The fox is not killed during the hunt; it lives to run again. The dogs' owners, listening on a hill, can recognize the voices of their Hounds, who seem to take pleasure in knowing the routes taken by individual foxes. The American Foxhound is also used, like the English Foxhound, in packs for hunting live fox or, in the West, coyotes, or for following a "drag" (artificial scent laid out before the hunt). To keep up with the hounds, devotees of the sport ride horses.

HEIGHT: Males, 22 to 25 inches; bitches, 21 to 24 inches.
WEIGHT: Not specified, but Hounds are lean and muscular, not heavy-bodied.
GAIT: True, great rear driving power, tireless.
COLOR: Any color.
HEAD: Skull: Fairly long, slightly domed at occiput, cranium broad and full, moderate stop. **Eyes:** Large, set wide apart, dark or hazel. **Ears:** Set low, nearly reaching tip of nose. **Muzzle:** Fair length, square-cut. **Teeth:** Not specified, but scissors bite normal. **Neck:** Medium length, not loaded, throat clean.
BODY: Shoulders: Sloping. **Forelegs:** Straight, well boned, strong pasterns. **Chest:** Deep, narrower than in English Foxhound, 28–inch girth in

24-inch-high dog, ribs carried well back, with 3-inch flank. **Topline:** Back moderately long, loins broad, slightly arched. **Hindquarters:** Stifles only slightly bent, hocks moderately so. **Tail:** Set moderately high, carried gaily, slight curve, very slight brush. **Feet:** Close and firm. **Coat:** Close, hard, medium length.

FAULTS: Skull flat, narrow across top, or with excess dome; small eyes; long, snipy muzzle; Roman nose or dish-face; cloddy neck and shoulders; throatiness; very long back, roach back, or swayback; splayed feet; upright shoulders; barrel chest or lack of depth; cow hocks; knees knuckled over; overshot or undershot; crooked forelegs.

FOXHOUND (ENGLISH)

No dog has been the subject of so much great literature as the English Foxhound, and literary descriptions of the sport in which it stars abound. A number of these Hounds are gathered in a pack and chase a red fox while they are followed over field, streams, and fences by horses and riders. Centuries of careful breeding have made the English Hounds superb specialists.

These dogs are heavier and slower than American Foxhounds. They are meant to stay in a pack and go at a pace that can be followed by riders who may have to jump fences, pick themselves up after a fall and remount, ford streams, open gates, and so on. There are still many packs of English Foxhounds in the United States, particularly on the East Coast.

HEIGHT: 24 to 25 inches, both sexes.

WEIGHT: Not specified, but heavier in body than the American Foxhound.

GAIT: Not specified, but true, good driving action.

COLOR: Not important, but Hound colors are black, tan, and white or any combination of these, plus pies (white with color of the hare, badger, or yellow).

HEAD: Girth of 16 inches before the ears. **Skull:** Fairly long, slightly domed at occiput. **Eyes:** Not specified, but normally brown. **Ears:** Set low, may be rounded by cutting off 1½ inches. **Muzzle:** Wide and 4½ inches long. **Teeth:** Level bite. **Neck:** Clean, no throatiness, not less than 10 inches from cranium to shoulder.

BODY: **Shoulders:** Sloping. **Forelegs:** Long upper arm, straight legs, strong pasterns, no knuckling over. **Chest:** Girth over 31 inches in a 24-inch Hound, back ribs very deep. **Topline:** Level, little tuck-up. **Hindquarters:** Heavily muscled thighs, straight stifles, hocks true. **Tail:** Carried gaily, but never squirrel fashion. **Feet:** Catlike, well-arched toes. **Coat:** Short, dense, hard, and glossy.

FAULTS: Knuckling over, lack of bone, cow hocks, elbows turning in or out, weak or fallen pasterns, splayed feet, squirrel tail.

DISQUALIFICATION: Undershot or overshot.

GREYHOUND

All the coursing dogs are of general Greyhound type. Although it cannot be known which variety was developed first, the Greyhound has been the best known throughout the world. Greyhounds have been used for coursing a variety of game wherever open country permitted such a sport.

In many countries today Greyhound racing competes with horse racing as a major sport. The dogs, eight to a field, pursue an artificial rabbit as it circles the track on a trolley. True coursing meets are also held, such as the famed Waterloo Cup race in England, which began in 1836. Coursing meets are still held in America's Midwest.

HEIGHT: Not specified.

WEIGHT: 65 to 70 pounds, males; 60 to 65 pounds, bitches.

GAIT: Extreme driving power derived from a "wheel back," which permits hind feet to drive past forefeet when dog is at a gallop.

COLOR: Immaterial.

HEAD: Skull: Long, narrow, fairly wide between the ears, little defined stop. **Eyes:** Dark. **Ears:** Small, folded, and semipricked when at attention (folded back against neck at other times). **Teeth:** Strong, level bite. **Neck:** Long, arched, no throatiness.

BODY: Shoulders: Set obliquely to upper arms, muscular, not loaded. **Forelegs:** Straight, elbows close, pasterns strong. **Chest:** Deep, ribs fairly well sprung. **Topline:** Back muscular, loins with good depth of muscle, well arched, belly well tucked up. **Hindquarters:** Long, heavily muscled over hip assembly and second thigh, stifles well bent, hocks well bent, close to ground, wide apart. **Tail:** Long, fine, tapering, curved at end. **Feet:** Hard and close, harefeet rather than cat feet, strongly knuckled up. **Coat:** Short, smooth, dense.

FAULTS: Yellow eyes, deep stop, erect ears, straight shoulders, loose elbows, flat feet, lack of stifle and hock angulation, poorly developed driving muscles.

HARRIER

The Harrier looks almost like an English Foxhound, but smaller, or just like a Beagle, but larger. Actually the Harrier is believed to have been bred down from the English Foxhound. The first known pack of Harriers, developed by Sir Elias de Midhope in about 1260, was maintained for some five hundred years.

Because hard hunting could be done on foot, Harriers were adopted by farmers and townsmen who might own only a single dog. They could combine their dogs to make a scratch pack for a morning of sport. In America Harrier packs have usually been followed on horseback, with a red fox as the quarry.

HEIGHT: 19 to 21 inches at the shoulder.
WEIGHT: Not specified.
GAIT: Not specified, but that of the Foxhound or Beagle.
COLOR: Those of the English Foxhound.
HEAD: Medium size with prominent forehead. **Eyes:** Dark brown. **Ears:** Those of the English Foxhound, but not artificially rounded. **Teeth:** Level or scissors. No disqualification for overshot or undershot as in English Foxhound. **Neck:** Long, clean.
BODY: Shoulders: Sloping. **Forelegs:** Straight, pasterns strong, elbows set away from ribs, but not turning out, slight knuckling over not to

be penalized. **Chest:** Deep, well-sprung ribs, carried well back, little tuck-up. **Topline:** Level, not dipping behind withers or arching over the loins. **Hindquarters:** Little angulation of stifles and hocks, hocks square, thighs muscular. **Tail:** Set high, carried Foxhound fashion. **Feet:** Round, catlike.

FAULTS: Those of the English Foxhound, plus exaggerated knuckling over.

IBIZAN HOUND

This Greyhound-type dog from the Balearic Islands of Spain has an Afghan-type gait but greater agility and jumping ability. The Ibizan Hound goes back more than five thousand years, for it was the hunting dog of the Pharaohs in Egypt. Artifacts from the tombs, including that of Tutankhamen, are clear evidence of this Hound's identity. The sea-faring Phoenicians were probably responsible for the breed's arrival on the Balearic island of Ibiza from which it takes its name. And it was the necessarily hardy people of this frugal land who bred their dogs carefully so that only the strongest and fittest survived. As a result, the Ibizan Hound today is a remarkably sound, healthy, strong dog. Ibizans were first imported to the United States in 1956, and the AKC gave recognition to the breed in 1978.

HEIGHT: Males, 23½ to 27½ inches at withers; bitches, 22½ to 26 inches.

WEIGHT: Males, about 50 pounds; bitches, 42 to 49 pounds. Slightly above or below okay.

GAIT: Graceful, driving.

COLOR: Solid white or solid red, red or lion (tawny colored) with white, or the reverse. Preponderant pattern is predominantly red with white feet and socks and white tail tip, chest, muzzle and forehead blaze. Other colors barred.

HEAD: Long, narrow cone. **Skull:** Long, flat, prominent occiput, little stop. Same length as muzzle. **Muzzle:** Slightly convex. **Ears:** Rigid, prick, base at level with eyes. **Eyes:** Oblique, small, amber to caramel in color. **Teeth:** Scissors bite. **Nose:** Extends beyond lower jaw. **Neck:** Long, slender, arched.

BODY: **Shoulders:** Sloping, withers loose. **Forelegs:** Long, straight forearms, pasterns straight, but flexible. **Chest:** Long, deep, prominent breastbone, ribs flat, but protruding slightly when dog is in working condition. **Topline:** Level to slightly arched loins and slightly sloping croup, less belly tuck-up than in Greyhounds. **Hindquarters:** Relatively vertical, hocks close to ground. **Tail:** Set low, long, carried sickle, ring, otter, or saber, according to mood. **Feet:** Harefeet, toes long, strongly arched, well furred between. **Coat:** Short, hard; or wirehaired, harsh, 1 to 3 inches long, possible mustache, longer hair on thighs and tail. Neither coat preferable to the other.

FAULTS: Deviations from standard; colors other than standard; flat, open-toed feet.

IRISH WOLFHOUND

Giant Irish Wolfhounds are known to have appeared in Roman arenas in the fourth century A.D. They are perhaps the only dogs the world has known big enough and fast enough to run down and kill wolves. After 1658, when famed wolf hunter Rory Carragh killed the last of the great Irish wolves, the breed languished.

Until very recently, the Irish Wolfhound was considered to be the tallest dog in the world. But today Great Danes and an occasional Borzoi may equal its height or, in the case of the Great Dane, surpass it.

A careful and successful effort has been made to save and revive interest in these Irish dogs. Although the first Irish Wolfhounds must have been quite savage, the modern dogs are remarkably gentle. They reach their minimum height and weight level by the time they are eighteen months old.

HEIGHT: Males, minimum of 32 inches at shoulders; bitches, minimum of 30 inches.

WEIGHT: Males, minimum of 120 pounds; bitches, minimum of 105 pounds.

GAIT: Sound when dog is at a trot, driving when dog is at a gallop.

COLOR: Gray, brindle, red, black, pure white, fawn, or any other color that appears in the Scottish Deerhound. Nose not specified, but usually black.

HEAD: Long. **Skull:** Moderately broad, frontal bones slightly arched, little stop. **Eyes:** Dark. **Ears:** Small, Greyhound carriage. **Muzzle:** Long, slightly pointed. **Teeth:** Not specified, but scissors bite normal. **Neck:** Long, muscular, without dewlap, free of throatiness.

BODY: Shoulders: Muscular, sloping. **Forelegs:** Heavily boned, straight, elbows set well under. **Chest:** Deep, breast wide. **Topline:** Rather long, loins arched, belly well drawn up. **Hindquarters:** Muscular thighs, second thigh long as in the Greyhound, hocks well let down. **Tail:** Long, slightly curved, well covered with hair. **Feet:** Well arched and closed. **Coat:** Rough, hard, especially wiry and long over eyes and under the jaw.

FAULTS: Head too light or too heavy, frontal bones too highly arched, large ears hanging flat to face, short neck, full dewlap, chest too narrow or too broad, sunken or straight back, crooked forelegs, cow hocks, spreading toes, lips or nose liver-colored or lacking pigmentation.

NORWEGIAN ELKHOUND

The Norwegian Elkhound belongs to the ancient Spitz family of northern forest dogs. Its general type is at least fifteen thousand years old and is seen in dozens of breeds, large and small. The Norwegian dog was developed for hunting elk (the North American moose). Some dogs are used for hunting a variety of game; others, for hauling sledges.

The dogs first appeared at a dog show organized by the Norwegian Hunters' Association in 1877. Norwegian Elkhounds have become very popular in the United States and Canada as pets and home guardians.

HEIGHT: Males, 20½ inches at the shoulder; bitches, 19½ inches.
WEIGHT: Males, about 55 pounds; bitches, about 48 pounds.
GAIT: Sound, effortless, with its back remaining level.
COLOR: Gray, with black-tipped outer coat, lighter on chest, stomach, legs, underside of tail, anal area. Nose not specified, but usually black.
HEAD: No loose skin, broad at the ears, forehead slightly arched. **Skull:** Slightly arched, in parallel plane with muzzle, stop small but clearly defined. **Eyes:** Brown, not protruding. **Ears:** Set high, erect, taller than wide, pointed. **Muzzle:** Medium length, tapering, but not pointed, lips tight. **Teeth:** Scissors bite. **Neck:** Medium length, no loose skin.
BODY: **Shoulders:** Not specified, but moderate slope. **Forelegs:** Straight, elbows close. **Chest:** Broad, deep, well-sprung ribs. **Topline:** Back short, compact, well-developed loins, very little tuck-up. **Hindquarters:** Moderate angulation of stifles and hocks. **Tail:** Set high, short, furred without brush, tightly curled, not carried too much to one side. **Feet:** Small, oblong, tight. **Coat:** Thick, hard, smooth-lying, longest on neck, chest, buttocks, undercoat light, soft, dense.

FAULTS: Lack of bold temperament, loose head and neck skin, yellow eyes, cow hocks, radical angulation at stifle joint, splayed feet, color too dark or too light, yellow markings or uneven colors.

DISQUALIFICATION: Any overall color (such as red, brown, solid black, white, or other solid color) other than the standard gray (as described).

OTTER HOUND

The Otter Hound was probably developed from the French Vendee Hound, but crosses with the Bloodhound and the extinct Southern Hound may have been used. Otter hunting seems to have become a sport around the year 1200. In the early 1300s William Twici, a huntsman, described it as a "rough sort of dog, between hound and terrier."

Otter hunting in the British rivers developed as a summer sport when other game could not be hunted. Otter Hound packs, which used to be numerous, are scarce today. The dogs are seldom seen at British dog shows, but have become popular in the United States and Canada as show dogs and gentle pets.

HEIGHT: Males, 24 to 27 inches at the shoulder; bitches, 22 to 26 inches.

WEIGHT: Males, 75 to 115 pounds; bitches, 65 to 100 pounds.

GAIT: At slow trot, hind feet step into prints of forefeet; may appear to shuffle. At faster gait, free and reminiscent of Bloodhound.

COLOR: Any color or combination. Nose black or liver, depending on coat color.

HEAD: Large, fairly narrow, 11 to 12 inches from occiput to nose tip in a 26-inch Hound. **Skull:** Long, rather narrow, slightly domed, stop not pronounced. **Muzzle:** Long, square. **Eyes:** Dark, but may vary with coat color, deeply set. **Ears:** Long, thin, pendulous, set low, tips reach to end of nose. **Teeth:** Scissors bite preferred. **Neck:** Medium length, appears short because of ruff of hair.

BODY: Shoulders: Sloping. **Forelegs:** Straight, heavy-boned, may have dewclaws. **Chest:** Wide, deep, ribs carried well back toward rear of trunk. **Topline:** Level. **Hindquarters:** Heavily muscled, moderately angulated, dewclaws removed. **Tail:** Reaches to hock, well feathered, carried sickle-fashion, but not over back when dog is in motion. **Feet:** Large, compact, strongly arched, webbed toes. **Coat:** Outer, coarse and crisp, 3 to 6 inches long on body, shorter on extremities, undercoat dense.

FAULTS: Grossly undershot or overshot, lack of undercoat, outercoat longer than 6 inches, haw more than slightly visible.

RHODESIAN RIDGEBACK

The Rhodesian Ridgeback was developed in Rhodesia and South Africa, where it was known as the Rhodesian Ridgeback Lion Dog, because it was used to hunt lions as well as other game. The dog gets its name from the ridge of hair that runs the opposite way along its back, starting at about the hips and widening into two crowns near the shoulders. This ridge was a characteristic of the native Hottentot hunting dog, with which the dogs of the Boer settlers undoubtedly interbred. A dermoid sinus (a kind of cyst) is sometimes found on the neck or under the ridge. Whether this abnormality is excised or not, it is a very serious flaw and such dogs should not be shown or bred.

Motion picture actor Errol Flynn helped to make the breed popular in the United States. American Kennel Club recognition came in 1955.

HEIGHT: Males, 25 to 27 inches at shoulder; bitches, 24 to 26 inches.

WEIGHT: Males, 75 pounds; bitches, 65 pounds when mature.

GAIT: Not specified, but sound.

COLOR: Light to red wheaten. White on toes and chest permitted. Nose black or brown.

HEAD: Skull: Flat, broad between the ears, free of wrinkles when in repose, stop reasonably defined. **Eyes:** Dark with black-nosed dogs, amber with brown-nosed dogs. **Ears:** Set high, medium size, folded. **Muzzle:** Long, deep, powerful jaws. **Teeth:** Level bite, well-developed canines. **Neck:** Strong, no throatiness.

BODY: Shoulders: Sloping. **Forelegs:** Straight, heavily boned, elbows close. **Chest:** Deep, capacious, not too wide, never barrel-chested. **Topline:** Level, loins heavily muscled and slightly arched, slight tuck-up. **Hindquarters:** Heavily muscled upper and second thighs, hocks well let down. **Tail:** Medium insertion, tapering, not coarse, carried with slight upward curve. **Feet:** Round, compact, protected with hair between toes and pads. **Coat:** Short, dense.

RIDGE: A distinctive breed characteristic. Starts behind shoulders with identical crowns on each side, tapers to a point between prominence of hips. Crowns not to extend more than one-third length of ridge.

FAULTS: Unsoundness of legs and feet, flesh-colored (Dudley) nose, white on belly or legs, incorrect ridge, woolly or silky hair.

SALUKI

The Saluki belongs to the group of hounds that was developed for coursing gazelles on the deserts and plains of Egypt, Arabia, Iraq, and Iran. The dog has great speed, unusually good vision, and the aptitude to hunt by sight rather than by tracking. The ancestry of these dogs goes back at least four thousand years.

Although the Saluki appeared in England in 1840, it did not come to America until 1920. The Saluki Club of America was formed in 1927, and the American Kennel Club gave the breed official breed recognition at that time. American Salukis have Egyptian, Arabian, English and Persian bloodlines. Salukis are now used in lure coursing in the United States and Canada. They exist in a wide range of colors, including white, golden, and tricolor, and in two varieties, with or without coat feathering.

HEIGHT: Males, 23 to 28 inches; bitches, slightly smaller.
WEIGHT: Not specified.
GAIT: Great foreleg reach, hind legs show great galloping and leaping power.
COLOR: White, cream, fawn, golden, red, grizzle, and tan, tricolor (white, black, and tan), black and tan. Nose black or liver.
HEAD: Long, narrow. **Skull:** Moderately wide between ears, little stop, in parallel plane with muzzle. **Eyes:** Dark to hazel, round, large, not protruding. **Ears:** Long, hanging close, covered with long, silky hair. **Teeth:** Level bite.
BODY: **Shoulders:** Sloping. **Forelegs:** Straight, long from elbow to knee. **Chest:** Deep, moderately narrow. **Topline:** Back fairly narrow, arched over loins, tuck-up pronounced. **Hindquarters:** Hipbones set wide apart, stifles moderately bent, hocks low to ground. **Tail:** Long, set low, slight curve, feathered on underside. **Feet:** Moderate length, toes long, well

arched, well feathered between toes. **Coat:** Smooth, silky, slight feather on legs, back of thighs, sometimes slight wool on shoulders and thighs. Smooth variety: No feathering.

FAULTS: Yellow eyes, undershot or overshot, radically angulated at stifles, cow hocks, splayed feet.

SCOTTISH DEERHOUND

The origins of the Scottish Deerhound and the Irish Wolfhound are almost certainly linked. Both descend from rough-coated gazehound stock. (The lighter Irish Wolfhounds may have been bred for the greater speed needed to hunt stags.) By 1600 the Scottish Deerhound breed type was well established.

The breed had been fostered — and chiefly owned — by Scottish clan chieftains. After the breakup of the clan system in 1745, the breed began to decline in popularity. It was rescued by Lord Colonsay and others about eighty years later. In recent years the breed has increased steadily in popularity in the United States and Canada.

HEIGHT: Males, 30 to 32 inches; bitches, 28 to 30 inches.
WEIGHT: Males, 85 to 110 pounds; bitches, 75 to 95 pounds.
GAIT: Typical gazehound drive, coupled with endurance.
COLOR: In order of preference: dark blue gray, darker or lighter grays or brindles, yellow and sandy red or red fawn, especially with black

ears and muzzles. White tail tip permitted. White on chest and toes permitted, but not desired. Nose black or blue.

HEAD: **Skull:** Flat, slight rise over eyes, but no true stop. **Eyes:** Dark brown to hazel. **Ears:** Greyhound type, always black or dark, hair short. **Muzzle:** Pointed, good mustache and beard. **Teeth:** Level bite. **Neck:** Long, but neck ruff may make it appear short.

BODY: Entire body like that of Greyhound, but taller. **Shoulders:** Sloping, little width between blades at withers. **Forelegs:** Straight, elbows close. **Chest:** Deep. **Topline:** Arched, good tuck-up, wide at hips, loins wide and powerful. **Hindquarters:** Long from hips to hocks, strong stifle angulation. **Tail:** Long, reaching to 1½ inches from ground, slight curve, covered with hair. **Feet:** Close, compact. **Coat:** Harsh, wiry; softer hair on head and chest.

FAULTS: Overshot or undershot, yellow eyes, prick ears, ewe neck, straight back, narrow rear, straight stifles, cow hocks, weak pasterns, splayed feet.

DISQUALIFICATION: White blaze or collar.

WHIPPET

The Whippet is almost identical to the Greyhound, except for size. It was developed about a hundred years ago by crossing Greyhounds and Terriers and later adding Italian Greyhounds. The English Kennel Club recognized the breed in 1891.

Because of their early use, Whippets were first called Snap Dogs and later Rag Dogs. Gamblers once made bets on how many hares a dog could snap (kill) in a given time. Later in race meets on a two-hundred-yard straightaway course, dogs were lined up at one end of the field, and the owners yelled and waved rags at the other end to get them to run. Today Whippets race from a starting box and run the distance by chasing a lure.

HEIGHT: Males, 19 to 22 inches; bitches, 18 to 21 inches.

WEIGHT: Not specified.

GAIT: Great reach in forelegs, strong drive behind, hind feet drive past forefeet when dog is at a gallop.

COLOR: Immaterial. Nose always black.

HEAD: Long, lean, barely perceptible stop. **Eyes:** Large, dark. Yellow or dilute colors to be strictly penalized. Both eyes must be same color. **Ears:** Semipricked at attention, folded back when at rest. **Teeth:** Scissors bite. **Neck:** Long, arched, free of throatiness.

BODY: **Shoulders:** Sloping, flat muscles. **Forelegs:** Long, straight, elbows close, not set far under the body, fair amount of bone. **Chest:** Reaching to elbows, ribs well sprung, but not barrel-chested. **Topline:** Arched, loins powerful, hips wide. **Hindquarters:** Long, powerful, stifles well bent, hocks well bent, close to ground, thighs heavily muscled. **Tail:** Long, tapering, should reach to hipbone when drawn under body. **Feet:** Thick pads, well-knuckled-up toes. **Coat:** Close, smooth, dense.

FAULTS: Nose other than black; flying ears; loaded shoulders; loose elbows; barrel chest; straight stifles; steep croup; tail carried higher than back when moving; thin, flat, splayed feet. An even bite is extremely undesirable.

DISQUALIFICATIONS: Blue or china eyes, undershot, overshot ¼ inch or more, ½ inch above or below specified height.

chapter thirty-seven
Working Breeds

Although a hunting dog may have to work until it is ready to drop from exhaustion, neither the owner nor the dog is likely to consider hunting to be work. It is sport. But that type of activity which is often very hard, often rather dull, and sometimes very dangerous is considered by man to be work. Working dogs pull sledges or formerly pulled small carts or wagons. They herd sheep or drive cattle or guard flocks, herds, buildings, private property, and military installations. They lead armed patrols, carry messages, search for people buried by avalanches, or do other rescue work. Some may be taught to attack.

AKITA

The Akita is the largest of a group of Japanese dogs belonging to the ancient Spitz family of northern forest dogs. It has been highly praised as a hunting dog, particularly with large game. It is also one of six breeds used for police and army work in Japan, in addition to being an excellent family pet and home guardian. The dog is alert, responsive, and dignified, yet aggressive to other dogs.

Helen Keller, the world-renowned blind and deaf woman who learned to talk, is said to have brought the first Akita to America in 1937. Widespread recognition of the breed in this country came when U.S. servicemen brought Akitas back home from Japan after World War II. The Akitainu Hozankai Society was organized in 1927 to oversee the continued purity of the breed and the Akita Club of America was founded in 1956. The breed received official American Kennel Club recognition in 1972.

HEIGHT: Males, 26 to 28 inches; bitches, 24 to 26 inches.
WEIGHT: Not specified.
GAIT: Moderate stride, hind legs move in line with forelegs.
COLOR: Any color, including white, but white has no mask. Pintos have white ground color, evenly placed patches on the head and on more than one third of the body. Nose black, but may be brown on white dogs, although this is not preferred.
HEAD: Massive. **Skull:** Free of wrinkles when at rest, shallow median furrow, stop well defined. **Muzzle:** A blunt triangle, little dewlap. **Ears:** Triangular, small, erect. If folded forward, tip should reach upper eye rim. When alert, ears form a continuation of the neck line. **Lips:** Black, not pendulous. **Eyes:** Dark brown, small, deep-set, rims black. **Tongue:** Pink. **Teeth:** Scissors bite preferred over even bite.
BODY: Longer than height. **Shoulders:** Moderate layback. **Chest:** Wide, deep. **Forelegs:** Heavy-boned, perpendicular to ground and parallel, fifteen-degree pastern slope. **Topline:** Level, moderate tuck-up. **Hindquarters:** Powerful upper thighs, stifles moderately bent, hocks well let down. **Feet:** Catlike, well knuckled up. **Tail:** Set high, carried over back or against flank in a three-quarter, full, or double curl, should reach hocks when let down. **Coat:** Double. Outer coat short, except at withers and rump, where it is about 2 inches long.
FAULTS: Unsoundness, poor gait, dewclaws on hind legs, pure white, white more than one third of ground color, splayed feet, lack of courage and alertness, a ruff or feathering.
DISQUALIFICATIONS: Butterfly nose or total lack of pigment, drop or broken ears, noticeably undershot or overshot, sickle or uncurled tail, males under 25 inches, bitches under 23 inches.

ALASKAN MALAMUTE

The Alaskan Malamute, the largest of the North American sled dogs, was developed by the Mahlemut Eskimos in Alaska. These people required a very strong freighting dog, capable of hauling heavy loads on sledges over the intensely cold, mountainous terrain of Alaska. Malamutes have been a part of many expeditions to the South Pole and many North Pole trips.

Mr. and Mrs. Milton Seeley of Wonalancet, New Hampshire, are credited with establishing the breed in the United States, and they were the principal authors of the breed standard. Their visit to the American Kennel Club with their dogs got the breed recognized in 1935. The parent club of the breed is the Alaskan Malamute Club of America.

HEIGHT: Males, 25 inches; bitches, 23 inches.
WEIGHT: Males, 85 pounds; bitches, 75 pounds.
GAIT: Hind legs move in line with front legs.
COLOR: Usually wolf gray to shadings of black, always white on underparts, legs, feet, and part of facial mask. White blaze on collar okay, but broken color extending over body in spots or uneven splashings not desired. Pure white is the only allowed solid color. Nose black.
HEAD: Skull: Broad, gradually narrows, slight furrow between eyes, little stop. **Muzzle:** Broad, deep. **Eyes:** Dark. **Ears:** Triangular, small in proportion to head, pointing forward when at attention, not set high. **Teeth:** Scissors bite. **Neck:** Arched.
BODY: Shoulders: Medium slope. **Forelegs:** Straight, heavily boned, pasterns short and vertical. **Chest:** Broad, deep. **Topline:** Back slopes slightly, not short-coupled, loins heavily muscled. **Hindquarters:** Moderate bend at stifles and hocks, hocks broad and short, dewclaws removed. **Tail:** Well furred, carried over back, but not curled. **Feet:**

Large, compact, well arched, furred between toes, pads thick. **Coat:** Coarse. Dense, oily undercoat, 1 to 2 inches long, outer guard hairs short, standoff, heavy around neck.

FAULTS: Splayed feet, light bones, stilted gait, long back.

AUSTRALIAN CATTLE DOG

This breed was developed in Australia. A New South Wales man named Hall imported two smooth-coated blue merle Collies from Scotland in 1840. They were only fair cattle dogs because they barked and did not heel properly. Hall crossed progeny of this pair with a dingo, whose trait is to creep up silently on its prey from behind and bite. About 1870 two brothers named Bagwood began to improve these dogs. Dalmatians were introduced, which changed the blue and red mottled colors to speckles. Kelpies were then added, which gave tan markings to blue dogs.

The dogs have had various names, including Timmons' Biter, Blue Heeler, Queensland Heeler, Australian Heeler, and finally Australian Cattle Dog. The present Australian standard was approved by the Australian National Kennel Council in 1963. Many of these dogs are now being imported into the United States.

HEIGHT: 18 inches, average.

WEIGHT: About 33 pounds.

GAIT: True, with remarkable dexterity in ducking kicks of wild cattle.

COLOR: Blue mottled, with or without black. Blue head may be marked with black and tan, and tan may be on legs. Or red speckled with darker red markings on the head. Nose black.

HEAD: V-shaped. **Skull:** Broad, slightly domed. **Eyes:** Dark, oval, medium size. **Ears:** Pricked, inclined outward. **Muzzle:** Medium long, tapering. **Teeth:** Scissors bite, lips tight. **Neck:** Medium length, exceptional strength.

BODY: **Shoulders:** Sloping. **Forelegs:** Straight, pasterns slightly bent. **Chest:** Deep, ribs well sprung. **Topline:** Straight, with strongly muscled, broad loins. **Hindquarters:** Moderately angulated at stifle and hock joints. **Tail:** Reaches to hocks, not carried above set-on, good brush. **Feet:** Round, deep, well arched, hard pads. **Coat:** Outer coat slightly harsh, moderately short except for leg feathering, undercoat soft and dense.

FAULTS: Cow or bow hocks, down in pasterns, out at elbows, stilted gait, dogs over or under 18 to 20 inches, bitches over or under 17 to 19 inches, tendency to grossness of body.

BEARDED COLLIE

The Bearded Collie is a Scottish breed, possibly with Komondors from Hungary as the basic stock, that is believed to have been developed in the fourteenth century, when trade between the two countries was important. The breed is also related to the Old English Sheepdog. A 1908 description says that the Bearded Collie was sleeker in build than the Old English and that it had a Dandie Dinmont head. However, the head of the modern Bearded Collie is more like that of the Scottish Deerhound.

The Bearded Collie was known as the Highland Collie in the 1900s. It was a drover's dog rather than a herding dog. Official recognition was given by the English Kennel Club in 1944 and by the American Kennel Club in 1977. The dog has a stable disposition, whether in the home or while working.

HEIGHT: Ideal for males, 21 to 22 inches; for bitches, 20 to 21 inches.

WEIGHT: Not specified.

GAIT: Lithe, supple, feet barely raised to cover ground, permitting quick turns, front and rear legs travel in parallel planes, moving inward to center line of body when dog is at a fast trot.

COLOR: All dogs are born either black, fawn, blue, or brown, with or without white markings. Blacks mature to gray or silver, browns will lighten from chocolate to sandy, fawns may grow lighter, and blues mature through shadings of slate or gray. White markings on face, neck, feet. Eye color and pigmentation of eye, mouth rims, and nose tends to follow dog's colors at birth.

HEAD: Skull: Broad and flat, stop moderate, cheeks well filled beneath the eyes. **Eyes:** Large, set wide apart, with eyebrows arched to sides to blend in with coat. **Ears:** Medium length, set level with eyes, covered with long hair. **Muzzle:** Length from nose tip to stop equals length from stop to occiput, nose square. **Teeth:** Scissors bite. **Neck:** Arched, rather long.

BODY: Longer than tall, in a ratio of 5 to 4 (from point of chest to point of buttocks). **Chest:** Deep, ribs reach to elbows. **Topline:** Level, merging into gentle curve or rump. **Shoulders:** Form right angle with upper arms, slightly wider at withers. **Forelegs:** Perpendicular to ground. **Hindquarters:** From hock to toes, perpendicular to ground at a line just behind point of buttocks, stifle joints well bent. **Feet:** Oval, arched, with thick pads. **Tail:** Set low, reaches to hocks, carried low with upward swirl when dog is standing; raised, but never beyond perpendicular, when dog is excited. **Coat:** Double. Undercoat soft and furry, outer coat flat and harsh, strong, shaggy, slight wave permitted, falls naturally to sides, never parted artificially, not so profuse as to hide the lines of the dog, hindquarters covered with shaggy hair, tail covered with abundant hair.

SERIOUS FAULTS: Snipy muzzle; flat or steep croup excessively long, silky hair; trimmed or sculptured coat; height over or under ideal.

BELGIAN MALINOIS

The Belgian Malinois is one of three breeds that are registered in Belgium and France as *Chiens de Berger Belge*. It stems from the same basic stock as the Belgian Sheepdog and the Belgian Tervuren. The Malinois is a fawn-colored, hard-coated dog with black-tipped hair over parts of its body and a black mask.

Until 1959 all three varieties were shown in the United States as Belgian Sheepdogs. Then the three were split into separate breeds, and the relatively rare Malinois was placed in the Miscellaneous Class. Regular imports brought full breed recognition in 1965.

HEIGHT: Males, 24 to 26 inches; bitches, 22 to 24 inches.

WEIGHT: Not specified.

GAIT: Quick and agile in starting and turning, legs move in line when dog is at a fast trot.

COLOR: Rich fawn to mahogany, black overlay, black mask and ears, underparts lighter fawn. Small white spot on chest and toe tips permitted. Nose black.

HEAD: Skull: Flattened, moderate stop, muzzle pointed, but not snipy, approximates skull length. **Lips:** Tight, black. **Eyes:** Dark brown. **Ears:** Triangular, stiffly erect, base not below eye level. **Teeth:** Level or scissors bite. **Neck:** Outstretched, arched, tight skin.

BODY: Shoulders: Oblique, long. **Forelegs:** Upper arms at ninety-degree angle with shoulders, bone round, pasterns slightly sloped. **Chest:** Reaches to elbow. **Topline:** Slopes to hips, loins short, croup slight slope. **Hindquarters:** Heavily muscled, sharp angles at stifles and hocks, dewclaws removed. **Tail:** Reaches to hocks, slight curve. **Feet:** Elongated, toes arched, nails black, except white at white toe tips. **Coat:** Dense undercoat, outer coat straight, slightly longer around the neck.

FAULTS: Washed-out fawn underparts, lips pink on outside, strong tuck-up or paunchy, extreme angulation.

DISQUALIFICATIONS: Hanging ears, cropped or stump tail, males under 22½ or over 27½ inches, bitches under 20½ or over 25½ inches.

BELGIAN SHEEPDOG

This is the breed known in Europe as the Belgian Groenendael, after the town of that name. In 1885, Monsieur Reul in Belgium mated a black bitch to a similar long-coated black dog, Piccard D'Uccle, from which succeeding generations of Belgian Sheepdogs came. These black dogs were so attractive that many people began to breed them exclusively.

The first Belgian Sheepdogs were brought to America in 1907; more were brought in 1912 and 1914. They were used in police departments, where they distinguished themselves, as they also did in Europe during World War I, when they served as messenger and Red Cross dogs. These Belgian dogs can be registered with the American Kennel Club provided that they can be proven to have three generations of only black ancestry.

HEIGHT: Desired for males, 24 to 26 inches; for bitches, 22 to 24 inches.

WEIGHT: Not specified.

GAIT: Agile, capable of quick starts and turns, legs move in line when dog is at a fast trot.

COLOR: Black. Small white patch on chest, white or gray frost on muzzle and tips of hind toes permitted. Nose black.

HEAD: Skull: Flattened, length and width equal, moderate stop, muzzle and skull approximately equal length. **Eyes:** Dark brown. **Ears:** Triangular, erect, base not lower than the center of the eye. **Lips:** Tight, black, no pink showing. **Teeth:** Level or scissors bite. **Neck:** Arched, skin tight.

BODY: Shoulders: Form ninety-degree angle with upper arms. **Forelegs:** Straight, parallel, oval bone, pasterns slight slope. **Chest:** Reaches to elbow. **Topline:** Slopes to hips, croup slight slope, abdomen neither tucked up nor paunchy. **Hindquarters:** Sharp angles at stifles and hocks, bone oval. **Tail:** Reaches hocks, slight end curve. **Feet:** Elongated, deep, arched, nails black, except white to match white toe tips. **Coat:** Guard hairs long, straight, slightly harsh, undercoat dense.

FAULTS: White on tips of front toes, snipy muzzle, undershot or overshot, poor temperament.

DISQUALIFICATIONS: Any color other than black, hanging ears, cropped or stump tail, males under 22½ or over 27½ inches, bitches under 20½ inches or over 25½ inches, viciousness.

BELGIAN TERVUREN

In conformation the Belgian Tervuren is almost identical to the Belgian Sheepdog. However, its color is much different and is described as a "blackened fawn." The breed began when M.F. Corbeel of Tervuren bred a bitch called Miss, which he sold to Monsieur Danhieux. He bred her to a black dog, Piccard D'Uccle, the same dog that founded the Belgian Sheepdog. Thereafter he bred very carefully to maintain the black-tipped fawn coat.

Most Belgian Tervurens were actually brought to this country from France, where the breed is very popular. Rudy Robinson, a noted Indiana dog breeder, imported many of the first Tervurens to America. Full breed recognition came in 1959.

HEIGHT: Males, 24 to 26 inches; bitches, 22 to 24 inches.

WEIGHT: Not specified.

GAIT: Agile for quick turns and starts, legs move in line when dog is at fast trot.

COLOR: Rich fawn to russet mahogany with black overlay, fawn hair black-tipped. Black overlay is especially pronounced on shoulders, back, ribs. Black mask and ears, dark or black tail tip. White on chest, white or gray frost on muzzle, and white toe tips permitted. Nose black.

HEAD: Skull: Flattened. Muzzle and skull same length, measured from stop. **Eyes:** Dark. **Ears:** Set high, triangular, base not lower than the center of the eye. **Teeth:** Scissors or level bite, distemper teeth not penalized. **Neck:** Arched.

BODY: Shoulders: Form a ninety-degree angle with upper arms. **Forelegs:** Straight, flat bone, elbows neither in nor out, pasterns slightly sloped. **Chest:** Reaches to elbow, belly neither tucked up nor paunchy. **Topline:** Horizontal, croup slightly sloped. **Hindquarters:** Stifles bent, upper thighs at right angles to hips, hocks moderately bent. **Tail:** Reaches to hocks, slight curve. **Feet:** Elongated, toes arched. **Coat:** Guard hairs long, medium harsh, straight, undercoat dense, collarette at neck, long, abundant on back of thighs and on tail.

FAULTS: Yellow eyes, unsoundness of legs and feet, undershot or overshot, splayed feet.

DISQUALIFICATIONS: Viciousness, hanging ears, cropped or stump tail, males under 23 or over 26.5 inches, bitches under 21 or over 24.5 inches, solid black or solid liver, white except as specified, severely undershot.

BERNESE MOUNTAIN DOG

This is a breed whose ancestry goes back to the Tibetan Mastiff and the Molossian Dog. It shows a similarity to other large dogs, such as the St. Bernard and the Newfoundland. The dog got its name from Berne, Switzerland, where it was used as a draft dog for hauling small carts. The breed's popularity declined during most of the nineteenth century, but Swiss dog fanciers restored it to favor about 1892. A specialty club was formed in 1907.

Bernese Mountain Dogs began to appear in America just before World War II, but the war held back their progress. Today they are becoming steadily more popular among those who like a strong, very muscular dog that is large, but not as large as the St. Bernard.

HEIGHT: Males, 23 to 27½ inches; bitches, 21 to 26 inches.
WEIGHT: Not specified.
GAIT: Not reaching, but powerful.
COLOR: Jet black, with russet brown or deep tan markings on all four legs, on each side of white chest markings, and spots over eyes. Brown on forelegs must be between black and white. White spot just above forelegs. White feet; white tip of tail, blaze, and star on chest; and a few white hairs on back of neck are considered desirable.
HEAD: **Skull:** Flat, defined stop. **Eyes:** Brown or dark hazel. **Ears:** V-shaped, set high, not pointed, short. **Muzzle:** Strong, with good bite. **Neck:** Not specified.
BODY: **Shoulders:** Not specified. **Forelegs:** Straight, muscular. **Chest:** Broad, deep. **Topline:** Back rather short, loins muscular. **Hindquarters:** Thighs well developed, stifles well bent. **Feet:** Round, compact, dewclaws removed. **Tail:** Fair thickness, well furred, but not to form a flag,

moderate length, upward swirl, carried gaily, but not over back or curled.
Coat: Soft, silky, long, slightly wavy.

   FAULTS: Too massive in head; light, staring eyes; too heavy or long ears; too narrow or snipy muzzle; undershot or overshot; pendulous dewlaps, too long a body; splayed feet or harefeet; cow hocks; white legs; poor tail carriage.

BOUVIER DES FLANDRES

   The Bouvier des Flandres (pronounced Boo-vee-ay day Flawn-druh) is another of the European working breeds that nearly died out as grazing lands were fenced, railroads were built to take cattle to market, and herding dogs were no longer needed. However, a few dogs remained, and two of these were exhibited at the International Exhibition in Brussels in 1910. Interest in saving the breed was immediately stimulated.

   During World War I the breed again suffered in popularity, but a few careful breeders remained to continue the dogs' line. One of the remaining dogs was the famous Champion Nic de Sottegem, who became the grand patriarch of the breed. In Europe many Bouviers des Flandres are police dogs or win police certificates in order to become champions. The present American standard was approved by the American Kennel Club in 1975.

   HEIGHT: Ideal for males, 26 inches; ideal for bitches, 25 inches. However, males can range from 24½ to 27½ inches; and bitches, from 23½ to 26½ inches. Those dogs that are over or under these heights are severely penalized.

WEIGHT: Not specified.

GAIT: Balanced fore and rear, back remains level.

COLOR: Fawn to black, pepper and salt, gray and brindle. White on chest permitted. Nose black.

HEAD: Medium long. **Skull:** Flat, longer than muzzle, brow arched, stop shallow. **Eyes:** Medium size, oval, nut brown. Black permitted. **Ears:** Set high, cropped to triangles, rough-coated. **Muzzle:** Wide, deep. **Teeth:** Scissors bite. **Neck:** Rounded, carried almost upright.

BODY: **Shoulders:** Long, sloping. **Forelegs:** Straight, moderate girth, elbows tight, legs well covered with rough hair. **Chest:** Reaches to elbows, moderate rib spring. **Topline:** Short and straight, loins slightly arched, rump broad and square, rather than sloping. **Hindquarters:** Hams powerful, stifles slightly angulated, hocks well let down. **Feet:** Round, toes arched, nails black. **Tail:** Set high, erect, docked to two or three vertebrae. **Coat:** Double. Outer coat rough and harsh.

FAULTS: Chocolate brown color with white spots; brown, pink, or spotted nose; light, staring eyes; narrow muzzle; weak back; cow hocks; loose elbows; soft coat; lack of undercoat.

BOXER

The boxer is a modern development of a variety of dogs that probably included the English Bulldog and the Dogue de Bordeaux. The undershot jaw and deep stop indicate Tibetan descent for all these dogs. The Boxer gets its name from its habit of sparring with its forepaws as a fight begins.

The great beauty of the modern dog did not come until after 1900. The first German registration was in 1904, and the first champion was crowned in 1915. However, its development was held back during the war years. Between the world wars the Boxer gained extraordinary popularity in the United States. This has since leveled off to a steady position as one of America's best-known breeds.

HEIGHT: Adult males, 22½ to 25 inches; adult bitches, 21 to 23½ inches.

WEIGHT: Not specified.

GAIT: Level-backed, ground-covering stride.

COLOR: Shades of fawn from light tan to deer red or mahogany, deeper colors preferred; brindle (black stripes on fawn background). White limited to one third of ground color. Nose black.

HEAD: Clean, no deep wrinkles. **Skull:** Slightly arched, distinct stop. **Eyes:** Dark. **Ears:** Set high, cropped long, carried erect. **Muzzle:** Nose tip higher than root, dark mask. **Teeth:** Undershot, lower incisors and fangs in line, upper incisors slightly curving. **Lips:** Meet evenly, with upper filling projection of lower jaw. **Neck:** Arched, no dewlap.

BODY: Square from ground to withers to rear projection of upper thighs. **Shoulders:** Long, sloping, form right angles with upper arms. **Forelegs:** Straight, perpendicular, parallel. **Chest:** Reaches elbows, ribs carried far back, arched, not barrel-shaped, light tuck-up, loins muscular. **Hindquarters:** Well angulated at stifles and hocks. **Tail:** Clipped. **Feet:** Strongly arched, rear toes longer than fore. **Coat:** Short, tight to body.

FAULTS: Bulldoggy head, either lip projecting beyond other, teeth showing, excessive flews, dark mask extending onto skull, tongue showing or hanging, dewlap, weak elbows, swayback or roach back, cow hocks, elbows turning in or out.

DISQUALIFICATIONS: White or black ground color, entirely white or black, any color other than fawn or brindle, more than one third white.

BRIARD

It is pleasant to speculate that the Sheepdogs of Brie (*Chiens Berger de Brie*) guarded the flocks on the plains of Brie (famed for Brie cheese). The breed is mentioned as early as 1809. Efforts to save the breed began late in the 1800s, when Les Amis du Briard (the Friends of the Briard) was organized. By 1900, the remaining stock was in the hands of careful breeders.

The dogs were used for messenger service and as Red Cross dogs in World War I. Today they serve as both farm guardians and home guardians. They are required to have two dewclaws on each hind leg.

HEIGHT: Males, 23 to 27 inches; bitches, 22 to 25½ inches.
WEIGHT: Not specified.
GAIT: Strong, flexible trot, legs move in line when dog is at fast trot.
COLOR: All solid colors except white. Dark colors preferred. Usually black, black with some white hairs, dark and light gray, tawny, and combinations of two of these colors, but with no marked spots. Nose always black.
HEAD: Long, medium width, forehead slightly rounded. **Skull:** Equal length with muzzle, stop distinct. **Eyes:** Dark, rather large. **Ears:** Set high, cropped or natural. If cropped, stand erect. If natural, not carried too flat. **Teeth:** Scissors bite. **Neck:** Muscular, distinct from shoulders.
BODY: **Shoulders:** Not specified, but sloping normal. **Forelegs:** Heavy bone, elbows tight. **Chest:** Broad, deep. **Topline:** Back straight, rump slightly sloped. **Hindquarters:** Well angulated at hocks, two dewclaws required on each hind foot. **Feet:** Strong, round. **Tail:** Well feathered, crook at end, reaches to hocks. **Coat:** Long, wavy, stiff, long on head, offstanding eyebrows.
FAULTS: Snipy muzzle; small, light eyes; white on chest; tail too short or carried over back; white nails.

DISQUALIFICATIONS: Nose any color other than black, yellow or spotted eyes, tail nonexistent or cut, fewer than two dewclaws on each rear leg, white coat, spotted coat, white spot on chest exceeding 1 inch in diameter, dogs or bitches under minimum sizes, white vent, white on feet.

BULLMASTIFF

The Bullmastiff was once known as the Gamekeeper's Night-Dog. It got its present name because of its background, which is about 60 per cent Mastiff and 40 per cent Bulldog. The Bullmastiff was developed on large estates after 1850 by gamekeepers who needed a dog that could knock down and hold but not injure poachers. Contests were held in which muzzled dogs and men with staves fought each other, with the dogs always winning.

The English Kennel Club recognized the breed in 1924, provided that the dogs were purebred (i.e., having no pure Mastiff or pure Bulldog breeding for three generations). Challenge Certificates were first awarded in 1928. The American Kennel Club recognized the breed in 1933.

HEIGHT: Males, 25 to 27 inches; bitches, 24 to 26 inches.
WEIGHT: Males, 110 to 130 pounds; bitches, 100 to 120 pounds.
GAIT: True and powerful, never cumbersome or ponderous.
COLOR: Red, fawn, brindle, with white chest spot permitted. Nose black. Dark mask on muzzle preferred.
HEAD: Broad, wrinkled, flat forehead. **Skull:** Large. **Eyes:** Dark, medium size. **Ears:** V-shaped, set high and close to head. **Muzzle:** Broad,

deep, one third the skull length, moderate stop. **Teeth:** Level bite or slightly undershot, flews not too pendulous. **Neck:** Arched, almost equals head in circumference.

BODY: Shoulders: Slightly sloping. **Forelegs:** Straight, elbows square, pasterns straight. **Chest:** Wide, well let down between forelegs, well-sprung ribs. **Topline:** Back short, loins wide, muscular, and slightly arched, fair depth of flank. **Hindquarters:** Well-developed second thighs, moderate stifle angulation. **Tail:** Set high, tapers to hocks, never carried Hound-fashion. **Feet:** Medium size, deep, pads thick, nails black. **Coat:** Short, dense.

FAULTS: Lack of foreface with nostrils set on top, long back, cow hocks, splayed feet, white other than chest spot.

ROUGH COLLIE

Collies descend from shepherd dogs of long ago. The known history of the breed begins in Scotland about 1800, when the dogs, called Scotch Collies, were about 14 inches tall at the shoulder. The origin of *Collie* is not known for certain. By 1860, when Collies were first shown at the great Birmingham, England, exhibition, they had reached their present height. Since then the breed has been refined to its present beauty.

In the United States the Rough Collie was first registered in the *American Kennel Club Stud Book* in 1885. Since then the dog has consistently been among the leading breeds at dog shows and has always ranked high among registrations. Albert Payson Terhune's Collie stories and Eric Knight's famous *Lassie Come Home,* plus the Lassie motion pictures, have helped to give the breed worldwide fame.

HEIGHT: Males, 24 to 26 inches; bitches, 22 to 24 inches.

WEIGHT: Males, 60 to 75 pounds; bitches 50 to 65 pounds.

GAIT: Sound, front and rear legs move comparatively close together at the ground, legs move in line when dog is at fast trot.

COLOR: Sable and white: Predominantly sable (light gold to dark mahogany), with white markings usually on chest, neck, legs, feet, tip of tail, and blaze on foreface or back of skull. Tricolor: Predominantly black, white markings as in sable and white, tan shadings about head and legs. Blue merle: Marbled or mottled blue gray and black, with white markings. White: Predominantly white, with sable, tricolor, or blue markings. No preference among colors.

HEAD: Blunted wedge, never massive, skull and muzzle of equal length and in parallel planes. **Skull:** Flat, arched eyebrows, slight stop. **Eyes:** Dark, set obliquely. In blue merles, one or both may be wall (whitish iris) or china (blue eye). **Ears:** When alert, carried high on back skull, three quarters erect, with one fourth tipping forward. **Teeth:** Scissors bite. **Neck:** Carried upright, heavily frilled with hair.

BODY: **Shoulders:** Sloping. **Forelegs:** Straight, well boned. **Chest:** Reaches to elbows, ribs well rounded. **Topline:** Level, croup sloped, loins arched. **Hindquarters:** Well angulated at stifles and hocks. **Tail:** Reaches to hock or below, swirl at tip, profuse brush, carried gaily. **Feet:** Small, oval. **Coat:** Outer coat abundant, harsh, and straight; undercoat soft and dense.

FAULTS: Massive or snipy head; too heavy ears; prick ears; large, full eyes; receding back skull; nonmatching eyes except in blue merles; lack of undercoat; cow hocks; straight stifles, loose elbows; poor gait.

SMOOTH COLLIE

It seems probable that the Smooth Collie was developed from other than Rough Collie stock and in northern England rather than in the Scottish Highlands. But the two breeds were interbred, and by 1885 both Roughs and Smooths were often found in the same litter. Smooth Collies are identical to Rough Collies except for the coat. This tends to accentuate or make more easily discernible some of the faults in both varieties.

BODY: Coat: Hard, dense, smooth.
FAULTS: Too narrow or too wide a front, ears so heavy that they are lifted with difficulty, too massive a head, cow hocks, other faults found in Roughs.

DOBERMAN PINSCHER

Louis Dobermann of Apolda, Thuringia, Germany, developed the dog that bears his name. He kept his breeding methods secret, but it is believed that he crossed Rottweilers, a black—and savage—Greyhound, and a Manchester Terrier. His breeding experiments covered a period of about twenty years; by 1890 he had the dog he desired. It was recognized in 1900. A Swiss dog owner of the period said it took a great deal of courage to own a Doberman because of its savage disposition.

Since then the dog's temperament has become milder within a household, yet the Doberman still maintains its alert guardian qualities. Alertness, intelligence, and easy trainability are breed characteristics. The breed is now enjoying worldwide popularity. It was recognized by the American Kennel Club in 1921.

HEIGHT: Males, 26 to 28 inches; bitches, 24 to 26 inches.

WEIGHT: Not specified.

GAIT: Balanced, great foreleg reach, strong hind leg drive.

COLOR: Black, red, blue, and fawn (Isabella). Rust markings sharply defined above eyes, on muzzle, throat, forechest, legs, feet, and below tail. Nose black, brown, dark gray, or dark tan to match coat color.

HEAD: Blunt wedge. **Skull:** In parallel plane with muzzle, flat on top. **Eyes:** Dark, but to match coat color. **Ears:** Set high, carried erect, normally cropped. **Teeth:** Scissors bite, all 42 teeth desired. **Neck:** Well arched, proportionate to body.

BODY: **Shoulders:** Form ninety-degree angle with upper arms. **Forelegs:** Straight, length from elbow to withers equals length from ground to elbow. **Chest:** Reaches to elbow, ribs well sprung, withers is highest point of body. **Topline:** Slopes to slightly rounded croup. **Hindquarters:** The angulation of the hindquarters is in line with the angulation of the forequarters. **Tail:** Docked to second joint. **Feet:** Cat feet, turning neither in nor out. **Coat:** Smooth, short, dense.

FAULTS: Deviations from standard. Shy or vicious dogs must be excused. Shyness: Refuses to stand for examination, backs away from judge at approach from either front or rear, shies at unusual noises. Viciousness: Attempts to attack the judge or its handler.

DISQUALIFICATIONS: Overshot more than $3/16$ of an inch, undershot more than $1/8$ of an inch, 4 or more missing teeth.

GERMAN SHEPHERD DOG

The German Shepherd is the most popular breed of dog in the world. It was developed about 1900 by crossing various shepherd breeds still remaining in Germany after herding dogs became unnecessary. Many breeds of dogs were used by the Germans during World War I, but it was the German Shepherd that stood out above the others. Its postwar world popularity was greatly helped by famous motion picture dogs Strongheart and Rin Tin Tin.

Refinement of the breed has developed a nearly effortless, tireless, trotting gait. The head has been refined to one of great beauty without losing strength. Aside from their use as police and war dogs, German Shepherds are used by most guide dog schools for the blind and for smelling out drugs and guns in the baggage of travelers.

HEIGHT: Males, 24 to 26 inches; bitches, 22 to 24 inches.
WEIGHT: Not specified.

GAIT: Legs move in a line, great foreleg reach and hind leg drive, with hind foot passing print of the forefoot.

COLOR: Most colors permitted except white.

HEAD: Long. **Skull:** In parallel plane with muzzle, wedge-shaped, with no abrupt stop. **Eyes:** Medium size, dark, set obliquely. **Ears:** Erect, parallel and perpendicular to the ground when dog is alert. **Teeth:** Scissors bite, with 42 teeth ideal. **Neck:** Long, clean.

BODY: Longer than tall as 10 is to 8½. **Shoulders:** Form ninety-degree angle with upper arms. **Forelegs:** Straight, pasterns angulated at twenty-five degrees from vertical. **Chest:** Reaches to elbows, ribs well sprung, little tuck-up. **Topline:** Slopes from withers to croup, loins broad, croup sloping. **Hindquarters:** Forelegs' angulation is parallel to shoulders. **Tail:** Bushy, reaches to hocks, slight curve at end. **Feet:** Short, compact. **Coat:** Medium length, double, close to body.

FAULTS: Missing teeth other than first premolars; sagging or roach back; shyness; tail hooked to one side; stilted, crabbing, or crossing-over gait; washed-out colors and blues or livers.

DISQUALIFICATIONS: Cropped or hanging ears, undershot jaw, docked tails, white dogs, dogs with noses not predominantly black, dogs attempting to bite the judge. Any dog showing pronounced indications of shyness, such as shrinking behind its handler, or of nervousness, such as looking upward or around with an anxious expression or tucking in its tail in response to strange sights or sounds, must be dismissed.

GIANT SCHNAUZER

The Giant Schnauzer was a cattle drover's dog, probably closely related to the Bouvier des Flandres. It is believed that Standard Schnauzers were crossed with the working dogs of Bavaria and Württemburg and with the progenitors of Bouvier. The dogs used to help shepherds herd their livestock in these rural areas. The desired height of the Giant Schnauzer seems to have been obtained by the use of a black Great Dane.

The three Schnauzer breeds (Giant, Standard, and Miniature) are look-alikes, but they are actually three distinct breeds that cannot be interbred. The Giant Schnauzer came to public attention during World War I, when it was recruited for army and police work. It was brought to America in the late 1920s but did not achieve prominence until after World War II.

HEIGHT: Males, 25½ to 27½ inches; bitches, 23½ to 25½ inches. Size never takes precedence over type, soundness, and temperament.

WEIGHT: Not specified.

GAIT: Free, balanced, vigorous, legs move in a line when dog is at a fast trot.

COLOR: Pure black, with white chest spot allowed, or equal mixtures of pepper and salt (acceptable shades of salt and pepper from dark iron-gray to silver-gray). Eyebrows, whiskers, cheeks, throat, chest, legs, and below the tail are slightly lighter but include "peppering." Nose black.

HEAD: Rectangular in appearance, elongated, in length one half the length of the body, withers to tail root. **Skull:** Of equal length and in parallel plane to muzzle, flat on top, moderately broad slight stop accentuated by the eyebrows. **Eyes:** Medium size, dark, oval, brows underarched and wiry. **Ears:** V-shaped, small, set high; if cropped, of equal length, carried high. **Teeth:** Scissors bite. **Lips:** Tight. **Neck:** Arched, tight skin at the throat.

BODY: Shoulders: Slanting, high withers, strongly muscled. **Forelegs:** Straight, pasterns straight. **Chest:** Reaches to elbows, breastbone visible. **Topline:** Back square from ground to withers to tail root, belly moderately drawn up. **Hindquarters:** Strongly muscled, well bent at stifles and hocks, hocks perpendicular to ground, second thigh almost parallel to an extension of the upper neckline. **Tail:** Cut at second or third joint, carried erect. **Feet:** Well-arched, compact, thick tough pads, nails dark. **Coat:** Hard, wiry, dense, not smooth or lying flat, harsh beard and eyebrows, coarse on skull top.

FAULTS: Dogs that repeatedly shrink from the judge or from approach from the rear, noise-shy dogs, dogs that try to bite the judge or handler. In each case the judge should dismiss the dog from the ring. An aggressive attitude toward other dogs should not be considered viciousness.

DISQUALIFICATION: Overshot or undershot.

GREAT DANE

The Great Dane is a German breed whose true name should be German Boar Hound. There is no real certainty about its direct ancestry, although the French eighteenth-century naturalist Georges de Buffon believed it to have an Irish Wolfhound background, and a contemporary, Baron Georges Cuvier, thought it had English Mastiff blood. In any case the dog belongs to the Molossian and Tibetan Mastiff group. The Germans adopted a breed standard in 1891, two years after the Americans and six years after the English. Despite being one of the largest of all dogs, the Great Dane has remained steadily popular and has usually been among the twenty leading breeds in registrations.

HEIGHT: Males, 30 inches minimum, but over 32 inches preferred; bitches, 28 inches minimum, but over 30 inches preferred.

WEIGHT: Not specified.

GAIT: Long, easy, springing, no tossing or rolling of body, back line remains parallel to ground.

COLOR: Brindle (golden shades, black stripes, deep black mask preferred), fawn (shades of golden, black mask), blue (pure steel blue), black (deep, glossy black), harlequin (pure white base, black torn patches irregularly distributed, never a black blanket). Less desired are small gray spots, salt and pepper colors. Nose black, but harlequins can have spotted noses. Pink nose is not desired.

HEAD: Long, narrow. **Skull:** Same length as muzzle and in parallel plane, distinct stop. **Eyes:** Medium size, dark. Not desired are lighter eyes in blues and walleyes or eyes of differing color in harlequins. **Ears:** Set high,

crease of folded ear above skull line, erect if cropped. **Teeth:** Scissors bite, full muzzle flews. **Neck:** Set high.

BODY: Shoulders: Sloping. **Forelegs:** Straight, including pasterns. **Chest:** Broad, deep. **Topline:** Slopes from withers to tail, moderate tuck-up. **Hindquarters:** Moderate angulation. **Tail:** Set high, reaches to hocks. **Feet:** Round, highly arched. **Coat:** Short, thick.

FAULTS: Deviations from standard.

DISQUALIFICATIONS: Under minimum height; white Danes without black marks (albinos); merles, a solid mouse gray color or a mouse gray base with black or white spots or both, or white base with mouse gray spots; harlequins and solid-colored Danes with a large spot that extends coatlike over entire body, so that only legs, neck, and point of tail are white; brindle, fawn, blue, or black Danes with white forehead line, white collar, high white stockings, and white belly; Danes with predominantly blue, gray, yellow, or brindled spots; any color other than those described under Color; docked tail; split nose.

GREAT PYRENEES

This dog is known in Europe as the Pyrenean Mountain Dog. It is another of the giant dogs whose ancestors came from Tibet and which descend from the Molossian Dog. Great Pyrenees were brought to Europe by 1000 B.C. The dog became a shepherd, as well as a companion dog to mountain sentries. The French nobility took up the breed in the late 1600s.

The first pair of Great Pyrenees to come to America was sent in the early 1800s as a present from General Lafayette to J. S. Skinner, America's first great dog authority. Although the dogs were recommended as the best possible guardian of sheep against the attack of wolves, the breed did not catch on at that time. The American Kennel Club recognized the Great Pyrenees in 1933. Since then, it has become reasonably popular, particularly because of its excellent disposition.

HEIGHT: Males, 27 to 32 inches; bitches, 25 to 29 inches.
WEIGHT: Males, 100 to 125 pounds; bitches, 90 to 115 pounds.
GAIT: Not specified.
COLOR: White, or white with markings of badger, gray, or shades of tan. Nose not specified, but always black.
HEAD: Ten to eleven inches from occiput to nose, crown rounded, furrow slightly developed. **Skull:** Large, wedge-shaped, no apparent stop. **Eyes:** Dark, set obliquely, dark brown, pigmented eyelids. **Ears:** V-shaped, set at eye level. **Lips:** Edged with black. **Teeth:** Not specified, but scissors bite normal. **Dewlaps:** Slight.
BODY: Square from ground to withers to tail root. **Shoulders:** Set obliquely. **Forelegs:** Not specified, but straight, elbows tight, pasterns erect, single dewclaws. **Chest:** Girth, 36 to 42 inches for males, 32 to 36 inches for bitches. **Topline:** Straight, ribs flat-sided, rump slightly sloped, loins short-

coupled. **Hindquarters:** Heavily boned, angulation not specified, but moderate, double dewclaws. **Tail:** Well plumed, reaches to below hocks. **Feet:** Compact, well arched. **Coat:** Heavy, harsh, long outer coat; dense, fine undercoat.

FAULTS: Unsound legs and feet, loose elbows, lack of heavy bone, insufficient coat, too heavy dewlap. No penalty for high tail carriage, either in movement or when standing.

KOMONDOR

The Komondor is a Hungarian shepherd dog whose ancestors came to that country during the Magyar migrations. The dog was used as a guardian against wolves and to protect homes and small farms. It is related to a dog of the Huns called the Aftscharka. The Komondor's heavily matted, or corded, coat served to protect it both from the weather and in fights with wolves.

The late motion picture actor Oscar Beregi was one of the earliest sponsors of the breed in the United States, beginning about 1937. The breed is not extremely popular partly because the art of developing the cords of its coat is not easy. The American Kennel Club still uses the Hungarian plural *Komondorok,* instead of *Komondors,* when referring to the breed.

HEIGHT: Males, 25½ inches and up; bitches, 23½ inches and up.
WEIGHT: Not specified.
GAIT: Leisurely, balanced, but long-striding.

COLOR: Pure white. Nose black. Dark gray or brown permitted, but not desired.

HEAD: Muzzle slightly shorter than skull, very broad, skull and muzzle in parallel planes, stop moderate. **Eyes:** Dark brown, eyelids gray. **Ears:** Set low, hanging, V-shaped. **Teeth:** Scissors bite, but level bite permitted. **Neck:** Arched, no dewlap.

BODY: Moderately long. **Forelegs:** Parallel, vertical columns, elbows close to body. **Chest:** Deep, powerful. **Topline:** Level, loins and back wide, rump slopes slightly to tail, moderate tuck-up. **Hindquarters:** Heavily muscled, stifles well angulated, dewclaws removed. **Tail:** Continuation of rump line, reaches to hocks, well furred. **Feet:** Large, close, well-arched toes, nails black or gray. **Coat:** Dense, soft, puppyish undercoat, coarser outer coat, formed into tassel-like cords. Cords longest at rump and loins; medium on back, shoulders, and chest; shorter on cheeks and around eyes, ears, and neck; shortest around mouth and on legs up to wrists and hocks.

FAULTS: Undersize; straight, silky coat; any missing teeth; short or curly tail; light eyes; erect ears or ears that move toward erect; dewlap; overshot or undershot.

DISQUALIFICATIONS: Blue-white eyes; color other than white; flesh-colored nose; bobtail; short, smooth hair on head and legs; failure of coat to cord by the time the dog is 2 years of age.

KUVASZ

The Kuvasz is a Hungarian breed, related to the Komondor, the Aftscharka, and other large working dogs that were brought by successive migrations from Asia into Eastern Europe. The Kuvasz also spread into Turkey, where it was known as the *kawasz*. King Matthias I of Hungary (1458–1490) was the first great fancier of the breed. He presented dogs from his own kennels to noblemen, who, in turn, bred them. Today the Kuvasz is primarily a family dog.

HEIGHT: Males, 28 to 30 inches; bitches, 26 to 28 inches.
WEIGHT: Males, 100 to 115 pounds; bitches, 70 to 90 pounds.
GAIT: When dog is at a trot, hind feet meet or drive past prints of forefeet.
COLOR: Pure white. Nose black.
HEAD: Length of head from nose to occiput less than half the height at withers, width one half the length. **Skull:** Elongated, stop well defined. **Muzzle:** In proportion to skull, inside of mouth preferably black, lips and flews black, tight to muzzle. **Teeth:** Scissors bite, but level bite acceptable. **Eyes:** The darker the better, almond-shaped; in profile, set slightly below plane of muzzle. **Ears:** V-shaped and slightly rounded, set between eye level and top of skull, to cover eyes if pulled down. **Neck:** Medium length, arched.
BODY: **Shoulders:** Sloping. **Forelegs:** Medium-boned, dewclaws not removed. **Chest:** Ribs nearly reach elbows, withers higher than back.

Topline: Level, croup slightly sloping, brisket deep, stomach well tucked up. **Hindquarters:** Moderately angulated, dewclaws removed. **Tail:** Reaches to hocks, curved at tip. **Skin:** Heavily pigmented, slate gray or black. **Coat:** Guard hairs moderately coarse, soft undercoat, medium length on body, short and smooth on head, ears, and paws.

FAULTS: Weak or hollow back, yellow saddle, lightly built loins, cow hocks, splayed or turned-out feet, yellow eyes, elbows turning in or out.

DISQUALIFICATIONS: Overshot or undershot, males smaller than 26 inches, bitches smaller than 24 inches, any other color than white.

· **MASTIFF**

The term *Mastiff* describes a large family of huge dogs that originated in Tibet and the surrounding mountains. Dogs of this type fought with the Assyrian armies and were used by the king when he went lion hunting. There are excellent bas reliefs made as early as 3000 B.C. that show dogs of Mastiff type. Caesar describes them in reporting the invasion of Britain in 55 B.C., when they and their masters fought side by side. Mastiffs were later taken to Rome to fight against dogs, other animals, and even men.

The present breed is more properly called the Old English Mastiff, which is its name in England. Most modern Mastiffs stem from the Lyme Hall kennels of Sir Peers Legh, whose bitch fought beside him on October 25, 1415, in the Battle of Agincourt, in which he was killed.

HEIGHT: Males, 30 inches minimum; bitches, 27½ inches minimum.

WEIGHT: Not specified.

GAIT: Not specified.

COLOR: Apricot, silver fawn, or dark fawn brindle. In brindles, fawn is ground color. Muzzle, ears, nose dark, the blacker the better. Similar color tone around eyes and brows.

HEAD: Short, blunted, narrowing very little at nose. **Skull:** Great width desired, marked skull wrinkles. **Muzzle:** One-half the length of skull. Brows moderately arched. **Ears:** Small, V-shaped, set wide at highest point of skull, the blacker the better. **Teeth:** Scissors bite or slightly undershot. **Neck:** Powerful, immense in girth, dry.

BODY: Shoulders: Sloping. **Forelegs:** Heavy-boned, straight, set wide apart, pasterns only slightly bent. **Chest:** Barrel-chested, but reaching to elbows, slight tuck-up. **Topline:** Straight, loins muscular. **Hindquarters:** Broad, second thighs well developed, hocks set back. **Tail:** Set moderately high, reaching to hocks or lower. **Feet:** Heavy, compact, arched toes. **Coat:** Outer moderately coarse, undercoat dense, short, close.

FAULTS: Teeth visible when mouth is closed, narrow skull, splayed feet, loose elbows, swayback or roach back, straight stifles, cow hocks.

NEWFOUNDLAND

The Newfoundland dog was developed in Newfoundland, but from unknown stock. One guess is that the Great Pyrenees was one of its ancestors. It probably was a true breed as early as 1775. The Newfoundland has an intense love of swimming and a great aptitude for it. The breed was immortalized by Lord Byron in a famous epitaph to his dog Boatswain, "Born in Newfoundland, May 1803."

HEIGHT: Males, 28 inches; bitches, 26 inches.

WEIGHT: Males, 150 pounds; bitches, 120 pounds.

GAIT: Slight roll, legs move straight forward, but toward the center of body when dog is at a fast trot.

COLOR: Black: Slight tinge of bronze or a white splash on chest and toes permitted. Blacks with only this white, plus white tail tip, are shown as blacks. Other than black: Almost any color, but following blacks with respect to markings. Bronze, or white and black, is preferred. Landseers (white and black) have black head, white blaze, evenly marked over the back, and black rump and tail.

HEAD: Massive, arched, distinct occiput, free of wrinkles. **Skull:** Broad, medium stop. **Eyes:** Dark, no haw showing. **Ears:** Set well back, rounded tips. **Teeth:** Scissors or level bite. **Neck:** Strong, long, heavy.

BODY: Square from ground to withers to tail root. **Shoulders:** Form ninety-degree angle with upper arms. **Forelegs:** Straight, pasterns slightly sloping. **Chest:** Reaches to elbows, broad. **Topline:** Back broad and level, croup slopes at thirty degrees. **Hindquarters:** Thighs long, stifles well bent, hocks wide, straight. **Tail:** Broad, heavily furred, reaches to below hocks. **Feet:** Cat feet, arched, webbing present. **Coat:** Double and water-resistant.

FAULTS: Round, protruding, yellow eyes; swayback or roach back; cow hocks; loose elbows; pigeon toes; tail kink; open coat.

DISQUALIFICATION: Markings other than white on solid-colored dog.

OLD ENGLISH SHEEPDOG

The history of the Old English Sheepdog goes back only about one hundred fifty years, and its origin is uncertain. One theory is that it was developed from the Scotch Bearded Collie; another guess is that it comes from the family to which the Russian Owtchar, Aftscharka, and Komondor belong. Although its name suggests that it was a shepherd dog, it seems actually to have been chiefly a cattle drover's dog.

The Old English Sheepdog has been called the Bobtail, not because it was born tailless, but because of the habit of docking (clipping short) its tail at the first joint. Because drovers were exempt from paying taxes on their dogs, the docking habit is said to have begun to distinguish these dogs from others. The present breed standard was adopted in 1953.

HEIGHT: Males, 22 inches and upward; bitches, slightly less.
WEIGHT: Not specified.
GAIT: Ambling or pacing, elastic when dog is at a gallop.
COLOR: Any shade of gray, bluish-gray, blue, or blue merle, with or without white markings, or the reverse. Shades of brown or fawn objectionable. Nose always black.
HEAD: Skull: Square, capacious, with arch over eyes, the whole covered with hair. **Eyes:** Vary with color of dog, very dark preferred. In blue dogs, walleyes or China blue eyes permitted. **Ears:** Medium size, carried close to skull. **Teeth:** Level bite. **Neck:** Long.
BODY: Lower at withers than at hips. **Shoulders:** Sloping. **Forelegs:** Dead straight, heavily coated. **Chest:** Deep, ribs well sprung, loin stout and arched. **Hindquarters:** Round, muscular, hocks well let down, hams more densely coated than any other part. **Feet:** Small, round, arched, close. **Tail:** None, or not more than 2 inches. **Coat:** Profuse, hard texture, not straight, but shaggy, undercoat a waterproof pile.
FAULTS: Narrow, Deerhound head; light eyes; flat-sided; loose elbows; cow hocks; soft or flat coat; lack of soundness in any part.

PULI

The Puli's origin goes back at least a thousand years. It was the smallest of the sheep dogs brought into Hungary from Asia by the Magyar invaders. In some respects it resembles the Tibetan Terrier, and originally it may not have been a sheep dog at all.

In any case the decline in the wolf population and the fencing of the range made sheep dogs less necessary, whereupon the Puli became the guardian of the home. In America dedicated owners are working to teach their Pulik sheepherding as a sport. The present breed standard was adopted in 1960.

HEIGHT: Males, 17 to 19 inches; bitches, 16 to 18 inches.
WEIGHT: Not specified.
GAIT: Not specified, but trot is quick and true.
COLOR: Solid colors—black, rusty black, shades of gray (an even mixture of colors), white. Black is usually rusty black or weathered. Nose black, as are flews and eyelids.
HEAD: Skull: Slightly domed, medium stop. **Eyes:** Deep-set, rather large, dark brown, though lighter brown not a serious fault. **Ears:** Set high, hanging, V-shaped. **Muzzle:** Medium length. **Teeth:** Level or scissors bite. **Neck::** Medium length, no throatiness.
BODY: Shoulders: Sloping, elbows close. **Forelegs:** Straight, well boned. **Chest:** Deep, fairly broad, ribs well sprung. **Topline:** Medium length, straight, level, belly well tucked up. **Hindquarters:** Muscular, well-bent stifles, dewclaws to be removed. **Tail:** Carried curled over back when dog is in motion, natural bobtail permitted, but not docked tail. **Feet:** Round, compact. **Coat:** Dense, double-coated, outer coat long, not silky, can be shown combed out or with tight, even cords.
FAULTS: Overshot or undershot; lack of undercoat; short or sparse coat; white markings on paws or chest; flesh-colored nose, flews, eyelids; down- or dish-faced; areas of two or more colors.

ROTTWEILER

The Rottweiler, one of the ancestors of the Doberman Pinscher, was named after the town of Rottweil in Germany, where Roman soldiers used the dogs to guard a supply dump nearby. Later it was known as the Butcher's Dog. When butchers left their walled towns to get cattle for slaughter, they often had to pass through forests inhabited by robbers, so they tied their money belts around the thick necks of their dogs. On the return trips the dogs would act as drovers, driving the cattle. Later these dogs pulled small produce and milk wagons. The number of Rottweilers decreased in the mid-1800s as they were no longer used for those functions. The breed was rescued from near–extinction just after 1900 when a special club was formed which drew up the first Rottweiler standard. The breed received official AKC recognition in 1931.

HEIGHT: Males, 24 to 27 inches; bitches, 22 to 25¾ inches.
WEIGHT: Not specified.
GAIT: Hind feet step into tracks of front feet and move to centerline at a fast gait.
COLOR: Black with tan-to-mahogany markings over eyes and on cheeks, muzzle, chest, and legs. White on chest or belly permitted, but not desired. Nose always black.
HEAD: **Skull:** Medium length, broad between ears, stop and occiput well defined. **Eyes:** Medium size, dark brown. **Ears:** Set high and wide, with break at skull level, comparatively small. **Muzzle:** Not as long as skull, flews not pronounced, black. **Teeth:** Scissors bite. **Neck:** Very muscular, not throaty.
BODY: **Shoulders:** Long, sloping. **Forelegs:** Elbows well let down,

but not loose, straight, well boned, pasterns erect. **Chest:** Broad, deep, well-sprung ribs. **Topline:** Straight, rather short, loins strong, no tuck-up, croup does not slope. **Hindquarters:** Muscular, stifles and hocks well bent, no dewclaws. **Tail:** Set high, docked close to body. **Feet:** Round, close, well-arched toes. **Coat:** Short, coarse, flat, undercoat required on neck and thighs, but not to show through.

FAULTS: Swayback or roach back; slab sides; long, narrow, or too plump head; light- or flesh-colored nose; lack of body substance or adequate bone.

DISMISS: Shy or vicious dogs.

DISQUALIFICATIONS: Undershot or overshot, four or more teeth missing, long coat, any base color other than black, total absence of markings.

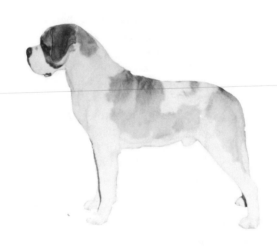

ST. BERNARD

The St. Bernard is named after St. Bernard de Menthon, founder of the hospice at the great Swiss Alpine mountain pass. The breed belongs to the family of the Molossian Dog of Tibet. About 1700, monks began to use the dogs as guides to smell out snow-covered crevasses and locate people buried due to avalanches. In 1810 some St. Bernards were brought into England. In the meantime, in Europe, the death of these dogs from distemper caused the monks to bring in other dogs, such as the Great Pyrenees and the Newfoundland, as guides. The crossing of short-haired St. Bernards with Newfoundlands resulted in longhaired St. Bernards.

An official breed standard was drawn up in Europe in 1887. The St. Bernard Club of America was organized the following year. The present breed standard was approved in 1959.

HEIGHT: Males, 27½ inches minimum; bitches, 25½ inches minimum.

WEIGHT: Not specified, but powerfully proportioned.

GAIT: Not specified, but ambling, legs move toward center line of body when dog is at a fast trot.

COLOR: White with various shades of red; brindle patches with white. Red and brown–yellow are of equal value. Required markings: White on feet, chest, tail tip, nose band, collar or spot on the nape. Nose black.

HEAD: Skull: Massive, broad, occiput not prominent, arched eyebrows. **Eyes:** Brown, lower lids not closed. **Ears:** Medium size, set high, standoff at crease. **Muzzle:** Greater depth than length. **Teeth:** Level or scissors bite or slightly undershot, black roof of mouth desired. **Neck:** Set high, very muscular.

BODY: Shoulders: Sloping, withers pronounced. **Forelegs:** Straight, extraordinarily muscled. **Chest:** Arched, not to reach below elbows. **Topline:** Straight to haunches, sloping to rump, belly slightly drawn up. **Hindquarters:** Well developed, moderately angulated at stifles and hocks. **Tail:** Broad, long, slight upward curve in lower third, never carried over back. **Feet:** Broad, high knuckles. **Coat:** Shorthaired: Dense, lying smooth, slightly bushy on rear of thighs and tail. Longhaired: Medium length, flat or wavy, never rolled, curled, or shaggy.

FAULTS: Swayback, long back, hocks too much bent, loose elbows, straight hindquarters, cow hocks, weak pasterns, any deviation from standard.

SAMOYED

The Samoyed is the largest of the white dogs belonging to the ancestral family of the Spitz, or northern forest dogs. It is named after the Samoyed people who used to live north of Iran but were forced north and east into the Arctic. The dogs seem to have been used both as reindeer-herding dogs and as sled dogs. A number of Arctic and Antarctic expeditions used them.

The Samoyed is a freighting dog, rather than a racing dog. However, in the Far North today, racing drivers may have teams of Siberian Huskies and Samoyeds. The Samoyeds will be used for Sunday dress parade. Samoyeds have lived in the huts and igloos of their owners and thus have a gentler disposition than, for instance, Greenland Eskimo dogs. The present Samoyed standard was approved in 1963.

HEIGHT: Males, 21 to 23½ inches; bitches, 19 to 21 inches.

WEIGHT: Not specified.

GAIT: Free, quick, agile trot, with feet moving to center line of body when dog is at a fast trot.

COLOR: Pure white, white with biscuit or cream, or all biscuit. All other colors disqualify. Black nose preferred, but brown, liver, or Dudley nose permitted.

HEAD: **Skull:** Wedge-shaped, not domed, stop well defined. **Eyes:** Dark, set well apart and deep, eye rims dark. **Ears:** Erect, thick, triangular, must be within border line of skull. **Muzzle:** Medium length and width, must be deep, lip edges black. **Teeth:** Scissors bite. **Neck:** Carried proudly.

BODY: **Shoulders:** Form forty-five-degree slope, 1 to 1½ inches apart at withers. **Forelegs:** Straight, parallel, and perpendicular, pasterns straight, but flexible. **Chest:** Reaches to elbows, ribs well sprung, but not barrel-chested. **Topline:** Straight to loins, medium length, loins arched, belly slight tuck-up. **Hindquarters:** Stifles bent to forty-five-degree angle with ground, hocks approximately 30 per cent of hip height. **Tail:** Reaches to hocks, profusely furred, carried over back, but not tight to back or side and not double-curled. **Feet:** Large, long, flattish. **Coat:** Double-coated. Outer coat stands straight out from body, undercoat dense, water-resistant.

FAULTS: Poor coat, hanging coat, cow hocks, straight stifles, swayback, too large ears, loose elbows, long back.

DISQUALIFICATIONS: Blue eyes, color deviations as noted.

SHETLAND SHEEPDOG

The Shetland Sheepdog is *not* a Toy Collie or a Miniature Collie. It was developed in the Shetland Islands from small herding dogs and crossed with the Border Collie and other dogs from Scotland and the Orkney Islands. Some Collie crosses were later used, but Collie fanciers made such an uproar that the English Kennel Club had to refuse to allow the breed to be called a Shetland Collie.

Shelties were first shown at Westminster in 1912, and championship classes were granted in 1914. Since then the breed has become popular throughout the world. The present standard was approved in 1959. The Canadian standard is virtually the same, but there are height differences in standards in England and other countries.

HEIGHT: 13 to 16 inches, both sexes.
WEIGHT: Not specified.
GAIT: At a trot, dog's legs move to centerline of the body.
COLOR: Black, blue merle, and sable, with varying amounts of white. Sable ranges from golden through mahogany.
HEAD: Long, refined wedge. **Skull:** Flat on top. Same length and in parallel plane with muzzle, stop slight. **Muzzle:** Well-rounded. **Eyes:** Medium size, brown, but may be merle in blue merles only. **Ears:** Small, set high, carried three-fourths erect, tips breaking forward. **Teeth:** Scissors bite. **Neck:** Arched.
BODY: **Shoulders:** Form forty-five-degree angle to ground, right angle with upper arms, one vertebra apart at withers. **Forelegs:** Straight, elbows equidistant from ground and withers, pasterns straight. **Chest:** Reaches to elbows. **Topline:** Relatively short, ribs well sprung, moderate tuck-up. **Hindquarters:** Well angulated at stifles and hocks. **Tail:** Reaches to hocks, carried gaily, but not over back, thick brush. **Feet:** Oval, compact, arched. **Coat:** Double. Dense undercoat gives long, straight outer coat its standoff quality, mane and frill abundant.
FAULTS: Lack of undercoat, two-angled head, prick ears, hound ears, receding back skull or underjaw, elbows turning in or out, feet turning in or out or splayed, harefeet or cat feet, croup higher than withers, cow hocks, tail too short or twisted at end, washed-out colors, more than 50 per cent white.
DISQUALIFICATIONS: Under 13 or over 16 inches, brindle color.

SIBERIAN HUSKY

The Siberian Husky is the peerless racing dog of the North. However, it is much more than that. Its original recognition came as a sled dog working for Siberian Eskimos. Leonhard Seppala, the famed racing driver, is credited with bringing the breed to world attention. Mr. and Mrs. Milton Seeley of Wonalancet, New Hampshire, are given major credit for gaining its recognition in 1930 by the American Kennel Club. Siberian Huskies supplied or located by the Seeleys took part in the Byrd Antarctic expeditions.

Siberian Huskies also received world attention for their work in the relay teams that carried diphtheria antitoxin to Nome during the epidemic in the winter of 1925. The breed has rapidly become popular, and sled dog racing has become part of the winter sporting scene in both the United States and Canada.

HEIGHT: Males, 21 to 23½ inches; bitches, 20 to 22 inches.
WEIGHT: Males, 45 to 60 pounds; bitches, 35 to 50 pounds.
GAIT: At fast trot, feet move to center line of body.
COLOR: All colors, from black to white. Caplike facial mask is typical. Nose black in gray, tan, or black dogs; liver in copper dogs; flesh-colored in pure-white dogs. Pink-streaked "snow nose" acceptable.
HEAD: Skull: Medium size, slightly round on top, same length as muzzle, distinct stop. **Eyes:** Almond-shaped, brown or blue, but one of each or part-colored okay. **Ears:** Medium size, triangular, rounded tips,

carried erect, well furred. **Teeth:** Scissors bite. **Neck:** Arched, medium length, extended when dog is moving.

BODY: Shoulders: Form a forty-five-degree angle to ground, upper arms angle backward from shoulders to elbows. **Forelegs:** Perpendicular to ground, parallel. **Chest:** Reaches to elbows. **Topline:** From tip of shoulders to rear point of croup longer than height, level, loin taut, narrower than rib cage, slight tuck-up. **Hindquarters:** Powerful, well angulated at stifles and hocks. **Tail:** Fox brush, carried in sickle curve, not snapped to back. **Feet:** Oval, compact, thick, tough pads, well furred between toes. **Coat:** Double. Dense undercoat supports straight, outer coat.

FAULTS: Heavy head or ears; eyes set too obliquely; weak, slack, or roach back; weak pasterns, soft or splayed feet; tail snapped flat to back; harsh, shaggy, or long coat; absence of undercoat except when shedding; short, thick neck; any bite other than scissors; short, choppy, prancing gait.

DISQUALIFICATION: Dogs over 23½ inches, bitches over 22 inches.

STANDARD SCHNAUZER

The Standard Schnauzer is the prototype of all three varieties of Schnauzer, all of which are registered as separate breeds. Many famed artists, dating back to 1490, have painted the breed, including Albrecht

Dürer, Rembrandt, Lucas Cranach the Elder, and Sir Joshua Reynolds. The breed was probably developed by crossing black Poodles, gray Spitz-type dogs, and Wire-Haired Pinschers. They were brewery guards and ratters.

The Schnauzer was first exhibited as a Wire-Haired Pinscher in Germany in 1879. A breed standard was set up the next year. By 1899 the breed was being shown at American shows. In 1918 the breed came under the control of the German Pinscher-Schnauzer Club. The Schnauzer Club of America (now the Standard Schnauzer Club of America) was formed in 1925. The first American champion was the imported Swiss bitch Resy Patricia. The present standard was approved in 1968.

HEIGHT: Males, 18 to 20 inches; bitches, 17 to 19 inches.

WEIGHT: Not specified.

GAIT: Free and true, back remains level, feet converge to center line of body when dog is at a fast trot.

COLOR: Pepper and salt (dark iron to silver gray) and pure black. Nose black.

HEAD: Rectangular, elongated. **Skull:** Same length and in parallel plane with muzzle, total length is one-half back length from withers to root of tail, slight stop accentuated by wiry brows. **Eyes:** Medium size, dark brown, turned forward. **Ears:** Set high. If cropped, carried erect. If uncropped, small, V-shaped, folded, carried high. **Teeth:** Scissors bite. **Neck:** Elegantly arched.

BODY: **Shoulders:** Form right angle with upper arms. **Forelegs:** Straight, vertical, set moderately apart, elbows close to body. **Chest:** Deep. **Topline:** Short, slight slope from withers to base of tail. **Hindquarters:** Well angulated at stifles and hocks. **Tail:** Erect, set high, docked to 1 to 2 inches. **Feet:** Small, compact, black nails. **Coat:** Double. Outer coat tight, wiry, 1½ inches on body, has eyebrows and beard; undercoat soft, dense.

FAULTS: Level bite; overshot or undershot; black coat mixed with gray or tan (except because of sun fading or age); brown, red, or yellow in black coat; toyish, racy, coarse.

DISQUALIFICATIONS: Viciousness, males under 18 or over 20 inches, bitches under 17 or over 19 inches.

WELSH CORGI, CARDIGAN

The Cardigan Welsh Corgi is believed to have been brought to Europe about the time of the Celtic invasion of Wales in 1200 B.C. It is descended from the same general family as that of the Dachshund and Basset Hound. But unlike those two breeds, Corgis have erect ears and, therefore, superior hearing.

The breed developed in Cardiganshire as a drover's dog, and it became adept at ducking the kicks of cattle as they were being herded. Today the Cardigan Welsh Corgi is a home guardian and faithful pet. The breed received official recognition from both the English Kennel Club and the American Kennel Club in 1934.

HEIGHT: Males and bitches, approximately 12 inches tall and between 36 and 44 inches from nose to tail tip.

WEIGHT: Not specified.

GAIT: Not specified, but legs should move in parallel planes.

COLOR: All shades of red, sable, all shades of brindle, black with or without tan or brindle points, blue merle (blue and gray mixed with black, marbled) with or without tan or brindle points. White flashings usually on chest, neck, feet, face, or tail tip. No preference in colors.

HEAD: **Skull:** Moderately wide and flat, stop distinct. **Eyes:** Brown, dark amber, one or both blue permitted in blue merles. **Ears:** Rounded tips, wide at base, carried erect. **Muzzle:** 3 inches long, or as 3 is to 5 with skull. **Teeth:** Scissors bite preferred, but level bite permitted. **Neck:** Muscular.

BODY: Long. **Shoulders:** Sloping. **Forelegs:** Short, strong, slightly bowed, distinct crook below the carpus, elbows close. **Chest:** Deep. **Topline:** Level, except slight slope at croup. **Hindquarters:** Muscular thighs, legs short, well boned. **Tail:** Long, fox brush, never carried over back. **Feet:**

Round, thickly padded. **Coat:** Medium length, slightly harsh, weather-resistant.

FAULTS: Flop ears; straight, terrierlike front; out at elbows; curled, rat, or whip tail; overly short or long coat; trimming to alter natural coat length.

DISQUALIFICATIONS: Over 50 per cent white, any merle other than blue, a distinctly long coat.

WELSH CORGI, PEMBROKE

Although the Pembroke Welsh Corgi may have come from the dogs brought into Europe by the Celts, its direct origin is believed to be quite different from that of the Cardigan breed. Some breed historians believe that it belongs to the Spitz family, to which the Keeshond and Pomeranian also belong, probably because Pembroke Welsh Corgis have a pointed muzzle and erect ear carriage.

Flemish weavers are believed to have brought the Pembrokes with them when they crossed the English Channel and settled in Pembrokeshire, Wales, in the early 1100s. It is indisputable that there have been crossings of the two Corgi breeds. The British royal family's interest in the Pembroke has helped its worldwide popularity. The American Kennel Club recognized the breed in 1934.

HEIGHT: Both sexes, 10 to 12 inches. Distance from high point of withers to base of tail should be 40 per cent greater than dog's height.

WEIGHT: Males, not exceeding 30 pounds; bitches, 28 pounds.

GAIT: Legs move in parallel planes, back remains level.

COLOR: Red, sable, fawn, black and tan, or with white markings on legs, chest, and neck. Some white permitted on head and foreface. Nose black.

HEAD: Foxy in shape. **Skull:** Wide and flat between ears, moderate stop. **Muzzle:** Length is in a ratio of 3 to 5 with the length of skull. **Eyes:** Well set, medium size, hazel or blend with coat color. **Ears:** Pricked, slightly pointed. When dog is alert, a straight line could be drawn from the nose through the eye and the tip of the ear. **Teeth:** Level or scissors bite. **Neck:** Fairly long.

BODY: Medium length, not short-coupled. **Shoulders:** Not specified, but normally sloping. **Forelegs:** As straight as a deep, broad chest will permit, but not terrierlike, elbows close. **Chest:** Deep, broad, ribs well sprung. **Topline:** Level. **Hindquarters:** Legs short, ample bone carried to feet, hocks perpendicular. **Tail:** Docked or naturally short. **Feet:** Oval, two center toes longer than outer toes. **Coat:** Medium length and dense, not wiry.

FAULTS: Fluffies (coat of extreme length, exaggerated feathering on ears, chest, legs, feet, underparts, and hindquarters); whitelies (body color white with red or dark markings); mismarks (colors with any area of white on back, between withers and tail, on sides between elbows, back of hindquarters, or on ears; black with white markings, no tan present); bluies (colored portions of the coat with bluish or smoky cast; this color associated with extremely light or blue eyes and liver or gray eye rims, nose, and lips); overshot or undershot bite, oversize or undersize.

DISMISS: Any vicious or excessively shy dog.

chapter thirty-eight
Terrier Breeds

The word *terrier* comes from the Latin word for earth, *terra*. Terriers are literally those dogs that "go to earth." They were bred to enter the lair of the fox, to follow the badger into its den, to dig out rats or to kill them when they had been dug out by their masters. Virtually all the Terriers have been developed in the British Isles (England, Scotland, Ireland, the Isle of Skye). Many were developed for use with Foxhounds. The Australian and the Silky Terriers are from Australia, but they were developed from a mixture of Terriers from the British Isles. The Miniature Schnauzer and Tibetan Terrier are exceptions; so is the Lhasa Apso (in those countries that consider it a Terrier).

AIREDALE TERRIER

Before the days of dog shows and stud books, English sportsmen had a variety of Terriers of various sizes. These stemmed from a now extinct dog called the Old English, or Broken-Haired, Terrier. They were black and tan and were used to track small game, including foxes, badgers, and otters. Eventually these Terriers were crossed with Otter Hounds. The progeny were called Bingley, or Waterside, Terriers.

These dogs appeared at dog shows as early as 1864. In 1879 they appeared at the Airedale Agricultural Society's show as Airedale Terriers. Thereafter other local shows gave classes for Airedales. Champion Master Briar, whelped in 1897, is considered the founding sire of the breed.

HEIGHT: Males, 23 inches; bitches, slightly less.

WEIGHT: Not specified.

GAIT: Legs move perpendicular to body and parallel.

COLOR: Head, ears, legs to thighs and elbows, underparts of the body and chest, and sometimes the shoulders are tan. Sides and back are black or dark grizzle. Red mixture sometimes found in black. Bit of white on chest permitted. Nose black.

HEAD: Skull and muzzle about same length. **Skull:** Long, flat, free of wrinkles, stop barely visible. **Eyes:** Dark, small, not prominent. **Ears:** V-shaped, fold above skull level, carriage to sides of head. **Teeth:** Level or scissors bite. **Neck:** Medium length.

BODY: Shoulders: Sloping, flat. **Forelegs:** Straight, elbows perpendicular to body. **Chest:** Deep. **Topline:** Short and level, loins muscular, little space between last rib and hip joint. **Hindquarters:** Muscular second thighs, stifles well bent. **Tail:** Set high, gay, but not curled over back. **Feet:** Small, compact. **Coat:** Hard, dense, wiry, lying straight and close, soft undercoat.

FAULTS: Toes turning in or out, cow hocks, yellow eyes, hound ears, white feet, soft coat, undershot or overshot, much oversize or undersize, poor gait.

AMERICAN STAFFORDSHIRE TERRIER

This breed is a cross between the Bulldog and one or more Terrier breeds. (No one knows for sure which Terriers were used.) In any case the English wanted to achieve a combination of the Bulldog's courage and tenacity and a Terrier's agility. The resulting breed was called the Bull-and-Terrier Dog, or the Pit Bull Terrier, and eventually the Staffordshire Bull Terrier. The dogs developed in America, known as American Bull Terriers, were larger, straight-legged dogs. The dogs were used mainly for pit fighting, a sport in which one dog was matched against another.

The American Kennel Club recognized the breed as the Staffordshire Terrier in 1935. To distinguish the larger breed from the English dog (the Staffordshire Bull Terrier), the AKC changed the former's name to American Staffordshire Terrier in 1972.

HEIGHT: Males, 18 to 19 inches; bitches, 17 to 18 inches.
WEIGHT: Not specified, but in proportion to height.
GAIT: True, agile, graceful.
COLOR: Any color, but not encouraged are all white, more than 80 per cent white, black and tan, and liver. Nose black.
HEAD: Medium length, very deep. **Skull:** Broad, pronounced cheek muscles, distinct stop. **Eyes:** Dark, set low in skull, far apart. **Ears:** Set high, cropped or uncropped, but uncropped preferred. If uncropped, short, held half rose or prick. **Teeth:** Scissors bite. Tremendous biting power a distinctive breed feature. **Neck:** Heavy, no loose skin.

BODY: Shoulders: Muscular, blades wide, sloping. **Forelegs:** Straight, set wide apart, pasterns erect. **Chest:** Deep, broad, ribs close and carried far back. **Hindquarters:** Well muscled, let down at hocks, turning neither in nor out. **Tail:** Short, set low, not curled or carried over back. **Feet:** Moderate size, well arched. **Coat:** Short, stiff, and glossy.

FAULTS: Pink eyelids, Dudley nose, light or pink eyes, tail too long or badly carried, undershot or overshot, weak elbows.

AUSTRALIAN TERRIER

In 1885 a dog called the Australian Rough Terrier was shown at the famed Melbourne Royal Dog Show. This short-legged, rough- or ragged-coated dog was later called the Australian Terrier. Some guesses about its ancestry are that it gets its long back from the Skye Terrier, its silky topknot from the Dandie Dinmont, its rough coat from the Cairn Terrier, and its blue and tan color from the Yorkshire Terrier.

The Australian Terrier was granted breed status in England (which seldom gives Terrier status to any dog not from Great Britain) in 1933. The American Kennel Club gave it full recognition in 1960, and the dog has since rapidly gained popularity.

HEIGHT: About 10 inches.
WEIGHT: 12 to 14 pounds.
GAIT: Straight and true, sprightly.
COLOR: Blue–black or silver–black, with rich tan markings on head and legs. Also sandy color or clear red. Nose black.
HEAD: Long. **Skull:** Flat, full between the eyes, moderate stop.
Eyes: Small, dark. **Ears:** Set high, small, pricked. **Muzzle:** Length equal

to length from eyes to occiput. **Teeth:** Scissors bite, but level bite acceptable. **Neck:** Long.

BODY: Low-set, longer than tall. **Shoulders:** Not specified, but normally sloping. **Forelegs:** Straight, slightly feathered to knees, pasterns strong. **Chest:** Medium wide, deep. **Topline:** Level. **Hindquarters:** Moderately angulated at stifles and hocks, medium bone. **Tail:** Set high, docked to two fifths, carried erect. **Feet:** Small, catlike. **Coat:** Outer coat harsh and straight, about 2½ inches all over body, undercoat short and soft, topknot on skull has finer texture, lighter color.

FAULTS: Light-colored or protruding eyes; any suggestion of sooty color in sandies is undesirable; poor gait.

BEDLINGTON TERRIER

In 1825 Joseph Ainsley of Bedlington in Northumberland mated his bitch, Coates Phoebe, to a male that he owned, Anderson's Piper. From this mating came the Bedlington Terrier. However, at first the breed was known as the Rothbury Terrier. Bedlington sportsmen took up the breed and used it for badger killing and ratting. In 1877 the National Bedlington Terrier Club was formed.

When its coat is in show trim, the Bedlington looks something like a lamb; and because of its ability in a fight, it has been called the "wolf in sheep's clothing." However, the dog is not particularly aggressive and has long been fancied by those willing to prepare its coat properly. The present American standard was approved in 1967.

HEIGHT: Males, 16½ inches; bitches, 15½ inches.

WEIGHT: 17 to 23 pounds, in proportion to height.

GAIT: Unique in being light and springy, must not cross over, weave, or paddle.

COLOR: Blue, sandy, liver, blue and tan, sandy and tan, liver and tan. In bicolors, tan is on legs and chest, under the tail, inside the hindquarters, over the eyes. Topknot lighter than body color. Nose black in blues and tans, brown in others.

HEAD: Narrow, deep, rounded. **Skull:** Shorter than muzzle, no stop. **Eyes:** Almond, well sunk. **Ears:** Triangular, rounded tips, set low, 3 inches at greatest width, tips reach mouth corners, tassels at tips. **Teeth:** Level or scissors bite. **Neck:** Long, no throatiness, erect.

BODY: Longer than height. **Shoulders:** Flat, sloping. **Forelegs:** Straight, wider at chest than at feet. **Chest:** Reaches to elbows, flat-ribbed. **Topline:** Natural arch over loins, definite tuck-up. **Hindquarters:** Well angulated. **Tail:** Set low, scimitar, tapering, reaches to hocks. **Feet:** Long, harefeet, compact, dewclaws removed. **Coat:** Mixture of hard and soft hair, standing out from skin, not longer than 1 inch in show trim except slightly longer on legs.

FAULTS: Under 16 inches or over 17½ for males, under 15 or over 16½ inches for bitches, straight stifles, cow hocks, loose elbows, lack of black lips in blue and tans, lack of brown lips in other colors.

BORDER TERRIER

The Border Terrier was developed by farmers and sportsmen living in the Cheviot Hills, which lie on both sides of the English-Scottish border. It is a small, rough-coated Terrier that is used against foxes, badgers, and rats and is leggy enough to follow horsemen riding to hounds. The dog was often exhibited at agricultural shows in the area but was seldom seen outside the Border (as the area is called).

Then in 1920 the English Kennel Club recognized the breed and gave championship classes for it. The American Kennel Club recognized the Border Terrier in 1950. Sporting people used the dogs, along with their horses, on hunts. The breed's progress has been slow, but it is now recognized as an excellent house dog.

HEIGHT: Not specified, but a 14-pound dog is 1 to 1½ inches taller than length from the withers to the tail root.

WEIGHT: Males, 13 to 15½ pounds; bitches, 11½ to 14 pounds.

GAIT: Straight and rhythmic.

COLOR: Red, grizzle and tan, blue and tan, or wheaten. White chest spot permitted. Nose black.

HEAD: Skull: Broad, flat between ears and eyes, stop is a curve, rather than an indentation. **Eyes:** Dark hazel, neither prominent nor small and beady. **Ears:** Small, V-shaped, set on side of head, crease not above skull level. **Muzzle:** Short, dark. **Teeth:** Scissors bite, large for dog's size. **Neck:** Muscular.

BODY: Behind shoulders, body could be spanned by a man's hand. Body length 1 to 1½ inches less than height at withers in a 14-pound dog. **Shoulders:** Long, sloping. **Forelegs:** Straight, moderate bone, set slightly wider than in Fox Terrier. **Chest:** Deep, narrow, ribs carried well back. Loins strong, no tuck-up. **Hindquarters:** Long thighs, stifles well bent, hocks well let down. **Tail:** Rather short, not set too high, carried gaily. **Feet:** Small, compact. **Coat:** Dense undercoat, covered with wiry, somewhat broken but close-lying outer coat, hide very thick and loose.

FAULTS: White on feet, any deviation from standard.

BULL TERRIER, WHITE

The Bull Terrier is the result of a cross between the Bulldog and the now extinct white English Terrier, and was bred originally for the purpose of dogfighting. In order to increase the dog's size, an additional cross was made with a Pointer or Spanish Pointer. In about 1860 James Hinks produced an all-white dog, which became very popular. However, lack of color and deafness are sex-linked, and therefore many of the pure-white dogs were deaf.

Great efforts have since been made to breed pure-white dogs with sound hearing. Because dogfights are no longer permitted, the temperament of the "white gladiator" has been softened. Today's Bull Terriers are friendly with people and not overly aggressive with other dogs.

HEIGHT: Not specified.
WEIGHT: Not specified, but 35 to 55 pounds is normal.
GAIT: Smooth, powerful, legs moving in parallel planes.
COLOR: White. Head markings permitted; markings on other parts of body not permitted. Skin pigmentation is not penalized. Nose black.
HEAD: In profile, a gentle curve from top of skull to nose. Face should be full, without indentations. **Skull:** Broad, flat across forehead. **Eyes:** Sunken, obliquely placed in triangular sockets, as dark as possible. **Ears:** Small, thin, placed close together, can be held erect. **Muzzle:**

Longer than skull, lips tight. **Teeth:** Level or scissors bite. **Neck:** Very muscular, arched, long.

BODY: **Shoulders:** Muscular, but not heavy. **Forelegs:** Big-boned, straight, dog stands squarely on them. **Chest:** Broad, deep, ribs well sprung, back ribs deep. **Topline:** Short, arched over loins, gentle tuck-up. **Hindquarters:** Stifles well bent, hocks short. **Tail:** Short, set low, thick at root. **Feet:** Cat feet. **Coat:** Short, flat, harsh.

FAULTS: Crooked forelegs, out at elbows, weak feet, any deviation from standard.

DISQUALIFICATION: Blue eyes.

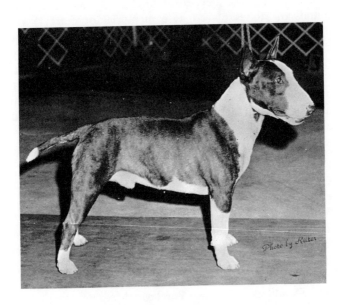

BULL TERRIER, COLORED

The standard for the Colored Bull Terrier is the same as that for the White except for color.

COLOR: Any color other than white, or any color, with white markings. Preferred color, brindle.

DISQUALIFICATIONS: Dog that is predominantly white, blue eyes.

CAIRN TERRIER

The Cairn Terrier was developed on the Isle of Skye to run over cairns (mounds of stones placed as a memorial or marker) and rocky ground in its work as a superb ratter. It was also used to search out foxes and weasels. The Cairn Terrier was recognized as a breed as early as 1845 and began to appear in dog shows just before World War I.

The dog's ragged coat needs little care. For show grooming, a certain amount of tidying up is permitted, but too much trimming is objectionable because it takes away from the Cairn's rough and sturdy appearance.

HEIGHT: Males, 10 inches; bitches, 9½ inches.

WEIGHT: Males, 14 pounds; bitches, 13 pounds.

GAIT: Free and agile.

COLOR: Any color except white. Dark ears, muzzle, tail tip desirable. Nose black.

HEAD: Skull: Broad, decided stop. **Eyes:** Set wide apart, sunken, hazel or dark hazel, shaggy eyebrows. **Ears:** Small, pointed, carried erect, free of long hair. **Muzzle:** Short. **Teeth:** Large, neither undershot nor overshot.

BODY: Shoulders: Sloping. **Forelegs:** Medium length and bone, elbows tight. **Chest:** Deep, well-sprung ribs. **Topline:** Level, medium length. **Hindquarters:** Strong, moderately angulated. **Tail:** Set at back level, short, well furred, but not feathery, carried gaily, but not curled over back. **Feet:** Compact, forefeet larger than hind feet, may turn slightly out. **Coat:** Hard outer coat, dense undercoat, skull furnished with hair softer than body coat, legs covered with hard hair.

FAULTS: Narrow skull; long muzzle; large, prominent, or yellow eyes; large ears with rounded points, set too high or too close; crooked forelegs; out at elbows; weak feet; body too short, too long, or weedy; low tail set; back not level; flesh-colored nose; white on chest, feet, or other parts.

DANDIE DINMONT TERRIER

The Dandie Dinmont was developed as early as 1700 in the Cheviot Hills, which lie on both sides of the Scottish-English border. Sir Walter Scott wrote of the breed in his novel *Guy Mannering,* which was published in 1814. A farmer named Dandie Dinmont and his dogs, which "fear naething that ever cam' wi' a hairy skin on't," were characters in the book. The dogs' names were Auld Pepper, Auld Mustard, Little Pepper, Little Mustard, Young Pepper, and Young Mustard. (Pepper and mustard are the colors of today's Dandie Dinmont breed standard.)

Because of its soft curves and long body, the Dandie Dinmont did not win the favor of early British dog show judges. Indeed, at the Birmingham show in 1867 the judge threw them all out, on the ground that they were only a pack of mongrels. Eventually the satirical name Dandie's Dinmonts became Dandie Dinmonts.

HEIGHT: 8 to 11 inches. Length not more than twice height, and 1 to 2 inches less is preferred.

WEIGHT: 18 to 24 pounds.

GAIT: Not specified, but true.

COLOR: Pepper (dark bluish black to light silver gray, intermediate shades preferred) and mustard (reddish brown to pale fawn, creamy white on head). Nose and inside of mouth black or dark.

HEAD: Skull: Broad, forehead domed, extraordinarily developed maxillary muscles. **Ears:** Set well back, hanging close to cheeks, 3 to 4 inches long, thin feather of hair starting 2 inches from tip. **Muzzle:** Should be 3 inches long, or as 3 is to 5 in proportion to skull. **Teeth:** Scissors bite, extraordinarily large canines. **Neck:** Very muscular.

BODY: Shoulders: Not specified, but should be somewhat erect so as to give downward curve to the back behind them. **Forelegs:** Immense muscular development, set wide apart. **Chest:** Set well down between legs, ribs well sprung and round. **Topline:** Downward curve behind shoulders and corresponding arch over loins, then slopes to root of tail. **Hindquarters:** Longer than forelegs, set wide apart. **Feet:** Slightly curved outward, not flat. **Tail:** 8 to 10 inches long, carried scimitar style, covered with wiry hair on top and lighter-colored, feathered hair 2 inches long on underside. **Coat:** 2 inches long from skull to root of tail, hard and soft hair mixed, lighter and softer on underparts.

FAULTS: Any deviation from standard, bandy legs, flat feet.

FOX TERRIER, SMOOTH

Although the Smooth and Wire Fox Terriers were crossbred for many years, they probably do not descend from common ancestry. The Smooth Fox Terrier is believed to come from smooth-coated Black-and-Tan Terrier, the Bull Terrier, and possibly the Greyhound and the Beagle. The breed dates back to at least 1790, when both a description and a painting of the dog were made.

The Smooth Fox Terrier is an older variety than the Wire; it appeared in dog shows for more than fifteen years beforehand. The Wire Fox Terrier is believed to be descended from rough-coated Black-and-Tan Terriers from Wales. The English standard was drawn up in 1876, and the only change since then has been to reduce the weight of males by 2 pounds. The American standard was approved in 1885.

HEIGHT: Males, 15½ inches; bitches, slightly less.

WEIGHT: Males, 18 pounds; bitches, slightly less.

GAIT: Legs move forward in a straight line and in parallel planes.

COLOR: White predominates. Markings of any color permitted except brindle, red, or liver, which are objectionable. Nose black.

HEAD: Skull and foreface about same length. **Skull:** Flat, moderately narrow, decreasing in width to the eyes; little stop. **Eyes:** Dark, round, small, deeply set. **Ears:** V-shaped, crease well above skull level, droop forward close to cheeks. **Muzzle:** Not dish- or down-faced. **Teeth:** Scissors bite. **Neck:** Clean, no throatiness.

BODY: **Shoulders:** Sloping, clear-cut at withers. **Forelegs:** Parallel at elbows and feet, pasterns erect. **Chest:** Deep, not broad. **Topline:** Level, not longer than 12 inches. **Hindquarters:** Long second thighs, stifles and hocks well bent, turning neither in nor out. **Tail:** Set high, gay, but not carried over back or curled. **Feet:** Round, compact, toes moderately arched. **Coat:** Smooth, flat, dense, abundant, belly not bare.

FAULTS: Yellow eyes, cow hocks, taller than 15½ inches, back longer than 12 inches, any other deviations from standard.

DISQUALIFICATIONS: White, cherry, or spotted nose; prick, tulip, or rose ears; much undershot or overshot.

FOX TERRIER, WIRE

Although it was once extensive, the practice of mixing Wire Fox Terriers and Smooth Fox Terriers has ceased. When the two were crossbred, it was to give the Wire a cleaner head and more white.

The Wire Fox Terrier resembles the Smooth in every respect except coat.

BODY: **Coat:** Broken; the harder and more wiry the texture, the better; dog must never look or feel woolly; no silky hair on skull or elsewhere. Coat should not be long enough to give dog a shaggy appearance, but it should show a marked and distinct difference from Smooth Fox Terrier all over.

IRISH TERRIER

Idstone's *Book of Dogs,* published in 1872, does not mention the Irish Terrier. However, three years later there was an Irish Terrier show in Dublin, in which nearly fifty dogs were entered. One dog was pure white, others looked like Cairns, and there was a class for Terriers weighing under 9 pounds. The first-prize winner, named Boxer, had an unknown pedigree.

A breed club for the Irish Terrier was organized in 1870, and a standard was drawn up that is similar to today's standard. In World War I, Irish Terriers served the British Army as messengers and Red Cross dogs. They were also taught to patrol railroad tracks to sound the alarm if rails were broken or if there was sabotage. The present American standard was approved in 1968.

HEIGHT: About 18 inches, either sex.
WEIGHT: 27 pounds for males; 25 pounds for bitches.
GAIT: Animated, lithe, and true.
COLOR: Whole-colored bright red, golden red, red wheaten, or wheaten. White permitted on chest, but not desired and a serious fault anywhere else on body. Nose and lips black.
HEAD: Skull and muzzle same length. **Skull:** Flat, no wrinkle, stop barely noticeable except in profile. **Eyes:** Dark, small. **Ears:** Small, V-shaped, crease above skull line, dropping closely to outside corner of eye. **Teeth:** Scissors bite. **Neck:** Fair length, arched, no throatiness.
BODY: Shoulders: Long, sloping into back. **Forelegs:** Moderately long, perfectly straight, pasterns short and erect. **Chest:** Deep, not full or side. **Topline:** Moderately long, no dip behind shoulders, ribs fairly sprung. **Hindquarters:** Stifles moderately bent, hocks near ground. **Tail:** Docked, one quarter taken off, not carried over back. **Feet:** Moderately small,

round, arched toes, pads free of corns. **Coat:** Dense, wiry, broken, undercoat soft and lighter-colored.

FAULTS: Any deviations from standard, lack of daredevil temperament, cow hocks, loose elbows.

KERRY BLUE TERRIER

The Kerry Blue Terrier is named after County Kerry in Ireland, but there is no proof that that is where the breed was developed. It was at the 1922 Cruft's Show in London that Mrs. Casey Hewitt of County Kerry exhibited the first of this breed ever shown in England. The first champion was Irish-bred Martell's Sapphire Beauty, which won at the National Terrier Show in 1923.

The first clubs to support the breed made no claim for County Kerry. The Irish club is the Irish Blue Terrier Club, and the English club is the Blue Terrier Club of England. Kerries were first shown in America at Westminster in 1922. The Kerry Blue Terrier Club of America was organized in 1926.

HEIGHT: Males, 18 to 19½ inches; bitches, 17½ to 19 inches.
WEIGHT: Males, 33 to 40 pounds, bitches, proportionately less.
GAIT: Not specified.
COLOR: Shades of blue gray or gray blue, from deep slate to light blue gray. Kerries are black at birth, pass through different shades until they reach mature color by 18 months. Black permitted on muzzle, head, ears, tail, and feet at any age; otherwise mature color must be uniform. Nose black.

HEAD: Skull and muzzle about same length. **Skull:** Flat, stop slight. **Eyes:** Small, dark, not prominent. **Ears:** V-shaped, folded, crease above skull level, drooping forward close to cheeks. **Teeth:** Level or scissors bite. **Neck:** Clean, moderately long.

BODY: Shoulders: Sloping, well knit. **Forelegs:** Straight when viewed from front or side, moderately long. **Topline:** Short and level, loins short, tuck-up slight. **Hindquarters:** Free of droop or crouch, stifles well bent, hocks close to ground. **Tail:** Set high, gay, straight. **Feet:** Round, moderately small, pads free of cracks. **Coat:** Soft, dense, wavy, body well covered, but head, cheeks, and ears clear, whiskers pronounced.

FAULTS: Short legs, loose elbows, feet turning in or out, lack of uniform color in mature dogs, heights above or below standard, yellow eyes.

DISQUALIFICATIONS: Solid black, dewclaws on hind legs.

LAKELAND TERRIER

The Lakeland Terrier's name reflects the fact that dogs of their type were shown at the Lake District agricultural fairs in the county of Cumberland, England. The preferred dogs were grizzle red, blue and tan, and wheaten in color. Since 1900 the breed has been refined to the popular dog we know today. The Lakeland's ancestry is uncertain, but there were probably crosses with Bedlington and Dandie Dinmont Terriers.

The name for the breed became official when a breed club was formed in 1921. Two years later, the dogs began to appear at championship shows in England. A Lakeland, Ch. Stingray of Derryabah, is the only dog in history to win Best in Show at both Cruft's (1964) and Westminster (1965).

HEIGHT: Males, 14½ inches, with ½-inch deviation permissible; bitches, as much as 1 inch less than males.

WEIGHT: Dogs at 14 ½ inches weigh 17 pounds; others, proportionate to height.

GAIT: True and free. Paddling, moving close, toeing in are faulty.

COLOR: Blue, black, liver, black and tan, blue and tan, red, red grizzle, grizzle and tan, or wheaten. Desired tan is light wheaten or straw color. Rich red or mahogany to be penalized. Nose black except liver in liver-colored dogs.

HEAD: Rectangle, skull and muzzle same length. **Skull:** Flat, little stop. **Eyes:** Small, oval, set wide apart, dark brown or black. **Ears:** V-shaped, folded, crease above skull line, falling close to cheeks. **Teeth:** Level or scissors bite. **Neck:** Arched.

BODY: Square from ground to withers to root of tail. **Shoulders:** Withers higher than back level. **Forelegs:** Straight, pasterns erect, elbows tight. **Chest:** Narrow, reaches to elbows. **Topline:** Level. **Hindquarters:** Well angulated stifles and hocks. **Tail:** Docked, not carried over back. **Feet:** Small, rounded. **Coat:** Outer coat hard and wiry, undercoat soft, plentiful furnishings on muzzle and legs.

FAULTS: Shyness, deviations from standard, except that size is less important than symmetry and proportion.

DISQUALIFICATION: Overshot or undershot.

STANDARD MANCHESTER TERRIER

The Standard Manchester Terrier was developed in Manchester, England, to kill rats and chase hares. John Hulme of Crumpsall is credited with developing the breed. A Black-and-Tan Terrier had been mentioned as far back as Dr. Caius's famous survey of British dogs in 1570. It is believed that Hulme crossed this dog and a Whippet, and undoubtedly other breeders did the same.

A famous dog named Billy was once matched against a hundred rats in a wooden pit. He killed them all in eight minutes and thirty seconds. On another occasion he killed one hundred rats in six minutes and thirteen seconds. When rat-killing contests and ear cropping were abolished in England, the breed languished. Many people ceased breeding the dogs after trying for a while to produce a dog with small button ears. Nonetheless, there are still dedicated fanciers of the dogs on both sides of the Atlantic. In the United States the Standard Manchester Terrier may be shown with cropped ears. (See also Toy Manchester Terrier.)

HEIGHT: Not specified.

WEIGHT: 12 to 22 pounds. American-bred and Open Classes may be divided into over 12 to 16 pounds and over 16 to 22 pounds.

GAIT: Not specified.

COLOR: Jet black and rich mahogany tan, with well-defined color divisions. Tan over each eye, on cheeks, and upper and lower jaws, extending under the throat; tan spots on each side of chest above legs. Black thumb mark on front of each leg between pastern and knee, black penciling running lengthwise on the top of each toe on all four feet. Remainder of forelegs tan to knees. Tan on hind legs almost to stifle joint on inside, black on outside. Tan on inside of tail and on vent. White on any part of body is a serious fault. Nose black.

HEAD: Long, narrow, tight-skinned. **Skull:** Flat, with median line furrow. **Eyes:** Small, black, set close together. **Ears:** Erect or button. If cropped, cut to a point and carried erect. **Teeth:** Level or scissors.

BODY: Moderately short, ribs well sprung behind shoulders. **Shoulders:** Sloping. **Forelegs:** Straight, parallel. **Chest:** Narrow, deep. **Topline:** Slightly arched over loins, falling to croup. **Hindquarters:** Hocks well let down, turning neither in nor out. **Feet:** Sound, well arched. **Tail:** Moderately short, set where arch of loin ends. **Coat:** Smooth, short, dense, glossy, not soft.

FAULTS: Unsound legs or feet, improper markings.

DISQUALIFICATIONS: White measuring as much as ½ inch on any part of body, over 22 pounds.

MINIATURE SCHNAUZER

The Miniature Schnauzer was developed in Germany by crossing the Standard Schnauzer and the Affenpinscher. It was exhibited as a distinct breed at German shows as early as 1899. The dog was considered a yard or stable dog. Neither Germany nor England will permit the breed to be called a Terrier.

The first Miniature Schnauzers are thought to have come to the United States just after World War I. The American Miniature Schnauzer Club was formed in 1933, and the American Kennel Club regards the dog as a Terrier. Matings between Miniatures and Standards are prohibited; that is, the offspring cannot be registered. The breed is now the most popular of all those in the Terrier Group.

HEIGHT: 12 to 14 inches, both sexes; ideal, 13½ inches.
WEIGHT: Not specified.
GAIT: Trots in a straight line, forelegs and hind legs move in parallel planes.
COLOR: Salt and pepper (shades of gray with tan shadings permitted), black and silver, and pure black. Gray fades to silver white on eyebrows, whiskers, cheeks, under throat, across chest, under tail, under body, and inside legs. Nose black.
HEAD: Rectangle, skull and muzzle same length. **Skull:** Flat, no wrinkles. **Eyes:** Small, dark brown, deep-set. **Ears:** Set high, cropped to points, carried erect. If uncropped, small, V-shaped, folding close to skull. **Muzzle:** Blunt-ended. **Teeth:** Scissors bite. **Neck:** Arched.
BODY: **Shoulders:** Sloping. **Forelegs:** Straight, parallel, elbows close, pasterns erect. **Chest:** Reaches to elbows, slight tuck-up. **Topline:**

Sloping from withers to tail. **Hindquarters:** Sufficient angulation to place hocks beyond tail. **Tail:** Docked short, only barely visible. **Feet:** Cat feet. **Coat:** Outer coat hard, wiry, not less than ¾ inch on body, never slick, furnishings thick, not silky, close undercoat, light underbody hair reaching above elbows, single tracking.

    FAULTS: Any deviation from standard, coarse skull, cow hocks, paddling gait, stilted gait, over-aggressive or timid, viciousness, undershot or overshot, level bite, light or prominent eye.

    DISQUALIFICATIONS: Dogs or bitches under 12 inches or over 14 inches, solid white, white body patches.

NORFOLK TERRIER

    This small, rugged, short-legged Terrier is considered an absolute demon for its size. Its temperament is steady and fearless. This dog, which is drop-eared, has now become a separately recognized breed; formerly it competed with Norwich Terriers in U. S. dog show competition.

    HEIGHT: Ideal, 10 inches.
    WEIGHT: 10 to 12 pounds.
    GAIT: Normal.
    COLOR: All shades of red, red wheaten, black and tan, or grizzle. White marks or patches permitted, but not desired.
    HEAD: Skull: Wide between ears, slightly rounded, well-defined stop. **Eyes:** Dark, bright, and keen. **Ears:** Neatly dropped, fold just above skull line, carried close to skull, not falling lower than outer corners of eyes,

slightly rounded tips. **Muzzle:** About one third less than distance from occiput to base of stop. **Teeth:** Scissors bite under tight lips. **Neck:** Medium length, strong.

BODY: **Shoulders:** Clean, well laid back. **Forelegs:** Short, powerful, as straight as possible. **Chest:** Ribs well sprung, deep. **Topline:** Not specified, but as nearly level as possible. **Hindquarters:** Heavily muscled, well turned at stifles, hocks well let down and straight when viewed from the rear, great propulsive power. **Tail:** Medium length, docked, carriage not excessively gay. **Feet:** Round, thick pads. **Coat:** Hard, wiry, straight, lying close to body, almost forming a mane of longer hair on neck and shoulders, short and smooth on head, ears, and muzzle except for eyebrows and whiskers, both of which are slight. **Scars:** Honorable scars not to count against.

FAULTS: Overshot or undershot; long, narrow head; trimming not desired.

NORWICH TERRIER

In England in the 1870s a man known as Doggy Lawrence made a living selling small red Terriers to Cambridge students. A master of Staghounds acquired some of these dogs, which are thought to have been small Irish Setters. This man had an employee named Jones, and at times the breed has been known as the Jones Terrier. Some American hunt clubs maintained small kennels of Jones Terriers.

In 1932 the English Kennel Club recognized the breed, giving it the official name of Norwich Terrier. In 1936 the American Kennel Club also recognized the breed.

HEIGHT: 10 inches, either sex.
WEIGHT: Ideal, 11 to 12 pounds.
GAIT: Not specified, but normal.
COLOR: All shades of red, wheaten, black and tan, or grizzle. White on chest permitted, but not desired.
HEAD: Skull: Wide, slightly rounded, stop well defined. **Eyes:** Very dark. **Ears:** Small, pointed, erect, set well apart. **Muzzle:** One-third skull length, foxy in appearance. **Teeth:** Scissors bite. **Neck:** Short, arched.
BODY: Moderately short. **Shoulders:** Clean. **Forelegs:** Short, as straight as is consistent with short legs. **Chest:** Deep. **Topline:** Level, ribs well sprung. **Hindquarters:** Heavily muscled, great propulsive power. **Tail:** Docked to medium length. **Feet:** Round. **Coat:** Outer coat straight, hard, and wiry, longer and rougher on shoulders and neck to form a mane, slight eyebrows and whiskers, definite undercoat. Excessive trimming to be severely penalized.
FAULTS: Long, narrow muzzle; square muzzle; light or protruding eyes; undershot or overshot; large, poorly carried ears; long, weak back; loaded shoulders; out at elbows; badly bowed or knuckled-over forelegs; cow hocks; white markings other than on chest; silky or curly coat; excessive trimming.
DISQUALIFICATION: Cropped ears.

SCOTTISH TERRIER

Dogs called Scottish Terriers were shown as early as 1860; however, these were in fact Skyes, Dandie Dinmonts, and even the forerunners of the

Yorkshire. Incensed Scottish breeders began a vitriolic campaign in newspapers and magazines, and in 1880 a fancier named J. B. Morrison drew up the first standard for the dog we now know as the Scottie. A joint Scottish-English club was formed in 1882. Still later, separate Scottish and English clubs were organized.

In 1883 John Naylor began importation of Scotties to America. He was followed by O. P. Chandler of Kokomo, Indiana, whose dog Dake was the first of the breed to be registered in this country. A famous dog named Whinstone is considered to be the founding sire of American Scotties. It is interesting to note that Henry Bixby, a former executive vice-president of the American Kennel Club, and Edwin Megargee, the famed dog artist, were on the committee that drew up the American standard in 1925. This standard was revised in 1947.

HEIGHT: Either sex, 10 inches.
WEIGHT: Males, 19 to 22 pounds; bitches, 18 to 21 pounds.
GAIT: Front legs incline in, hind legs move true.
COLOR: Steel or iron gray, brindled or grizzled, black, sandy, or wheaten. Slight white permitted on chest. Nose black.
HEAD: Skull: Slightly domed, slight stop, muzzle and skull about same length, but nose protrudes beyond muzzle. **Eyes:** Set wide apart, small, almond-shaped, dark brown or nearly black, set well under brows. **Ears:** Small, prick, rather pointed, set high. **Teeth:** Level or scissors bite. **Neck:** Short.
BODY: Shoulders: Sloping. **Forelegs:** Straight or slightly bent, elbows close, very heavy bone. **Chest:** Broad, very deep, well let down between forelegs. **Topline:** Moderately short, deep flanks. **Hindquarters:** Well-bent stifles, heavy bone, hocks straight. **Tail:** About 7 inches long, carried in slight curve, but not over back. **Feet:** Round, thick. **Coat:** Intensely hard, wiry, about 2 inches long, dense undercoat.
PENALTIES: Soft coat, round or light eyes, overshot or undershot, oversize or undersize, shyness, failure to show with head and tail up. Never to be given Winners or Best of Breed unless true Terrier fire is shown.

SEALYHAM TERRIER

Captain John Edwardes of Haverfordwest, Wales, developed the Sealyham Terrier between 1850 and 1890. Edwardes was sometimes called the Mad Captain, and it was said that he made litters of pups battle an otter. If they showed fear, he had them killed. If any pups were courageous enough to fight to the death, he rebred their parents. Whatever the truth of the story, Captain Edwardes did breed a very spirited dog, equally adept at fighting badgers and otters.

In 1908 the Sealyham Terrier Club of Haverfordwest was formed, and a breed standard was drawn up. Sealyhams appeared at English shows in 1910, and the breed received official recognition in 1911. The American Kennel Club recognized the breed the same year, and the American Sealyham Terrier Club was formed in 1913. Modern Sealyhams have excellent dispositions with people and are not objectionably aggressive with other dogs.

HEIGHT: About 10½ inches, both sexes.
WEIGHT: Males, 23 to 24 pounds; bitches, slightly less.
GAIT: Not specified.
COLOR: All white or white with lemon, tan, or badger markings on head and ears. Heavy body markings or excessive ticking to be discouraged. Nose black.
HEAD: Long, broad, powerful, three quarters of height at withers or 1 inch longer than neck, breadth between ears slightly less than one half of head length. **Skull:** Very slightly domed, median line furrow. **Muzzle:** In proportion to skull. Jaws level, square. **Eyes:** Very dark, set deeply, medium size, oval. Lack of eye rim pigment not a fault. **Ears:** Folded level with top of head, reach to eye corners, lie close to cheeks. **Teeth:** Scissors bite or level. **Neck:** Slightly less than two thirds of body height.
BODY: **Shoulders:** Well laid back. **Forelegs:** Strong, as straight as is

consistent with shortness and chest depth and breadth. **Chest:** Well let down between forelegs, well-sprung ribs. **Topline:** Level, back about 10½ inches long. **Hindquarters:** Strong second thighs, stifles and hocks well angulated, hocks protrude beyond tail. **Tail:** Docked, set high, carried upright. **Feet:** Large, compact. **Coat:** Dense, soft undercoat; hard, wiry outer coat.

FAULTS: White, cherry, or butterfly nose; light, large, protruding eyes; prick, tulip, rose, or hound ears; straight shoulders; thin, spread, or flat feet; cow hocks; roach back or swayback; down on pasterns; knuckled over; bowed forelegs; out at elbows; silky or curly coat.

SKYE TERRIER

Four hundred years ago, in the book *Of Englishe Dogges,* Dr. John Caius (physician to Edward VI, Queen Mary I, and Queen Elizabeth I) wrote of "a cur brought out barbarous borders fro' the uttermost countryes northward . . . which, by reason of the length of heare, makes showe neither of face nor of body." Skye Terrier historians believe that this is a description of their breed. However, Queen Victoria's Skye, Rona, did not have this heavy coat. Aside from Rona, the breed's most famous dog was Greyfriar's Bobby, who belonged to a poor Edinburgh shepherd. When he died, Bobby slept on his grave for nearly ten years.

The Skye came from the Isle of Skye near Scotland, and it became a rugged individualist, along with its masters. A saying among dog judges is: "If you examine a Skye on the table, it won't bite you. At other times, treat it with respect." The breed's long hair served as protection not only against foul weather but also against adversaries, who got mostly a mouthful of hair in a fight.

HEIGHT: Males, 10 inches; bitches, 9½ inches. Length not more than twice the height.

WEIGHT: Not specified.

GAIT: Legs travel in a straight line.

COLOR: One color at skin. Full coat is varying shades of black, blue, dark or light gray, silver, platinum, fawn, or cream. Black points on ears, muzzle, tail tip desired. No trace of pattern in coat. Nose black. A 2-inch white spot on chest permitted.

HEAD: About 8½ inches long, powerful. **Skull:** Moderately wide at ears, tapering to strong muzzle, slight stop. **Eyes:** Dark brown. **Ears:** Prick or drop. If prick, medium size, set high, carried erect, wider at peak than at skull. If drop, larger, set lower. **Teeth:** Level or scissors bite. **Neck:** Long, arched, carried high.

BODY: Long, low. **Shoulders:** Sloping. **Forelegs:** Short, straight as possible, elbows close. **Topline:** Level. **Chest:** Deep, with oval ribs. **Hindquarters:** Well angulated. **Tail:** 9 inches long, well feathered, carried at back level. **Feet:** Large, harefeet. **Coat:** Undercoat short, soft, woolly; outer coat hard, straight, flat, 5½ inches long, with no extra credit for longer. Coat hangs straight down on each side and is parted along spine from head to tail. Head hair shorter and softer but veils forehead and eyes and forms beard and apron. Long feathering on ears falls from tips and outer edges.

FAULTS: Any deviations from standard; temperament other than fearless, good-natured, reserved with strangers; males under 8 inches; bitches under 7½ inches.

DISQUALIFICATION: Dudley, flesh-colored, or brown nose.

SOFT-COATED WHEATEN TERRIER

The Kerry Blue Terrier may be the most barbered dog in the world (next to the Poodle), and the Soft-Coated Wheaten Terrier has been called the least groomed. Both breeds come from Ireland. The ungroomed Soft-Coated Wheatens have been slow in gaining popularity, but recently show dogs have been so beautifully groomed that the breed's future in America seems assured.

The ancestry of the Wheaten Terrier is in doubt, but it is claimed to be related to both the Kerry Blue Terrier and the Irish Terrier. Some Irish Terriers are also wheaten in color. The Irish Kennel Club recognized the breed in 1937; the English governing body gave its recognition in 1943; and the United States followed suit in 1973. The first dogs shown in America (in the Miscellaneous Class) arrived about 1946.

HEIGHT: Males, 18 to 19 inches; bitches, slightly smaller.
WEIGHT: Males, 35 to 45 pounds; bitches, slightly less.
GAIT: Graceful, straight leg action fore and aft.
COLOR: Wheaten. Nose black. Lips black.
HEAD: Moderately long, skull and muzzle equal length. **Skull:** Flat on top, good stop, cheeks clean-sided. **Eyes:** Small to medium size, dark hazel or deep brown. **Ears:** Set high and dropped. **Teeth:** Level or scissors bite. **Neck:** Moderately long, clean at throat.
BODY: Compact. **Shoulders:** Sloping. **Forelegs:** Straight. **Chest:** Deep, well-sprung ribs. **Topline:** Short. **Hindquarters:** Thighs heavily

muscled, well-bent stifles, well-let-down hocks. **Tail:** Docked, carried above body line. **Feet:** Compact, well-arched toes. **Coat:** Abundant over entire dog, moderately long, slightly wavy, soft, and silky. Stabilizes at 18 to 24 months. May be tidied up, but never clipped, plucked, or stylized. Ear fringe may be trimmed.

FAULTS: Undershot or overshot; any color except wheaten, but deviation permitted up to 18 months of age; woolly or coarse coat texture in mature dogs; dewclaws on hind legs.

STAFFORDSHIRE BULL TERRIER

Before 1900 this breed was registered by the United Kennel Club as the American Bull Terrier. The dog, which originated in England, is a mixture of Bulldog and probably a variety of Terriers. Early specimens were used in bullbaiting; later ones, in dogfights.

Although these dogs have been noted for their aggressiveness toward other dogs, they have been equally noted for their gentleness with children. As the Staffordshire Bull Terrier, the breed became recognized by the English Kennel Club in 1935. The American Kennel Club recognized the breed in 1974, and championship classes were first held in 1975.

HEIGHT: 14 to 16 inches.

WEIGHT: Males, 28 to 38 pounds; bitches, 24 to 34 pounds.

GAIT: Not specified, but agile and springy.

COLOR: Red, fawn black, blue, or any of these colors with white; white; brindle; or brindle and white. Nose black.

HEAD: Short, deep. **Skull:** Broad, short foreface, pronounced cheek muscles, distinct stop. **Eyes:** Dark or lighter, depending upon coat color, set to look straight ahead. **Ears:** Rose or half-pricked, small. **Teeth:** Scissors bite. **Neck:** Muscular, short.

BODY: Close-coupled. **Shoulders:** Sloping. **Chest:** Deep brisket, well-sprung ribs. **Topline:** Level. **Forelegs:** Straight, set wide apart, not loose at elbows, strong pasterns, feet turned slightly out. **Hindquarters:** Heavily muscled, stifles well bent, hocks well let down, legs parallel when viewed from behind. **Tail:** Medium length, set low, slight curve. **Feet:** Medium size, well padded. **Coat:** Smooth, short, close.

FAULTS: Light eyes, pink eye rims, tail too long or curled, over or under weights or heights, full drop or pricked ears, Dudley nose, badly overshot or undershot. Ears must never be cropped.

DISQUALIFICATION: Black–and–tan or liver color.

WELSH TERRIER

The Welsh Terrier is of very old lineage, descending from a dog called the Black-and-Tan Wire Haired Terrier or Old English Terrier. The breed has not changed much since 1886, when the English Kennel Club allotted one class for "Welsh, or Old English Wire Haired Black and Tan Terriers." The Welsh Terrier was first exhibited under its present name in Caernarvon, Wales, in 1884 and 1885.

Welsh Terriers began to appear in America as early as 1888, but it was not until 1901 that regular classes were allotted for the breed at American dog shows. Since then it has maintained a steady position as one of the most popular of the Terrier breeds.

HEIGHT: Males, 15 inches; bitches, slightly shorter.

WEIGHT: Males, 20 pounds; bitches, in proportion.

GAIT: Free and true.

COLOR: Black and tan or black grizzle and tan, free of black penciling on toes. Nose black.

HEAD: **Skull:** Flat, wider between ears than that of a Fox Terrier, and with a deeper, more punishing jaw. **Eyes:** Small, not too deeply set or protruding, dark hazel in color. **Ears:** V-shaped, small, set high, carried forward and close to the cheeks. **Muzzle:** Fair length. **Teeth:** Not specified but scissors bite normal. **Neck:** Moderate length, arched.

BODY: **Shoulders:** Long, sloping, well laid back. **Forelegs:** Straight, muscular, erect pasterns. **Chest:** Deep, moderate width, well ribbed up. **Topline:** Short, loins strong. **Hindquarters:** Muscular thighs, good length, hocks well let down, moderately straight. **Tail:** Set moderately high, not carried over back. **Feet:** Small, round, catlike. **Coat:** Wiry, hard, very close, abundant.

DISQUALIFICATIONS: Nose white or cherry or spotted to a considerable extent with these colors; prick, tulip, or rose ears; undershot or pig jaw; black below hocks or white to an appreciable extent.

WEST HIGHLAND WHITE TERRIER

The West Highland White Terrier is probably related to both the Scottish Terrier and the Cairn Terrier. Its relationship to the Dandie Dinmont and the Skye is less certain. Apparently the Malcolm family of Poltalloch, Scotland, began a pure strain of white terriers at least a hundred years ago. Earlier names for the breed were the Poltalloch Terrier and the Roseneath Terrier (after Roseneath, the duke of Argyll's estate in Dumbartonshire).

HEIGHT: Males, about 11 inches; bitches, 10 inches.
WEIGHT: Not specified.
GAIT: Free and true.
COLOR: White. Black pigmentation desired on lips, eye rims, pads of feet, nails. Nose black.
HEAD: Skull: Broad, slightly domed, distinct stop. **Muzzle:** Slightly shorter than skull. **Eyes:** Medium size, dark, set wide apart, slightly sunken. **Ears:** Small, carried erect, set wide apart, pointed, hair short, trimmed free of fringe. **Teeth:** Large for dog, level or scissors bite. **Neck:** Muscular, medium length.
BODY: Shoulders: Sloping. **Forelegs:** Straight, short, set under shoulder blades. **Chest:** Reaching to elbows, good breadth. **Topline:** Level, broad loins. **Hindquarters:** Short, sinewy, thighs muscular, not set too wide apart, hocks well bent. **Tail:** Short, not higher than top of skull, covered with hard hair, but no feathering, straight. **Feet:** Front feet larger than hind feet, may turn slightly out, round, strongly arched, covered with thick hair, hind feet arched, strong. **Coat:** Outer coat straight, hard, about 2 inches long, shorter on neck and shoulders, properly blended, undercoat dense.
FAULTS: Any color other than white; nose other than black; much over or under 11 inches; long, narrow skull; long muzzle; undershot or overshot; round-pointed, drop, broad, large ears; mule ears; ears not fully erect; light eyes; shallow chest; long, weak back; steep shoulders; cow hocks; stiff, stilted gait.

chapter thirty-nine

Toy Breeds

Giantism has been a way of life for many species ever since life on earth began. But as though in revolt against it, man has dwarfed many things, including cherry trees, cattle, and dogs. Many of the Toy breeds represent dwarfs of present-day dogs. But some have been dwarfed for so long that no one truly knows how they got that way or from what parent stock they came. Yet, the Chihuahua, at 1½ to 4 pounds, is as much a true dog as the 200-pound St. Bernard. A few of the so-called Toy breeds are not really Toys anymore. For example, some Pugs and many Shih Tzus are really outsized toys at the very best.

AFFENPINSCHER

In German the word *Affenartig* means "monkeylike." (The verb *äffen* means "to hoax.") And so the funny-looking little dog that some people say looks like a monkey — though it really doesn't — is called an Affenpinscher. The name has been translated as "monkey dog," which continues the hoax.

It is claimed that the breed was known in the seventeenth century and that it is the progenitor of the Brussels Griffon. The two breeds may be cousins, but there is little proof that one developed from the other. Nor does anyone wish to hazard a guess about the origin of the Affenpinscher. Suffice it to say that the Affenpinscher was recognized by the American Kennel Club in 1936 and that it has a small but dedicated group of fanciers.

HEIGHT: 10¼ inches either sex, the smaller the better.

WEIGHT: 7 to 8 pounds.

GAIT: Not specified, but normal.

COLOR: Black preferred, but black with tan markings, red, gray, and other mixtures permitted. Nose black.

HEAD: Skull: Round, domed forehead. **Eyes:** Round, large, black. **Ears:** Small, set high, pointed, erect, usually clipped to a point. **Muzzle:** Short, pointed, upper jaw longer than lower. **Teeth:** Should close together, but slightly undershot permitted; teeth should not show when mouth is closed. **Neck:** Short, straight.

BODY: Shoulders: Not specified, but moderately sloping. **Forelegs:** As straight as possible. **Chest:** Deep. **Topline:** Straight, equals height at shoulder, very little tuck-up. **Hindquarters:** Not much bend at stifles, hocks set well under the body. **Tail:** Cut short, set and carried high. **Feet:** Round, compact, turning neither in nor out, black pads and nails preferred. **Coat:** Hard, wiry, longer on legs and around the eyes, nose, and chin, thus giving monkey look.

FAULTS: Any deviations from standard.

BRUSSELS GRIFFON

The Brussels Griffon has been termed the "Belgian street urchin." It is claimed that this dog is the result of mating German Affenpinschers with somewhat larger, hard-coated street dogs that were mongrels, although they conformed fairly well to type. Another theory is that a Pug was mated with a Belgian street dog. As in the case of the Affenpinscher, there is little proof about its ancestry. However, the two breeds seem close enough to be cousins.

Whatever its ancestry, the Brussels Griffon is a homely and — perhaps for that reason — an attractive little dog, intelligent and remarkably sturdy in body. There are two varieties. The rough-coated dog is called simply the Brussels Griffon; the smooth-coated variety is usually called a Brabançon. The Pug may be responsible for the Brabançon's smooth coat.

HEIGHT: Not specified.
WEIGHT: 8 to 10 pounds; should not exceed 12 pounds.
GAIT: Not specified.
COLORS: Four allowed in rough-coated variety: Reddish brown, with a little black permitted in whiskers and on chin; black and reddish brown mixed, with black whiskers and chin; black, with uniform reddish brown markings on legs, under chin, eyebrows, around edges of ears, and around vent; solid black. In smooth-coated variety, solid black not allowed. In either variety, any white hair except chin frost in the black of mature dogs is a serious fault. Nose black.

HEAD: Skull: Large, domed. **Eyes:** Large, black, prominent, eyelashes long and black, eyelids edged in black. **Ears:** Small, set high, semi-erect if cropped. **Muzzle:** Extremely short, laid back. **Teeth:** Undershot, lower jaw broad, neither teeth nor tongue to show when jaw is closed.

BODY: Forelegs: Straight, set wide apart, pasterns erect. **Chest:** Deep, broad. **Topline:** Level, short. **Hindquarters:** Stifles and hocks well bent. **Tail:** Docked to one third, set high. **Feet:** Round, compact, turning neither in nor out, black pads and nails preferred. **Coat:** Rough-coated dogs: Hard, wiry, no wool or silk, not shaggy except at chin, eyes, nose, and cheeks. Smooth-coated dogs: Short, no trace of wire, similar to that of Boston Terrier.

DISQUALIFICATIONS: Dudley or butterfly nose, white anywhere, hanging tongue, overshot jaw, solid black in a smooth-coated dog.

CHIHUAHUA, SMOOTH COAT

There are many theories about the origin of the Chihuahua. One is that it was developed by the Toltecs as early as A.D. 900 and called a Techichi. However, *chichi* seems to have been the Aztec root word for a mammal, and the prefix *te* was Aztec for "wall." In Mexico *chichi* now is slang for "breasts." Another theory of the Chihuahua's ancestry is that the Chinese brought these dwarf dogs to Mexico.

In' about 1900 people were observed along the Mexican border, carrying Chihuahuas in their pockets. Many dog fanciers became interested in the breed. All modern Chihuahuas, including those in Mexico, stem from American breeding.

HEIGHT: Not specified.

WEIGHT: Not to exceed 6 pounds; 2 to 4 pounds ideal.

GAIT: Not specified, but should trot in a straight line.

COLOR: Any color. Nose black; in tans, blues, chocolates, it is self-colored; in blonds, it may be pink.

HEAD: Skull: Rounded apple dome, with or without molera (hole in the head), cheeks and jaws lean. **Muzzle:** Slightly pointed. **Eyes:** Full, set well apart, dark, ruby, or luminous, light eyes in blonds permitted. **Ears:** Large, erect when dog is alert, but flaring to sides at forty-five-degree angle when dog is in repose. **Teeth:** Level or scissors bite. **Neck:** Arched.

BODY: Shoulders: Sloping, with slight ruff of hair on neck and shoulders. **Forelegs:** Strong, straight. **Chest:** Deep. **Topline:** Level, back slightly longer than height at withers, but shorter backs desired in males, ribs rounded. **Hindquarters:** Muscular, hocks well apart, true. **Tail:** Moderately long, carried sickle-fashion and out or over body, or in a loop over back, with tip just touching back, never tucked under, furry. **Feet:** Small, toes well split up, not spread. **Coat:** Soft, close, glossy. Heavier coats with undercoat permitted, with slight neck ruff, but scanty on head and ears.

DISQUALIFICATIONS: Cropped tail, bobtail, broken down or cropped ears, any dog over 6 pounds.

CHIHUAHUA, LONG COAT

The standard is the same as for the Smooth Coat Chihuahua, except for the following. Its coat should be of a soft texture, either flat or curly, with undercoat preferred. Ears fringed (heavily fringed ears may be tipped slightly, but never down), feathering on feet and legs, and pants on hind legs. Large ruff on neck desired and preferred. Tail full and long (as a plume).

DISQUALIFICATIONS: Thin coat. Other disqualifications the same as in the Smooth Coat Chihuahua.

ENGLISH TOY SPANIEL

Diminutive spaniels of English Springer Spaniel type have been known in England for centuries. Mary, Queen of Scots, bred them. One of her executioners reported that he "espied her little dog which was crept under her clothes which could not be gotten forth except by force." And Samuel Pepys wrote of King Charles II, "All I observed there was the silliness of the King playing with his dog all the while and not minding his business."

As time passed, the small Spaniels developed a domed skull and a shortened muzzle. It seems likely that they were crossed with Japanese Chins and possibly with Pugs. A Pekingese cross has also been suggested.

HEIGHT: Not specified.
WEIGHT: 9 to 12 pounds.
GAIT: Not specified.
COLOR: There are four varieties of English Toy Spaniel: King Charles, Ruby, Blenheim, and Prince Charles. King Charles and Ruby are solid colors, though the King Charles is really black and tan. Blenheim and Prince Charles are broken colors. King Charles: Glossy black with deep mahogany tan on muzzle, chest, legs, and over eyes. A few white hairs permitted on chest, but not a white patch or any white elsewhere. Ruby: Rich, chestnut red. Blenheim: Red and white, with white ground color and red evenly distributed in large patches, ears and cheeks red, white blaze; clear spot of red in center of blaze at the top of

forehead. Prince Charles: Tricolored (white, black, and tan), with white ground color, black evenly distributed in large patches, tan spots over eyes and on muzzle, chest, legs; ears and vent lined with tan. No forehead spot. Nose black in all varieties.

HEAD: Skull: Domed, semiglobular, protruding over eyes, nearly meets upturned nose, deep stop comparable to that of Bulldog. **Eyes:** Nearly black, enormous pupils, eyelids square to the line of the face. **Ears:** Measure 20 to 22 inches tip to tip, heavily feathered. **Muzzle:** Square, deep, turned-up underjaw. **Teeth:** Concealed, tongue not to show when jaws are closed. **Nose:** Turned up between eyes.

BODY: Compact, resembling that of Pug. **Shoulders:** Not specified. **Chest:** Wide. **Topline:** Broad and short. **Forelegs:** Parallel, straight, strongly boned. **Hindquarters:** Well developed. **Feet:** Firm, round. **Tail:** Cut to 1½ inches, feather 3 to 4 inches long. **Coat:** Long, silky, wavy, but not curly, profuse mane, feathers on ears and thick on feet. On King Charles, ear feather exceeds that on Blenheim by 1 inch or more.

DISQUALIFICATIONS: King Charles and Ruby: White patch on chest, white on any other part.

ITALIAN GREYHOUND

The Italian Greyhound is a Toy Greyhound. It seems to have been developed in Roman days or earlier as a result of man's passion for making diminutives of admired breeds. Many of the great artists of the sixteenth and seventeenth centuries, including Veronese, Van Dyke, and Watteau, painted the breed. In 1790 the engraver Thomas Bewick described the dogs as "exquisitely beautiful and delicate." Italian Greyhounds were among the breeds shown at the first Westminster dog show more than a hundred years ago.

HEIGHT: 13 to 15 inches.
WEIGHT: Not specified.
GAIT: High-stepping, free, forelegs and hind legs move in straight line.
COLOR: Any color and markings are acceptable except brindle markings and the tan markings normally found on black-and-tan dogs of other breeds.
HEAD: Skull: Long, almost flat. **Eyes:** Large, bright. **Ears:** Thrown back, or folded at right angles to head when alert. **Muzzle:** Long, fine. **Teeth:** Scissors bite. **Neck:** Long, gracefully arched.
BODY: Shoulders: Long, sloping. **Forelegs:** Straight, well set under shoulders. **Chest:** Deep, narrow. **Topline:** Arched, drooping at the hindquarters. **Hindquarters:** Thighs muscular, hocks well let down, stifles

well bent. **Tail:** Long, fine, carried low. **Feet:** Long, harefoot. **Coat:** Skin fine and supple, hair thin, glossy as satin.

FAULTS: Light or partially pigmented nose, undershot or overshot mouth, erect or button ears. Ring tail a serious fault.

DISQUALIFICATIONS: Brindle markings, tan markings of the kind normally found on black-and-tan dogs of other breeds.

JAPANESE CHIN

The Japanese Chin is a centuries-old breed that probably originated in China and was then developed to its present perfection by the Japanese. Commodore Perry brought the first dogs to America after opening Japan to foreign ships in 1853. A pair of Chins was sent to Queen Victoria of England. In the following years sailors bought or stole Chins to sell to Americans and Europeans. But the dogs were not hardy, and many died at sea.

World War II brought a severe reduction in the Chin population in Japan, as well as in other countries. Revived interest in the breed in Japan and elsewhere is under way. For more than a century the Chin was known in English-speaking countries as the Japanese Spaniel, but in the

United States this name was discontinued in August 1977. The parent club name has been changed to the Japanese Chin Club of America.

HEIGHT: Not specified.

WEIGHT: Varies. In shows with a large number of entries, Open Classes may be divided into under 7 pounds and over 7 pounds.

GAIT: Not specified, but stylish.

COLOR: Black and white or red and white. Red includes all shades of sable, brindle, lemon, and orange; but the brighter and clearer the red, the better. Nose black in black-and-whites; flesh color in red-and-whites.

HEAD: Large for size of dog. **Skull:** Broad, rounded at forehead. **Eyes:** Large, dark, set wide apart. **Ears:** Small, V-shaped, set high, wide apart, carried slightly forward. **Neck:** Short, thick.

BODY: Length about equals height. **Shoulders:** Sloping. **Forelegs:** Slender, well feathered. **Chest:** Wide. **Tail:** Profusely covered with long hair, must be well twisted to either side, carried over back, with hair flow to opposite side. **Feet:** Small, somewhat long, dog tends to stand high on toes. If feathered for a showy appearance, tufts to increase in length of foot, but not in width. **Coat:** Profuse, long, straight, rather silky, free of wave or curl, not to lie too flat, tendency to stand out, especially at the neck to give a mane or ruff, profuse feathering on thighs and tail.

DISQUALIFICATION: Nose other than black in black-and-whites.

MALTESE

At the beginning of the first century A.D., the Roman historian Strabo wrote: "There is a town in Sicily called Melita whence are exported many beautiful dogs called Canis Melitei." John Caius, a physician and author who wrote during the time of Queen Elizabeth I, noted that they are "called Melitei from the Island of Melita. They are very small indeed and chiefly sought after for the pleasure and amusement of women who carried them in their arms, their bosoms, and their beds." Maltese are pert, healthy dogs.

The breed has remained steadily popular among the aristocracy ever since Roman days, but ownership throughout the world is now no longer limited to the aristocracy. Since World War II it has become the most popular breed in Japan, where there is a passion for diminutiveness in many things — in dogs and even in trees.

HEIGHT: Not specified.
WEIGHT: Under 7 pounds; 4 to 6 pounds ideal.
GAIT: Jaunty, smooth-flowing; forelegs and hind legs move in line.
COLOR: Pure white. Light lemon or tan on ears permitted, but not desired. Nose black.
HEAD: Medium length, in proportion to size of dog. **Skull:** Slightly rounded, stop moderate. **Ears:** Low-set, heavily feathered with

long hair, hanging close to head. **Muzzle:** Medium length, tapering, not snipy. **Teeth:** Level or scissors bite. **Neck:** Sufficient to hold head erect.

BODY: Length of body equals height from ground to withers to root of tail. **Shoulders:** Sloping. **Forelegs:** Straight, pasterns erect, elbows close. **Chest:** Deep. **Topline:** Level, ribs well sprung, loins taut, slight tuck-up. **Hindquarters:** Moderately bent stifles and hocks. **Tail:** Long-haired plume, carried over back, tip lying to one side. **Feet:** Small, round, pads black. **Coat:** Single, hangs long, flat, silky, nearly to or to ground, long head hair may be tied into topknot. Kinky, curly, woolly hair objectionable.

FAULTS: Cow hocks or any suggestion of hind legs toeing in or out, deviations from standard.

MANCHESTER TERRIER (TOY)

The Toy Manchester Terrier is a smaller size of the standard Manchester Terrier. The breed has been known under many names over the centuries. In England, its original name was Toy Manchester Terrier, which was changed to Toy Black-and-Tans and then to Miniature Black-and-Tans. Today the official English title is English Toy Terrier (Black and Tan).

In the United States they are known by their original name, but for nearly a hundred years people called them Rat Terriers or Toy Rat Terriers, reflecting their early use as ratters, either in pits or around farmhouses and stables.

HEIGHT: Not specified.

WEIGHT: Not exceeding 12 pounds. American-bred and Open Classes can be divided by weight. 7 pounds and under, and over 7 pounds but not exceeding 12 pounds.

GAIT: Not specified.

COLOR: Jet black and rich mahogany tan, with well-defined color divisions. Tan over each eye, on cheeks, upper and lower jaws, and extending under the throat; rosettes on each side of chest above legs. Black thumb mark on front of each leg between pastern and knee, black penciling running lengthwise on the top of each toe on all four feet. Remainder of forelegs tan to knees. Tan on hind legs almost to stifle joint on inside, black on outside. Tan on inside of tail and on vent. Nose black.

HEAD: Long, narrow, tight-skinned. **Skull:** Flat, with median line furrow. **Eyes:** Small, black, set close together. **Ears:** Of moderate size, set high on skull, rather close together, thin, moderately narrow at base, pointed tips, carried erect. **Teeth:** Level or scissors bite.

BODY: Moderately short, ribs well sprung behind shoulders. **Topline:** Slightly arched over loins, falling to croup. **Chest:** Narrow, deep. **Forelegs:** Parallel, straight. **Feet:** Compact, arched. **Hindquarters:** Well angulated at the stifles, hocks let down, turning neither in nor out. **Tail:** Moderately short, set where arch of loin ends. **Coat:** Smooth, short, dense, glossy, not soft.

FAULTS: Unsound legs or feet, improper markings. White on any part of the body. Wide, flaring or blunt-tipped ears.

DISQUALIFICATION: Cropped or cut ears.

MINIATURE PINSCHER

The Miniature Pinscher is incorrectly referred to as a Miniature Doberman Pinscher or a Toy Doberman. Actually the breed is much older than the Doberman, although its specific origin is unknown. Breeding on a national scale did not start in Germany until the formation of the Pinscher-Schnauzer Club after World War I. (*Pinscher* is the German word for "Terrier.") This breed has also been called the Reh Pinscher.

The Miniature Pinscher was shown in the Miscellaneous Class in American dog shows until it had become reasonably popular all over the country. The Miniature Pinscher Club of America was formed in 1929. The breed is popular both as a show dog and as a home pet.

HEIGHT: 11 to 11½ inches.
WEIGHT: Not specified.
GAIT: A spirited, high-stepping (hackney) gait.
COLOR: Solid red or stag red; lustrous black with sharply defined tan or rust red markings on cheeks, lips, lower jaw, throat, twin spots above eyes and on chest, lower half of forelegs, inside of hind legs, and on vent, black penciling lines on toes; solid brown or chocolate with rust or yellow markings. Nose black, may be chocolate color with brown coat.
HEAD: Skull: Wedge-shaped, in parallel plane with muzzle. **Muzzle:** Strong, little stop. **Eyes:** Full, oval, dark to black, set wide apart. **Ears:** Upstanding. If cropped, pointed and erect. **Teeth:** Perfect alignment. **Neck:** Gracefully arched.
BODY: In males, height (ground to withers) equals length (withers to root of tail); in bitches, length is slightly greater. **Shoulders:** Sloping. **Forelegs:** Straight, elbows close, parallel, perpendicular to ground. **Chest:** Reaches to elbows. **Topline:** Sloping or level, tuck-up slight, croup sloped thirty degrees. **Hindquarters:** Well angulated at stifles and hocks. **Tail:** Cropped close to body, set high. **Feet:** Catlike, arched toes. **Coat:** Smooth, hard, short, covering entire body.

MAJOR FAULTS: Thick skull, loose elbows, feet turning in or out, undeveloped stifles, cow hocks, poor gait, swayback, roach back.

DISQUALIFICATIONS: Thumb marks or any area of white on feet or forechest exceeding ½ inch in longest dimension, a dog of either sex under 10 inches or over 12½ inches tall.

PAPILLON

This dog's name (pronounced *Pah-pee-yown*) is French for "butterfly." And, in truth, the dog's delicate, well-fringed, wide-flaring ears remind one of a butterfly's wings. However, there is a variety of Papillon whose ears are down, called Phalène (meaning "moth") in France and Epagneul Nain ("dwarf spaniel") or Phalène in America. The breed apparently originated in Spain in the 1500s, but the chief breeders were in Italy, near Bologna. Marie Antoinette and Madame de Pompadour owned them, as did Queen Charlotte Sophia of England, as seen in paintings of these women with their dogs.

The English Kennel Club recognized the breed in 1923, and the American Kennel Club did so in 1935.

HEIGHT: 8 to 11 inches.

WEIGHT: In proportion to height.

GAIT: Free and graceful, not paddle-footed or with stiff hip movement.

COLOR: Always parti-color, white with patches of any color. Color other than white must cover both ears and eyes. Nose, eye rims, and lips well-pigmented black. Clearly defined and symmetrical white blaze and nose band preferred.

HEAD: **Skull:** Medium width, rounded, stop distinct. **Eyes:** Dark, inner corners of eyes in line with stop, eye rims black. **Ears:** Erect type carried obliquely, movement suggests that of the spread wings of a butterfly. Drop type droop completely down. **Muzzle:** One third of total head length, abruptly narrower than skull. **Teeth:** Scissors bite, tongue not to show when mouth is closed.

BODY: Longer than height. **Shoulders:** Well developed. **Forelegs:** Straight. **Chest:** Medium depth, ribs well sprung. **Topline:** Level. **Hindquarters:** Well angulated, dewclaws must be removed. **Tail:** Long, set high, plumed, carried arched over body. **Feet:** Thin, elongated. **Coat:** Abundant, long, fine, straight, profuse neck frill, no undercoat, ears well fringed, leg feathers.

FAULTS: Overshot or undershot; ears small, pointed, set too high; one ear up; ears partly down; feet turning in or out; low tail set; poor tail carriage; over 11 inches tall; nose not black.

DISQUALIFICATIONS: Over 12 inches at the withers, an all-white dog, a dog with no white.

PEKINGESE

The Chinese had small pet dogs as early as A.D. 565, when a dog from Persia named Red Tiger (Ch'ih Hu) was owned by the emperor. Emperor Kou Tzu had a pair of small dogs said to be only 6 inches tall. No one knows whether these were truly Pekingese. However, by the time of Emperor Ch'ien Lung in the eighteenth century, Pekingese were much as we know them today.

According to tradition, four Pekingese dogs were seized when the Chinese royal palace was sacked by the British in 1860. One of these was presented to Queen Victoria. Some have doubted that these were the royal palace dogs. However, dogs of true Pekingese type did appear in England later, although they were not shown there until 1893. The American Kennel Club recognized the breed in 1909.

 HEIGHT: Not specified.
 WEIGHT: Maximum, 14 pounds.
 GAIT: A slight roll.
 COLOR: All colors. Black masks, spectacles, and lines to ears desired. Parti-colors: Broken patches, no large portion of one color, white shown on saddle. A solid color with white feet and chest is not a parti-color. Nose black.
 HEAD: **Skull:** Massive, flat between ears, wide between eyes, stop deep. **Eyes:** Large, prominent. **Ears:** Heart-shaped, not set high, not to reach below muzzle, drooping, long feathering. **Muzzle:** Broad, wrinkled,

very short, flat, not overshot or pointed, broad underjaw. **Teeth:** Not to show when jaws are closed.

BODY: Heavy in front, well-sprung ribs. **Chest:** Broad, falling away lighter behind. **Topline:** Level, not too long. **Forelegs:** Short, bowed, firm at shoulder. **Hindquarters:** Lighter, but firm. **Tail:** Set high, lying well over back to either side; long, profuse feathers. **Feet:** Flat, toes turned out, dog should stand on feet, not ankles. **Coat:** Long, thick undercoat, straight, flat, not curly or wavy, rather coarse, feathering profuse, profuse mane extending beyond shoulder blades.

FAULTS: Protruding tongue, badly blemished eye, overshot or wry mouth.

DISQUALIFICATIONS: Over 14 pounds, Dudley nose.

POMERANIAN

The Pomeranian is the smallest of the Spitz family of northern sled and herding dogs. It appears to have been bred from sled dogs. A larger ancestor was probably the German wolf spitz, which weighed thirty pounds or more. Sometimes the Pomeranian's aggressiveness toward other dogs seems to indicate that it does not realize that it is a toy dog. As the Spitzdog, the breed was recognized in England in 1870. The name was later changed to Pomeranian, after the country of its origin, Pomerania, a former province of Prussia.

The Poms of the early 1900s were heavier-boned and larger than the present dogs. Refinement has come during the last fifty years. The American Kennel Club recognized the breed in 1900. The first specialty show of the American Pomeranian Club was held in 1911.

HEIGHT: Not specified.
WEIGHT: 3 to 7 pounds; 4 to 5 pounds ideal.
GAIT: Not specified.
COLOR: Any solid color, any solid color with lighter shadings of the same color, any solid color with sable or black shadings, parti-color, sable, and black and tan. Black-and-tan is black with tan or rust sharply defined above eyes, on muzzle, throat, forechest, all legs and feet, and below tail. Parti-color is white with any other color in even patches on body and with a white blaze. Eye and lip rims and nose must be black, but may be self-colored in browns and blues.
HEAD: Foxlike, wedge-shaped. **Skull:** Not domed, pronounced stop, muzzle fine, but not snipy. **Eyes:** Dark, medium size. **Ears:** Small, set high, carried erect. **Teeth:** Scissors bite. **Neck:** Short, profuse mane of hair.
BODY: **Shoulders:** Sloping. **Topline:** Short, level, well ribbed. **Forelegs:** Straight, parallel. **Hindquarters:** Sound, hocks perpendicular to the ground. **Tail:** Turned over back, set high, carried flat, profusely covered with long, spreading hair. **Feet:** Small, dog stands well up on toes. **Coat:** Double. Undercoat dense, outer coat standoff, straight, harsh, legs well feathered.
FAULTS: Deviations from standard; round, domed skull; too large ears; undershot; light or Dudley nose; out at elbows; flat-sided; cow hocks; soft, open coat.

POODLE (TOY)

Poodles are not separated by varieties in the *American Kennel Club Stud Book*. Thus, if a Toy Poodle is disqualified by height as a Toy, it can move into the classes for Miniatures. This means that all Poodles share foundation bloodlines. However, it seems likely that other Toy breeds were used in dwarfing Poodles to Toy size. Early pictures suggest that the Maltese or a dog once called the Maltese Poodle may have been used.

In any case the modern Toy Poodle is so nearly identical to the larger varieties that the same breed standard applies to both the Miniature Poodle and the Standard Poodle except, of course, for size. Faults that are more common in the Toys than in the other varieties are flat feet and tearstained faces. (See Standard Poodle, pp. 449–450, for the breed standard.)

HEIGHT: 10 inches or under at the withers.
WEIGHT: Not specified.
GAIT: Sound and merry, with forelegs and hind legs moving in line.
DISQUALIFICATION: Any Poodle that is more than 10 inches at the shoulders shall be disqualified from competition as a Toy Poodle. However, such a Poodle could compete at later shows as a Miniature Poodle, provided it is entered as such.

PUG

The Pug appears to have originated from a smooth-coated Chinese dog closely related to the Pekingese. The Dutch East India Company brought the dog to the Netherlands. It became known as the Dutch Pug because it was from the Netherlands that importations into England were made.

Meanwhile a black strain was apparently introduced from Japan. One might say that the Pug grew larger while the Pekingese became smaller and hairier.

The Pug enjoyed extraordinary popularity in Great Britain during the Victorian era, after which its popularity declined. The breed's resurgence began with the publicity given to the Pugs belonging to the Duke and Duchess of Windsor. In the United States the Pug's popularity has been steady for at least three quarters of a century.

HEIGHT: Not specified.
WEIGHT: 14 to 18 pounds is desirable.
GAIT: Not specified, but forelegs and hind legs move in line.
COLOR: Silver or apricot fawn. Clearly defined dark markings: muzzle mask, ears, moles on cheeks, thumb mark or diamond on forehead, trace along spine. Only other allowed color is black.
HEAD: **Skull:** Large, massive, round, not apple-headed, no stop. **Eyes:** Dark, very large, globular, bold, prominent. **Ears:** Thin, soft (as black velvet), may be rose or button, but button preferred. **Muzzle:** Short, blunt, square. **Teeth:** Not specified, but usually level or slightly undershot. **Facial wrinkles:** Large and deep.
BODY: Short, well ribbed up. **Chest:** Wide. **Topline:** Flat. **Forelegs:** Very strong, straight, moderate length, well set under. **Hindquarters:** Not specified, but reasonably angulated. **Tail:** Tightly curled over hip, a double curl is perfection. **Feet:** Compact, well-split-up toes, black nails. **Coat:** Fine, smooth, soft, glossy.
FAULTS: Lean, leggy dog, dog with short legs and long body, long harefeet or round cat feet, deviations from standard.

SHIH TZU

The known history of the Shih Tzu (pronounced *Sheed-Zu*) begins with the Manchu Dynasty in China. Royal visitors to Tibet were given pairs of the dogs, which were taken back to Peking. There they were bred and became well established. The name is said to mean "lion dog" in the Tibetan language. It seems certain that Shih Tzus were crossed with Pekingese — if not in China, then in England.

General Sir Douglas Brownrigg and his wife brought the breed to England in 1930. At first, progress was slow. In the United States registrations were refused at first, until it could be shown that the dogs had not been crossed with Pekingese in the last three generations. American Kennel Club recognition came in 1969, and on the first day of competition classes, a Shih Tzu made history by winning Best in Show.

HEIGHT: 9 to 10½ inches ideal; never more than 11 inches, nor less than 8 inches.

WEIGHT: 12 to 15 pounds ideal; never more than 18 pounds.

GAIT: Slight roll, moves with head held high.

COLOR: All colors. Nose and eye rims black, but may be liver in dogs with liver markings.

HEAD: Skull: Broad, round between eyes. **Muzzle:** Short, square, definite stop. **Eyes:** Large, dark, round, but not prominent. **Ears:** Large, with long leathers, drooping, set slightly below crown of skull. **Muzzle:** Square, about 1 inch long, not wrinkled. **Teeth:** Level or slightly undershot.

BODY: Longer than tall. **Chest:** Broad, deep. **Topline:** Level.

Forelegs: Short, well boned, appear massive because of hair. **Hindquarters:** Short, thighs massive, no cow hocks. **Tail:** Heavily plumed, curved well over back, set high. **Feet:** Good size, firm, hair between pads, hind dewclaws removed; if on front legs, may be removed. **Coat:** Long, dense, may be slightly wavy, but not curly, undercoat woolly, hair on head may be tied up.

FAULTS: Narrow head; overshot bite; snipiness; pink on nose or eye rims; small, light eyes; legginess; sparse coat; lack of definite stop.

SILKY TERRIER

The Silky Terrier is descended from a number of sources, primarily from a Tasmanian dog known as the Broken-Haired Terrier, which was developed by using Skyes (to give length of back, short legs, and color), Scotties (for broken coat), and Dandie Dinmonts (for topknot). In turn the Australians crossed the breed with Yorkshire Terriers. The first standard was drawn up in 1909, although the breed, then known as the Sydney Silky, had first been shown in 1907.

Silkies were first shown in Great Britain in 1928. Australian imports to the United States and Canada began in the early 1950s. Official American Kennel Club recognition came in 1959.

HEIGHT: 9 to 10 inches, should never be less than 8 inches.
WEIGHT: 8 to 10 pounds.
GAIT: Free, light-footed, and straightforward.
COLOR: Blue and tan (blue may be silver, pigeon, or slate; tan, deep and rich). Blue extends from base of skull to tip of tail, down legs to pasterns and hocks. Blue should be very dark on tail. Tan on muzzle, cheeks, over eyes, at base of ears, below pasterns and hocks, and around vent. Topknot is silver or fawn. Nose black.

HEAD: Wedge-shaped. **Skull:** Longer than muzzle, stop shallow. **Eyes:** Small, dark. **Ears:** Small, V-shaped, pricked, carried erect. **Teeth:** Scissors bite.

BODY: One-fifth longer than tall. **Forelegs:** Straight, fine-boned. **Chest:** Reaches to elbows. **Topline:** Straight. **Hindquarters:** Well angulated at stifles and hocks. **Tail:** Set high, docked, carried erect. **Feet:** Small, catlike, point straight ahead. **Coat:** Flat, glossy, 5 to 6 inches on mature dogs, topknot on skull, coat parted along the spine, legs free of long coat below pasterns and hocks.

FAULTS: Ears flaring obliquely, light eyes, overshot or undershot, white- or flesh-colored nails, toeing in or out, under 8 inches tall.

YORKSHIRE TERRIER

Just after 1850 the name Scotch Terrier seems to have applied to a variety of dogs. But at the Leeds show in 1861 there was only one such dog, and it was large and clumsy. The breed was refined until it became the Yorkshire Terrier we know today. Yorkshiremen bred them in large numbers but kept their breeding methods secret. The English authority Stanley Dangerfield believes the ancestors may have been Black-and-Tan Terriers, perhaps the Maltese, and Skye Terriers. The breed's characteristic excessive coat was supposedly developed to protect the dogs from bites while ratting.

Britain recognized the Yorkshire Terrier in 1886, six years after its introduction to the United States, but at that time it did not breed true to type. Today it is a thoroughly well-established breed around the world and at times has been the third most popular breed in Great Britain and among the fifteen most popular breeds in the United States.

HEIGHT: Not specified.

WEIGHT: Not to exceed 7 pounds.

GAIT: Lively, head erect, forelegs and hind legs move in line.

COLOR: Blue and tan. Blue is dark steel blue, not silver blue, not mingled with fawn, bronze, or black. It extends from back of neck, over body, to end of tail, which is darker than body color. Tan hair is darker at roots, gradually lightens, should not be mingled with sooty or black hair. Tan is rich golden on head and hair overhanging the face, deeper at sides of head, at ear roots, muzzle, and ears, and does not extend down neck. Tan on chest and legs is bright and rich, and should not extend above elbows or stifles. Puppies are born black and tan; black must clear to blue by age 18 months. Nose black.

HEAD: Small. **Skull:** Flat on top. **Eyes:** Medium size, dark. **Ears:** Small, V-shaped, carried erect. **Muzzle:** Not long. **Teeth:** Scissors or level bite.

BODY: Height equals length. **Topline:** Level, short. **Forelegs:** Straight, elbows close. **Hindquarters:** Stifles moderately bent, hocks straight. **Tail:** Docked to medium length, carried just above back level. **Feet:** Round, black nails, dewclaws removed. **Coat:** Glossy, silky, long, perfectly straight, may be trimmed to floor length if desired to give better movement, headfall may be tied with one bow or parted and tied with two, body coat is parted down middle from base of skull to tail tip, ear tips and feet usually trimmed.

FAULTS: Any deviation from standard, toes turning in or out, overshot or undershot, cow hocks.

chapter forty
Non-Sporting Breeds

When the American Kennel Club had finished placing most of the breeds into proper groups, it found some breeds left over that rather defied classification. The Bulldog had been bred for bullbaiting, which had long since been outlawed. The Poodle had once been a water dog. The Dalmatian had been a coaching dog, following and guarding the passengers of horse-drawn vehicles. No one was certain what the purpose of the Lhasa Apso might have been. The AKC dealt with the situation by placing these breeds and varieties into a special division, the Non-Sporting Group.

BICHON FRISE

The name *Bichon* once referred to a family of small dogs, usually white, that originated on the shores of the Mediterranean Sea. Among these were the Bichon Maltais and the Bichon Teneriffe. As a family the dogs have a history dating back to Roman times. The Teneriffe Bichon was a favorite of King Francis I of France, who reigned from 1515 to 1547.

An official French standard for the breed was approved in 1933. Madame Nizet de Leemans, a European all-breeds judge and then president of the Fédération Cynologique Internationale (FCI), proposed the name Bichon Frise (meaning "frizzy-haired Bichon") when that organization recognized the breed in 1934. In English, *frizzy* means "tight curls," but in French, when referring to the dog, it means "loose curls."

The first Bichons Frises were brought to the United States in 1956. Since then the breed has gained an astonishing popularity. It was given full American Kennel Club recognition in 1973.

HEIGHT: 9½ to 11½ inches, ideal.

WEIGHT: Not specified.

GAIT: Not specified, but lively and straightforward.

COLOR: Solid white, or white with cream, apricot or gray on the ears and sometimes on the body. Nose black.

HEAD: Proportionate in size to the body, 3 parts muzzle to 5 parts skull. **Skull:** Broad, somewhat round, stop definite. **Eyes:** Large, black or dark brown, rims black or brown. **Ears:** Dropped, reaching halfway to the nose, covered with long, flowing hair. **Muzzle:** Medium long. **Teeth:** Scissors bite. **Neck:** Rather long, proudly carried.

BODY: Slightly longer than height at withers. **Shoulders:** Well laid back. **Forelegs:** Elbows close to body, legs as straight as possible. **Chest:** Well developed, with good rib spring. **Topline:** Inclines gradually to slight rise over muscular loins. **Hindquarters:** Well angulated at stifle and hock joints. **Feet:** Tight, round, cat feet. **Coat:** Profuse, silky, loosely curled, definite undercoat. Minimum adult coat not less than 2 inches long.

FAULTS: Cow hocks, snipy muzzle, poor pigmentation, protruding or yellow eyes, undershot or overshot, missing teeth, corkscrew tail, black hair in coat, shadings over 10 per cent of body coat except in puppies.

BOSTON TERRIER

In 1870 Robert C. Hooper of Boston had a dog named Hooper's Judge, which was a cross between a Bulldog and the now extinct white English Terrier. Judge was a leggy dog, weighing 32 pounds. He was bred to a "low and square" bitch named Gyp, weighing 20 pounds. From this mating descend almost all purebred Boston Terriers. At first the breed was called the American Bull Terrier, then the Round Head. In 1891 the name became Boston Terrier. However, thousands of owners still speak of their dogs as Boston Bulls or Toy Bulldogs.

The American Kennel Club recognized the breed in 1893. Since 1900 the breed has been greatly refined and standardized. At one time it was the most popular breed in America. The breed still has its dedicated fanciers, but the number of dogs has decreased, partly because so many of them must be born by Cesarean section.

HEIGHT: Not specified.

WEIGHT: Not to exceed 25 pounds, but divided into three classes for the show ring: lightweight, under 15 pounds; middleweight, 15 to under 20 pounds; heavyweight, 20 to not over 25 pounds.

GAIT: Graceful, forelegs and hind legs move in line.

COLOR: Brindle with white markings (brindle evenly distributed and distinct, white muzzle, even white blaze, white on collar, breast, part or all of forelegs, hind legs below hocks). Black and white permitted, but brindle preferred. Nose black.

HEAD: Skull: Flat, free of wrinkles, abrupt brow, well-defined stop. **Eyes:** Large, round, set wide. **Ears:** Cropped or natural bat, carried erect, set near corners of skull. **Muzzle:** Free of wrinkles, shorter in length than width, length not exceeding one third of skull length, parallel to top of skull. **Teeth:** Even, or undershot to square muzzle. **Neck:** Arched.

BODY: Deep, good width, ribs carried well back. **Shoulders:** Sloping. **Chest:** Deep. **Topline:** Short, rump curving to set-on of tail. **Forelegs:** Set on line of shoulders, elbows close. **Hindquarters:** Bent at stifles, short from hocks to feet. **Tail:** Set low, short, straight or screw, not carried above back line. **Feet:** Round, well arched. **Coat:** Short, fine.

FAULTS: Domed skull, too long or short for breadth; eyes small, sunken, light, or walleye; muzzle wedge shallow; down-faced; protruding teeth; poor ear carriage; ewe neck; loose shoulders or elbows; straight hind legs; cow hocks; weak pasterns; rolling, paddling, or weaving gait; tail elevated above root, long, gnarled, or curled against body.

DISQUALIFICATIONS: Solid black, black and tan, liver or mouse colors, Dudley nose, docked tail.

BULLDOG

Bullbaiting became a popular sport around the year 1200. It was cruel, and many dogs lost their lives in combat. Those that did not die were exceedingly ferocious. In 1835 dogfighting and consequently bullbaiting became illegal in Great Britain. But Bulldog owners wanted to perpetuate their breed, and so there followed a long period during which the breed lost its vicious, aggressive demeanor.

Today the Bulldog is both gentle and affectionate, yet stubborn and determined when it wants to be. Its exaggerated form — long-slung in front, light in rear, pushed-back nose — shows qualities its ancestors needed to adapt to their brutal life as bullbaiters.

HEIGHT: Not specified.

WEIGHT: Maximum for males, 50 pounds; maximum for bitches, 40 pounds.

GAIT: Distinctive, loose roll, shuffling sidewise movement.

COLOR: In order of preference: red brindle; all other brindles; solid white; solid red, fawn, or fallow; piebald; inferior shades of previous colors. A perfect piebald preferred to a muddy brindle. Solid black undesirable, but black may appear in moderate degree in piebald patches. Nose black.

HEAD: Circumference in front of ears at least equals height of dog, forehead flat. **Skull:** Broad, square, stop deep, with median furrow.

Eyes: Low in skull, in line with stop, as wide apart as possible, dark, not showing haw. **Ears:** Rose ears preferred, set wide, as far from eyes as possible. **Nose:** Turned upward, set back deeply between eyes; distance from stop to tip not greater than distance from tip to edge of underlip. **Lower jaw:** Projects, is turned upward; chops overhang lower jaw, meet to cover or nearly cover teeth. **Neck:** Very short, thick. **Teeth:** Large, strong, even bite.

BODY: Body well let down between shoulders, broad behind shoulders, narrow at loins. **Shoulders:** Very heavy, widespread, slanting outward. **Forelegs:** Short, straight, set wide, bowed outline, but not bandy-legged, elbows low, stand out from body, loose. **Chest:** Very broad, deep. **Topline:** Slight fall behind shoulders, rising to loins (higher than shoulders), dropping sharply to tail. **Hindquarters:** Longer than forelegs, stifles turned outward, hocks slightly bent, approaching each other. **Tail:** Hangs low, straight or screwed. **Feet:** Compact, highly knuckled up, forefeet, straight or turned outward, hind feet pointed well outward. **Coat:** Short, straight, lying flat, close.

DISQUALIFICATION: Brown or liver-colored nose.

CHOW CHOW

The Chow Chow, which originated in China, is a descendant of the northern forest and Spitz-type dogs. It dates back to the Western Han Dynasty, about 150 B.C., when it served as a hunting dog. The Chow Chow and the polar bear (no relationship suggested) are said to be the only mammals in the world having a blue tongue. A China specialist whom I have talked with suggests that the blue tongue is a late development in the breed and that the Chow Chow is related to a now–extinct Chinese dog called the Five Pinks. Others propose that the dog's heavy coat was developed in Great Britain.

The first Chows may have been brought to England in 1780, but regular importations did not begin until about 1880. Queen Victoria's interest helped to popularize the breed. Chows were first shown in the United States in 1890.

HEIGHT: Not specified.

WEIGHT: Not specified, but dog is massive in appearance, partly because of its standoff coat.

GAIT: Short and stilted because of straight hocks.

COLOR: Any clear, solid color, with lighter shadings on ruff, tail, and buttocks. Nose black, but blue Chows may have solid blue or slate-colored noses.

HEAD: Large, massive in proportion to dog's size. **Skull:** Broad and flat, well filled under the eyes, moderate stop. **Eyes:** Dark, deep-set. **Ears:** Small, slightly rounded at tips, stiffly erect, set wide apart, forward tilt. **Muzzle:** Short in comparison to skull length, broad, length equals depth. **Teeth:** Scissors bite, tongue blue–black, mouth tissues black. **Neck:** Strong.

BODY: Shoulders: Slightly sloping. **Forelegs:** Straight, upright pasterns, heavy bone. **Chest:** Broad, deep, well-sprung ribs. **Topline:** Short, loins powerful. **Hindquarters:** Straight-hocked, heavy-boned. **Tail:** Set high, carried close to back on spine line. **Feet:** Round, catlike. **Coat:** Dense, straight, standoff coarse in texture, undercoat soft and woolly.

FAULTS: Undershot or overshot, narrow chest, loose elbows, feet turning in or out.

DISQUALIFICATIONS: Nose spotted or other than black except as noted for blue Chows; tongue red, pink, or obviously spotted with red or pink; drop ear or ears. Underside of tongue need not be all there.

DALMATIAN

The Dalmatian supposedly originated in Dalmatia, a region of Yugoslavia on the eastern shore of the Adriatic Sea. The dogs accompanied gypsies on their journeys throughout the world, trotting alongside their wagons. The breed was introduced in England under various names, including English Coach Dog and Plum Pudding Dog. After coaches and carriages were no longer in use, the breed languished for a time.

The Dalmatian has become well known as the traditional firehouse dog. It has also shown exceptional clowning ability in circus acts. Dodie Smith's book and Walt Disney's movie *101 Dalmatians* caused worldwide renewed interest in the breed.

HEIGHT: 19 to 23 inches desirable.
WEIGHT: Not specified.
GAIT: Steady, in rhythm of 1-2-3-4. Legs and feet should not interfere with each other, no weaving or crossing over.
COLOR: Pure white ground color, spotted with black or liver. Spots should be separate and distinct, and should range from dime to half-dollar size. Spots on face, head, ears, legs, and tail smaller than body spots. Nose black in black-spotted dogs, brown in liver–spotted dogs.
HEAD: **Skull:** Flat, broad between ears, free of wrinkles, moderate

stop. **Eyes:** Dark or blue in black-spotted dogs; golden, brown, or blue in livers; eye rims black in black-spotted dogs, brown in livers; never flesh-colored in either. **Ears:** Set high, wide at base, preferably spotted. **Muzzle:** Of fair length. **Teeth:** Scissors bite. **Neck:** Fairly long, arched.

BODY: Shoulders: Oblique, muscular. **Forelegs:** Straight, heavy bone, elbows close. **Chest:** Deep, rather than wide, ribs never barrel. **Topline:** Powerful, loins strong and arched. **Hindquarters:** Muscular, hocks well let down. **Tail:** Reaches to hocks, not set low, carried with slight upward curve. **Feet:** Compact, arched, nails black or white or both in black-spotted dogs, brown or white or both in livers. **Coat:** Short, hard, dense, fine.

FAULTS: Ring or low-set tail, undersize or oversize. **Major faults:** Butterfly or flesh-colored nose, cow hocks, flat feet, lack of pigment in eye rims, shyness, trichiasis (abnormal position or direction of eyelashes).

DISQUALIFICATIONS: Any color or markings other than black or liver, over 24 inches at withers, tricolors, undershot or overshot, patches (a true patch is a solid, sharply defined mass of black or liver, appreciably larger than any of the markings on the dog).

FRENCH BULLDOG

The French Bulldog probably originated in Spain. A bronze plaque — dated Burgos, 1625, and marked "Dogue de Burgos, España — shows an unmistakable Bulldog head, but with bat ears, rather than the rose ears characteristic of the English Bulldog. The dogs were used in bullfighting, and Burgos was the home of the sport.

The breed was taken up by French nobility, and crosses were made with English Bulldogs. Very small English dogs were used for this purpose.

The French Bulldog Club of America was organized in 1898 and was the first club to sponsor the breed. A specialty show was held at the Waldorf-Astoria Hotel that year. In 1913 the breed made history when one hundred dogs were entered at the Westminster show. It was in America that the breed's bat ears were brought to their present perfection.

HEIGHT: Not specified.

WEIGHT: Two classes: lightweight, under 22 pounds; heavyweight, 22 pounds but not over 28.

GAIT: Not specified, but slight roll usually seen, otherwise true.

COLOR: All brindle, fawn, white, brindle and white, or other colors except those that disqualify. Nose black, lighter in lighter-colored dogs.

HEAD: Skull: Flat, but forehead slightly rounded, stop deep. **Muzzle:** Broad, deep, short, laid back. Flews match nose color, are thick, cover lower jaw, meet in front to cover teeth. Underjaw deep, undershot, turned upward. **Eyes:** Dark, set as low as possible in skull, not sunken or bulging, no haw or white showing when dog is looking forward. **Ears:** Bat ears, broad at base, round at top, set high, but not too close, carried erect, with orifice to the front. **Neck:** Thick, arched, loose skin at throat.

BODY: Forelegs: Short, straight, set wide apart. **Chest:** Broad, deep, well ribbed up. **Topline:** Roach back, slight fall behind shoulders, arched at loins, but narrow, belly tucked up. **Hindquarters:** Longer than forelegs in order to arch loins above shoulders, hocks well let down. **Tail:** Short, hung low, straight or screw, not curly. **Feet:** Compact toes, well split up, high knuckles. **Coat:** Fine, short, smooth, skin loose, forming wrinkles on head and shoulders.

DISQUALIFICATIONS: Other than bat ears, black and white, black and tan, liver, mouse, solid black (black means with no trace of brindle), eyes of different colors, nose color except as specified, harelip, any mutilation, over 28 pounds in weight.

KEESHOND

The Keeshond (pronounced *Caze-hawnd,* plural *Keeshonden*) is a Dutch breed of the Spitz family. It was a fairly common dog in the sixteenth and seventeenth centuries. However, towards the end of the eighteenth century, in the great social war in the Netherlands between the partisans of the Prince of Orange and the Patriots, the dog suddenly won national acclaim. The Patriot leader, Kees de Gyselaer, had one of the dogs, which he called Kees. The dog, which was portrayed in cartoons and drawings, was known as Kees' Hound and was regarded as a dog of the people. It has also been called the Dutch Barge Dog.

The breed nearly died out, but it was kept pure by riverboat captains, some of whom kept stud records. The Dutch Baroness van Hardenbroek searched out these dogs and began a large breeding operation. The Dutch Kennel Club accepted the breed in 1933. It appeared in England about 1925, and subsequently came to America.

HEIGHT: At 2 years old, males, 18 inches; bitches, 17 inches, but type considerations take precedence over height.

WEIGHT: Not specified.

GAIT: Should be brisk, with forelegs and hind legs in line.

COLOR: Outer coat a mixture of gray and black, varying from light to dark. No deviation from gray-and-black mixture permitted. Delicate penciling and markings form required spectacles. Tail plume light gray, black-tipped. Hair on legs and feet cream. Undercoat pale gray or cream. Nose and muzzle black.

HEAD: Skull: Wedge-shaped, distinct stop. **Eyes:** Dark, set obliquely, not protruding. **Ears:** Small, triangular, set high, length about distance from outer eye corners to nearest ear edges. **Teeth:** Scissors bite. **Neck:** Arched.

BODY: Forelegs: Straight. **Chest:** Deep, barrel well rounded. **Topline:** Slight slope from withers to rump, moderate tuck-up. **Hindquarters:** Legs of good bone, hocks only slightly bent. **Tail:** Set high, tightly curled over back, lying flat, plume well feathered. **Feet:** Catlike, arched. **Coat:** Outer coat long, straight, harsh, standoff, undercoat thick and downy, profuse mane from under jaw over forechest and shoulders, short on pasterns and hocks.

FAULTS: Silky, wavy, or curly coat; part in coat down back; tail not carried up when dog is moving; ears not erect when dog is at attention; apple head; absence of stop; protruding or light eyes. **Very serious faults:** Entirely black or white, any other solid color.

LHASA APSO

The Lhasa Apso originated in Tibet. There is some confusion regarding the origin of its name. One theory is that it comes from *Abso Seng Kye* ("Bark Lion Sentinel Dog") because the Apso was used to guard the inner courts of dwellings. Another theory is that *Apso* is a corruption of the word *rap-so,* meaning "goatlike" — which is descriptive of the dog's hardy constitution. It is certain that there has been crossbreeding of the Lhasa Apso and the Shih Tzu.

The dogs, along with other Tibetan breeds, arrived in England about 1930 and in America shortly afterward. In England the breed is called the Tibetan Apso. In the United States the breed is placed in the Non-Sporting Group; in Canada, it is in the Terrier Group.

HEIGHT: Males, 10 to 11 inches; bitches, slightly smaller.
WEIGHT: Not specified.
GAIT: Not specified, but good reach in front and excellent drive with hind legs.

COLOR: All colors. Nose black.

HEAD: Skull: Narrow, falling away behind the eyes to a marked degree, not quite flat, foreface straight and of good length (about one third of total length from nose to occiput). **Eyes:** Dark brown, medium size and placement. **Ears:** Pendant, heavily feathered. **Teeth:** Level or slightly undershot.

BODY: Length from point of shoulders to buttocks longer than height at withers. Well ribbed up, strong loins. **Shoulders:** Sloping. **Topline:** Level. **Chest:** Fairly deep. **Forelegs:** Straight. **Hindquarters:** Well developed. **Tail:** Well feathered, carried well over back in a screw, may have a kink at end. **Feet:** Round, catlike, thick pads, well feathered. **Coat:** Heavy head furnishings with good fall over eyes, body coat heavy, straight, hard, of good length, very dense, feathering on legs heavy.

FAULTS: Square muzzle, small or sunken eyes, large and full eyes, a low tail carriage, poorly developed thighs, domed skull.

POODLE (MINIATURE)

The history and standard for the Miniature Poodle are the same as those for the other two varieties of Poodles; only the height differs. (See

Standard Poodle (below); and Toy Poodle, p. 428.) A Miniature Poodle is over 10 inches, up to and including 15 inches, in height. A Poodle disqualified as a Toy because it is over 10 inches tall can compete as a Miniature. But as a small Miniature it might not be able to win in today's heavy Poodle competition. Similarly a dog disqualified as a Miniature because it is too tall can compete as a Standard, but again it is doubtful that such a dog could win.

POODLE (STANDARD)

Many people refer incorrectly to this dog as a French Poodle. In France it is called a *Caniche,* but in Germany the breed has been called a

Wasserhund (water dog) or *Pudel*. (The English name is obviously derived from the German.)

The dog appears to have originally been a retriever of water birds. It later appeared in circuses, where the present system of clipping probably started. Poodles have also been used in France to sniff out the location of the underground delicacy, the truffle.

The Standard Poodle is without question the most barbered dog in the world. Even so, grooming standards in dog shows are strict.

The three sizes or varieties of poodles — Toy, Miniature, and Standard — are registered as one breed. In theory at least, all three stem from common ancestors.

HEIGHT: Over 15 inches.

WEIGHT: Not specified.

GAIT: Straightforward trot, head and tail carried high.

COLOR: An even, solid color at the skin. In blues, grays, silvers, browns, café au laits, apricots, and creams, clear colors are preferred, but coat may show varying shades of the same color without penalty. Brown and café au lait dogs have liver-colored noses, eye rims, and lips, dark nails, and dark amber eyes. Black, blue, gray, silver, cream, and white dogs have black noses, eye rims, and lips, black or self-colored nails, and very dark eyes. Apricots have liver-colored noses, eye rims, and lips; amber eyes are permitted, but not desired.

HEAD: **Skull:** Slightly rounded, about the same length as the muzzle, slight stop. **Eyes:** Set far apart, oval. **Ears:** Set at or below eye level, long, wide, thickly feathered. **Teeth:** Scissors bite. **Neck:** Long, arched.

BODY: Dogs appear square, measured from breastbone to tip of rump and from ground to highest point of withers. **Shoulders:** Laid back, blades about same length as upper arms. **Forelegs:** Straight, parallel. **Chest:** Deep, back short, slightly hollowed, loins short, well muscled. **Hindquarters:** Stifles well bent. **Tail:** Docked, straight, set high, carried up. **Feet:** Small, oval, toes well arched, toes neither in nor out, dewclaws may be removed. **Coat:** Curly, harsh, dense; or corded.

CLIP: Only these clips are recognized in dog show competition: Puppy (for dogs under 1 year old), English Saddle, Continental, and Corded.

PUPPY CLIP: Coat long. Face, throat, feet, base of tail shaved. Pompon left at end of tail. Slight coat shaping permitted, but excessive scissoring to bring dismissal. Dogs 1 year old or older disqualified for this clip.

ENGLISH SADDLE CLIP: Face, throat, feet, forelegs, base of tail shaved, leaving puffs on forelegs and a pompon at end of tail. Hindquarters are left with a short blanket of hair except for a curved, shaved area on each flank and two shaved bands on each hind leg. Rest of body in full coat, but may be shaped.

CONTINENTAL CLIP: Face, throat, feet, and base of tail shaved. Hindquarters are shaved with pompons (optional) on hips. Legs are shaved, leaving bracelets on hindlegs and puffs on forelegs. Pompon at end of tail. Entire shaved foot and a portion of shaved foreleg above the puff are visible. Rest of body in full coat, but may be shaped.

In all clips, topknot may be held in place by a barrette or elastic band. Hair only long enough to present a smooth outline.

CORDED CLIP: Essentially the Continental clip but with hair in unclipped areas allowed to cord.

DISQUALIFICATIONS: Any Poodle that is over or under the specified height limit, a clip other than those listed above, parti-colors (two or more colors at the skin).

SCHIPPERKE

The Schipperke originated in the Flemish areas of Belgium. Its name has been translated to mean "little captain," "little skipper," or "little boatman." The breed was favored by Belgian cobblers, who used to parade their tail-less dogs in Sunday promenades. One theory of the dog's origin is that it is a member of the Spitz family; in fact, Belgian cobblers called their dogs Spitz. Another theory is that the Schipperke descends from a black Belgian sheepdog called the Leauvenaar.

By 1880 the breed had become very popular. The first registration of a Schipperke, a dog named Tip, was in 1882. Monsieur Renssens of Belgium began breeding the dog in 1822 and is considered the father of the breed. American Kennel Club recognition came in 1904.

Schipperkes are often born tail-less. In the United States colors other than black are disqualified, but in Canada and most other countries all solid colors other than white are permitted.

HEIGHT: Not specified.
WEIGHT: Up to 18 pounds.
GAIT: Not specified, but forelegs and hind legs move in line.
COLOR: Solid black. Nose black.
HEAD: Foxlike. **Skull:** Fairly wide, narrowing at eyes, appears slightly rounded when viewed in profile, stop medium to slight. **Eyes:** Dark brown, small, oval, neither protruding nor sunken. **Ears:** Very erect, small, triangular, set high, so strongly made they cannot be lowered except in line with the body. **Muzzle:** Tapers, but neither elongated nor blunt. **Teeth:** Level bite, but tight scissors bite acceptable. **Neck:** Rather short, arched.
BODY: Short, thick-set, broad behind shoulders. **Shoulders:** Sloping. **Forelegs:** Straight, medium bone. **Chest:** Broad, deep. **Topline:** Strong, short, straight, level or slightly sloping from withers to tail set, loins muscular, tuck-up medium. **Hindquarters:** Lighter than forelegs, but muscular and powerful. **Tail:** Docked to no more than 1 inch in length. **Feet:** Small, round, tight, not splayed. **Coat:** Abundant, slightly harsh to touch; short on ears, front of legs, and hocks; fairly short on body, but longer around neck, beginning back of ears, forming a ruff and a cape; a jabot between front legs; and forming a culotte on rear. Culotte should be as long as ruff. Undercoat dense, forcing ruff to stand out.
FAULTS: Light eyes; ears too long or too rounded; head too narrow; elongated or blunt muzzle; domed skull; lack of undercoat; curly or silky coat; body coat more than 3 inches long; slightly overshot or undershot; swayback; straight hocks; straight stifles; cow hocks; feet turning in or out.
DISQUALIFICATIONS: Any color other than solid black, drop or semierect ears, badly overshot or undershot.

TIBETAN TERRIER

An ancestry of nearly two thousand years is claimed for this dog from Tibet. It was kept there at the monasteries in an area known as the Lost Valley. Dr. Greig, an Englishwoman who was practicing medicine in India, went to Tibet, where she was given one of these dogs by the husband of a Tibetan woman she had cured. Back in India Dr. Greig is said to have bred more of them, although where she got her additional breeding stock is unknown. Upon her return to England her family established a kennel.

The breed is sometimes called a Miniature Old English Sheepdog. However, it is not born tail-less, and its tail is not bobbed but carried in a curl over its back. Also, the dog's gait is that of a Terrier, not that of the Old English Sheepdog. The breed was recognized in India in 1920, in England in 1937, and in the United States in 1973.

HEIGHT: 14 to 16 inches.
WEIGHT: Average, 22 to 23 pounds, but may be 18 to 30 pounds.
GAIT: Unspecified.
COLOR: Any color or colors, including white. Nose black.
HEAD: Medium length, with muzzle and skull of equal length, hair to fall forward over eyes, small beard. **Skull:** Medium length, rather flat, stop definite. **Eyes:** Dark, set wide apart, eyelid rims dark. **Ears:** Medium

length, V-shaped, not too large, heavily feathered, rounded tips. **Neck:** Arched. **Teeth:** Level bite preferred.

BODY: Compact and powerful. **Shoulders:** Sloping. **Forelegs:** Straight, connecting to sloping shoulders. **Topline:** Level, length of back from withers to tail equals height at withers. **Hindquarters:** Sturdy, hocks well let down. **Tail:** Medium long, well feathered, carried in curl over back, sometimes kinked at tip. **Feet:** Large, round, well coated with hair between the toes. **Coat:** Double. Undercoat soft and woolly, outer coat long, straight, rather fine in texture.

FAULTS: Any deviation from standard.

chapter forty-one
Miscellaneous Breeds

There was a time when the American Kennel Club might give full recognition to a breed when it could be shown that there were one or two dozen members of the breed in the country. But it is expensive to open the stud book in such cases and to provide regular classes and championships for such breeds at field trials and dog shows. Moreover, there is no certainty that the breed will prosper. Today the American Kennel Club requires that breed fanciers keep their own stud book according to AKC rules, and it may require that as many as 600 properly registered dogs are well scattered over the country. The breeds admitted to the Miscellaneous Class are deemed by the Board of Directors of the AKC to have reached near-recognition status. There must be nationwide interest and activity in the breed, a parent club that promotes the welfare of the breed, and serious, growing breeding programs throughout the country. If these and other conditions have been met, the breed may be granted full recognition. Until then, such breeds are listed in the Miscellaneous Class and are not eligible for championship points.

AUSTRALIAN KELPIE

The word *kelpie* is of Gaelic origin and means "water sprite." And it was a dog named Kelpie that gave her name to the breed. In 1872 Kelpie won the first sheep dog trial ever held in Australia. Kelpie's dam, also called Kelpie, had been mated to a dog named Caesar. Caesar was the son of two dogs called Fox Collies that had been imported from Scotland and that had been mated aboard ship. Two of the pups, including Caesar, were black and tan; the third was red.

It is notable that two black Kelpies will produce both red and black pups, but two red Kelpies will produce only red offspring. The Kelpie is a superb sheep dog and vies with the Border Collie as the most intelligent and most easily trained of all dogs, in the opinion of sheepmen. The present Australian standard was approved in January 1963.

HEIGHT: Males, 18 to 20 inches; bitches, 17 to 19 inches.

WEIGHT: Males, 25 to 30 pounds; bitches, proportionately smaller.

GAIT: Sound, very quick at sudden stops, turning, dropping.

COLOR: Black, black and tan, red, red and tan, fawn chocolate, and smoke blue. Nose black, blue, or brown to conform to body color.

HEAD: Skull: Slightly rounded, broad between ears, stop pronounced. **Muzzle:** Tapers, refined in comparison with skull. **Eyes:** Brown, lighter in blues. **Ears:** Pricked, including outward. **Teeth:** Scissors bite. **Neck:** Fair length, arched.

BODY: Shoulders: Close-set at withers, sloping. **Forelegs:** Straight, refined bone, well muscled. **Chest:** Deep, rather than wide. **Topline:** Level, loins well muscled, little tuck-up, rump broad, sloping, set at corresponding angle to shoulders. **Hindquarters:** Broad and muscular, stifles well turned, hocks well let down. **Tail:** Reaches hocks, not carried above back. **Feet:** Round, deep, arched. **Coat:** Outer coat moderately short, flat, straight; undercoat dense, forms brush on tail.

FAULTS: Unsoundness, ponderous gait, cow or bow hocks, out at elbows, weaving gait, lack of alertness, intractable disposition.

BORDER COLLIE

The Border Collie and the Australian Kelpie are without question the world's finest sheep dogs. Border Collies have been competing in sheep dog trials in Scotland and England since 1873, only a year after the first trials in Australia. They have been known as Farm Collies and Working Collies. They are not seen in dog shows in Great Britain, and they can enter only in the Miscellaneous Class in the United States. However, they do compete for show championships in Australia.

In most countries the breed has its own stud book registry, and dogs are not registered until they have proven themselves at herding. Sheep dog trials are held in both Canada and the United States. To watch these dogs work is to watch a miracle.

HEIGHT: Males, 18 inches; bitches, 17 inches. In Australia, standard is 2 inches taller for both sexes.

WEIGHT: Males, 35 to 45 pounds; bitches, slightly smaller.

GAIT: True, with remarkable dexterity at sprinting, sudden stops, turns, and dropping.

COLOR: Usually black and white, sometimes gray and white or blue merle and white, and rarely black, white, and tan. Nose black.

HEAD: Skull: Broad between ears, moderate stop. **Eyes:** Large, dark, set wide. **Ears:** Medium size, broad at base, carried semiprick. **Muzzle:** Slightly blunt. **Teeth:** Scissors bite. **Neck:** Long, arched, muscular.

BODY: Slightly longer than height. **Shoulders:** Sloping. **Forelegs:** Straight, muscular. **Chest:** Deep, reaching to elbows. **Topline:** Level to loins, then slight muscular arch. **Hindquarters:** Heavily muscled, well angulated at stifle and hock joints. **Tail:** Thick brush, set low, with upward swirl, never carried above back. **Feet:** Oval, well-arched toes. **Coat:** Long, silky.

FAULTS: Coarseness, weediness, lumbering gait, flat or splayed feet, shyness, viciousness, lack of alertness.

CAVALIER KING CHARLES SPANIEL

The much smaller, short-nosed King Charles English Toy Spaniel has been known for centuries, but it was not shown until 1920. An American named Eldridge began to offer large prizes at English shows, starting at Cruft's, for an old-fashioned, long-nosed, sound, diminutive version of the Cocker Spaniel. A breed club was formed in 1928, and the English Kennel Club gave the Cavalier King Charles Spaniel official recognition in 1944.

The Cavalier King Charles Spaniel remains in the Miscellaneous Class at American Kennel Club shows because careful breeders refuse formal recognition. They choose to maintain their own stud book and conduct their own championship shows. The breed is fully recognized in Canada and Australia.

HEIGHT: 12 to 13 inches, either sex.
WEIGHT: 13 to 18 pounds, either sex.
GAIT: True Sporting Dog movement.
COLOR: Black and tan, ruby (whole-colored, rich red), Blenheim (white ground color with rich chestnut markings, red ears, white blaze between the ears in the center of which is the Blenheim spot), tricolor (white ground color, jet black markings, and tan markings over eyes, inside of ears).
HEAD: **Skull:** Slightly rounded, appearing flat because of high ear carriage, shallow stop. **Eyes:** Large, round, dark, luminous. **Ears:** Set high, long, well feathered. **Muzzle:** Tapered, 1½ inches from stop to tip or longer. **Teeth:** Scissors or level bite. **Neck:** Long, arched, not throaty.
BODY: **Shoulders:** Moderately sloping. **Forelegs:** Straight, elbows tight. **Chest:** Moderately wide, deep. **Topline:** Level, loins muscular, little tuck-up. **Hindquarters:** Well angulated at stifle and hock joints. **Feet:** Compact. **Tail:** Set and carried level with the back. If docked, only one third removed; in broken colors, docked to leave white tip. **Coat:** Long, silky, waves but not curls permitted.
FAULTS: Straight stifles, cow hocks, weak pasterns, open feet, out at elbows, barrel-chested, curly coat, weedy specimens, white marks on whole-colored dogs, heavy ticking on Blenheims and tricolors.

MINIATURE BULL TERRIER

Although there are various histories of the Miniature Bull Terrier, it seems likely that this dog is simply a smaller white Bull Terrier. (The two breeds bear a close physical resemblance.) After 1900, special classes were given for Bull Terriers weighing under 16 pounds, but these classes were seldom filled with dogs that qualified. Efforts to maintain the smaller dogs at between 12 and 14 pounds or even under 16 pounds were unsuccessful.

A breed standard was set up in England, and the English Kennel Club gave official recognition in 1943. The present American standard is 18 pounds.

HEIGHT: Not to exceed 14 inches, either sex.
WEIGHT: Not to exceed 20 pounds.
GAIT: Gait is free, but springy.
COLOR: White or with patches of color, preferably brindle. Nose black.
HEAD: Skull: Oval or egg-shaped, particularly when viewed in profile, well filled under the eyes, entirely lacking in stop. **Muzzle:** Not snipy, underjaw deep and strong. **Eyes:** Sunken, obliquely set, dark. **Ears:** Small, thin, stiffly erect. **Teeth:** Level or scissors bite. **Neck:** Moderately long, arched, tight skinned.
BODY: Shoulders: Sloping. **Forelegs:** Straight, elbows close to body, nearly upright pasterns. **Chest:** Rounded and deep. **Topline:** Flat, except for

slight loin arch, little tuck-up. **Hindquarters:** Well angulated at stifle and hock joints. **Tail:** Short, set low, heavy at root, tapering, carried horizontally off the body. **Feet:** Round, catlike, compact, with highly arched toes. **Coat:** Short, tight-fitting, harsh to touch.

FAULTS: Any deviations from standard.

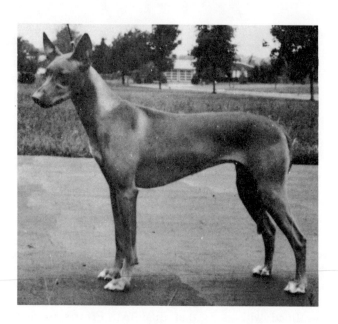

PHARAOH HOUND

The Pharaoh Hound was added to the list of breeds eligible to be shown in the Miscellaneous Class at dog shows on January 1, 1979. The dog belongs to the sight hound, or coursing, group, and traces its origin back to ancient Egypt.

HEIGHT: 23 to 25 inches for males; 21 to 24 inches for bitches.

WEIGHT: Not specified.

GAIT: Free and flowing, with head held high; legs and feet should move in line with the body; any tendency to throw the feet sideways, or a high stepping "hackney" action is a fault.

COLOR: Ranging from tan to rich tan to chestnut with white markings as follows: White tip on tail desired; white on chest (called "the Star"); white on toes and slim white snip on center line of face permissible; flecking or other white undesirable. Nose flesh colored.

HEAD: Skull: Long, lean, and chiselled. Foreface slightly longer than the skull; top of skull parallel with the foreface to represent a blunt wedge. Slight stop. **Eyes:** Oval, moderately deep, amber. **Ears:** Medium high set, carried erect when alert, but very mobile, broad at the base. **Teeth:** Scissors bite. **Neck:** Long, lean and muscular with a slight arch and clean throat line.

BODY: Length from breast to haunch bone slightly longer than height of withers to ground. **Shoulders:** Sloping, strong without being loaded. **Chest:** Deep brisket almost to point of elbow. **Topline:** Almost straight with slight slope from croup to tail. Moderate tuck-up. **Forelegs:** Straight and parallel. Elbows well tucked in, pasterns strong. **Hindquarters:** Strong with moderate anulation, well developed second thigh, parallel. **Feet:** Neither cat nor hare but well knuckled, paws well padded, dewclaws may be removed. **Tail:** Medium set, fairly thick at the base and tapering whip-like, reaching below the hock in repose, curved when in action, should not be tucked between the legs. A screw tail is a fault. **Coat:** Short and glossy, ranging from fine and close to slightly harsh with no feathering.

FAULTS: "Hackney" action, screw tail, accidental blemishes should not be considered as faults, any deviation from standard must be penalized.

SPINONE ITALIANO

The Spinone Italiano is an all-purpose sportsman's dog that was developed in Italy. Many European sportsmen desired a dog that could be used for pointing upland game birds, tracking larger game, and retrieving waterfowl from rivers and lakes. Spanish and European Pointers were accordingly crossed with Hounds. To get a coarse, weather-resistant wire coat, Griffons were added.

The Spinone Italiano was the result. It probably reached perfection in the Piedmont region of northern Italy. The Spinone Italiano has been slow to catch on in the American sporting scene.

HEIGHT: 20 to 26 inches, with 24 to 25 inches average.
WEIGHT: Averages 56 pounds.
GAIT: Normal for a Sporting Dog.
COLOR: All white or white with yellow or light brown. Nose flesh-colored or light brown.
HEAD: Long. **Skull:** Moderately wide, slightly domed, shallow stop. **Eyes:** Light brown or yellow, set under bushy eyebrows. **Ears:** Large, hanging close to cheeks. **Muzzle:** Long, square. **Teeth:** Level bite. **Neck:** Arched.
BODY: **Shoulders:** Sloping. **Forelegs:** Straight, rather long. **Chest:** Deep, but not too broad. **Topline:** Strong and straight, but arched over loins. **Hindquarters:** Muscular and well angulated at stifle and hock joints. **Tail:** Docked, carried at back level or slightly upward. **Feet:** Round, toes close, high arched. **Coat:** Rather short, rough, hard, wiry, undercoat smooth and dense, bushy over eyes.
FAULTS: Any deviations from standard and from soundness.

TIBETAN SPANIEL

The Tibetan Spaniel is, as its name suggests, a small Spaniel-type dog from Tibet. It is called a Spaniel just as the Pekingese was once called a Spaniel. A few of the dogs reached Britain about 1900. However, no progress was made until 1934, when the English Kennel Club gave the breed separate classification. Most of those that have come since, either to Britain or to America, have come by way of Sikkim or Nepal, and Indian traders brought some into northern India.

In 1977 the American Kennel Club felt that sufficient numbers had been brought to the United States to place the breed in the Miscellaneous Class. If larger numbers appear, and the breeders' private stud book records are accurate, full recognition for the Tibetan Spaniel will follow.

HEIGHT: Ideal, 10 inches.
WEIGHT: 9 to 15 pounds.
GAIT: Quick-moving, straight, free.
COLOR: All colors and mixtures of colors. White markings permitted on feet. Nose black.
HEAD: Small in proportion to body. **Skull:** Slightly domed, stop slight, but present. **Eyes:** Dark, oval, set fairly well apart, eye rims black. **Ears:** Medium, pendant, set high, slight lift, but do not "fly." **Muzzle:** Medium length, blunt, free of wrinkle. **Teeth:** Slightly undershot, evenly placed, full dentition desired, teeth not to show when jaws are closed. **Neck:** Short, covered with a shawl or mane.

BODY: Longer than height. **Shoulders:** Sloping. **Chest:** Deep. **Topline:** Level. **Forelegs:** Slightly bowed. **Hindquarters:** Moderate angulation at stifles, hocks well let down. **Feet:** Harefeet, small, feathering between the toes. **Tail:** Set high, richly plumed, gay curl over back when dog is moving. **Coat:** Double. Outer coat silky, moderate body length, lying flat, smooth on face and front legs, except back side of legs well feathered, ears well feathered, buttocks and longer tail hair. Males have longer hair than bitches.

FAULTS: Large, full eyes; broad, flat muzzle; very domed or flat, wide skull; deep stop; weak or wrinkled muzzle; overshot mouth; very bowed forelegs; straight stifles; cow hocks; protruding tongue; light eyes; long, plain, down face without stop; cat feet; nervousness.

chapter forty-two
Rare Breeds

There are literally several hundred rare breeds in the world. Here I have selected half a dozen that should prove to be of interest to American and Canadian readers. These breeds may become sufficiently popular to enter the Miscellaneous Class and later gain official recognition in the AKC Stud Book.

AUSTRALIAN SHEPHERD

If you ask an Australian sheepman or cattle man about the Australian Shepherd, he will look at you blankly and say that he has never heard of the breed and that no such breed exists in Australia. He will be right. Actually there are a number of theories about this breed's origin. One is that Basque shepherds brought their dogs to Australia, left after a few years, taking their dogs with them, and moved to the American West.

A second theory is that bobtailed Smithfield cattle dogs in Australia were crossed with a Dingo by a man named Timmins. His dogs were called Timmins Biters. Some believe that smooth-haired blue merle Collies were added about 1840; others say that a wolflike merle or grizzle dog known as a German Coulie was added. Their owners then came to America with the dogs. (For the history of the Australian Cattle Dog, see p. 333.)

For many years the Australian Shepherd was registered in a privately owned stud book in the United States. Now there is a national parent club, the Australian Shepherd Club of America, and the breed is working toward AKC recognition.

HEIGHT: 18 to 23 inches, but 21 inches ideal.
WEIGHT: Not specified.
GAIT: Quick, true, agile at turns and stops.
COLOR: Blue or red merle, black, all with or without tan markings. Eyes and ears entirely surrounded with color other than white. Nose black, liver in red and red grizzle dogs.
HEAD: Head and muzzle nearly equal length. **Skull:** Flat or slightly domed. **Eyes:** Set wide apart, may be blue, brown, one of each, or blue flecked with brown, neither too prominent nor too sunken. **Ears:** Tips carried forward, breaking one to three quarters above base. **Teeth:** Scissors bite. **Neck:** Arched, free of throatiness, moderate ruff.
BODY: Shoulders: Sloping. **Forelegs:** Straight, pasterns slightly sloped. **Chest:** Deep, ribs well sprung, but not barrel-chested. **Topline:** Level, loins powerful, croup sloping. **Tail:** Natural bob, or docked if long. **Hindquarters:** Stifles well angulated, hocks well let down, placed slightly under the body. **Feet:** Oval, strongly arched toes. **Coat:** Moderate length, undercoat short and thick, shorter hair on head, ears, feet, front of forelegs.
DISQUALIFICATION: More than one third white.

CANAAN DOG

Pariah Dogs, to which there are references in the Bible, have existed in a semiwild state for at least four thousand years, living by their wits in a generally inhospitable land. They are closely related to the first domesticated dogs.

An authority on the senses of dogs, Mrs. Rudolphina Menzel, came to Israel from Austria. She began to breed and train Pariah Dogs for messenger, Red Cross, and mine-detecting work. By 1948 she had a fixed type, a breed now known as the Canaan Dog. This breed has been winning gradual acceptance in the United States because of its intelligence and trainability.

HEIGHT: 19 to 24 inches, either sex.
WEIGHT: 40 to 60 pounds.
GAIT: True, long reach, legs move in line when dog is at a fast trot.
COLOR: All shades of brown (sandy to reddish), black, and solid colors with white. White with large markings of black, brown, or red is desirable. Gray not permitted. Facial mask. Nose dark.
HEAD: Skull and muzzle equal in length, or muzzle slightly shorter. **Skull:** Stop medium. **Eyes:** The darker the better, slightly slanted. **Ears:** Prick desired, tips slightly rounded, set low. **Muzzle:** Blunt, lips tight, well pigmented, not pendulous. **Teeth:** Scissors bite. **Neck:** Arched, not heavy.

BODY: Shoulders: Sloping. **Chest:** Reaches to elbows, belly well tucked up. **Topline:** Level, not falling at croup, which is broad. **Forelegs:** Straight, medium bone. **Hindquarters:** Heavily muscled, well angulated at stifles, never cow-hocked or bowed. **Feet:** Catlike, well up on pasterns. **Tail:** Set high, bushy, curled over back. **Coat:** Short.

FAULTS: Gray and/or brindle, white mask, aggressiveness toward people.

LOWCHEN

The Lowchen, whose name means "little lion," is a lively little dog belonging to the Bichon family. Only recently it was the rarest breed in the world, but now it is rapidly gaining in popularity. The British standard is given here, but the parent club is asking for a weight increase to 12 pounds and to permit lighter-colored noses in dogs other than black.

HEIGHT: 8 to 14 inches.
WEIGHT: 4 to 9 pounds.
GAIT: Not specified, but lively and straightforward.
COLOR: Any color permissible. White, black, and lemon gold are most sought-after. Nose black.
HEAD: Short. **Skull:** Wide in proportion to length. **Eyes:** Round, large, intelligent, dark in color. **Ears:** Pendant, long, well fringed. **Teeth:** Not specified.
BODY: Short, well proportioned. **Shoulders:** Not specified. **Forelegs:** Straight and fine-boned. **Hindquarters:** Straight when viewed

from rear, with good turn of stifles. **Tail:** Medium length, curves over back, clipped with tuft left on end to form pompon. **Feet:** Small and round. **Coat:** Fairly long and wavy, but not curly, hindquarters and legs clipped in Poodle-fashion (Continental), hair left on lower legs and feet.

FAULTS: Any departure from standard, to be judged according to the seriousness of the departure.

PORTUGUESE WATER DOG

This breed is known in Portugal as the Cao d'Agua de Pêlo Ondulado (long-coated variety) and Cao d'Agua de Pêlo Encaracolado (curly-coated variety). As far back as the fourteenth century these dogs were companions and helpers to Portuguese fishermen because they were adept swimmers. As methods of fishing changed, the breed began to decline in numbers and was chiefly found in Portugal's Algarve region. It is almost certainly related to the Poodle and may be an ancestor of the Irish Water Spaniel. The long-haired variety is the better known.

Americans discovered the breed and began importing dogs from Portugal in 1970. Today there are more of the dogs in the United States than in Portugal, and progress toward recognition is rapid. The Portuguese Water Dog is intelligent, gentle, and an exceptional swimmer. It is also easily trained.

HEIGHT: 20 inches ideal.
WEIGHT: 40 pounds ideal.
GAIT: Not specified.

COLOR: Black, white, various tones of brown, and combinations of black and brown with white. Skin is usually bluish. Nose black, brown in brownish-colored dogs.

HEAD: **Skull:** Slightly longer than muzzle, occiput pronounced, stop well defined, median skull furrow. **Eyes:** Medium size, set well apart and slightly oblique, eyelids black, no haw. **Ears:** Heart-shaped, thin, set above eye level, tips should not reach below neckline, well feathered. **Muzzle:** Narrows slightly to nose, lips thick, inner corner not to show when jaws are closed, roof of mouth and under tongue black or black-ticked. **Teeth:** Scissors or even bite. **Neck:** Rounded, short, held high.

BODY: **Shoulders:** Well angulated. **Forelegs:** Parallel, may be held slightly forward of perpendicular, pasterns strong. **Chest:** Reaches to elbows, ribs well sprung. **Topline:** Short, level, croup slightly inclined, wide, well fleshed. **Hindquarters:** May be inclined slightly forward of hocks, which are set under. **Tail:** Not to reach below hock joints. **Feet:** Round, rather flat, toes webbed, nails slightly turned up, nails black or to match coat color. **Coat:** Profuse, adult coat trimmed Poodle-fashion (Continental), clipped from middle of chest back, tail tuft left on, feet and legs clipped clean.

DISQUALIFICATIONS: Very long, narrow, flat, or pointed head; muzzle funnel-shaped or too pointed; nose flesh-colored or discolored in whole or in part; eyes light-colored, differing in form or size, sunken, or too prominent; ears set incorrectly, too large, too small, or having folds; deafness, either inherited or acquired; tail docked, rudimentary, or nonexistent; tail heavy, droopy in action, or held perpendicular; dewclaws on hind legs; coat other than described; albinism (white with red eyes and reddish skin color); overshot or undershot.

TELOMIAN

The Telomian, originally discovered in the jungles of Malaysia, bears a resemblance to the Basenji of Africa and the Dingo of Australia. A wrinkled forehead, erect ears, an annual breeding cycle, and vocalization are similar for these three breeds.

Dr. Orville Elliot, a doctoral student of Anthropology at Harvard University, found Telomian dogs along the Telom River in Malaysia in 1963. He sent a pair to Dr. John P. Scott at the Jackson Memorial Laboratory at Bar Harbor, Maine, where canine behavioral studies were underway.

Dr. Scott, a world-famous student of canine behavior, became interested in them and began a breeding colony. He took the dogs with him to Bowling Green State University in Ohio in 1965. Others became interested and a Telomian Dog Club of America was organized in September 1970.

The dog's voice, between a bark and a howl, is called a *crow*. The breed has a catlike ability to use its paws.

HEIGHT: 15 to 19 inches.
WEIGHT: 18 to 28 pounds.
GAIT: Single track.
COLOR: Shades of sable and white.
HEAD: Skull: Medium to wide width, square from ears to eyes, wrinkles should appear on forehead and temples. **Neck:** Arched, slightly full at base of throat. **Ears:** Pointed and erect. **Eyes:** Dark pigmented lids, almond-shaped. **Nose:** Black. **Mouth:** Direct or scissors bite.

BODY: Firm, muscular, elongated. **Chest:** Deep, ribs well sprung. **Topline:** Straight with pelvis, slightly higher. **Forequarters:** Straight. **Hindquarters:** Strong and muscular. **Feet:** Moderate size, well arched toes. **Coat:** Short and smooth. **Tail:** Carried gaily over the back.

FAULTS: Walleye or no pigment in eye, dewlap, tail tightly curled.

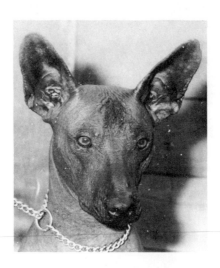

XOLOITZCUINTLI

This is perhaps the best known of a group of hairless or nearly hairless dogs that includes the Peruvian Orchid, Mexican Hairless, Turkish Naked Dog, and Chinese Crested Dog. The Mexican Hairless was recognized by the American Kennel Club in 1883. Recognition has now been withdrawn in the United States due to the decline of interest and breeding, although it continues in Canada.

The Xoloitzcuintli is Mexican in origin, but it cannot have been the animal of that name which the conquistadores found in Mexico, an animal said to have been four feet long. However, there was a hairless dog called the Pelon along the Mexican-American border in the first quarter of the nineteenth century. Its size indicates that it may have been the dog now called Xoloitzcuintli.

Like other hairless dogs, the "Cholo" is missing its side teeth. Because the dog has no insulating blanket of hair, its skin feels hot to the touch, a fact that has given rise to the erroneous impression that its temperature is higher than that of other dogs. The breed is recognized by the Mexican Kennel Club and the Fédération Cynologique Internationale, in Belgium.

HEIGHT: 12 to 20 inches.

WEIGHT: Unspecified.

COLOR: Elephant gray, uniform dark bronze, black, or pink and brown blotched.

HEAD: **Ears:** Erect, nearly four inches long. **Muzzle:** Longer than the skull.

BODY: Well made; legs and feet are sound; a few bristles of hair are sometimes found on the forehead and feet.

DISQUALIFICATIONS: Hanging ears, cut or broken tail, albinism.

Appendixes

Glossary of Dog Show Terms

Almond eyes: Eyes set in tissue of almond shape.
Angulation: The angles formed by bones of the shoulders and upper arms and the upper and lower thigh bones.
Apple head: A domed but irregularly shaped skull.
Apron: Long hair on the lower throat and chest of some dogs.
Barrel-chested: Ribs sprung into a rounded, barrel shape.
Bat ear: Erect, broad-based ear with rounded tip, as in the French Bulldog.
Belton: Mixture of colored and white hairs giving a somewhat smoky effect.
Bench show: A dog show in which the dogs in competition are confined in stalls mounted on platforms.
Bilateral cryptorchid: A dog with neither testicle descending into the scrotum.
Bitch: Female dog.
Bite: Position of upper and lower jaws and teeth. (See also *level bite, scissors bite, pig jaw, undershot, overshot.*)
Blanket: A solid color stretching from neck to tail and down the sides.
Blaze: White stripe between the eyes.
Bloom: Said of a coat in perfect health.
Blue merle: Blue and gray mixed with black. Also called *marbled.*
Bone: The relative size of the leg bones in circumference.
Brace: Two dogs shown together.
Brindle: Tawny ground color with streaks of black; black hairs with lighter streaks of tan, brown, or gray.
Brisket: Body below the chest and between the ribs.
Broken-haired: Roughed-up wire coat.
Broken-up face: Receding nose with deep stop, as in the Pekingese.
Brush: A bushy tail.
Burr: Irregular formation in the cup of the ear.

Butterfly nose: Dark-colored nose spotted with pink or flesh color.

Button ear: Ear folding forward, tip touching skull, pointing toward eye.

Canidae: The group that comprises true dogs, wolves, coyotes, foxes, and so on.

Canines: Fangs; long, pointed teeth; two in each jaw.

Castrate: To remove the testicles of the male.

Cat foot: Rounded, compact foot with short third digits.

Chalk: Drying powder.

Champion (Ch.):   Title given to a dog that wins 15 championship points, twice with 3 points or better, under different judges in conformation competition.

Chest: The part of the body enclosed by the ribs.

China eye: A clear blue eye.

Chiseled: Clean-cut head, especially below the eyes.

Chops: Pendulous flesh of lips and jaw, as in the Bulldog.

Clip: Pattern of trimming the dog, as in the Poodle.

Cloddy: Low-set, heavy, clumsy mover.

Close-coupled: Short between neck and hipbones; sometimes said of dogs short between the last rib and the thigh.

Coarse: Not refined; rough.

Cobby: Short-backed.

Collar: White neck band of hair.

Companion Dog (CD):   Title given to a dog that wins three legs in Novice Class obedience competitions.

Companion Dog Excellent (CDX):   Title given to a dog that wins three legs in Open Class obedience competitions.

Conformation: Arrangement of parts according to the breed standard; a dog's form and structure.

Coupling: Body between the ribs and pelvis; also the loin.

Cow hocks: When the hock joints turn inward, forcing lower legs and feet to point outward, rather than in line with the body.

Crop: To cut and trim the ears.

Croup: The rump; the hind part of the back.

Cryptorchid: Unilateral, one testicle undescended into the scrotum; bilateral, neither testicle descended.

Culotte: Long, heavy hair on the back of the thighs.

Cushion: Thickness of upper lip, as in the Boxer and Pekingese.

Dam: The mother of puppies.

Dappled: Mottled markings with no color predominating.

Dewclaw: Useless, rudimentary fifth (in some breeds, fifth and sixth) toe.

Dewlap: Pendulous skin under the throat.

Dish-faced: Concave nasal bone between stop and nose tip; the opposite of Roman-nosed.

Distemper teeth: Pitted or discolored teeth, the result of distemper, nutritional deficiencies, or other diseases.

Dock: To shorten or remove the tail.

Dog: A male dog; also used as a general term for the genus.

Domed: Evenly rounded top skull.

Double coat: A soft, dense undercoat covered with a heavier coat of guard hairs.

Down-faced: Muzzle inclining downward from the stop or from the skull above the eyes.

Down in pastern: Pastern, or metacarpus, set at a pronounced angle from the vertical; sometimes, fallen pastern.

Drop ears: The ends of the ears fall or droop forward.

Dry neck: Skin tight to the neck.

Dual champion: A dog that has won both conformation and field trial championships.

Dudley nose: Flesh-colored.

Elbow: Joint between upper arm and forearm.

Ewe neck: A weak, concave neck.

Eyeteeth: The upper canines.

Fall: Hair falling over the face.

Fangs: The four long canine teeth.

Fawn: A color ranging from cream to deep gold.

Feathering: Fringe hair on the ear tips, legs, body, and tail.

Fiddle front: Out at elbows, pasterns close, feet turned out.

Flank: The sides of the body between the last rib and the hip.

Flare: A blaze that widens on the skull.

Flat bone: Leg bones whose girth is elliptical.

Flews: Upper lips pendulous, especially at the corners.

Flying ears: Ears that should fold but stand straight up instead.

Forearm: The foreleg between the elbow and pastern.

Foreface: The front part of the head; muzzle.

Foul color: Color not characteristic of the breed.

Frog face: Extended nose, receding jaw, undershot mouth.

Furnishings: Long hair on certain breeds.

Furrow: Median line indentation down the center of the skull.

Futurity Stake: A competition at a show or field trial for which the young dogs were nominated at or before birth.

Gait: Dog's movement at various speeds; sometimes used as a command: "Gait your dog."

Gay tail: One carried above the back line.

Goose rump: A steep or falling croup.

Guard hairs: Long, straight, slightly harsh hair that grows through the undercoat.

Hackles: Hair on the neck and back raised in fright or anger.

Hackney: Raising the front legs high when trotting; wasted energy.

Harefoot: A long foot, with long third digits.

Harlequin: Patched colors, usually black and white, often including an undesirable gray or blue merle.

Haw: A third eyelid that is exposed when the lower lid drops.

Heat: Mating cycle in the female; estrus.

Hock: The tarsus bones of the hind leg forming the joint between the second thigh and the metatarsus; the heel.

Hucklebones: The tops of the hipbones.

Inbreeding: A contraction of "incestuous breeding"; the mating of very closely related dogs—for example, brother and sister.

Incisors: The teeth between the canines in both jaws.

Isabella: Fawn or light gray color seen in some Doberman Pinschers.

Kiss marks: Tan spots on the cheeks and above the eyes.

Knuckling over: Structural fault of the wrist that permits it to double forward; permitted in the Harrier.

Lay back: Angle from vertical of the shoulder blade.

Leather: The flesh of the ear flap.

Level bite: Upper and lower incisors meet edge to edge.

Linebreeding: Mating within a family but not as close as inbreeding.

Lippy: Pendulous, loose-fitting lips.

Liver: Deep reddish brown, often shining.

Loaded shoulders: Shoulder blades apart at withers by overdeveloped muscles.

Loin: Area on each side of the spinal column between last ribs and hips.

Lumber: Too much fat.

Mane: Long hair on the neck.

Mantle: Dark, shaded color on the shoulders and back.

Mask: Dark shading on the foreface.

Match show: Usually an informal dog show at which championship points are not awarded.

Merle: Blue–gray color with flecks of black.

Miscellaneous Class: Competition class at shows for dogs that are purebred but not sufficiently numerous to have complete AKC recognition and be included in one of the six breed groupings.

Mismarks: Improper color markings in some breeds.

Molera: Misspelling of the Spanish word for fontanel, the hole in the head caused by failure of skull bones to unite; seen in the Chihuahua.

Occiput: Upper, back point of the skull, which protrudes in some dogs.

Open Class: Competition class at shows in which all dogs 6 months or over, including champions, and foreign-bred dogs can enter.

Otter tail: Very thick at the root, round, tapering hair parted on the under side; desired in the Labrador Retriever.

Outcrossing: Mating unrelated dogs of the same breed.

Overhang: Pronounced brow, as in the Pekingese.

Overshot: Upper incisors overlap lower ones, leaving a gap between.

Pace: Feet on one side move forward at same time, followed by those on the other side.

Paddling: Moving with forefeet swinging wide.

Pads: The tough soles of the feet.

Paper feet: Thin pads, usually combined with flat toes.

Pastern: Area between the wrist and the toes.

Penciling: Black lines dividing the tan on the toes of a Manchester Terrier.

Pied: Large patches of two or more colors; parti-colored.

Pig jaw: Severely overshot.

Pigeon breast: Protruding breastbone.

Points: A color on the face, legs, tail, and so on, that contrasts with the body color.

Pompon: Shaped tuft of hair left on the tail of a Poodle.

Premium list: A brochure listing the details for a forthcoming dog show.

Prick ear: Carried erect and pointed at the tip.

Professional handler: A person who is paid a fee by owners for showing their dogs.

Puppy: A dog under 12 months old.

Purebred: A dog whose ancestors have belonged to the same breed for many generations.

Put down: To prepare a dog for a show; also refers to a dog that does not place in competition. It is used colloquially to mean euthanasia.

Rat tail: Thick hair at the base, growing hairless toward the end.

Ring tail: Tail carried up and around, in the shape of a circle.

Roach back: Convex curvature of the spine toward the loin.

Roan: A fine mixture of colored and white hairs, such as blue roan.

Roman nose: A convex curvature of the nasal bone from stop to nose tip.

Rose ear: Drop ear that folds over toward the back to show the burr.

Ruff: Thick mane of neck hair.

Saber tail: Carried in a semicircle.

Sable: A lacing of black hairs over a lighter ground color, which may be brown, from golden to mahogany, in the Collie and the Shetland Sheepdog.

Scissors bite: The outer side of the lower incisors touches the inner side of the upper ones.

Sedge: The deadgrass color seen in the Chesapeake Bay Retriever.

Semiprick ears: Erect, with only the tips falling slightly forward.

Shelly: A dog without sufficient bone or depth of chest and narrow-bodied.

Sickle tail: Carried up in a semicircle.

Single track: Gait in which the forelegs and hind legs move in parallel planes.

Sire: The male parent.

Snipy: A pointed, narrow, and weak muzzle.

Spay: To remove the ovaries of the female; ovariectomy.

Specialty Show: Competition in which only one breed competes.

Splay foot: An open, flat foot in which the toes spread widely.

Squirrel tail: Carried in a curve forward over the back.

Standoff coat: One in which the outer guard hairs stand off from the body.

Staring coat: A harsh, dry coat; in some breeds, curling at the hair tips.

Stern: The tail, usually spoken of a Sporting Dog or Hound.

Stifle: The dog's knee; the joint between the thigh and the second thigh.

Stop: Indentation between the muzzle and forehead.

Straight stifle: Lack of angulation between the two thighs.

Supercilliary arches: The ridge or prominence of the frontal bones over the eyes.

Swayback: Concave curvature of the spine between withers and hips.

Team: Four dogs shown together.

Thumb marks: Black spots on the front of the pasterns.

Ticked: Small areas of colored hair on a white dog.

Trace: A dark stripe down the spine of a Pug.

Tracking Dog (TD):   A title given to a dog that passes the AKC tracking test.

Tricolor: White, black, and tan.

Trumpet: Small depression on the side of the dog's skull, just behind the eye socket.

Tuck-up: Shallow belly back of the chest.

Tulip ear: Ears carried slightly forward.

Turn-up: Foreface tilted upward.

Undershot: Lower incisors project beyond the upper ones when the mouth is closed.

Unbenched show: Dog show in which the dogs are required only to appear in a ring for judging.

Upper arm: The humerus; foreleg bone between the shoulder blade and the elbow.

Utility Dog (UD):   A title given to a dog that has won three legs toward the title in Utility Class obedience competition.

Variety group: Refers to Sporting, Hound, Working, Terrier, Toy, and Non-Sporting breeds classifications.

Vent: The rectal or anal opening.

Walleye: A whitish iris; a blue eye.

Weaving: Crossing of the forefeet and hind feet when trotting.

Weedy: Lacking in sufficient bone.

Wheel back: The arched back line seen in many racing dogs.

Withers: The highest point of the shoulders at the junction with the neck.

Wrinkle: Folding, loose skin on the forehead and foreface.

Wry mouth: Lower jaw out of line with upper jaw; often one side meets upper jaw, but the other does not.

Glossary of Field and Hunting Terms

Babbler:　A Hound that barks on trail; also can refer to a dog that should hunt silently but does not.

Back:　A brace dog honors its mate's point by also pointing.

Back cast:　Casting back over territory already covered; casting behind a handler.

Bay:　Voice of a Hound on a hot trail.

Blinker:　A dog that points a bird but then leaves it; a Spaniel that, upon sighting game, does not go in to flush it.

Bolt:　To startle an animal from its burrow or earth.

Brace:　A pair or a couple of dogs.

Breaking shot:　Failure to remain on point after the shot; a Spaniel that chases the bird after the shot and before being ordered to retrieve.

Bye:　The odd dog in a field trial series after the other dogs have been paired.

Cast:　Search made by a field dog without making an abrupt turn.

Challenge:　First Foxhound to give voice after the scent is found.

Couple:　Two Hounds.

Coursing:　Sight-chasing of a hare or jackrabbit or artificial lure.

Cut:　Sheep culled from a flock to be taken to market.

Derby:　A field trial stake for dogs usually 1 to 2 years old.

Drag:　Trail made by dragging a bag of scent along the ground. For Coonhound trials it can be a bag of raccoon droppings.

Drawing:　Pairing dogs by lot before the trial begins.

Dropper:　A cross between two bird dog breeds (e.g., Pointer and an English Setter).

Field Champion:　Title earned in field trial competition.

Field trial:　Competition in which a dog's performance and style in a number of tests of hunting skills are judged.

Flag:　The tail of a bird dog carried high.

Flush:　To startle game from its cover.

Full cry:　Chorus of a hound pack running at full speed.

Futurity Stake:　A competition for dogs who were nominated at or before birth.

Gazehound:　A dog that hunts by sight.

Gundog:　A dog that hunts with its master and his or her gun, as distinguished from a field trial dog.

Gun-shy: Afraid of noise, smell, or sight of a gun.

Hie on: A command used to start or urge on a fielddog.

Hot trail: Distinct scent of a trail.

Hup: A command used by Spaniel trainers to make the dog drop to flush or to stop it as it hunts.

Lure coursing: Chasing a fur piece being drawn by a machine.

Music: The baying of a Hound on a hot trail.

Mute: A dog that hunts silently.

Non-slip Retriever: A Retriever that is not used for actual hunting but is kept at heel and sent out only to retrieve dead or wounded game, such as pheasants or waterfowl. Retriever field trials are for non-slip dogs.

Potterer: A dog that dwells too long on a scent, often said of a Hound or Spaniel.

Retrieve: To bring back game to the handler.

Run out: Sheep dog going out after sheep.

Set and crawl: Crouching and crawling action of a sheep dog to move sheep slowly in the proper direction.

Stake: A class designation at field trials (e.g., open all-age stake).

Staunch: To remain steady on point; in some countries, to remain in a sitting position when birds are flushed (or flushed and shot).

Wearing: Action of a sheep dog to keep sheep from bolting in the wrong direction.

Wind: To catch the wind-borne scent of game.

Credits for Breed Photographs

Sporting Breeds

Pointer   Ch. Cumbrian Seabreeze; owned by Pat and Dick Frost, Shodell Kennels, *p.269*

German Shorthaired Pointer   Ch. Conrad's Brio; owned by Galen and Nancy Conrad; photo by William P. Gilbert, *p.271*

German Wirehaired Pointer   Ch. O'Dells Gustav Von Zinsley; owned by Pat and Dick Frost, *p.272*

Chesapeake Bay Retriever   Ch. Teal's Tiger; owned by Susan Hatfield Steuben; photo by Bennett Associates, *p.273*

Curly-Coated Retriever   Ch. Siccawei Black Rod v. Windpatch; owned by N. Dale Detweiler; photo by William P. Gilbert, *p.275*

Flat-Coated Retriever   Ch. Bramcroft Dandy, U.D.; owned by Terroux Kennels, *p.276*

Golden Retriever   Ch. Misty Morn's Sunset; owned by Peter Lewesky, *p.277*

Labrador Retriever (yellow)   Ch. Augustin deGregorio, C.D.; owned by Victoria K. DePalma; photo by John Ashbey, *p.279*

Nova Scotia Duck Tolling Retriever   photo by Little River Kennels, *p.280*

English Setter   Ch. Thenderin Miss O'Dell of Delta; owned by Dick and Pat Frost; photo by Johnnie McMillan, *p.281*

Gordon Setter   Loch Adair Diana of Red Chico; owned by Carol Chevalier; photo by Evelyn M. Shafer, *p.283*

Irish Setter   Ch. Glendee's Diamond in the 'Ruff; owned by Mr. & Mrs. Thorne D. Harris, Jr.; photo by Richard Anderson, *p.284*

American Water Spaniel Ozark Prince Aaron; owned by Mary Beth Flowers, *p.285*

Brittany Spaniel   Ch. Millettes Dirty Harry; owned by Gary M. Tate, *p.287*

Clumber Spaniel   Ch. Andronicus Winchester; owned by Eunice C. Gies, Andronicus Kennel; photo by Evelyn M. Shafer, *p.288*

American Cocker Spaniel   Ch. Centerbury's Mr. Accessor; owned by Donna B. Neal; photo by Earl Graham, *p.289*

English Cocker Spaniel   Ch. Ancram's Simon; owned by Joyce Scott-Paine, Ancram Kennels, *p.291*

English Springer Spaniel   Ch. Good-Will Crowd Pleaser; owned by Paul Pagel; photo by MikRon Photos, *p.292*

Field Spaniel   Ch. Flowering May of Mittina, owned by Mr. & Mrs. R. Squier; photo by Norton of Kent, *p.293*

Irish Water Spaniel   Ch. Oaktrees' Irishtocrat; bred and owned by Anne Embree Snelling, *p.295*

Sussex Spaniel   Sedora Quettadene Damon, owned by Eunice C. Gies, *p.296*

Welsh Springer Spaniel   Ch. DL'Car Gottonwin; owned by Mrs. D. L. Carswell; photo by William P. Gilbert, *p.297*

Vizsla Am. & Can. Ch. Napkeltei Bajos Perri; owned by Dr. W. Jean Dodds, *p.298*

Weimaraner Ch. Wetobe's Dusty Zeus, S.D., N.R.D.; bred and owned by Mrs. H. B. Barnett; photo by Alexander Photo, *p.299*

Wirehaired Pointing Griffon   Fieux Du Val De Tonnerre; owned by Mr. & Mrs. A. Peila; photo by Ritter, *p.301*

Hound Breeds

Afghan Hound   Ch. T. Flite's Cavalier; owned by Rosemarie Crandahl; photo by Martin Booth, *p.302*

Basenji   Ch. Betsy Ross' Kingola of Ber Vic; owned by Betsy and Ross Newman, Betsy Ross Kennels; photo by Rudolph Tanskey, *p.304*

Basset Hound   Ch. Het's Joe of Smith Farms; owned by Mr. & Mrs. William Smith, Smith Farms Hounds; photo by Morry Twomey, *p.305*

Beagle (13 inch)   Ch. Page Mill Lone Star; owned by Mr. & Mrs. David Arnold; photo by Morry Twomey, *p.306*

Black and Tan Coonhound   Ch. Karlena's Musical C. Note; bred and owned by Miss Mignon Murray; photo by Evelyn M. Shafer, *p.308*

Bloodhound   Am. & Can. Ch. The Rectory's Rebel Yell; owned by The Rev. & Mrs. G. E. Sinkinson, *p.309*

Borzoi   Ch. Jobi Reyas Rohan; owned by Joanne B. Jelke, *p.310*

Dachshund (smooth)   Ch. Sheen V. Westphalen; owned by Mrs. Peggy Westphal, *p.312*

Dachshund (wirehaired)   Ch. Vantebe's Draht Timothy; owned by Mrs. Peggy Westphal, *p.313*

Dachshund (longhaired)   Ch. Midas' Fancy Decision; owned by Mrs. William Burr Hill, *p.313*

Foxhound (American)   Ch. Kentucky Lake Admiral; owned by Mrs. Rose Minnick, *p.314*

Foxhound (English)   Ch. Baynor Whitebluff Dan; owned by Virgil D. Johnson; photo by Earl Graham, *p.315*

Greyhound   Ch. Hewly Highbrow; bred and owned by Stanley D. Petter, Jr.; photo by John L. Ashbey, *p.316*

Harrier   Ch. Lady Elizabeth of Byron Mews; owned by Joan R. Nolan; photo by William P. Gilbert, *p.318*

Ibizan Hound   Electra's Cassandra, C.D.; owned by Ron and Judy Bauer, Gallantree Ibizans; photo by Ritter Photo, *p.319*

Irish Wolfhound   Ch. Irish Paddy of Ulaid; owned by Paul Burczycki, *p.320*

Norwegian Elkhound   Ch. Vin-Melca's Nimbus; owned by Patricia V. Craige and Harold Shuler, *p.322*

Otter Hound   Ch. Fernbank Madrigal; owned by Fernbank Kennels, Reg., *p.323*

Rhodesian Ridgeback   Am. & Can. Ch. Geoni's Gyni; owned by Dr. F. George Walker, Geoni Kennels, Reg.; photo by William P. Gilbert, *p.324*

Saluki   Ch. Crown Crest Summer Song; owned by Bruce and Mary Dee Huntsman, *p.326*

Scottish Deerhound   Ch. Shanid's Iolanthe; bred and owned by Frieda and Paul Pilat, Shanid Kennel, Reg., *p.327*

Whippet   Ch. Highlight's Legacy; bred and owned by Margaret C. Hodge, *p.328*

Working Breeds

Akita   Akemi's Buf-Lo-Go; owned by Akemi Kennels; photo by Lee Scanlan, *p.330*

Alaskan Malamute   Ch. Glacier's Storm Kloud, C.D.; owned by Nancy C. and Robert G. Russell, Timberlane Kennel; photo by Bennet Associates, *p.332*

Australian Cattle Dog   Aust. Ch. Ravoredalen Ranger; owned by T. J. Brennan; photo by Peter Hatherly Photography, *p.333*

Bearded Collie   Am. & Can. Ch. Brambledale Blue Bonnet, C.D.; owned by Mr. & Mrs. Robert Lachman, *p.334*

Belgian Malinois   Ch. Lagardaire de la Mascotte Royale, C.D.; owned by Mrs. Dale M. Diamond; photo by William P. Gilbert, *p.336*

Belgian Sheepdog   C. Jolly Roger Anbigen, C.D.; owned by Mrs. D. H. Greer, Jr., Black Knight Kennels, *p.337*

Belgian Tervuren   Ch. Yamin Van't Hof Melyn; owned by Vice Admiral & Mrs. Thomas Walker; photo by Rich Bergman, *p.338*

Bernese Mountain Dog   Ch. Sanctuary Woods Gordo; owned by Joseph and Susanne Gagnon; photo by William P. Gilbert, *p.340*

Bouvier des Flandres   Ch. Bibarcy's Soldat de Plumb; bred and owned by Arthur M. and Mary E. Pedersen; photo by Morry Twomey, *p.341*

Boxer   Ch. Eldic's Darius; bred and owned by Mr. & Mrs. R. Haeberle, Jr.; photo by William Brown, *p.342*

Briard   Ch. Quassus D'el Pastre, CAC, CACIB; owned by Harold Marley, *p.344*

Bullmastiff Am. & Can. Ch. Ramapo Torne's Red Steve; owned by Virgil Millett; photo by William P. Gilbert, *p.345*

Rough Collie Ch. Briahill High Voltage; owned by Molly and Dick Bishop, Esprit Collies, *p.346*

Smooth Collie Peterblue Roderick; owned by Mrs. Everett M. Cooper, *p.348*

Doberman Pinscher Am. & Can. Ch. Votag's Great Goliath; owned by Bob and Polly Yarnall, Kimbertal Kennels, *p.349*

German Shepherd Dog Ch. Covy-Tucker Hill's Finnegan; owned by Ralph and Mary Roberts, *p.350*

Giant Schnauzer Ch. Quedame de la Steingasse; owned by Mr. & Mrs. Jack A. Beutel, *p.352*

Great Dane (fawn) Ch. Waco's Faro of Apollo; owned by Frank and Lorraine Smega; photo by E. H. Frank, *p.354*

Great Dane (harlequin) Ch. Kato's Baccarat; owned by Tom and Kathleen Anderson, Malibu Kennels; photo by Rich Bergman, *p.355*

Great Dane (brindle) Ch. Nandane's Sweet Silhouette; owned by Evelyn Niedenthal, Fourleaf Danes, *p.355*

Great Pyrenees Ch. Quibbletown's Juggernaut; owned by Dr. Gordon Keller; photo by William P. Gilbert, *p.356*

Komondor Ch. Shaggyrock Aranyes; owned by Rosemary Franck, *p.357*

Kuvasz Ch. Hamralvi Demost Happy Fella; bred by Dr. & Mrs. Z. M. Alvi, Hamralvi Kennels; owned by Miss Barbara Colyear, *p.359*

Mastiff Ch. Grand Duke O'Fern; owned by Blanche M. Fontaine, *p.360*

Newfoundland Ch. Edenglen's Mr. Christian; owned by Jean Quandt; photo by Martin Booth, *p.361*

Old English Sheepdog Ch. Loyalblu Hendihap; bred and owned by Dr. & Mrs. Hugh Jordan; co-owned by Mr. & Mrs. Richard Boerner, *p.363*

Puli Ch. Sasvolgyi Puszi Pajtas; owned by Barry Becker and Leslie Benis; bred by Leslie Benis, Hunnia Puli Kennels, *p.364*

Rottweiler Ch. Rodsden's Axel vh Brabant; owned by Joan R. Klem, Rodsden's Rottweilers, Reg., *p.365*

St. Bernard Ch. Engler's King Edward; owned by Edward A. and Laura Turner, *p.366*

Samoyed Ch. Frostriver Drumson of Snopaw; owned by Steve and Shirley Mangini, *p.368*

Shetland Sheepdog Ch. Halston's Peter Pumpkin; owned by Thomas W. Coen, Macdega Kennels, *p.369*

Siberian Husky Ch. Bundas Boston Blacky; owned by Dr. Gabriel Mayer, Bundas Kennels; photo by William P. Gilbert, *p.371*

Standard Schnauzer (salt and pepper) Ch. Erik von Hahlweg; owned by Sue Baines, *p.372*

Welsh Corgi, Cardigan Ch. Hillsborough Kelly; owned by Dr. W. E. McGough; photo by William P. Gilbert, *p.374*

Welsh Corgi, Pembroke Ch. Jan Dons' Miss Sable; owned by Mr. G. Albertson and Mr. J. Stewart; photo by Rich Bergman, *p.375*

Terrier Breeds

Airedale Terrier   Ch. Cyndale Coke N'Copper; owned by Mrs. Glen Huey; photo by Ritter, *p.377*

American Staffordshire Terrier   Ch. Archer's Dixie; owned by Dorothy M. Archer, *p.379*

Australian Terrier   Aust. Am. Ch. Tinee Town Talkbac R.O.M. of Pleasant Pastures Kennels; owned by Mrs. Milton Fox; photo by William P. Gilbert, *p.380*

Bedlington Terrier   Ch. Mr. Blue of Tamarack; bred and owned by Sally A. DeKold, *p.381*

Border Terrier   Ch. Dandynow Bitter Shandy; owned by George Seeman, Jr.; photo by Evelyn M. Shafer, *p.382*

Bull Terrier, White Am. & Can. Ch. Bejobos Jack Frost; owned by Jon Cole, *p.384*

Bull Terrier, Colored   Ch. Highland's Big Ben; owned by Forrest and Agnes Rose; photo by Ritter, *p.385*

Cairn Terrier   Am. & Can. Ch. Rogerlyn Sea Hawk's Salty Sam; bred by Mr. & Mrs. Robert Cox; owned by Betty Hyslop, *p.386*

Dandie Dinmont Terrier   Eng. Am. Ch. Hendell Colislinn Loelia; owned by Mr. & Mrs. C. Nelson, *p.387*

Fox Terrier, Smooth   Ch. Foxden Warpaint; owned by Mr. & Mrs. James A. Farrell, Jr.; photo by William P. Gilbert, *p.388*

Fox Terrier, Wire   Eng. and Am. Ch. Harwire Hetman of Whinlatter; owned by Frederick Jones; handler, Clifford Hallmark, *p.390*

Irish Terrier   Ch. Nutbrown Leprechaun; owned by Rudolph Jensen; photo by Alexander Photo, *p.391*

Kerry Blue Terrier   Ch. Ruan's Native Dancer; owned by Rita L. Modler; photo by Earl Graham, *p.392*

Lakeland Terrier   Ch. Schlosshaus's Jo-Jo The Red; bred by Tom W. Castles, Jr.; owned by Capt. Jean L. Heath, MSC, USN (ret.) and William H. Cosby, Jr., *p.393*

Standard Manchester Terrier   Ch. Chatham's Mitzie; owned by Mrs. Ruth Turner, *p.394*

Miniature Schnauzer   Ch. Classic Imperial Sky Jumper; owned by Bill and Dorothy Culley, *p.396*

Norfolk Terrier   Eng. Ch. Ickworth Peter's Pence of King's Prevention; bred by Miss Alice Hazeldine; owned by Mrs. Sterling Larrabee; photo by Sally Anne Thompson, *p.397*

Norwich Terrier   Ch. Shawnee's Cricket; owned by Mrs. S. Powel Griffitts, *p.398*

Scottish Terrier   Ch. Dunbar's Democrat of Sandoone; owned by Richard Hensel, Dunbar Kennels; photo by MikRon Photos, *p.399*

Sealyham Terrier   Ch. Lord Mitchell of Surgen Pride; owned by Mrs. Olive R. Surgen, Surgenpride Sealyhams; photo by Tauskey, *p.401*

Skye Terrier   Ch. Talisker's Dark Knight; owned by J. Roy and Elaine T. Lee, *p.402*

Soft-Coated Wheaten Terrier   Ch. Abby's Postage Dhu O'Waterford; owned by

Marjorie C. Shoemaker, Waterford Wheatens; photo by John Ashbey, *p.404*

Staffordshire Bull Terrier Can. Ch. Terrco's Richard the Gentleman; bred and owned by Lt. Col. N. E. and Dr. P. M. Cooke, *p.405*

Welsh Terrier Ch. Alokin Achievement; owned by Janterrs Kennels, *p.406*

West Highland White Terrier Am. & Can. Ch. Dancing Hannah of the Rouge; owned by Mrs. J. H. Daniell-Jenkins, Kennels of the Rouge, Reg.; photo by Rob Gordon, *p.408*

Toy Breeds

Affenpinscher Int. Ch. Vinzenz v. Greifensee; owned by Lucille E. Meystedt; photo by Twomey, *p.409*

Brussels Griffon Ch. All-Celia's Beau Brummel; courtesy of Iris de la Torre Bueno, All-Celia Kennels; photo by Evelyn M. Shafer, *p.411*

Chihuahua, Smooth Coat Ch. Dartan's Blazon Dragan; owned by Edward Dragan, *p.412*

Chihuahua, Long Coat Ch. Dartan's Batman; owned by Darwin and Tanya Delaney, *p.414*

English Toy Spaniel Ch. Carefree Prince David; owned by S. R. Snider, Jr.; bred by Diane Christiansen; photo by Earl Graham, *p.415*

Italian Greyhound Ch. Padre Berta Joh-Cyn; owned by Rev. Robert E. Watson; photo by Earl Graham, *p.417*

Japanese Chin Ch. Tenson Uigo; owned by Mrs. Michael Pym; handler, Dorothy White, *p.418*

Maltese Ch. Tennessa's Fitzhue of Weewyte; owned by Kathleen and Robert Blackard; bred by Annette Feldblum; photo by William P. Gilbert, *p.420*

Manchester Terrier (Toy) Int. Ch. Lilac Farm Peach Honey; owned by Lourene Wishart, *p.421*

Miniature Pinscher Ch. Bo-Mar's Road Runner; owned by Mr. & Mrs. William Kleinmanns, *p.423*

Papillon Am. & Can. Ch. Kenrennie Udell; owned by Sally and Harold Gell; bred by Betty Kenworthy; photo by John L. Ashbey, *p.424*

Pekingese Ch. Dan-Lee Dragonseed; owned by Michael Wolf; photo by Evelyn M. Shafer, *p.426*

Pomeranian Gold Blackacre Honey Gold; owned by Gold Blackacre Kennels; photo by Frasie, *p.427*

Poodle (Toy) Ch. Sundown Sassafras Bootblack; owned by Mrs. James P. Goodson, *p.428*

Pug Am. & Can. Ch. Wolf's Li'l Joe; bred and owned by Gus and Esther Wolf; photo by Don Petrulis, *p.429*

Shih Tzu Taramont's Encore Chopsticks; owned by Joan and Bill Kibler, *p.431*

Silky Terrier Ch. Koala I'm Casey's Dandy; owned by Doreen and Jason Gross, "Koals" Silky Terriers; photo by Bill Francis, *p.432*

Yorkshire Terrier Ch. Cede Higgens; owned by Barbara and Bill Switzer, *p.433*

Non-Sporting Breeds

Bichon Frise Teeny Tepee's Cherokee Prince; owned by Betty Shehab; photo by Joseph F. Lynch, *p.435*

Boston Terrier Ch. Jacque Cyr; courtesy of Mary C. Piazza, *p.437*

Bulldog Burgess' Harbor Master; owned and bred by Willis W. Burgess, *p.439*

Chow Chow Ch. Ky-Lin's Red Buddha; owned by Mary Ann and William Chambers; photo by Elaine Johnson, *p.440*

Dalmatian Ch. Viking's Bret D.; owned by Marie D. Zink; photo by Martin Booth, *p.442*

French Bulldog Ch. Ralanda Ami Pierre; owned by Mrs. Ralph West; photo by E. H. Frank, *p.443*

Keeshond Am., Can., & Mex. Ch. Brynhaven Johan van Saga; owned by Miss Linda Loucks; photo by Lloyd W. Olson Studio, *p.445*

Lhasa Apso Multiple Best In Show Champion Yojimbo Orion; bred and owned by Elaine Spaeth; photo by Don Petrulis, *p.446*

Poodle (Miniature) Ch. Round Table Boucanier; owned by Mrs. A. V. Keene, *p.447*

Poodle (Standard, Puppy clip) Ch. Lou Gin's Kiss Me Kate; owned by Barbara and Terri Meyers, *p.448*

Poodle (Standard, Continental clip) Ch. Lou Gin's Kiss Me Kate; owned by Barbara and Terri Meyers, *p.448*

Schipperke Ch. Wilsons Flash Lightning; owned by James E. and Clazina M. Wilson; photo by Don Petrulis, *p.450*

Tibetan Terrier Ch. Kontan's Kori-Nor Bu-Tsa Lhor; owned by Mr. & Mrs. Stephen P. Furman, *p.452*

Miscellaneous Breeds

Australian Kelpie Aust. Ch. Kefalin Storm Sun; owned by Mrs. C. T. Higgins, *p.455*

Border Collie owned by Carl H. Bradford, Sr.; Bradford's Border Collies, *p.456*

Cavalier King Charles Spaniel Ttiweh Granaldon Maigret, C.D.; owned by Juanita Waite Howard; photo by Action Photography, Jayne Langdon, *p.457*

Miniature Bull Terrier Imperial Apple of My Eye; owned by Jackie McArthur, *p.459*

Pharaoh Hound Sakkara's Isis; owned by Linda DeFeo, *p.460*

Spinone Italiano courtesy Ente Nazionale Della Cinofilia Italiana, *p.461*

Tibetan Spaniel Ch. Am-Ku Niblet; owned by Beatrice Karstadt, Von Karstadt Kennels, *p.463*

Rare Breeds

Australian Shepherd Stumpendo of Gefion; owned by Frieda Mazzone; photo by The Louis Studio, *p.465*

Canaan Dog Aleph of Star Pine; owned by Jay C. Sheaffer, Spatterdash Kennels, *p.467*

Lowchen Eng. Ch. Littlecourt Arela; owned by Freda McGregor, Littlecourt Kennels; photo by Sally Anne Thompson, *p.468*

Portuguese Water Dog owned by Joseph Gratton, Portuguese Water Dog Club, *p.469*

Telomian courtesy of Audrey M. Palumbo, Telomian Dog Club of America, *p.471*

Xoloitzcuintli Mex. and World F.C.I. Ch. Quetzalcoatl; President Lascelles de Premio Real, Federacion Canofila Mexicana, *p.472*

Index

Origin of the Dog Breeds

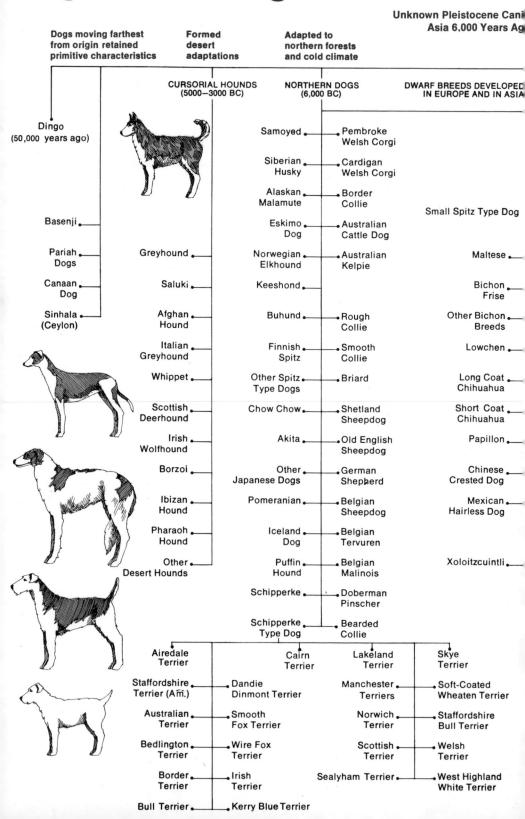

Unknown Pleistocene Cani
Asia 6,000 Years Ag

Dogs moving farthest from origin retained primitive characteristics	Formed desert adaptations	Adapted to northern forests and cold climate	
	CURSORIAL HOUNDS (5000–3000 BC)	NORTHERN DOGS (6,000 BC)	DWARF BREEDS DEVELOPED IN EUROPE AND IN ASIA
Dingo (50,000 years ago)		Samoyed → Pembroke Welsh Corgi	
		Siberian Husky → Cardigan Welsh Corgi	
		Alaskan Malamute → Border Collie	Small Spitz Type Dog
Basenji		Eskimo Dog → Australian Cattle Dog	
Pariah Dogs	Greyhound	Norwegian Elkhound → Australian Kelpie	Maltese
Canaan Dog	Saluki	Keeshond	Bichon Frise
Sinhala (Ceylon)	Afghan Hound	Buhund → Rough Collie	Other Bichon Breeds
	Italian Greyhound	Finnish Spitz → Smooth Collie	Lowchen
	Whippet	Other Spitz Type Dogs → Briard	Long Coat Chihuahua
	Scottish Deerhound	Chow Chow → Shetland Sheepdog	Short Coat Chihuahua
	Irish Wolfhound	Akita → Old English Sheepdog	Papillon
	Borzoi	Other Japanese Dogs → German Shepherd	Chinese Crested Dog
	Ibizan Hound	Pomeranian → Belgian Sheepdog	Mexican Hairless Dog
	Pharaoh Hound	Iceland Dog → Belgian Tervuren	
	Other Desert Hounds	Puffin Hound → Belgian Malinois	Xoloitzcuintli
		Schipperke → Doberman Pinscher	
		Schipperke Type Dog → Bearded Collie	

Airedale Terrier	Cairn Terrier	Lakeland Terrier	Skye Terrier
Staffordshire Terrier (Am.) → Dandie Dinmont Terrier		Manchester Terriers → Soft-Coated Wheaten Terrier	
Australian Terrier → Smooth Fox Terrier		Norwich Terrier → Staffordshire Bull Terrier	
Bedlington Terrier → Wire Fox Terrier		Scottish Terrier → Welsh Terrier	
Border Terrier → Irish Terrier		Sealyham Terrier → West Highland White Terrier	
Bull Terrier → Kerry Blue Terrier			